# Sonic Bodies

SOUND IN HISTORY

Emma Dillon, *Series Editor*

# SONIC BODIES

Text, Music, and Silence in
Late Medieval England

Tekla Bude

**PENN**

UNIVERSITY OF PENNSYLVANIA PRESS

PHILADELPHIA

Published by
University of Pennsylvania Press
Philadelphia, Pennsylvania 19104-4112
www.upenn.edu/pennpress

Printed in the United States of America on acid-free paper
10 9 8 7 6 5 4 3 2 1

A Cataloging-in-Publication record is available from the
Library of Congress
ISBN 978-0-8122-5370-2 (hardback)
ISBN 978-0-8122-9832-1 (eBook)

*For Carson, Steve, Biko, Fela, Cala, and Naima*

# Contents

# Acknowledgments

A first book, at least in my experience, is about the art of losing, inscribed in 12-point font and peer-reviewed, and the story of this book is one of letting go: of places I love, both begrudgingly and unabashedly (Ann Arbor, Oxford, Philadelphia, Johannesburg, Cambridge, Cleveland); of material possessions that couldn't, for reasons of space or expense, travel with me as I moved (I sold all of my books, in 2013, to a secondhand bookstore in Melville). Over the course of its writing, I have lost parts of myself to surgery and lost a child through miscarriage. I have charted the loss of relationships, some forever, others happily resutured; of time (I began to conceive of this book as a young adult, and now am teetering on the edge of middle age); and of words—so many words!—both less material and more personal than these other things.

But of course, it's not all loss, and the move I'm going to make here, from negativity to positivity, is as earnest as it is hackneyed. When I set out to write acknowledgments in my undergraduate honors thesis in 2006 and then, the next year, my master's thesis, I couldn't think of anyone to thank, or to dedicate the text to. I was lonely, angry, and not in a mood to thank anyone, even if thanks were due.

I couldn't feel more differently now, and the list of friends, colleagues, and mentors to thank here—for their companionship and their brilliance— should, rightly, take up the rest of these acknowledgments, because if this book is anything but loss, it is because of them.

To the wonderful English faculty at the University of Michigan who gently warned me about the dangers of going to graduate school, all while supporting me unconditionally, in particular Marjorie Levinson and Jonathan Freedman; to Vincent Gillespie, my master's adviser, who intimidated and molded me in equal measure; to my PhD advisers, whose unparalleled guidance, acuity, and kindness shaped this project and my career: David Wallace, Emily Steiner, Rita Copeland, Emma Dillon, and Ann Matter; to my fellow

PhD students at Penn, whose intellectual and political rigor should be a template for all grad students everywhere: Claire Bourne, Kara Gaston, Bronwyn Wallace, Simran Thadani, Lucia Martinez, Marissa Nicosia, and Marie Turner; to the open-hearted, sarcastic, and ironizing wit of my friends in South Africa, who upheld me at my weakest moments: Colette Gordon, Judy Sikuza, and Michelle Schenck; to the women at Cambridge whose conversation kept me tethered: Alex Vukovich, Fiona Stewart, and Sarah Harris; to the wonderful women of the pre-tenure writing group at Oregon State University, who are friends and guardians who model how to be unflinching yet caring professors: Ana Milena Ribero, Trina Hogg, Rena Lauer, Megan Ward, Lily Sheehan, Cari Maes, and Mila Zuo; to my colleagues in SWLF and at OSU, who supported me both personally and institutionally: Rebecca Olson, Tara Williams, Christopher Nichols, and my department chair, Peter Betjemann; to my medieval community more broadly, especially those who took the time to talk with me about this book: Sarah Baechle, Ruen-Chuan Ma, Sarah Watson, Liza Strakhov, Laura Saetveit Miles, Rosemary O'Neill, Carissa Harris, Megan Cook, Jen Jahner, Lucy Allen-Goss, Julie Orlemanski, Andrew Albin, and Christopher Michael Roman; to the readers and editors of this manuscript, who gave more of themselves than was required, especially Andrew Hicks and Elizabeth Lyon, whose excellent Latin translations are a pivotal part of this book; to the institutions—to the corporations of people—without whom this book could not have come to be: the Mellon Foundation, Newnham College, and the Oregon State Center for the Humanities, all of which gave me time to think and to write when time was sorely needed; and, finally, to my husband, my cat, my dogs, and my daughters, who (in that order, temporally) have accompanied me and sacrificed for me as I've worked to complete this book.

If this book is constituted by my serial losses, it is also comprised of their presence.

Introduction

# Writing Sonic Bodies

## Music, Odd Bodies, and Sonic Embodiment: Thinking About This Book

Sometime around 1320, a certain *magister artium* at the University of Paris named Jacobus sat down to write a treatise summarizing contemporary Parisian music theory and performance.[1] The resulting book was an encyclopedic, seven-volume magnum opus entitled the *Speculum musicae* that is best known today for its colorful diatribes against the *moderni*, composers of the *ars nova*. The *moderni's* complex polyphonic compositions and innovative text-setting elicited a colorful tirade from the author that, in its vitriol, rivals Theodor Adorno's invectives against jazz:[2]

> O what great abuse, what great brutishness, what great beastliness, when an ass is taken for a human, a she-goat for a lion, a sheep for a fish, a serpent for a salmon! For the concdords (*concordiae*) are so different from the discords (*discordiis*) that one is in no way like the other. . . . There are also some who do not observe the good manner, although they have learned a little to sing discant (*discantare*). They sing discant too frivolously, they multiply superfluous notes. Some of them apply hocket (*hoketant*) too much, they break consonant (*consonantiis*) notes too often, run up and divide up, they leap in unsuitable places, they clash, they bellow (*saltant, hurcant, iupant*), and they yelp and bark in the manner of dogs (*ad modum canis hawant, latrant*), and like insane people, they take nourishment from a disorganized and convoluted ruckus, they use a harmony that is far removed from nature.[3]

If this passage evokes an aging man in his doorway, waving his fist in anger at the young musicians on his front lawn, it also serves as a fitting example of the concerns of this book, which are about the relationship of music to the body in the medieval period, and the way that music and the body have material effects on each other. Jacobus's curmudgeonly attitude toward the *moderni* and their new art presents a semiotic system that weaves hermeneutics and materiality together; it is one that relies on existing norms about relative animal and human value for its legibility.[4] In this passage, Jacobus consciously mingles the technical vocabulary of fourteenth-century music ("concord and discord," "discanting," "hocketing," and "consonance"—*concordie a discordiis, discantare, hoketant, consonantiis*) to a series of vivid embodied and material metaphors (the *moderni* "break," "run up," "divide up," "leap," "clash," "bellow," and "yelp and bark like dogs"—*frangunt, scandunt, dividunt, saltant, hurcant, jupant, ad modum canis hawant, latrant*). In Jacobus's estimation, the *ars nova* makes humans bestial, inverting the normative hierarchy of creation that places animals below humans in a spectrum of rationality and rational behavior. The resulting music is both aesthetically and ethically suspect. In order for this invective to land, however, Jacobus's readers must already implicitly agree that the human is a nobler being than the ass, the lion more regal than the goat, and the embodied practices of clashing, bellowing, yelping, and barking less salubrious forms of movement and sonic production than more staid forms of musical performance.[5] The songs and practices of the *moderni* are "unnatural" to the extent that they are classified, in medieval animacy hierarchies, as *less than human*.[6] If musical performance delineates the bodies it inhabits, cultural assumptions about bodies, in turn, help to articulate judgments about whether a given sound is musical or if it is simply noise.[7]

Jacobus's judgment of the *moderni* is one of the most famous in the *Speculum*. Its logic is a vivid reminder that music and the body always exist in a discursive relationship to each other, but it does more than remind us of that fact. It also suggests that music and the body are literally contingent upon each other. Although Jacobus claims that the difference between good and bad music is a purely intellectual one, he cannot help but elide bodies and minds, thereby yoking together what the body is, what the mind is capable of, and what music is. In Jacobus's case, he hears the *ars nova* as noise in part because he imagines the bodies of its singers as animals; conversely, the bodies of the *moderni* are bestial because the songs they perform are—at least in his estimation—noisy. These two judgments cannot be divorced from each other. Jacobus's fractious description of the *ars nova* explicitly addresses the difference between old music and new, but its claim rests upon the implication that pronouncements about music and the body are co-constitutive and linguistically entangled. Jacobus's curmudgeonly account is both vivid and humorous, but in its coupling of music and the body, it is far from unique among medieval accounts.

This book argues that music and the body are entangled practices that emerge out of social and textual environments so diverse that these musical bodies reach the very limits of what we understand music and the body to be. These are what I call *sonic bodies*: mutually dependent, relational, historically contingent, and co-emergent processes that rely on dialectics of materiality. From the immaterialism of angelic song to the material musicality of monastic friendship, from the (im)materiality of silence to the matter of disabled bodies, *Sonic Bodies: Text, Music, and Silence* follows a series of late medieval writers—from mystics to spiritual autobiographers, from Langland to Chaucer—to show how sound and the body are co-emergent forms. While these bodies refer to and are accountable to matter (as Jacobus is with his animal-like singers), the sonic bodies imagined by medieval writers sometimes make this accounting by *rejecting* matter. Thus sonic bodies arise not only out of matter itself, but also out of a dialectic of materiality that also includes the immaterial.

In its attention to music, texts, and embodiment, *Sonic Bodies* is an inherently transdisciplinary project, building on over thirty years of incisive work in the fields of medieval musicology, sound studies, and medieval literary studies. Although medieval music theory divides into two types—speculative and practical—and practical music theory has always been, as the name suggests, about the *practice* of singing, for much of the twentieth century, scholars believed that medieval speculative music theory had little, if anything, to do with the body. Notated music and speculative music theory was seen as primarily an academic exercise, more like geometry than art, because speculative theory was written in an arcane vocabulary of mathematical proportions that rarely discussed affect or emotion, and polyphonic music, especially fourteenth-century polyphony, was thought to be overly complex, bizarre, and sometimes simply bad.[8] But, at the beginning of the twentieth century, a series of seminal studies began to overturn this conventional narrative. As Daniel Leech-Wilkinson has shown, work by Gilbert Reaney, Craig Wright, and Christopher Page proved the singability of music by Machaut and others, demonstrating the carnality of song not only in academic arguments, but also by performing the music in vocal ensembles. In his pivotal *Music, Body, and Desire in Medieval Culture: Hildegard of Bingen to Chaucer* (2001), Bruce Holsinger argued that medieval music was a practice of the flesh, a deeply sensual artistic mode imbued with pain and pleasure, desire and repulsion. For Holsinger, not just music, but "all conceptual systems, philosophical or otherwise" are "rooted in the body and tempered and constrained by lived, corporeal experience."[9] Not just practical music and the singing of plainchant, but also speculative music and more complex polyphony are inhabited by performing bodies. Looking beyond speculative music theory to literary and historical texts that described musical experience, these writers argued that the strange polyphony of the high medieval period was not just a mental exercise, but instead, was a practice of the material body.[10]

It is now, therefore, impossible to write about medieval music today without in some way thinking about matter and the material body. In *Singing the New Song: Literacy and Liturgy in Late Medieval England* (2008), Katherine Zieman notes that song's intimate connection to language, literature, and society politicized, gendered, and disciplined the flesh. Emma Dillon, in *The Sense of Sound: Musical Meaning in France, 1260–1330* (2012), proposes that musical listening in the medieval period subordinated the meaning of words to their sonic effects on the world around them, from the cityscape to the cries of the mentally ill.[11] One of the central tenets of Andrew Hicks's *Composing the World: Harmony in the Medieval Platonic Cosmos* (2017) is that the medieval Neoplatonic conception of *musica mundana*, or the harmony of the universe, is "materially grounded," and that the "human ability to hear the cosmos is predicated upon the transduction of an extrasonic signal . . . into a sonic representation accommodated to human sensory realities."[12] In *The Monstrous New Art*, Anna Zayaruznaya argues that formal properties of medieval music "evoke or embody" a creaturely way of thinking.[13] As this cursory but exemplary sample of recent literature suggests, for a twenty-first-century medievalist, medieval music is now ineluctably and powerfully bound to the flesh. In this way, modern studies of medieval music echo the recent material turn in academia more generally. From object-oriented ontology to new materialisms, and from hyperobjects to vibrant matter and assemblages to intra-actions, the last twenty years have seen new and incisive arguments about matter's significance within discursive frameworks.[14] Language, culture, and meaning arise out of material considerations in complex and fascinating ways, and *Sonic Bodies* builds on contemporary philosophy's

more general turn to materialism(s) as well as the material turn more specific to medieval studies.

But this book also wants to push back against scholarship on medieval
music and its all-too-easy elision of *flesh* with *body*, and to explore what is
lost when we equate the two. What does it mean to consider musical embodiment beyond the sensorium of a single, delimited human form? What
are the possibilities for sonic embodiment if the bodies are collective, figural, or somehow immaterial, as, for instance, angels were thought to be by
many philosophers in the medieval period? In collapsing body into flesh, we
run the risk of simplifying the relationship between these two terms: of reading the body as strictly bounded by skin, of understanding the body as a
shell or surface, or of reading all uses of the word "body" as metaphors for
materiality.[15] But perhaps most importantly, in equating the body with its
culturally hegemonic definition as a spatially organized tactile object, we
overlook the ways in which sound might constitute embodiment differently
than sight: how does a sensorium that demotes visuality and promotes aurality limn a different understanding of, and capacity for, embodiment? The
*sonic body,* this book argues, is a different sort of body, one that has access to
forms of subjectivity, power, ways of being, and linguistic meaning that do
not accrue to the visible or visio-tactile body. Matter might be at the heart
of this body, but so too might immateriality.[16] What *are* bodies if (im)matter
is sound? Sound may—but then again may not—be a practice of the flesh.
What productive work might we do with music and the body when we probe
the strange forms of embodiment that exist beyond normative, individualized, human forms, or when we imagine not music as operating *on* the body
or the body as *performing* music, but instead when we think about the ways
in which "music" and "the body"—whatever those things are—mutually co-
constitute each other and emerge as simultaneous sites of performance? *Sonic
Bodies* outlines the multiple and evasive sonic bodies at play in medieval literature, arguing not only that "music" and "the body" are uniquely intertwined, but that their existence determines—and is determined by—literary
form and social function.

This is not simply a case of placing modern theories of immateriality
and embodiment onto the medieval. After all, the medieval period had multiple and complex understandings of embodiment and materiality. As Ernst
Kantorowicz famously outlines, medieval theology and political theory recognize multiple bodies: the king has "two bodies" (one natural and one mystical), as does Christ (his human, material body and the Church); the Church

itself (which is both a material location and a mystical corporate entity) has multiple bodies; and the polity (a material city and a mystical body of collected human beings, both living and dead) is similarly doubly incorporated.[17] More recently, Caroline Walker Bynum traces the difference between "the body" (*soma* or *corpus*) and "the flesh" (*sarx* or *caro*) in medieval theologies of the resurrection, suggesting that the problem's thorniness and its persistence are inherently related.[18] As Patricia Dailey argues, the Western Christian tradition understood the body not as a simple organic unity, but instead as a body comprised of both inner (intellectual) and outer (sense-perceptual) persons, both of which were culturally and socially determined.[19] In other words, medieval writers had multiple ways of understanding and describing the body and its erotics, pains, and ecstasies—feelings that might not exist in the flesh at all even though they referred back to the body as a metaphor.

Just as *Sonic Bodies* expands the accepted boundaries of the medieval body, this book also explores the acceptable range of definitions for "music" in the medieval period. "Music" is a capacious term, and it means something different in medieval poetry than it does in mystical texts, philosophical discussions, manuscripts of notated music, or texts in the speculative musical tradition; each of these written forms of music are different still, because they are inscribed in texts, from the ephemeral performances of music in *viva voce* song. What types of music have been overlooked in current critiques of the medieval period? As will become clear throughout the chapters of this book, some of the most interesting music of the medieval period dwells in texts not normally considered musical, and whose sounds commingle music and noise, silence, and the quotidian sounds of daily life. If this book is about expanding the boundaries of the body, it is also about expanding the *corpus* of medieval music.

The sonic bodies that are the subjects of this book, then, challenge normative conceptions of embodiment and musicality. Sonic embodiment is labile and ductile, manifold and ever changing, as it asks us to exchange the eidetic forms conjured by the word "body" with auditory replacements.

Each of the chapters of this book looks to specific late medieval textual scenarios in which sonic embodiment is at work, sometimes in radically different ways.

Chapter 1 explores in detail two fourteenth-century attempts to define and describe angelic song. Angelic song provides a helpful framework for thinking about sonic embodiment because of the role that angels played in medieval hierarchies of being based on the types of bodies and intellects they were thought to have. Medieval writers believed that, like humans, angels sang. But most theologians and philosophers believed that, unlike humans, angels lacked physical, material flesh. Because of this, many writers posited that the songs angels sang were also immaterial, incapable of propagating through matter as sound waves. And yet, humans claimed to hear angels' song, and medieval mysticism, literature, and art were full of singing angels.[20] With what ears did these humans hear their impossible music? What sorts of bodies did human audiation of angelic song necessitate? How did writers express the ineffability of this music in language? The answers to these questions provide a glimpse into the strange world of sonic embodiment, and the two discursive arenas that this chapter considers provide divergent answers to these questions. In the first, late medieval speculative music attempts to define and describe angelic song; in the second, Richard Rolle, the early fourteenth-century English mystic, thinks about the relationship between embodiment and his experience of angelic song as *canor*.

Beginning in the late thirteenth and early fourteenth centuries, speculative music treatises like Jacobus's *Speculum* began to look for a space for angelic song among the preexisting, tripartite division of music articulated by Boethius (d. 524) in his *De musica*.[21] Was angelic song *musica mundana* (the music of the spheres), *musica humana* (the music of the human body-soul), or *musica instrumentalis* (instrumental music)? Each of these forms of music concerned physical matter, but, again, most medieval philosophers argued that angels were not fleshly creatures. Because angels' song seemingly broke down the traditional taxonomy of music, speculative music treatises like Jacobus's *Speculum* tentatively proposed a form of music that added to the old Boethian tripartite model: *musica celestis*. For Jacobus, angelic song inhabits a body that is "transcendental" or "metaphysical." As Jacobus says, *musica celestis* "considers transcendental things that pertain to metaphysics or theology."[22] Although Jacobus was the only late medieval music theorist to account for angelic song in great detail, other theorists of the same period, taking cues from Scholastic philosophy's discussions of angelic embodiment, seem to have thought about angelic song in a similar way.

Around the same time, Richard Rolle, an English mystic, began to describe angelic song too. Although Rolle did not know Jacobus or his *Speculum musicae*, Rolle's mystical writings treat angelic song as an embodied reality much like Jacobus does. For Rolle, angelic song—which he calls *canor*—is a physical sonorous experience that separates the soul from the body, removing the fleshly restrictions that typically constrain human hearing, audiation, intellection, and musical performance (such as images, phantasms, temporal divisions, and even the necessity to speak normative human language). As Rolle listens to *canor*, his material body is overwhelmed by his spiritual body, and he begins to speak, quite literally, an angelic language—one that is mimicked in his written work through florid alliteration and prosopoetics. In Rolle's account, *canor* actively creates the metaphysical organ of its audiation; it also affects the formal properties of the written word. If Jacobus and other late medieval music theorists postulate the existence of angelic song as a form of metaphysically embodied music, Rolle's accounts *perform* its effects in writing.

Both medieval music theory and mysticism describe a spiritual body—and a metaphysical sensorium—that performs and tunes in to angelic song. For Jacobus and Rolle, the "music" that angels make is silent, and the "body" that performs and hears this music is not made of matter. Both Jacobus and Rolle argue that there is such a thing as the metaphysical sonic body, and they saw its potential for performance. However, in the generations that followed, some writers—far from being excited about the prospects for immaterial sounds—were downright suspicious of them and sought to contain the potential theological harm that the human experience of angelic song might effect. Angels' song, the thinking went, might encourage its listeners to neglect religious orthopraxis for heterodox, personal, and potentially heretical mystical experiences.

In this vein, Chapter 2 explores the work of one such skeptic, Walter Hilton (d. 1396), whose *Of Angels' Song* both describes metaphysical music and admonishes his reader to stay away from it, focusing on the psalms, hymns, and anthems of the Church instead. In this little-studied but provocative treatise, Hilton describes angels' song as a form of "gastly" touch that can be "feled and a persayved in a saule, but it may noght be shewed." (Hilton's assessment is borne out in visual art of the period, where touch between humans and angels is almost never depicted; there was, it seems, real anxiety around "showing" the impossible, invisible interface between human bodies and angelic ones.)[23] Nevertheless, in spite of his misgivings, Hilton posits a convincing description of angelic songs and the human organs that perceive them.

Hilton juxtaposes the interior, spiritual, and fluid noneidetic body that hears angelic song to an exterior, material, and visual body that performs the liturgy and is open to discipline, punishment, and social conformity.

Because Hilton calls angels' song a sort of *inner touch,* this chapter considers the role that touch or *tactus* played in the embodying discourses of medieval medicine and music. Throughout the medieval period, the word *tactus* was used in a variety of metaphorical ways: first, it connoted the musicality of the heartbeat (an interoception that could be felt but not shown); and later, in the fifteenth century, *tactus* came to refer to a fundamental unit of musical time.[24] As each *mensura* or *tactus* passed, a singer tapped their partner or partners on the shoulder to indicate time's passing. The notion of the "touch," then, has both interior, noneidetic meanings and exterior, disciplinary ones. While Hilton ultimately rejects angelic songs and the "ghostly bodies" touched by them as imprudent, nevertheless, he still describes a body that is noneidetic, that is not flesh, and yet is distressingly real, so real that Hilton marshals the disciplinary logic of exteroceptive touch and (exterior songs) as a containment mechanism.

For Hilton, hearing is a synaesthetic experience out of which the body emerges: angelic song is neither truly eidetic (it cannot be "shown") nor physical (it is "ghostly"). Instead, the body that emerges out of angelic song is a process-oriented one, a body of simultaneous and undifferentiated feeling or affect.

Chapter 3 continues this investigation of sonic embodiment, sound, and silence in mysticism and life-writing, arguing that Margery Kempe (d. ca. 1438) constructed her spiritual autobiography—*The Boke of Margery Kempe*—as a type of sonic body. More specifically, her sonic body is social and inter-subjective: Margery deftly leverages the intervals between sound and silence to create in her audience a sense of participatory rhetorical expectation and attendance. This chapter argues that Margery's sonic embodiment is what the twentieth-century sound theorist Jacques Attali might have called a "noisy silence" or what Lisbeth Lipari refers to as an "ethics of attunement" That is, sonic meaning accrues at the social intersection of silence and noise, and listening is at the heart of all communicative acts.[25] Margery's noisy weeping—her most famous attribute—is, throughout her *Boke,* balanced and given meaning by moments of tactical silence that bring the listener into attunement with her vocal performances.[26]

Because of its focus not just on the sensation of sound and silence, but on sound as a marker of communication between two people or groups of people, this chapter develops the notion of the sonic body begun in Chapters 1 and 2. However, whereas the first two chapters make a single "self" the focus of sonic embodiment, Chapter 3 opens up the self to the listening other, arguing that the sonic body can also be intersubjective. Here, I build on Julie Orlemanski's conception of Margery's sonority as a form of "distributed expressivity."[27] For Margery Kempe, the sonic body arises out of interdependence; the *Boke* is simultaneously congenial and unsettled because *canor* and the self are always dependent on the experience of the other.

Chapter 4 continues the exploration of intersubjective sonic bodies in mysticism that Chapter Three began. In the margin of folio 33v of the sole surviving manuscript of *The Boke of Margery Kempe,* next to a moment that describes Margery's vociferous weeping, there is a cryptic reference to two Carthusian monks: "so fa RM & f Norton of Wakenes & of the passyon." Who are "RM" and "f Norton," and what was their relationship to Margery's noisy performance of Rollean *canor*? This chapter answers these questions in the first modern study of the mystical diary of John Norton (from a unique manuscript, Lincoln Cathedral MS 57), which I read alongside its partner-text, the mystical diary of Richard Methley (also contained in a unique manuscript, Trinity MS O.2.56).[28] Both men lived and wrote in the Charterhouse of Mount Grace in the late fifteenth century, and their manuscripts perform an intersubjective, textual sonic body.

As the multiple similarities, borrowings, and exchanges in their manuscripts show, Methley's and Norton's manuscripts were written collaboratively: both contain accounts of their mystical experiences, which are in large part indebted to Rollean *canor.* Both also rely heavily on intertextuality in order to encompass their experiences: the manuscripts share an extensive array of formal, generic, and thematic qualities.[29] Carthusians sang their offices together less frequently than other monastic orders; in this chapter, I argue that Methley and Norton displace sonic embodiment onto their texts. Their manuscripts show a sense of friendly responsibility and kinship, not only to each other, but also to the unique needs of their Carthusian community, where their musical intertexts produce a sonic body that is itself open to other readers and overhearers. In the words of John Norton, *canor* is the unbounded spiritual love that exists between brothers.

Chapters 5 and 6 turn away from forms of sonic embodiment in life-writing or literature that imagines itself as nonfiction to explore sonic bodies in narrative and lyric poetry of the fourteenth century.

In Chapter 5, I argue that William Langland's figural or allegorical personifications are sonic bodies. This chapter uses Pierre Schaeffer's notion of the *objet sonore* (sound object) to argue that William Langland's *Piers Plowman* is an experiment in reifying sound and in making music—literally—matter.

For Schaeffer, sounds themselves could become objects according to the principles of Husserlian adumbration. Schaeffer, a composer and electronic musician, took sounds out of their original context and clipped, distorted, and looped them; when he did so, the sounds became unrecognizable, forcing the listener to attend to them merely as sounds without any of their original intentionality or causal referents. Out of Schaeffer's early experiments arose a discourse—inflected by contemporary sound studies—that understood sounds as objects: ones not bounded by space or tactility, but instead by temporality and memory. Like Schaeffer's music, *Piers Plowman* is built of sonic objects, from the aural loops of its alliterative long lines to its resonating personifications and its final passus, which experiment with the ramifications of sonic objecthood for the Christian commune. All of these forms of sonic embodiment are related, as *Piers Plowman*'s soundscape enacts subjectivities that are mutable, profoundly incorporative, and methexic rather than mimetic. The poem's sonic landscape is the ground on which the interrelatedness, interpenetration, and intersubjectivities of the text are built, the source of its ethics, assimilatio, and protreptics. In the context of the sonic object, *Piers*'s musical moments can be seen as experiments in communitarian thinking—moments in which bodies are formed not around individual identity, but instead around the belonging of communal performance. For Schaeffer and other sound studies scholars—Michel Chion, Brian Kane, Mladan Dolar, and Rey Chow among them—sound studies is primarily reliant on the possibility for iterable auditory phenomena that the phonograph and pursuant technologies of the last century or so have allowed. But, I argue, *Piers Plowman*, in giving sounds bodies, imagines this reification of sound avant la lettre.[30] Reading *Piers Plowman* for the way it reifies sound opens an avenue for sound studies prior to the invention of modern recording technology.

In the final chapter, I argue that Chaucer makes the notions of musicality as disability, loss, and absence central to his poetics. Chaucer crips medieval music theory's definition of itself as mental and physical capability, instead showing that musical not-having, lack, and delay allow his work—which is uniquely antagonistic to music among his fourteenth-century contemporaries—to inhabit the potency of music tout court. In Chaucerian poetry, the body of music is quite literally an absence or aporia, and by casting the body of music into the elsewhen/elsewhere, Chaucer authorizes his poetic project as the reparative site of musical lack. Music in Chaucer's poetry frequently exists in spaces of embodiment beyond the body, a maneuver that Chaucer makes intentionally, challenging the assumption that the voice indicates presence and text is a form of absence. Poetry becomes *poesis* in the moment it emerges from dichotomous notions of embodiment as presence and text as absence. I call this poetic endless deferral of musical ability an *advental body*. The chapter investigates the body of Echo in the Franklin's Tale, the lyric *I* in the triple ballad *Fortune*, which has resonances in the formal structure of Chaucer's dream poems, and Troilus's body in *Troilus and Criseyde*. Each of these bodies inhabits sonorous asynchronies, delaying music for the purposes of poesis.

*Sonic Bodies* attempts to break down ways of thinking about the body that conflate the normative physical form, the flesh, and the body, and to imagine a more capacious body and a more capacious musical landscape that includes intersubjective subjects as well as forms of discourse on the fringes of organized sonority. The project of sonic embodiment is a project of recuperation, of trying to imagine the ways in which sound or music—sensations that we generally think of as transient or fleeting—might take on some of the qualities of "the body," and, in doing so, challenge our notions of the body's limits.

# Chapter 1

# *Musica Celestis* and *Canor*

## Angelic Song in Speculative Music Theory
## and Rollean Mysticism

But another species of music can, as it seems, to be added to these,
which can be called "celestial" or "divine." This species of music
considers things separated from motion and perceptible matter,
and according to their being and according to the intellect:
namely, transcendental things pertaining to metaphysical or
divine knowledge.

—Jacobus, *Speculum musicae*

In the seventh book of his *Speculum musicae*, Jacobus passes judgment on the
songs and singers of the *ars musica* in an extended, bestial metaphor: the *ars
nova* is bad because its music sounds animalic, and its singers are like dogs
because of the animalistic bodily contortions the musical style requires.[1] This
passage is colorful and evocative, and has garnered much scholarly attention
as a result. But in a much less well-known and less commented-upon moment
in the *Speculum*, Jacobus considers a different type of singing body and the
music that flows from it. These are the metaphysical bodies of separate substances (or what we moderns might think of, simplistically, as angels), who
have bodies that are not part of the material world. Their songs are as divine
as the songs of the *ars nova* are demonic. "Celestial or divine music (*musica
celestis vel divina*)," Jacobus says, is music that considers "transcendent things
pertaining to metaphysical [knowledge] or divine knowledge."[2] In a passage
of the *Speculum* devoted to outlining the three Boethian categories of music

(*musica mundana, musica humana,* and *musica instrumentalis*), Jacobus adds *musica celestis vel divina* as a logical—if metaphysical—extension to the list.

Although Jacobus is often thought of as an arch-conservative, it is difficult to understate how radical his addition of *musica celestis* to the existing taxonomy of music is. For over eight hundred years, Boethius's (d. 524) tripartite division of music in *De musica* had been the standard for the medieval period's understanding of music. Boethius classified music according to the three types of bodies in which it adhered: in *musica instrumentalis*, it took up residence in instruments or the mouths of singers; in *musica humana*, the human body served as the material container for the incorporeal soul; and in *musica mundana*, stellar bodies whirled about the heavens, making music as they went.[3] In imagining that there is a type of music that is made by "things separated from motion and perceptible matter," Jacobus is allowing that metaphysical bodies—the bodies of angels—could also be entwined with song, even though those bodies did not attach themselves to matter and their songs were phenomenally silent. That music might be *silent* was not such a departure from earlier music theory (indeed, of the three Boethian forms of music, *musica humana* and *musica mundana* either made no sound or made sounds so rarified that humans could not hear them). But what *was* radical was the assertion that a type of real, legitimate music might exist without matter in which to resound.

As Aristotelian philosophy made its way into the curricula of European universities—particularly Paris and Oxford—over the course of the thirteenth and fourteenth centuries, it made possible a new way of interrogating and organizing creation. Jacobus's articulation was a response to these new ways of thinking. Although music (as one of the quadrivial or mathematical arts) was never a central focus of study in the medieval university, it, too, took on a particularly Aristotelian flavor, its definition shifting as it did so.[4] Whereas for Boethius (and early medieval speculative music theory by extension) music was about cosmic relations, by the late Middle Ages, the discipline of music was understood to pertain primarily to sound. By 1250, the current definition of music had shifted from *numerus relatus* to *numerus relatus ad sonos* and then, later, it was defined more specifically as follows: "Music is number related to sound, from which relations consonances are made; therefore, music concerns consonance."[5]

But what, then, is the sound of angels singing? If medieval music, as Boethius claimed and as later medieval music theorists argued, was music practiced by and upon bodies—instrumental, human, and planetary—then the ontological taxonomies of the medieval period themselves posed a problem for a definition of angelic song. Angels sang, as Scripture and medieval devotional literature illustrate: Isaiah 6:3 records two seraphim singing antiphonally; the angelic visitors of the Nativity sing the *Gloria* in Luke 2:14, and in Revelation 5:11 and 7:11 John hears the angels praising God; medieval visionary literature from Pseudo-Dionysius to Hildegard von Bingen and from Richard Rolle to Bridget of Sweden all describe, in vibrant detail, interactions with angels and their songs.[6] Medieval literature, too, contains countless references to the angelic song of the *Gloria* and the *Sanctus*, from Dante's *Commedia* to the plays of the *Corpus Christi* cycle.[7] "The song of the angels," Augustine says, "is poured out exultantly."[8]

But, crucially, most medieval philosophers held that angels did not have material bodies, and that their songs were silent. In the early medieval period's Neoplatonic worldview, all existing entities in the universe were ranked in a hierarchy of being that placed pure spirit—God—at the top of the hierarchy and pure matter—rocks and stones—at the bottom. Later medieval taxonomies perpetuated this hierarchy, albeit with new terms of art borrowed from Aristotelian philosophy. As pure form, God's fully actuated essence could be in no place and in all places at once, with instantaneous perfect knowledge of all particular things and abstract ideas. On the other end of the spectrum, on the lowest rung of that hierarchy, were nonliving things made of pure matter—rocks and minerals—who did not have souls at all.[9] Between God and the mineral world lay a wide spectrum of ensouled bodies: plants, endowed with a vegetative soul, which grew and reproduced but did not "think" or locomote; animals, with a sensitive soul, who had the capacity not only to grow and propagate, but also to sense the world around them, to move, to remember, and to desire; and humans, who in addition to possessing a vegetative and sensitive soul, also possessed an intellective soul that gave them the ability to reason and to form abstract conclusions from specific sense impressions. Human reason required a material or empirical connection to the world and the body—in the act of hearing, for instance, a physical perturbation of the air acted on human ears, which received the species of sound—but this sense-input inspired the higher functions of the common sense, the imagination, and the estimative faculty to draw broader conclusions.[10] *Musica mundana*, *musica humana*, and *musica instrumentalis* slot easily into this hierarchy, as, thus far, all the potentially musical bodies are also material ones.

But unlike humans and the rest of the created world, angels lacked material bodies. Augustine, for instance, noted that "angels [. . .] do not have bodies that can be felt."[11] John Damascene (d. 749) called angels "intellectual substance," nearly six hundred years later, Aquinas called them "separate substances" and "incorporeal substances," concluding that they must exist because God intended for the universe to—as nearly as possible—mirror his own goodness, and because "God produces the creature by his intellect and will. Hence the perfection of the universe requires that there should be intellectual creatures."[12] Placed between humans and God in the ontological hierarchy, angels were a little like humans—delimited in their ability to know, circumscribed in their powers, and, compared to God, "material and corporeal"[13]—even though they did not, in Aquinas's view, have "anything corporeal in them." While angels might temporarily assume material bodies in order to communicate with other material bodies (namely, humans), these bodies were not, as Aquinas argued, real bodies, but only *simulacra*, and their speech in these moments is "not real speech but a certain resemblance by the likeness of effect."[14] This ventriloquism was different from natural angelic song; divorced from sensuality and sense-perception, angels normally did not require flesh to hear, perceive, or communicate.

There were numerous debates about angels—how they communicated, what they knew, when they had come into being, whether they had free will, whether they existed in place and space or not—in the thirteenth and fourteenth centuries, and I am greatly simplifying these debates here.[15] Bernard of Clairvaux (d. 1153) seems to have anticipated these debates in his *Commentary on the Song of Songs*:

> Whether the bodies of angels be natural to them as bodies are to men; whether, immortal though they be, their bodies have an animal nature like man's, which in this life is not immortal; whether they change these bodies and turn them into whatever form and figure suits them when they wish to become visible, imparting to them the density and solidity that fits their purpose, while at the same time, in the reality of their own nature with its essential subtlety, they remain impalpable to us and beyond our power of vision; or whether again, while continuing to exist as simple spiritual substances, they merely assume bodies when they find a need for them and then, once the need has passed, allow them to dissolve again into the elements from which they were formed—all these are questions which I prefer that you should not ask me. The Fathers seem to have held divergent views on the problem, and I must confess

that I cannot come to a decision about the view I might be justified
in teaching. But I am of the opinion that knowledge of these matters
would not contribute greatly to your spiritual progress.[16]

Bernard's weary tone anticipates the next two centuries of debate on the subject of angelic bodies.[17] If the early medieval period addressed angelic embodiment as part of the plenitude of creation, the later medieval period, with
its Scholastic syllogisms and argumentative methodology, formalized a number of logical problems about angelic bodies that early medieval writers had
also discussed, and that, for his part, Bernard seems keen to elide. Aquinas,
Bonaventure (d. 1274), Henry of Ghent (d. 1293), Richard of Middleton (d.
1308), John Duns Scotus (d. 1308), Giles of Rome (d. 1316), Durandus of Saint-
Pourcain (d. 1334), and William Ockham (d. 1347) all addressed the difficult
problem of angelic embodiment, and while their conclusions are nuanced,
the immateriality of angelic substance was, with the exception of Bonaventure, largely axiomatic in thirteenth- and fourteenth-century philosophy.[18]
Separate substances were not bodies, but they were not *not* bodies, either.

     In short, medieval philosophy was not in total agreement about angelic
bodies, but in general held them to be untiring and often metaphysical;
their vocal cords—such as they were—could sing ceaselessly. Moreover, their
songs were disentangled from human rhetoric, grammar, and logic, possessing a divine logic of their own. And yet, in spite of this, angelic song
was, in some shadowy sense, performed through human writing and liturgical performance.

     If medieval music is a practice that unites mind to flesh and ideation to
substance, then singing angelic bodies force a reconsideration of what is actually meant by the terms *flesh, substance,* and *matter.* Angels sing, but their
song is immaterial, and because their bodies are not made of "hard" matter,
their songs cannot propagate through the air or make a sound.[19]

     When Jacobus wrote his "conservative" *Speculum,* then, he also tasked
himself with making space for a totally current philosophical discussion
across mysticism, literature, and liturgical practice, taking the common claim
that angelic song *could be heard,* and squaring this with philosophy, which
held the opposing view. The *Speculum musicae* formally acknowledged angelic song by granting it space alongside *musica munda, humana,* and *instrumentalis,* naming angelic song *musica celestis vel divina* (heavenly or divine
music).[20] Jacobus devotes two chapters of his *Speculum musicae* to *musica celestis*; in a treatise that runs through seven volumes, the addition to the

Boethian taxonomy of music seems small, but it is radical in its expansion
of the possible bodies that might emerge from, contain, or perform music.
Jacobus posits that the most rarified, perfect type of music is not in matter
at all—not the human body, the heavens, or anywhere else—but in the resonant space of transcendent things—angels.

According to Jacobus, *musica celestis* "considers things (*res*) that are separated from motion and sensible matter, both according to their being and
according to their understanding: namely, transcendent things that pertain
to metaphysics or theology."[21] Aristotle, Jacobus argues, arrived at knowledge of separate substances by observing the motion of sensible matter:
because sensible matter moved, the intellect should, too. Jacobus takes this
thought-experiment a step further: if melody can exist in "corporeal, natural, or substantial numbered things," then it should also exist in "metaphysical things" as well; Jacobus is effectively positioning music in all three
divisions of philosophy: physics, mathematics, and metaphysics.[22] If music
is about the relative and proportional movement of things, then some of those
things should be cognitive things. Moreover, the very word "music" connotes
its relationship to immateriality. The word, Jacobus says, comes from *muso
sas*, which means "to inquire by thinking," and if, in turn, the things that
pertain to wisdom are metaphysical things, why should there not be a form
of music that is metaphysical?[23] Music is everywhere, and there is nothing
that is without music; this everywhere, naturally, extends to the realm of
metaphysical things.[24]

The *Speculum* presents an alternative medieval taxonomy of music to
those available to earlier writers, proposing a new meaning for "heavenly
music." When, a generation earlier, Jerome of Moravia (d. 1272) wrote about
the *sonus caelestium corporum* in his *Tractatus de musica*, the sound of heaven
to which he referred was the sound of the planets and stars, or Boethius's
*musica mundana*.[25] Jacobus's *musica celestis* refers to something else entirely,
and the immaterial angelic song he argues for exists in the realm of metaphysical, rather than physical, inquiry.[26]

Jacobus's *Speculum musicae* survives in only one complete and two partial copies, and it appears never to have circulated broadly nor to have been
widely cited in Jacobus's day.[27] Although Jacobus's addition of *musica celestis*
to the ambit of musical investigation presented a novel space for speculative
music in the late medieval period, the *Speculum* was never popular in his generation or the ones that followed, and his fascinating discussion of *musica
celestis* is an intellectual dead end. If there is a tendency in thirteenth- and

fourteenth-century music theory to accommodate metaphysical song, Jacobus's *musica celestis* is a symptom of a broader cultural and philosophical movement rather than its etiology. Like Jacobus, a number of other music theorists of the fourteenth and fifteenth centuries—who were also embedded in Scholastic debates about the nature of angelic being—also touched on the notion of angelic song and came to similar (if less thorough) conclusions. As a result of increased speculation about the nature of angelic being, language, and embodiment in the wider intellectual field of late medieval philosophy, angelic song is briefly contemplated in a handful of speculative music treatises of the late medieval period.

Among these is Johannes de Grocheio's (1255–1320) *Ars musicae,* which deploys immaterial angelic embodiment in order to define angelic song as the antithesis of *musica instrumentalis*:

> Since, therefore, among everything created by God, man, after the angels, receives more—that is, to understand and to reason—he ought to applaud Him through his good works and to praise him night and day. However, in this office, the angels have more power on account of the nobility of their nature and because they do not use organs that are sensitive and fatigable. But man cannot continue this labor for a long time, because his form is in bodily material and he operates with bodily organs; but also because it is necessary for him to repeat other operations frequently, like eating and drinking, and sleeping, and many other operations accompanying these.[28]

Johannes asserts that angelic song exists, and that angels, who have a "nobility of nature" (*nobilitatem . . . naturae*), are unwavering singers. Humans have intellects, and this makes them good singers, but they cannot be perfect singers like the angels because their bodies—their corporeal matter—get in the way; their ears and vocal cords tire, they need to eat and drink, and their feet can stand in the choir only so long before failing. Angels, on the other hand, have no such weaknesses, not being possessed of physical flesh.

This angelic ability to sing without ceasing is referenced repeatedly in speculative music treatises of the late medieval period, where it is often described as an eternal *Sanctus* or *Gloria*. However, it is distinguished from its liturgical counterpart by its distended performance, an elongation of the repetitive cycle of liturgical time into the atemporality of celestial time. Angelic song is "unending,"[29] "ineffable," and "untiring."[30] In the *Practica artis musice* (1271) Amerus suggests that the *Sanctus* and *Gloria* often attributed to angels is a sort of otiose linguistic performance done for the pleasure and edification of human ears, but that in essence angels' song does not need— or have—human "grammar or logic."[31] This was a common sentiment in the period. Real angelic song, as Dante asserts in the *Convivio*, is "perfect peace," without the "sophistical arguments" that mark the very human debates about angelic embodiment.[32]

Other pronouncements of angelic song as metaphysical are glancing, but nonetheless suggest a similar investment in Scholastic debates about their embodiment. In the third decade of the fourteenth century, Henricus Helene (fl. 1335) indicates the separation of the nine orders of angels from the nine planetary spheres, calling angelic song not *musica celestis* but *musica supercelestis*—literally music above the heavens.[33] In the *Compendium musicale* of 1415, Nicholas of Capua names the music played in heaven, in the presence of God, *musica angelica*.[34]

Late medieval debates about the bodies of angels—reflected most fully in Jacobus's *musica celestis* and to a lesser extent by some of his contemporaries— exemplify a form of immaterial, silent sonic embodiment: neither a practice of the flesh nor purely an academic exercise of the mind, angels' song enacts a metaphysical body that transgresses the limits usually placed both on embodiment and on musicality.[35] *Musica celestis* emerges out of music theory's reconciliation of Scholastic philosophy with authoritative scriptural and experiential accounts of angelic song, the results of which are a categorical addition to the types of bodies and musics thought possible by music theory: a body without lips, tongue, vocal cords, or ears that could nonetheless hear and sing, and a song that was transcendentally silent. The concepts of metaphysical bodies and metaphysical song developed alongside each other, as writers like Aquinas, Bonaventure, and Ockham wrestled with angelic being and speculative musicians like Johannes de Grocheio and Jacobus considered the ramifications of angels' newly articulated bodies for music theory.

But what was perhaps an even more critical change in late medieval music pedagogy at the university and elsewhere was the increasing demand that speculative music treatises address *both* theory and contemporary musical performance practice. That is, not only *speculative* music but *practical* music treatises of the period had to wrestle with angelic embodiment. The "practical" nature of angelic music is perhaps most obvious in Johannes Ciconia's (1372–1412) *Nova musica,* a treatise that is interested in both practical and speculative music, combining Scholastic musical theory with experiential learning.[36] Tellingly, Ciconia opens his treatise by relating angelic song to the practice of *musica instrumentalis*:

> The holy fathers said that celestial harmony is the melody of the angels, [harmony] which they sing without end in the celestial father-land, in praise of the Creator. For when anyone who is blessed is led there, he will no longer have sadness or grieving anymore, because in seeing God, he will rejoice with him forever. Therefore to you, O prudent reader, let my discourse be made. Although you seek earthly harmony, which we promise to give to you, however, do not forget to seek from God that celestial harmony, which is so much sweeter than the heaven is seen to be higher than the earth.[37]

Ciconia's exhorts his reader to seek "celestial harmony" (*armoniam . . . cele-stem*) above all things. For Ciconia, angelic song is more than just a philosophical curiosity, but rather the goal of musical study, and, in its promise of reward in the afterlife, an ethical structuring principle of musical practice.

The type of metaphysical sonic body explored by Jacobus and others is unique to its particular discursive argot; when music theorists approach angelic song as a philosophical problem, the very formal and generic characteristics of their writing delineate and determine the types of bodies involved; mystics or poets, for whom personal narrative or fictionality, and not systematic philosophy, were the goal, necessarily produce different textually embodied forms from those writing in and for the university. *Musica celestis* is exemplary, but not determinative, of an immaterial form of sonic embodiment.

## Richard Rolle's *Canor:* Getting Beyond the Body with Audible Sound

The experiences recorded by medieval mystics provide another way of thinking about angelic song, as these writers—whose access to formal training in music varies widely—chart ways of understanding the relationship between sonic experience and embodiment along a diverse spectrum of generic and formal registers. As a result, descriptions of angelic song in mysticism differ from the more systematic accounts in treatises like Jacobus's *Speculum*, sometimes paralleling, but never identifying with, *musica celestis*.

From Pseudo-Dionysius's *Celestial Hierarchy* in the sixth century to Bernard of Clairvaux's sermons on guardian angels in the twelfth and Bridget of Sweden's account of heavenly visions in the fourteenth, medieval mystical treatments of sonic embodiment are marked by idiosyncratic and hyperindividualized experiences of angelic song that simultaneously and paradoxically engage in very conventional textual borrowing and citation.[38] These accounts are varied and fecund, and to treat them as a monolithic account of angelic song would do disservice to them all. Nevertheless, there is one writer for whom angelic song and sonic embodiment is vital: the fourteenth-century mystic Richard Rolle.

Rolle is important for a study of sonic embodiment for a number of reasons. Not only was the spiritual sensation of song absolutely fundamental to his mystical practice (he called this song *canor*), but his written corpus also had a deep impact on later medieval English mysticism and devotional writing. If Jacobus's *Speculum* appears to be an intellectual dead end, the work of Richard Rolle, Jacobus's contemporary, is the opposite: during his lifetime and in the century or so after his death, Rolle was widely read; more English manuscripts from the fourteenth and fifteenth centuries include texts written by or attributed to Rolle than any other English author, and today, the accepted Rollean corpus runs to over thirty prose pieces and at least fifteen verse compositions.[39]

Rolle's popularity stems in large part from the stunning range of his work. Even if, as Nicholas Watson argues, Rolle considered himself a "spiritual elitist," many of his works have a populist effect: Rolle translated the Psalms into English, he penned empathetic vernacular epistles, and his poems—meant for affective devotional practice—were copied and read by laypeople, Lollards, and orthodox Carthusians alike. While Rolle wrote Latin commentaries on the Psalter and the Song of Songs as well as more difficult original treatises on contemplation in Latin in an effusive, highly alliterative, and ornate style, he never seems to have finished university (and may never have gone, even though he is traditionally thought to have attended Oxford); his writing shows the influence not of Scholastic writing practice but of the affective mysticism of the Franciscan and Bernardine tradition: the *Stimulus amoris*, Anselm's *Orationes sive meditationes*, the *Itinerarium mentis in Deum*, and Bernard's sermons on the Song of Songs.[40] Rolle never took holy orders, either, but instead worked as a private spiritual counselor, first for the family of John de Dalton, and then for the Cistercian nuns of Hampole, specifically Margaret Kirkeby. The close personal connections Rolle had to those whom he served as a spiritual guide eventually grew into a cultish following, as is evidenced by the *Officium et miracula,* a liturgical office written in a (fruitless) attempt to have him beatified in the fourteenth century.[41] Many writers from the later fourteenth and fifteenth centuries quote Rolle at length, mimic his style, respond critically to his affective mysticism, or in some way refer back to his work; perhaps the most famous example is Margery Kempe, who cites Rolle along with Walter Hilton, Bonaventure, and Bridget of Sweden as one of the *auctores* of her own spiritual practice. It is nearly impossible to imagine the rise of the written English vernacular without Rolle, and if there is a surfeit of mystics writing about angelic song in late medieval England, it is in large part due to Rolle's influence on their reading *habitus.* Most scholars today read Rolle as a mystic who privileged emotion over intellect, and whose spiritual practice—indebted more to Bonaventure than to Aquinas—was rugged, idiosyncratic, and sometimes strange. Katherine Zieman's reading is typical: Rolle's implicit privileging of affect over academic understanding led later writers to carry out cautious revisions of his work; but precisely because later writers felt the need to sanitize his work in this way, we can understand just how powerful Rolle's affective style was.[42]

If the scope of Rolle's writing is broad in its themes, genres, and its audience, it is nevertheless unified by its repeated focus on three integral embodied and spiritual sensations: a burning heat felt in the breast (which Rolle called *fervor* or *calor*), a taste of sweetness on the tongue (*dulcor*), and a heavenly melody heard by the ears (*canor*). Rolle borrowed *calor* and *dulcor* from Victorine and Bonaventurean sources, but *canor* was his own creation. With his experience of *canor*, argues Nicholas Watson, Rolle "passes beyond the traditional language of affective spirituality" into a space "where his own life is by far his most significant source."[43] The identification of *canor* with an experience that is specific and unique to Rolle has made it a central element of Rollean scholarship.[44]

For Rolle, the sonic body of *canor* is not a specific ontological category; it is not, as *musica celestis* is, the song of a metaphysical substance like angels, even though Rolle describes *canor* as "angelic song" (*angelica cantica*) and "angelic sweetness" (*angelica suavitas*).[45] Instead, tautologically, *canor* is the fleshly process of transcending the very flesh that animates *canor.* The work of *canor* is to tune the body so that it becomes the space into which sensory *qualia* enter and, through *canor*, become mystical.

*Canor* achieves this effect not by forcing the mystic to renounce fleshly sensation, but instead by soothing the mystic's physical body into a sleep that opens it up, making it more available to divine experience. *Canor*, Rolle says, is a "resting song" (*canticum quiescentes*), and "continual calm of mind and body" should be the goal of the mystic.[46] Moving around disturbs contemplation, for, "when wearied by the body, their balmy breast doesn't boil over with ballads," that is, when the body's physical demands tap its spiritual resources, mystics are unable to attain *canor*.[47] So, Rolle says, the mystic should aim for a sort of physical inertia. Rolle elaborates on this rest in the *Ego dormio*, glossing the Song of Songs. "I slepe and my herte waketh," he says, "for al the melody, al the richesse, al the delites that al the men of this world can ordeyne or thynke, semeth and is bot noy and angre to a mannes herte that verraily is brennynge in the loue of God, for he hath mirth and melody and ioy in angels songe."[48] Comfort is central to Rolle's strategy vis-à-vis his flesh, which is not strictly renunciatory, but rather, ambivalent in the literal sense of the word: the body participates in the process of finding *canor* by sleeping; Rolle calls flesh to participate in the immanence of the divine not through weeping or excessive penance, but rather by letting the body be *comfortable*. This rejection of renunciation itself is a sort of metarenunciation that deconstructs systems of renunciation. Here, if the flesh is left behind, it is left behind in a way that makes its continued maintenance of central importance to its absence. For Rolle and for *canor*, stillness and quietude of the corporeal body is not a simple rejection of the body, but a particular type of tuning in to it, a medieval sensory deprivation chamber, a type of mindfulness meditation in which the body becomes central to the same practice that forgets it.

That *canor* and exterior music operate on the body in different ways—*canor*, like a lullaby, soothing the body into somnolence, and exterior songs actively blocking the work of *canor*—is apparent in Rolle's *Contra amatores mundi*: "But the active rejoice in exterior songs; we, set on fire by divine contemplation fly beyond earthly things in the sound of feasting; . . . no one has been able to rejoice in the love of God who has not first relinquished the vain comforts of the world."[49] The renunciation of "vain comforts" applies specifically to the types of songs practiced by the embodied world, which Rolle rejects in favor of a heavenly song that is both *outside* and *within* the mystic: "All earthly melody (*melodia mundialis*), and all corporeal music (*corporalis musica*) played skillfully on musical instruments (*instrumentis organicis*), however much they may be pleasing to active people, or to secular men entangled in their affairs, they will not be desirable for contemplatives. Rather, they avoid hearing corporeal sound, because contemplative men have already received heavenly sound (*sonum celestem*) within themselves."[50] Rolle's language here does not use the exact Boethian terminology of *musica mundana*, *humana*, and *instrumentalis*, but it does engage the same general ideas of "earthly melody" and instrumental music that recall the materially embodied divisions of the *De musica*. These earthly forms of music must be rejected by the mystic in order to hear "celestial sound" (*sonum celestum*) that resides in the interior space of the mystical body. Simultaneously beyond the physical body and inside it, *canor* is outside the flesh to the extent that it refers to heaven, and inside it to the extent that it belongs, uniquely and personally, to the mystic's experience. *Canor* makes the transcendental familiar, and this familiarity, in turn, makes *canor* affective. Rolle understands the "bodies" at work in contemplation to be twofold: there is the exterior, physical body that sings in jumbled, earthly noises and which must be lulled to sleep, and there is the interior, spiritual body that, informed by *canor*, exists both inside and beyond itself.[51]

As the mystic begins to experience *canor*, their physical and mental spacetime is altered, and it becomes akin to the angelic intellect that sings *musica celestis*: "Lo, everlasting laudation is lodged within [me]. Melody miraculously remains in my mind; my ears overhear angelic amenity and a canorous canticle is conceived in my core."[52] Just as with angelic song in the speculative musical repertoire, which typifies angelic song as belonging to beings without "sensitive and fatigable organs," so too does the *iubilus* of *canor* operate in a sempiternal manner, and, in turn, makes the human mind more like the rational intellect of separate substances than a human mind: once a human being has attained a certain experience of *canor*, that knowledge is *always* present to them. In other words, here, Rolle suggests that the experience of *canor* leaves a mystic with a type of continually active knowledge; it is a process of the intellect and affect (*mente/corde*), and, rather than knowing something *in potentia*—which is how humans know most things—the mystic comes away from an experience of *canor* with the ability, like angels, to be in perpetual, actual knowledge of heaven at all times. "His melody-moderated mind is mutated (*mutetur*) so misgivings don't dismay it; his charity-chafed heart changes to chant to chime its strains in its chores for the Champion," says Rolle.[53] The mystic is *always* present, and always perpetually capable, and this capability is what replaces the physical body with a sonic one, even using the language of music theory (*mutetur*)—the shift of the hexachord from hard (*dura*) to soft (*mollis*)—to express his point.[54]

*Canor* is a continual, hierophanic outpouring that turns Rolle's mental, spiritual, or "psychological" makeup into song; it then draws him, through the phatic expression of the *iubilus*, away from mundane, material music. The final development of *canor* allows Rolle to remain in a constant musical relationship to God, no matter the actions of the outside world upon him, as his being is the resonant space of *canor* itself. "I do not know how to be silent," Rolle says, so that even when he is surrounded by ill-wishers, he is "sacredly subsisting by sitting in solitude, warbling and warm and gigantically jubilant."[55] *Canor* separates mind from body, removing the mundane restrictions that typically constrain human intellection (such as images, phantasms, or temporal divisions), even including the articulation of particular words, so that Rolle begins to speak, quite literally, another language—an angelic one. This is reminiscent of the postulate that angels do not need "grammar or logic" in order to communicate, as these are sensorial tools of the body. Those who are perfected by *canor* "will accordingly be crowned amid choristers choiring the canticle of canticles in the Creator's court, and they'll honorably be accepted as equals among angels for adoring so ardently and scorning carnal corruption."[56] *Canor* is not, then, *musica celestis*. It is the process by which the mystic attains something like it.

The processual nature of *canor* is poignantly illustrated in one of the most important devotional miscellanies to survive from late medieval England. British Library Additional MS 37049 is a Carthusian manuscript copied sometime in the last half of the fifteenth century. Studied extensively in Jessica Brantley's *Reading in the Wilderness*, the manuscript is a stunning compilation of didactic texts, poetry, and amateur images that, in Brantley's words, "seek to reproduce the experiential effects of dramatic performance."[57] An astounding variety of texts and images is represented in the manuscript—John Mandeville's *Travels*, quotations from the Heinrich Suso's *Horologium sapientiae*, selections from the *Danse macabre,* and extracts from the *Prick of Conscience*, as well as many full-page diagrams of trees, morbid drawings of corpses being eaten by worms, devotional images of the *arma Christi* and depictions of the five wounds—and it is no surprise that Rolle, too, appears in the manuscript on multiple occasions. Images of the hermit appear on folios 37r and 52v. In the first image, Rolle is seated; above him is a scroll surrounded by angels on which is written what Andrew Albin describes as a "fully singable" notated *Sanctus*.[58] Rolle holds a book open on his lap; the only legible word is *Ego*, a reference to the *Ego dormio*, four paragraphs of which are included a few pages earlier, on folios 30v–31r, under the image of a reclining man (who looks much like the picture of Rolle on 37r) who is depicted saying the Rollean phrase "I slepe and my hert wakes." This is an attempt to depict how sleep and the anti-renunciation of the flesh becomes *canor,* as folio

Figure 1. BL Additional MS 37049, fol. 84v: a man plays a harp;
above and to his right is a blank musical stave.

52v shows Rolle once more, this time seated, the Rollean lyric "I syt and synge
of luf langyng" beneath his feet, the words *armonia, odas, canora* written
above it.[59] For the Carthusian reader, these images and their accompanying
texts efficiently illustrate the complex embodiment of *canor*, which is both of
the sleeping body and not of it, both above it and internal to it.

But perhaps the most interesting image in the Carthusian miscellany is
on folio 84v (Figure 1). Here a figure—this time, if his blue robe, red stock-
ings, and well-trimmed hair are any indication, it is not Rolle—is seated in
a chair, playing a harp. The text that accompanies this image is a Middle
English adaptation and elaboration of Job 30:31 (*Versa est in luctum cithera
mea et organum meum in vocem flencium*; "Allas ful warly for wo may I synge /
For into sorow turned is my harpe"). Above the poem and to the right of the
musician is a five-line stave of music. Unlike the *Sanctus* on folio 37r, however,
the stave is blank; the poem is unsingable. While the five-line stave indicates
that the anticipated song is not chant, but instead polyphonic music, its empti-
ness dictates silence, the renunciation of sound in the performance of contrite
contemplation.[60] If the Rollean images that precede folio 84v portray the

performance of Rolle's nonrenunciatory practice of *canor,* the imagetext on folio 84v depicts a sonic body, quietly waiting, resonating with the spiritual longing for and receptivity of *canor*'s silence.

The preceding examples of *musica celestis* and of *canor* show that the sonic body contemplated by music is never straightforward; it is not necessarily ideational, nor is it purely carnal even when it draws on the logics of material embodiment (as *musica celestis* does, by analogizing the motion of separate substances to that of sensible matter) or uses material metaphors to surpass that very materiality (as Rolle does with *canor*). Both *musica celestis* and *canor* demonstrate late medieval writers wrestling with the types of bodies possible for music, and, in turn, the types of music that emanate from such bodies, specifically, what "music" means when it is materially silent, and what "the body" means when it is not made of matter. They suggest that music and the body are more capacious terms than eidetic carnality allows.

# Chapter 2

# Touching Music
## Walter Hilton, Angels' Song, and Synaesthesia

Heard melodies are *sweet,* but those unheard
Are *sweeter;* therefore, ye *soft* pipes, play on;
Not to the sensual ear, but, more endeared,
Pipe to the *spirit ditties of no tone.*
                    —John Keats, *Ode on a Grecian Urn*

When a saule es purified by luf of God, illumynd be wysdom,
stabild be the myght of God, than es the egh of the saule opynd to
behald gastly things, and vertus, and angels, and haly saules, and
hevenly thyngs. Than es the saule abil, because of clennes, to fele
the *touchyng,* the *spekyng* of goode aungels. *Thys touchyng and
spekyng, it is gastly, noght bodele.*
                    —Walter Hilton, *Of Angels' Song*

## Synaesthesia and the Failure of Language

In his *Ode on a Grecian Urn,* John Keats uses poetic language to create a hierarchical relationship between the music of the physical world and the silent
music of rumination on the aesthetic object. "Heard melodies are *sweet,*" Keats
says, "but those unheard / are *sweeter.*" Although heard music is "sweet," a
metaphor of taste so frequently applied to music that it lands, dead, on the
ears, unheard music is "sweeter," a distension of the original metaphor that
shocks the original, banal adjective into liveliness. The comparative "sweeter"

does real work here, as it creates a sense of relative worth between these two musics even though neither is fully defined. To do the impossible work of comparison between material music and spiritual music—the music of sound and the music of art—Keats marshals a synaesthetic vocabulary of gustation and tactility. In these lines spiritual music does more than just taste "sweeter"; it is also "soft." Within the space of a single line, spiritual aurality mutates seamlessly from a taste into a texture, a sensation that, in the following line, does not merely *touch*, but also engages the subject in a heightened sort of feeling, "endearing" the listener in an affective embrace. The metamorphosis of sound into touch marks a shift from the distal to the proximal senses as the poem charts a changing relationship between the sensing subject and the external world. Usually, the distance between the object of sensation and the subject or organ that senses it is what marks hearing, along with vision, the other distal sense, as both more objective and more rational than the other senses, like touch, where skin is both the medium of sensation and the place where it occurs.[1] But in Keats's poem, hearing becomes a type of touch, collapsing the spatial distance between object and subject.[2]

Through these metaphors, Keats's "unheard" music—whatever that might be—plays to ears that do not simply hear, but also can be oversweetened, touched, and clasped. At the same time, the language Keats uses to achieve this ouster creates a pressing problem: insufficient to the task of describing "the spirit ditties of no tone," unsure of whether poetry has the power to speak the very regimes of synaesthetic sensation that the art object—the urn, or the poem itself—induces in the viewer, the poem fails to actually represent the art object. Instead, it can only leave the reader with a suggestion toward finding their own experience of art: feel it, the poem seems to say, with your whole body simultaneously.[3] This is a poem where language fails, leaving sensation to fill the gap between experience and its articulation. But if this poem fails, it fails purposefully: by imagining a set of aesthetic sense-organs that cross sense-modalities—a set of ears that can hear, touch, and be touched—Keats's *Ode* creates a body whose job it is to acquiesce to the imperfect expressions of language.

Although written around four hundred years before the *Ode*, Walter Hilton's (d. 1396) *Of Angels' Song* uses a similar language of synaesthesia to plot the relationship between normative song and its metaphysical analogue. *Of Angels' Song* is a short epistle of advice (running to about six pages in modern editions, and only a few folios in the handful of manuscripts that contain it) that the Augustinian monk wrote to a "dere brother in Crist" in the final decades of the fourteenth century. Taking the title on its own, Hilton's treatise on angelic song promises to provide esoteric Scholastic philosophy on angelic embodiment.[4] But the anxieties that actually motivate Hilton's treatise are a series of pressing human issues about sensation and the interpretation of sense-data, as Hilton voices concern about how intense spiritual exercise can affect his fellow contemplative's perceptions. In *Angels' Song*, Hilton calls angels' song a "touchyng and spekyng," and, like Keats, says that the spiritual organs that hear it must be tuned not only to auditory phenomena, but also to the spiritual sensation of tactility. Like Keats's *Ode,* Hilton's treatise fails with a purpose: the sonic body that he proposes is one that calls into question the ability of sense-perception itself to provide epistemological certainty, and, as such, encourages resignation to religious orthodoxy.

The treatise can be summarized briefly.[5] In *Of Angels' Song,* Hilton argues that angels do not have material bodies, and so their songs are fundamentally different from the vibrating matter that physical human ears and minds interpret as music. Most reported instances of "angelic song" are not angels' song at all, he says, but instead different forms of spiritual or physical illness: deceptions of the devil, auditory symptoms of psychosomatic stress brought on by excessive spiritual exercise, or the slippage of a spoken/reiterated mantra (like the word *Ihesu*) into melodiousness through the process of repetition.[6] However, Hilton admits that on very rare occasions, a devout contemplative might be granted an ineffable experience of heaven where she hears angels singing a song that "may noght be descried be na bodely liknes." This song is experienced as a "gastly" or spiritual touch whose effects occur beyond symbolic or imaginary frameworks. Angels' song "may be feled and a persayved in a saule, but it may noght be shewed," Hilton says.[7] The letter ends with an admonishment to the "dere brother" that, because of the dangers and uncertainties surrounding this rare phenomenon, he avoid angelic song if at all possible. "It suffices me," Hilton says in a closing line, "to live in trouth principally, and noght in felyng."[8] Hilton's pragmatic valedictory suggestion is that the mystic forgo the excessive and unbridled outbursts symptomatic of angelic song, replacing them instead with the "psalmes and ympnes and antymps of haly kyrk."[9]

It is the failure of Hilton's treatise to accurately address or fully define the very subject it purports to speak about—angelic song—that, ultimately, proves to be the text's raison d'être and its most compelling foray into an anthropology of auditory embodiment. In fact, the text fails on multiple occasions, each time building up to a final climax and then a denouement of purposeful failure. First, Hilton fumbles through a description of ineffability and disembodiment using metaphors of the body: angelic song may not be described by bodily likeness, he says; nevertheless, it is like a spiritual "touching," as this chapter's epigraph notes. Next, Hilton asserts that angelic song exists, and attempts to describe it, but, recognizing the impossibility of his task, admits that he does not really know what it is. In the final lines of the treatise, Hilton says that it suffices him to live not in "felyng," but in "trouth" (*troth*), validating an allegiance to the meaning-making hegemony of the liturgy (the "psalmes and ympnes and antymps of haly kyrk") that obviates the need for the music of angels in the first place. This is the goal of Hilton's text: not to educate the "dere brother" on angels' song, but instead to persuade him away from the perilous individuality of spiritual music and toward the policed subjectivity its liturgical counterpart requires.

We do not know who Hilton's "dere brother" was—whether he was a real individual or a handy rhetorical fiction—and the concerns of the letter are, at the end of the day, as patronizing as they are fraternal, marking a stark contrast to the other set of monastic friends this book will investigate in Chapter 4, the Carthusian *confreres* Richard Methley and John Norton.[10] Nevertheless, the "dere brother's" identity is less important than the real, implied target of Hilton's letter: *Of Angels' Song* is generally found, both in manuscript and in early print, alongside treatises on the discernment of spirits and Rollean material. In the half century between his death and when Hilton picked up his pen, Richard Rolle (d. ca. 1349)—the mystic, biblical exegete, and poet—had become one of the most popular English authors in England. For Rolle, mystical song—*canor*—was a type of music that overwhelmed the body, sometimes going so far as to paralyze it, and as a result, Rolle's mysticism encouraged its listeners to neglect the liturgy and other forms of orthopraxis for their own personal and private experience of heavenly song. By the late fourteenth and early fifteenth centuries, the highly individualized and effusive practice of Rollean *canor* had become problematic even as—and because—it had grown in popularity.[11] *Of Angels' Song*, then, responds not only to the unnamed "dere brother" to whom the text is explicitly addressed, but also to Rolle's readers, followers, and cult more generally, serving as a corrective to the more effusive Rollean oeuvre. By the time he wrote *Of Angels' Song,* Hilton had already penned a longer critique of Rolle in his *Scale of Perfection* and *De imagine peccati,* where he suggested that Rolle's obsession with the body in mystical experience missed the point of religious contemplation; in Hilton's opinion, the goal of mystical experience was mastery over and rejection of the flesh rather than the dangerous entanglement of body and soul he saw operating in Rolle's work, particularly in his experience and expressions of *canor,* which so thoroughly affected the flesh as to overwhelm it.[12]

Hilton's career marks the beginning of one of the most important periods of epistemological anxiety surrounding popular religion and populist religious movements—and their connection to *soth* versus *trouth*—in English history. The Peasants Revolt of 1381 (in which the Lollard John Ball played a large role) and then the dismissal of John Wycliffe from the University of Oxford that same year ushered in a century of suspicion of lay devotion and religious practice that would not end with the Reformation of the sixteenth century, but only be heightened.[13] *Of Angels' Song* was written and then later circulated in the time of Henry IV's publication of *De heretico comburendo* (1401), Arundel's *Constitutions* (1407), the condemnation of Lollardy (1410), and the Oldcastle Revolt (1414). In light of the late medieval religious context—where Rolle's mysticism abutted a newfound anxiety around individual spiritual experience—*Of Angels' Song* is not an esoteric, narrow, or provincial topic, but, rather, a central one.

*Of Angels' Song,* then, is not just about defining angelic song: it is also about using the inability to define angelic song to throw private, personal sensory experience into question. From a contemporary perspective, skepticism seems to serve the purpose of the individual; indeed, in its early modern, Enlightenment, and modern instantiations from Pico della Mirandola (d. 1494) and the humanists to American Christian anarchism, skepticism has often worked as a tool of popular revolt. But in the thirteenth and fourteenth centuries, empirical skepticism was often deployed by the arbiters of orthodoxy in order to delegitimize the sensations of specific classes of laypeople, particularly women, as the vituperative work of men like William of Auvergne and Jean de Gerson (who, most famously, inveighed against Joan of Arc's visionary experience) shows.[14] If the senses might be the foundation of belief, it is difficult for authoritative power structures to invalidate individual spiritual practice, but by negating affect as a legitimate mode of devotional experience, those same power structures cast doubt on the individual's perceptual abilities, and consequently compel them to deny their own personal religious practice. That is, while, in general, the Middle Ages did, as Steven Justice argues, "believe in their miracles" in more than a parabolic sense, there were specific political and social moments in which the power of miraculous sensation might also pose a challenge to orthodoxy. Skepticism—particularly the sort of skepticism Hilton encourages in *Of Angels' Song*—is merely one such example, a useful hegemonic tool for the rift in the orthodox fabric the Augustinian monk identified.[15] Far from being a revolutionary philosophical position, skepticism might be the tool of a reactionary power structure against practitioners who reach the event horizon of that structure.

But if Hilton's allegiance to *trouth* over *felyng* betrays a desire to dwell in the articulatable space of normative religious practice, in doing so, it also proves the existence and incantatory power of this form of music through the very attention it gives the topic. On the one hand, there is the inscribable and imaginable body that hears the "psalmes and ympnes and antymps of haly kyrk" and that he leaves the reader with at the end of the text. On the other hand, there is the impossible, unpoliceable, and much more *interesting* spiritual body that emerges out of the audiation of angelic song. Like Keats's *Ode*, which builds a case for the aesthetic object by failing to circumscribe it in language, Hilton's failure to describe angelic song can be read as an apophatic mystical engagement with the very object it so critically opposes. Angels' song, he says, "may noght be discried be na bodely liknes, for it es gastly, and aboven al maner ymaginacioun and reson. It maybe feled and persayved in a saule, but it may noght be shewed."[16] Hilton never says that angelic song does not exist, but only that descriptions using "bodily likeness" fail. On one level, this is unsurprising: the failure of language to describe mystical experience is absolutely essential to the genre; without ineffability topoi, mystical treatises would easily collapse into more mundane spiritual genres.[17] It is therefore not particularly interesting—nor is it possible—to determine just how close to the "soth" Hilton's description of angelic song might have come. In spite of what seems to be a willful *failure* here, the treatise nevertheless leaves its reader with room to dwell in the impossible space of spiritual sound. When Hilton describes angelic song as a sort of "ghostly touch," he is positing a form of spiritual embodiment that invokes the language of interiority, of synaesthesia, and of affect, marking a spiritual body that is fashioned—or indeed, remains unfashioned and indeterminate—and that evades the formal or symbolic and subjectivizing forces placed upon the material body with its externalizing, self-to-world direction of fit. Though Hilton ultimately rejects this body as imprudent and impossible to describe, it is there. And it has repercussions for the way we understand what the sonic body of medieval musical experience is. Elsewhere, as in the epigraph at the head of this chapter, Hilton describes angelic song as a type of touch. The important question, then, is not so much why Hilton failed to describe angelic song (angelic song is ineffable), but rather, why Hilton's treatise fails to describe its object by using touch as its metaphor.

Medieval philosophy borrowed its theories of the sensation of touch primarily from two sources: Aristotle on the one hand (in particular *De anima* II.II), and Avicenna on the other. For these authors and their Scholastic readers, the senses of touch and taste were distinct from the other three senses (smell, sight, and hearing) in terms of the relationships they drew between the objects, mediums, and organs of perception. On the one hand, sights, sounds, and odors, which are the objects of vision, hearing, and smell, all radiated from their sources through the air and were received by their respective organs (the eyes, ears, and nose). Seeing, hearing, and smelling were defined in part by distance (hence their appellation as "distal" senses); they worked because there was a physical divide between the sensing human and the object of perception. Touch and taste, on the other hand, collapsed these spatial distances: according Aristotle, the flesh was the medium of touch and the heart its organ, and for Avicenna, the organ of touch was the flesh. In spite of differences in the Aristotelian and Avicennan framework, the distinction between the proximal senses (touch and taste) and the distal ones is clear: touch brings the object and subjects of sensation into contact with each other.[18] By calling angelic song a type of touch, Hilton is implying that metaphysical audiation works with the immediacy and proximity of touch, that the organ receptive to angelic song is not the ear, but the heart, and that angelic song has the capacity to bypass physical sonic media, to collapse the distance between its source (the angel) and its target (the heart).[19]

Hilton, who had been a student at Cambridge before becoming a solitary, would have been well aware of Aristotelian and Avicennan models of physical sensation when he wrote *Of Angels' Song*, and so it seems reasonable to read his commingling of the senses of hearing and touch as an intentional blending of the proximal and distal senses.[20] In spite of itself, *Of Angels' Song* depicts a spiritual sensorium that is synaesthetic and that is uniquely tuned

to spiritual music. This is the sonic body of angelic audiation: a dedifferentiated, immediately integrated, and always already transcendent body.

## Spiritual Sensation, the Internal Senses, and the Synaesthetic Body

At the same time, there is another tradition working alongside the Scholastic
models of sensation in Hilton's treatise, and that is spiritual sensation. Whereas
the physical senses are primarily concerned with *external objects,* spiritual sensation is processual and non-object-oriented, focused primarily on feelings or
affects, and it is impossible to understand how the synaesthesia at work in
Hilton's treatise operates without an understanding of spiritual sensation.

From Origen to Bonaventure and Albert the Great to Nicholas of Cusa,
many Christian philosophers of the late classical and medieval periods wrote
about spiritual sensations. While the specific qualities of spiritual sensations
are often unique to the individual writer, some basic characteristics can be
outlined.[21]

In the first place, the spiritual senses are (usually, though not always)
depicted as something distinct from the five Aristotelian internal senses
(common sense, imagination, estimation, fantasy, and memory), although
they are often aligned with them. In the *Opus maius,* for instance, Roger
Bacon (d. 1292) treats the spiritual senses as a unique form of "internal knowledge" that is apprehended and operated upon by the internal senses, and
Albert the Great (d. 1280) compares the spiritual senses to different aspects
of internal sensation: spiritual sight and hearing are connected to the intellect, and spiritual taste, touch, and smell are connected to the *affectus* or will
in his commentary on the *Sententiae.*[22] From common sense to imagination,
estimation, fantasy, and memory, each progressive level of internal sensation
adds a corresponding layer of abstraction to the input from physical sensation, synthesizing the preceding sense in order to make diverse and discrete
data available to the rarified and immaterial intellect. The internal senses
are the means by which the external world becomes accessible to the immaterial soul. In this system, the spiritual senses remain distinct from the
internal senses; they are not a part of cognition, but prior to it.

The spiritual senses operate in a manner analogous to the five external
senses (exteroceptions), and in fact actually sense things. The objects of their
perception just happen to be immaterial things. In spiritual sensation, ex-

teroceptive language, that is, language that uses the five external senses as metaphor, is deployed to describe different ways of experiencing God, angels, or other metaphysical beings. But spiritual sensation is more than just metaphor. Not only does spiritual sensation appropriate the language of physical sensation, but it also operates *like* physical sensation. In his seminal study on the subject, Augustin Poulain, the early twentieth-century Jesuit theologian, described spiritual sensation as a type of intellectual sense "having some *resemblance* to the bodily senses" that "in an *analogous manner* and in diverse ways is able to perceive the presence of pure spirits, and the presence of God in particular."[23] Spiritual sensation, then, is expressed in language that slips between the analogical and the metaphorical, actively blurring the distinction between real resemblance and poetic language.[24]

When, for instance, Origen (d. 253), the earliest writer to articulate a doctrine of the spiritual senses, describes spiritual sensation in his *Contra Celsum*, he speaks in terms borrowed from physical sensation. Spiritual sensation includes "a sight which can see things superior to corporeal beings, the cherubim or seraphim being obvious instances," "a hearing which can receive impressions of sounds that have no objective existence in the air," "a taste which feeds on living bread that has come down from heaven and gives life to the world," "a sense of smell which smells spiritual things," and "a sense of touch . . . [that] has handled with hands 'of the Word of life.'"[25] In Origen's foundational description, each of the external senses is mirrored by a corresponding spiritual one, and the two bodies—the spiritual and the physical—are linked by a common language that draws on the flesh for its impact. Origen's language here discloses vital information about the way he understands each spiritual sensation to operate. Spiritual sense is, like physical sense, multifarious and multimodal, distinguishing different properties of the same object through different sensory means. Just as different qualities of a dog—its color, the sound of its bark, its odor, and the texture of its fur—are perceived by different physical senses (sight, hearing, smell, and touch), so too do the different spiritual senses perceive different aspects of spiritual objects, metaphysical bodies, or God.

Pseudo-Dionysius (ca. sixth century) articulates a similar operation of the spiritual senses in the *Celestial Hierarchy*:

One could say that the powers of [spiritual] sight suggest [the angelic] ability to gaze up directly toward the lights of God and, at the same time, to receive softly, clearly, without resistance but flexibly,

purely and openly the enlightenments coming from the Deity, yet
without emotion. The powers to discern smells indicate their capacity to welcome fully those fragrances which elude the understanding and to discern with understanding those opposites which
must be utterly avoided. The powers of hearing signify the ability
to have a knowing share of divine inspiration. Taste has to do with
the fill of conceptual nourishment and their receptiveness to the divine and nourishing streams. Touch is understanding how to distinguish the profitable from the harmful.[26]

Pseudo-Dionysius's taxonomy analogizes between outer and inner, between
the physical and spiritual senses, creating a spiritual body that registers divinity just as the body registers the physical world: across multiple modalities and in different ways.

At the same time, however, one thing becomes apparent from an analysis of spiritual sensation from Origen and Augustine to William of Auxerre
and Nicholas of Cusa: while writers on the subject understood spiritual sensation to operate in an *analogous* manner to external sensation, the purpose,
intent, or mode of each spiritual sensation was far more unstable than its
exteroceptive counterpart. While external sensations might mingle, mix, and
complicate each other—as synaesthesia does—by and large, each external
sense-modality retains a relationship to a specific sense-organ that gives it a
sort of concreteness. Spiritual sensation lacks this specific relationship between specific organs of sensation and their objects, and as a result, descriptions of the spiritual sensorium are remarkably fluid. Each writer on the
subject seems to have their own understanding of it. For Origen, for example, spiritual hearing "receives impressions of sounds with no objective existence"; this is different from Pseudo-Dionysius's description of spiritual
hearing, which is that it signifies "an ability to have a knowing share in divine inspiration," which is different still from William of Auxerre's (d. 1231),
that through spiritual hearing "we will be delighted by the symphony of
God."[27] Sometimes, too, the taxonomies of the spiritual senses fracture under
the weight of the affective ends to which they are deployed. In his *Sermones
in Cantica canticorum*, Bernard of Clairvaux (d. 1153) notes that faith touches
Christ "with the eye of the intellect."[28] Alexander of Hales (d. 1245) articulates various spiritual senses, but also admits that "to see [spiritually] is the
same as to hear [spiritually]."[29] In other words, spiritual sensation's direct
parallels to physical sensation's objects are fragile, and the boundaries be-

tween each sense are permeable according to the affective, emotional, or poetic needs of each writer.

Hilton's interests in angelic audiation as a sort of "spiritual touch" reflect the influence of spiritual sensation as a broader trope in Western Christianity: they are, paradoxically, both distinct and inchoate. For Hilton, the metaphysical body affected and effected by the act of audiation does not have representable "ears" distinct from "skin," and so hearing and touch collapse onto each other. Elsewhere, too, Hilton recognizes the spiritual faculties as particularly receptive to synaesthetic experience. In the *De imagine peccati*, Hilton highlights the synasethesis at the heart of spiritual sensation: "You will have a sharp (*acutum*) and penetrating (*perspicacem*) spiritual vision (*visum spiritualem*) in the contemplation of spiritual things; you will feed on these things, and your heart will be satisfied with this delicacy. And you will hear, moreover, the praise of God without the sound of the body (*sine sono corporis*), in the pure understanding of the mind (*puro intellectu mentis*), sung by every creature with a sweet melody (*dulci modulamine*)."[30] Taste, hearing, vision, and touch are mixed here: the melody (sound) is sweet (taste), it occurs simultaneously with a spiritual vision (sight) that is both sharp (touch, perhaps taste) and penetrating (vision, again, despite its tactile English resonances: the Latin *perspicax* comes from *per* + *specio*). Hilton's repeated engagement with spiritual sensation in general and angelic song in particular is dependent on a rhetorical movement between different types of sensation.

Synaesthesia, which is remarkable in normal exteroception—modern research suggests that only 2 to 4 percent of the population are synaesthetes—is absolutely fundamental to medieval articulations of spiritual sensation. Although there are no formal discussions of synaesthesia in medieval philosophy, synaesthetic language is a common expressive tactic in medieval literature more generally. For instance, in the *Inferno,* the she-wolf pushes Dante back to where "the sun is silent";[31] in *Pearl,* the poet is not just touched, but literally knocked out by the pleasant aroma of the bankside: "Suche odour to my hernes shot / I slode upon a slepyng-slaghte."[32] In synaesthesia, the stimulation of one sense automatically and simultaneously stimulates another sense, thus welding and incorporating sensory organs as one has an immediate effect on another.[33]

Mystical literature in particular is a fertile ground for synaesthesis, and a long-form study of the operation of synaesthesia in medieval mysticism is long overdue. Tellingly, modern accounts of synaesthesia describe it in language that is just as applicable to medieval mysticism: synaesthetic experiences are "transcendent," "telescoping,"[34] or "transformative";[35] "oneiric . . . surreal . . . strange" and "magical" experiences of "heightened mystery."[36] More importantly, they produce feelings of "imaginative sympathy"[37] in "fused" experiences that are viscerally "affective in any subsequent recall."[38] Synaesthetic experiences feel "no real borderline between perceptions and emotions."[39] "The emotion of the synaesthetic experience . . . serves as a marker of its significance."[40] In contemporary accounts, then, synaesthesia and affect are inextricably linked together.

Something similar happens in Hilton's account of song as spiritual touch. In medieval faculty psychology, the *sensus communis* commingles sense-inputs as one step in the intellective process. However, in the synaesthetic experience Hilton describes in *Of Angels' Song,* the spiritual senses are already commingled prior to their abstraction. Unlike the physical body, which locates and understands itself through separate and distinct exteroceptions, the metaphysical body cannot use the self-reflexive experiences of spiritual sensations to do the same. The nonconceptual, process-oriented experiences of spiritual sensation give birth to a fluid, ever-changing body that cannot be "shown"— that is, it cannot be analyzed and its parts cannot be assigned specific functions—but instead is "felt" or "perceived" as an amorphous, preorganic whole. Spiritual sensation is a process of dedifferentiation, immanence, and immediacy.[41] Like Deleuze and Guattari's body without organs, the body of spiritual sensation is not an organism, but a surreal assemblage of affects.[42]

Spiritual sensation's "surreal assemblage" has ramifications for the way Hilton imagines the metaphysical body that hears angelic song. On the one hand, the physical exteroceptions of sight, hearing, touch, taste, and smell not only objectify the world, but also give the physical body a conception of itself: one might think about the cortical homunculus as a helpful way for thinking about how physical sensation—exteroception—understands the body: as each sense palpates the world around it, it also provides a mental map of the sensing body that assigns to that very body its own organs of sensation. Although the "body" that emerges from this sensory autodepiction is grotesque (the mind enlarges the sense-organs because of how vital they are to an organism's self-preservation), it is, nonetheless, an image. The perception that emerges out of exteroception is eidetic. In other words, the bodies mapped by external sensation can, in Hilton's words, be "shown." But the spiritual body's organology, on the other hand, is evasive. Spiritual sensation has no analogue to the cortical homunculus. It actively bars such body-mapping, existing, in Hilton's words, on "feeling."

When Hilton describes angelic song, he uses synaesthetic language to trip the trigger-wire of a sensorium that mimics the inchoate objects of its perception. Angels' song "may noght be discried be na bodely likens," he says, "for it es gastly, and aboven al maner of ymaginacioun and resoun."[43] Angels' song might be "felt and perceived," but it cannot be "shown." The fundamental problematic inhering in the accommodation of the symbolic order to angelic song is not simply that angelic song is ineffable—too large, too magnificent to be captured in language—but also, that the sensation of angelic song belongs to a set of organs, and to a body, that itself can only be described as nonconceptual and presymbolic. The interior or spiritual senses, which are syncretic, and which deconstruct neat and independent perceptions, yoke multiple properties of an object together simultaneously in a sensorial cacophony, resulting in the layered synaesthetic rhetoric of Hilton's treatise. Angels' song can be felt. It can be perceived. But it cannot be visually objectified for the purposes of mimesis. Spiritual sensations are nonrepresentational and processual.

A useful modern analogue for considering spiritual sensation can be found in the modern biophysiological concept of the interoception.[44] If exteroceptions map a body-to-world direction of fit, registering the world that, being "outside" the body, acts on it, then interoceptions focus on what is "inside" the body, that is, the sense-perceptions of events that occur within the body and are frequently tied to emotional states.[45] These are feelings that relate a sense both of self and of ill- or well-being. Some interoceptive feelings are immediately familiar to us: vasodilation of the skin registers embarrassment, stretch receptors in the bladder create discomfort, and the stomach flips in moments of nervousness. Other interoceptions are less familiar, humming along below the level of consciousness: chemoreceptors in the circulatory system monitor blood salt levels and trigger feelings of thirst, pulmonary stretch receptors control respiratory rates and feelings of ease or panic, and the beating of the heart registers relaxation or arousal. Through exteroceptors, we can understand and can develop a functional image of the environment. Interoceptors, on the other hand, are used to guide intentional action.

Unlike exteroceptions, which find and assess objects in the world, interoceptions generally produce an awareness of the *act* of feeling itself. Imagine, for instance, looking at an apple (an exteroceptive act). When you look at it, you see the *object* of your visual perception (an apple); you make a judgment about where it is (in front of you, on the table); perhaps you have an involuntary appetitive reaction to it (you become hungry); you may even go one step further and make some sort of decision based on that object (that you will pick it up and eat it). However, when looking at an apple, you rarely consider—unless you are engaging in meditative practice—the experience of *seeing* in and of itself (what it feels like to view objects, how your eyes and your brain register the undifferentiated world around you and make judgments about it). In most instances, the purpose of vision is to see objects rather than to experience visuality. In interoception, on the other hand, the focus tends to be on the feeling itself rather than on the object at the center of that experience. When the stomach churns in hunger, we think of ourselves as hungry, and only secondarily do we imagine ourselves as a toroid of flesh whose invaginated inner surface is expanding and constricting. This is not always the case, of course—instead of focusing on the interoceptive experience of the heart beating, we might focus on the object of that experience, that is, the beating heart (and worry that we are having a heart attack)—but even in moments where the interoceptive experience dims behind the object of that experience, the lack of visual availability makes interoception *seem* more about the experience of experience than the object of that experience. As such, interoceptions open themselves up more to states of feeling than their analogous exteroceptive counterparts; they also remain largely noneidetic.

Although interoceptions cover a broad array of interior experiences that are distinct from exteroceptions, the language most frequently used to describe them appropriates, as Hilton's *Of Angels' Song* does, exteroceptive language. More specifically, they use the language of touch. Interoceptions strike (the heart "beats"), pull (the bladder "stretches"), press (the stomach is "full"), are irritated (tired eyes "itch"), ache (overworked muscles "burn"), and pulse (the migrainous head "throbs"). As the most intimate of exteroceptions, touch is perhaps the most appropriate sensation to describe interiorized affective and sensory states.

Current research into interoceptions using fMRI data tie this linguistic tic to neurobiology: the part of the brain that is recruited in interoception is the same part of the brain that is stimulated by soft touches of the skin, known in scientific literature as "social" or "affective" touch.[46] Furthermore, interoceptions are routed through one region of the brain, where they register as physical sensations, and then are re-represented elsewhere in the brain, where they are re-processed emotionally as sadness, anger, anxiety, pain, panic, joy, pleasure, sexual arousal, and so forth.[47] Contemporary research suggests a neurological link between interoception and emotion.

Hilton's description of angels' song is also concerned with affect and emotion, though he obviously uses a medieval framework and not a contemporary neuropsychological one. Like interoceptions, medieval theories of the emotions use tangible metaphors: the two primary categories of emotion described in medieval philosophy—the concupiscible and the irascible passions—served to push the feeler toward desirable things or to pull them away from undesirable ones, respectively. In fact, these emotions were, quite literally, meant to effect local motion of the body.[48] Much has been written about the relationship of touching to medieval affective devotion, and to the collaborative symbolic registers that enmesh tactility and bodily experience in the production of emotion.[49] In spite of the fact that touch was considered one of the lower, more animalistic senses by medieval philosophical frameworks, the importance of touch for what Katie Walter calls "ethical epistemological modes" as well as "lived experience" appears again and again in both Latin philosophy and vernacular writing of the later medieval period.[50] Affect and touch are linked at the level of metaphor and, simultaneously, in medieval philosophy's schemata used to understand human behavior. It is nearly impossible to describe emotional engagement without recruiting the vocabulary of tactility (we "feel" emotions; we are "touched" by a kind gesture; we are "moved" by a sad song).[51] Hilton represents the affective capacity of angelic song as a sort of touch, an affective strum, something that might lead the practitioner to action.

Modern notions of interoceptions built from neurobiological data use the same language that medieval expressions of spiritual sensation do. While it is not my intention to identify medieval sensory affects and the modern biopsychological understandings of internal states with one another, the common language used to articulate both suggests that there is something transhistorically fitting—appropriate—about imagining emotionality and interiority as tactile.[52] This language pegs both spiritual sensations and interoceptions as labile, tactile, and more proximal to emotion than the external senses. Interoceptions, like spiritual sensations, are always already open to synaesthetic metaphors; the unique feelings of the heart beating, of the stomach churning, and so forth are interpreted as touch. Interoceptions, like spiritual sensations, are invested in the experience of the sensation itself more than in the object of that sensation: as Hilton says, it is impossible to say what, exactly, angelic song is, but it exists, and can be perceived.

Unlike interoceptions, however, spiritual sensations are explicitly metaphysical. This distinction is critical. Whereas interoceptions describe physical states of a material body understood through a modern discourse of neuro-psychology, Hilton is operating with an entirely different understanding of the faculties of the mind, body, and spirit that admits the possibility of the separability of *corpus* and *anima*, a dualism that modern biological material-ism denies. Nevertheless, a consideration of interoceptions—and the type of relationships they allow between sensation, embodiment, and affect—is a helpful tool for understanding the ramifications of medieval discourses of spiritual sensation for understanding the body. The spiritual body, like the interoceptive one, is a series of states of being, one that understands the body not as visualizable (not the homunculus, or as a form), but instead as a continuously changing set of feelings. In both cases, the language of physi-cality and external sensation—particularly tactility—are recruited to under-stand an invisible region of the body as a process. The tactility of angelic song collapses the space of experience into an intimate spiritual haptics. By calling angelic song a sort of "ghostly touch," Hilton is both using a synaes-thetic metaphor for poetic effect and making a specific claim, rooted in a long theological tradition of spiritual sensation, about the metaphysical body: it is dedifferentiated, immediately integrated. If touch charts the depth of human flesh, spiritual tactility charts the depth of the soul.

## An Impossible Haptics: Angelic Touch as *Utopos*

The interface between angelic bodies and human bodies exists outside of representation, Hilton argues. But Hilton is not the only medieval writer to make this claim, which is also borne out in striking fashion in medieval vi-sual art: although medieval artists represented angels as embodied and drew or carved their anthropomorphic forms interacting with all sorts of objects—musical instruments, clouds, buildings, heavenly saints, objects of devotion, disembodied parts of Christ's body, and other angels (Figure 2)—angels only exceedingly rarely touch humans in Western medieval art.[53] If, as Hilton says, angels' song can be felt but not shown, visual art also seems to support this position.

In most manuscripts where human-angelic touch might occur, great care has been taken on the part of the illuminator specifically to avoid depicting it. In the Holkham Bible Picture Book, for instance, an angel appears to the shepherds at the Nativity (Figure 3). Here, the angel stands on the ground next to the shepherds, squeezed into a packed manuscript page. Because of

Figure 2. BL Additional MS 88929 (1485–1509), prayer roll of Henry VIII and
Catherine of Aragon: two angels hold a disembodied side-wound of Christ.

the image's tight confines, the illustrator had every opportunity here to have
the angel reach out and touch the shepherd, but nonetheless seems to have
taken great care to do the opposite: as the shepherd throws his arm up to
shield his eyes from the brightness of the revealed star, the angel's wing grace-
fully dodges the shepherd's elbow. Even in a manuscript whose spatial economy leaves little negative space, a bit of air intervenes between the heavenly
body and the earthly one.

This tendency appears again and again in medieval art.[54] In a Book of
Hours that depicts the Christ's appearance to Mary Magdalene, Mary Jacobi, and Mary Salome after the Resurrection, the angel evades human flesh
(Figure 4). Only a few millimeters separate the angel's hand and the Magdalene's arms, raised in shock and surprise. In fact, the angel comes so close
to touching her that he grazes the sleeve of her dress. And yet, Mary remains untouched. The noli me tangere of the gospel lesson here applies not

Figure 3. BL Additional MS 47682 (1327–1335), the Holkham Bible Picture Book, fol. 13r: the angel appears to the shepherds at the Nativity.

only to the Magdalene's and Christ, but to the moment of communication between her and the angel.

A thirteenth-century Belgian manuscript of the life of Christ and the saints presents multiple forms of angelic touch evasion. In an Annunciation scene, on folio 20v, the angel Gabriel is separated from the Virgin by a thin column supporting a Gothic arch, the architectural space presenting a handy excuse for the lack of contact between the angelic messenger and his charge (Figure 5). This is a common divisorial tactic in such scenes, with countless illuminated images of the Annunciation using lecterns, arched columns, cirboria, thrones, and even potted plants to imply the impossibility of tactile engagement between Gabriel and Mary. But this is not the only form of evasiveness in the manuscript. Elsewhere, human figures have been erased in order to avoid the possibility of angels and humans interacting, as is the case with Saint Michael on folio 56r (Figure 6). At his feet is a shadowy figure, still legible as a woman at prayer, kneeling with her hands at her breast and her head covered in a wimple. The original intent appears to have been to have a woman praying at the feet of the angel; however, the confines of the manuscript page would have required the human figure and the angelic one

Figure 4. Walters MS W.102 (ca. 1300), Book of Hours, fol. 7v:
the angel appears to the three Marys on Easter morning.

to touch each other. As a result, the human has been washed with blue paint, erased; she has literally become a wall. So great was the concern over depicting human and angelic touch that the artist dissolved the human form entirely.[55]

Perhaps one of the most striking visual depictions of angel-human interaction occurs not between angels and human bodies, but between angels and the human soul. If the preceding has discussed, specifically, the necessity of imagining the interface of human-angelic interaction as occurring not in the physical world, but in a metaphysical, nonrepresentational dimension analogous to it, then it is these depictions that can tell us the most about

Figure 5. BnF NAF 16251 (ca. 1285–1290), fol. 20v: the Annunciation.

the illegibility of such interaction. Such depictions are rare but illuminat-
ing. In two Italian examples, a twelfth-century stained-glass roundel in the
Church of St. Orso and in Guariento di Arpa's magnificent fourteenth-
century paintings of angels, angels are depicted holding human souls.[56] In
both cases, the angels suspend the soul in a piece of cloth; an integumen-
tum is placed between the angelic hand and the human spirit, not only pro-
hibiting direct tactile contact, but also, more specifically, hiding the space
of angelic contact from the eyes of the viewer. These cloths present a dou-

Figure 6. BnF NAF 16251 (ca. 1285–1290), fol. 56r: Saint Michael.

bling of the mystifying presence of absence that mimics the palpable impossibility of angelic touch: it can be perceived and felt, but not shown.

A similar blindness is registered in the very few and notable exceptions to the practical prohibition of angelic touch in medieval art.[57] One example occurs within a miniature found in an Office of the Guardian Angel, which depicts a winged angel standing behind a Benedictine nun.[58] His hand rests on her shoulder, but she does not turn to acknowledge his presence. Instead, the nun casts her gaze downward, to the written text of her book or perhaps to her own hands, which are clasped in prayer. The intimacy depicted between the nun and her angel is a single instance of angelic touch, and one that attempts to depict a theory of communication between angels and humans. Even though this image highlights the importance of embodied form for the moment of human and angelic touch, it also seems to want to deny that same material reliance: the nun turns away, blind to the angel standing behind her. The prayer that accompanies the image highlights the angel's corporeal absence-in-presence: "Angel who is my guardian, save, defend, and guide me, who was committed to you by [the] Supernal Piety. O sweet angel who stays with me, although you do not speak with me face-to-face, I ask that you watch over my soul, along with my body—this is your duty to which you are assigned. O blessed angel, messenger of our God, rule my thoughts and actions to the desire of God most high."[59] The angel is invested in the human as a composition of thoughts (*cogitatus*) and actions (*actus*), of body (*corpus*) and soul (*anima*). The angel responds to the needs of the human as simultaneously material and spiritual, intimately attached to the complexity of form that comprises the human being. Even though he rules the external behaviors and internal states of the human mind (*cogitatus et actus meos regula*), the angel is also radically detached: he is not permitted—by his own nature, or by God—to speak to his human charge. This relationship between human and angel is integumental: the moment of touch is symbolic, and that symbol is itself represented as a sort of evasion. The miniature that accompanies this prayer depicts the nun at prayer as the angel calmly places his hand on her shoulder so that she might feel his touch, even though he remains invisible to her.

The total number of angels depicted in the medieval West runs to the many thousands, and a complete survey of these images will necessarily uncover some exceptions to the rule that angels and humans do not touch each other in medieval art; the example above is one such moment. Nevertheless, the great majority of angelic-human interactions evade depicting the moment of angelic touch.

In one of the very rare cases where integumenta do not come between angels and the human form, another complicated relationship between touch and music is brought to the fore instead. At the top of a page of poetry in the famous Carthusian miscellany British Library Additional MS 37049, a group of four angelic musicians leads a human figure across a field; one angel holds the soul by the hand, and another presses a hand into its back (Figure 7). "Here is a saule led with myrthe and melody of angels to heuen," the caption underneath reads.[60] Underneath the procession, the manuscript records a version of the Angels' Second Song Within Heaven, and English translation from the *Pèlerinage de l'âme*.[61] Of course, the text below the im-

Figure 7. BL Additional MS 37049, fol. 74v: a soul is led to heaven
in mirth and melody; the song of angels appears beneath.

age is not actual angelic song: there are no notes for performance; the music
is implied but not present. This is a textual, logocentric approximation of
music. Just as this angelic song is a metaphor—a physical analogue for a spiritual sensation—so too is the angelic touch exteroceptive, a synaesthetic
analogue for an invisible interoception.

Normally, when material bodies are presented in art, touch and vision
coexist in a mutual representative logic that makes tactile sense out of the
spatial organization of matter in space. Visual forms depict *touch* by representing one object occluding or infringing another object's spatial domain.
(We might pause to think about how unique it is among sensation that one
sense—sight—is able to observe another sense—touch—in this way: we do
not smell sounds, hear tastes, or smell visual objects; this should make us
question whether we actually "see" touch at all, or whether, instead, we have
a long-held cultural assumption about the relationship between physical bodies, their spatial arrangement, and the heuristics of visualization which in
turn manifest in visual art, where the visual language of overlapping signals
tactile engagement. Cubism and other forms of abstract art directly challenge the visio-tactile heuristic.[62]) That is, visual art performs synaestheti-
cally. However, when the bodies involved are immaterial, depictions of touch

become impossible—a recognition of the failure of sight, on its own, to be able to *feel*. Touch can be *felt* but it cannot be *shown*.

As Herbert L. Kessler suggests, visual art of the medieval period—broadly speaking—accomplishes two tasks: it provides a material means of understanding the divine; and it makes clear that the intellect, rather than the senses, is the only human faculty that might truly approach an understanding of God.[63] Medieval art is participatory, its visuality evoking not only mental images, but also provoking emotional states in the viewer and providing a means of accessing affective devotional or contemplative experiences.[64] As Beth Williamson's work on images of angels in medieval depictions of music-making shows, images of angels produce "imagined" and "interior" or spiritual sounds on the part of the viewer.[65] When angelic touch is depicted in medieval art as an evasion, as allegorical, symbolic, or, perhaps most importantly, as impossible to visualize, these images register not only the intellectual and spiritual capacities of sight, but also produce affective engagement, in part by recognizing vision's own shortcomings—its inability to adequately accommodate the interface between material and spiritual bodies.

When Hilton describes angelic song as a type of noneidetic inner touch, he is pointing out that cultural assumptions about visual representation do not hold when the bodies and sensory systems involved are metaphysical. Angelic singing-touching is a type of internal sensation, invisible and affective, constitutive of embodied reality even though it is itself an imaginary boundary where the logics of occlusion, overlap, or spacing are revealed to simply be another form of metaphorical discourse. Visual art performs this same gesture.

## *Tactus*, Meter, and Disciplining Angelic Song

So much for interoception, spiritual sensation, and angelic song. But exteroception—physical touch—also illuminates the spatial impossibilities of touch and how it marks the body. In the quotidian exteroceptive sense of "making physical contact," touch occurs at a point or a surface, that is, at a one- or two-dimensional interface. One- and two-dimensional objects are *real* in the ideational sense of the word, but not actually physically real at all. All physical objects subsist in three spatial dimensions; touch, at most, encounters only surfaces, or two dimensions. Touch, therefore, occurs in a sort of imagined space; it never totalizes, never grasps the reality of its object; even if it can feel an object's volume or three-dimensionality, it can never plumb its depths or assay beneath its surface.[66] Even touch as the subject-enabling Merleau-Pontian "place of the fold" occurs not in pre-extant three-dimensional space, but in an act of bending that asks surfaces to imagine their three-dimensionality as a process rather than a metaphysical a priori. In the physical world, touch is an imaginary point out of which "embodiment" emerges as a field of play.

Middle English use of the word "touch" reflects this geometrical reality-in-impossibility. John Trevisa's translation of the *De proprietatibus rerum* defines a corner as "þe *toche* and *metynge* of tweye lynes so þat aþir touche oþir."[67] In a treatise on geometry found in British Library Sloane MS 213, "touch" is the intersection of two perpendicular lines: "mark where þe perpendicle falles, þan counte þe poyntes fro þe begynnyng of þe side of þe vmbre to þe *touche* of þe perpendicle."[68] In both of these instances, touch glances off its object; it is an invisible moment of contact that brings higher-order dimensions into being. The skin is a no-place, a utopia of encounter, and space depends upon and arises from these nonexisting points of touch.[69]

The impossible physics of touch—the singularity into which touch collapses—allows it to fluctuate across modes of sensation and cognition. In rhetoric, *touche* takes the sense of "to touch upon," that is, to address a specific topic within a broader argument.[70] Here, "touch" metaphorically expands to cover rhetorical acts with the same pointed focus of the word's literal meaning. One does not "touch upon" an entire argument, but only pieces of it; the fragment of an argument encompassed by a "touch" metonymically illuminates the whole argument but is not identical to it. *Touche* might also apply to time: in her *Revelations,* Julian of Norwich repeatedly uses touch to refer to a time-outside-of-time in which the visions showed to her "understanding" occur: "This was schewed me in a toch, and redely passed ouere into comforth."[71] The *shewings* exist beyond physical experience in a non-quantifiable internal tactile register where the senses are literally squeezed into the same place, into nothingness, like the *scintilla* or *synderesis*. Tactility does not encompass its object; instead, it marks momentary situations of experience out of which time, space, and affect arise.

Medieval medical treatises recognized this imaginary capacity of touch to do body-defining work, both interoceptive and exteroceptive, both temporal and spatial. The rhythm of the pulse, known as the *tactus*, indicated the presence of the soul in the body as a type of *musica humana*.[72] Beginning with Avicenna (d. 1037), it was commonplace among medieval medical treatises to refer to the pulse as a sort of musical inner touch that could in turn be sensed on the skin. Because physicians, as ordained *doctores*, were forbidden from drawing blood, the rate and rhythm of the heartbeat was used as a diagnostic tool. The pulse and its musicality served as surrogates for the flow of blood in the body. In the hands of the physician, the bloodiness of the flesh was sublimated to the neo-Pythagorean demesne of the quadrivium: the science of arsis and thesis, systole and diastole, touched, but did not invade, the flesh.

For this reason, physicians were expected to have training in music. As Avicenna says in his *Canon*, "I am surprised to think how many of such relations could be perceived by the sense of touch, and yet I am confident that it can be done if one is habituated to the use of it, and can apportion metre and beats of time."[73] Following Avicenna, many of the most important medical writers of the later medieval period continued to study musical rhythm to understand the pulse, supporting the notion of pulse-musicality even if they remained largely skeptical of its use in diagnosis. One of the few outliers in the literature is Roger Bacon (d. 1292), who, as Nancy Siraisi notes, suggests that even though the pulse operates according to musical principles, it is *not* musical because it does not refer to hearing, "but only to touch."[74] For Bacon, in other words, the sine qua non of music is that it makes a sound.[75] And yet, in spite of Bacon's position, most of his contemporaries and colleagues understood the pulse to be a type of music, and, as Juan Gil de Zamora and other music theorists show, recognized, in a Neoplatonizing and Boethian sense, that the very connection between *caro* and *anima* was *harmonia* expressed through the beating of the heart.[76]

It is no surprise, then, that late medieval music theory treatises refer to units of time as *tactus* (touch). In late medieval music performance—especially the performance of polyphony—singers kept time by gently touching each other on the shoulder, a touch that was first called the *mensura* in the fourteenth and early fifteenth centuries, but which was referred to as *tactus* by the second half of the fifteenth century.[77] Adam de Fulda gives a lengthy treatment of the term *tactus* in the *De musica* of 1490.[78] When medieval music theory treatises attempt to describe the duration of the *tactus*, they describe it in terms of the heartbeat or the pulmonary push-and-pull of breathing.[79] For instance, Ramis de Pareja, in the *Musica practica* (1482), says that the singer should "move his foot or hand or finger, touching in some place, like this pulse."[80] As each *mensura* or *tactus* passed, one singer tapped their partner or partners on the shoulder to indicate movement forward in musical time. Although the time contained between two *tactus* was not the smallest acknowledged unit of time—each *tactus* might be broken up into smaller units—it *was* the smallest temporal unit that occurred in common between singers voicing different parts. The touch itself—the *tactus*—technically occurred in time, "was comprised of time, was measured by and measured time," as Ruth DeFord argues.[81] But the *tactus*—the touch itself—was also a vanishingly small point in a continuum of time that marked time's passing and that, in its striking, marked the possibility for group norming within time. The regular, perceptible time units delimited by the beating of the heart— nonrepresentational interoceptions—are, in very real sense, the habitable space of the *tactus*, the region in which mensuration makes personal sense.[82]

Tactus—the beating of the heart and the musical beat—is simultaneously internal and external, both interoceptive and exteroceptive. In both cases, an experience that registers self with self (the beating of the heart, the movement of air through lungs and vocal chords) and the other is registered as corporate experience that can be measured and modified, policed and adjudicated, diagnosed or harmonized. Exteroceptive touch, an impossible-to-visually-represent thing, is deployed in order to make equally nonrepresentational interoceptions count as social action. And, as social action, touch is ritualized, routinized, and disciplined by orthodoxy. In the medieval church, touch was vital. During Mass, the pax board, sometimes decorated with intricate scenes of the Crucifixion, would be passed from layperson to person for devotional osculation, an intermingling of sight and sound and touch. Illuminated images of Christ's side-wound and the *arma Christi* in devotional manuscripts betray the well-worn paths of fingers and lips, as the body of Christ was assayed in manuscript form, his side-wound and the nails that pierced his hands and feet sometimes appearing alongside legends that note the painted wounds to be the exact size as the historical originals, offering devotional readers the opportunity to take a measure of the size of their devotion as their fingers glanced across and then tenderly caressed a simulacrum of their suffering Lord.[83]

Physical touch's impossibility does not make it any less available to discipline: exteroceptive touch is of a piece with being policed and brought to account. The body is not a physical thing that preexists its engagement with tactility; it is the act of accounting out of which the physical body emerges. Exteroceptions and interoceptions, or, put in medieval terms, physical sensations and spiritual sensations, share a vocabulary and a discursive framework but nevertheless remain distinct. However, the linguistic ties that bind spiritual sensation to physical sensation serve as a site of potential containment for and enforcement of behavior. The *tactus* of music theory is like angelic song-touch: a vanishing point, a relationship, an ideational fiber out of which real time, and real music, are spun.[84] Like angels' song, the *tactus* is inaudible, but could nonetheless be felt: singers silently tapped their fellow singers as the music pulsed forward.

## Hilton, Touch, and Impossible Angels

The interpenetration of external sensation and internal or spiritual sensation allows for pastoral guidance, discipline, and, ultimately, the containment of heretical or problematic performances of mystical experience, and it is this work that Hilton's *Of Angels' Song* is ultimately trying to do. Although the treatise purports to be about the phenomenon of angelic song, that is, of solving a thought-exercise for its reader, its answer to the problem—which is that angels' song is unknowable through normal rational means, and the ways in which it can be *felt* are mutable and complex—breeds skepticism about the experience of angelic song. In both his description of angelic song as spiritual haptics and his "failure" to adequately describe it, Hilton actually ends up installing doubt at the heart of the very experience he purports to describe. "Sum man," he says,

> When he has longe traveld bodili and gastli in destroyng of syns and getyng of vertus, . . . he gadres his wittis be violence to sekyn and to byhalde hevenly thynges, or his egh be mad gastly be grace, and overtravels be ymaginacioun his wittis, and be undiscrete travelyng turnes the braynes in his heved, and forbrekis the myghtis and the wittis of the saule and of body. And than, for febilnes of the brayn, him thynk that he heres wonderful sownes and sangs; and that is nathyng els bot a fantasy, caused o trublyng of the brayn; als a man that es in a fransy, hym thynk that he heres and sese that nan other man dos, and al es bot a vanite and fantasy of the heved, or els it be wirkyng of the enemy that feynes swylk soun in his heryng.[85]

This passage employs a startling medicalizing vocabulary that aims to discredit the auditor of angels' song, who has his "wits" or "braynes in his heved" "gadre[d] . . . be violence" and "overtravel[ed] be ymaginacioun" so that he literally, materially, breaks his mind. He "turnes the braynes in his heved";

he falls into a "fransy"; angels' song is described as a "fantasy of the heved." Each one of these phrases is not a simple assignation of illegitimacy to the experience of angelic song, but a turn to medical language that materializes and pathologizes the individual experience of spiritual sensation. "Turning of the brain" is a phrase commonly used in medieval medical literature to describe vertigo; "fransy" is defined by Bartholomeus Anglicus as an insanity or delirium in which the sufferers "sometimes sing, sometimes laugh, sometimes cry . . . rarely are they silent, and they shout a lot. These people are very dangerously ill, and yet they do not realize they are ill"; and "fantasy" is commonly defined in medieval texts not only as one of the mental faculties, but as this mental faculty gone awry, become delusional, and engaged in false recall and bad imaginative work.[86] All three of these descriptions relate auditory revelations to a lack of self-awareness—whether of proprioception (vertigo), of infelicitous performance (frenzy), or of breaks from reality (the delusions of grandeur that attend fantasy)—across all the levels of sensation, perception, and embodiment that this chapter has outlined. Hilton's psychopathologizing move is deeply skeptical: it might be possible for a "dere brother in Crist," devout and yet not perfected, to be mistaken about his own mental state. Not only might his senses fail, but his perception might, too. If percepts themselves might be no more than "vanite and fantasy of the heved," the scaffolding for a reliable intellectual truth begins to fall apart. Mystical experience, even mystical experience based on interior changes of behavior and mental or emotional states, simply does not *suffys*.[87] Hilton makes an admonition that the auditor of angelic song be treated by a doctor—to reach outside the self to the palpation and the reading of the medical *tactus*.

"Sothly I can noght telle the for syker the sothnes" of angelic song, Hilton says at the opening of the treatise.[88] The following argument delegitimizes the very search for truth—or "soth"—that is the treatise's explicit stated goal. Hilton's failure to describe angelic song is not merely an ineffable account of an ineffable experience, but in fact an attempt to negate the experience of angelic song as a worthwhile sensory pursuit. Not only is angelic song unimportant, Hilton says, but so is the attempt to understand what it might *be*. "I have tald the in this mater a litel as me think," he says, "noght affermand that this suffys, ne that this es the *sothfastnes* in this mater. . . . It suffys to me for to lif in *trouth* principali, and noght in *felyng*.[89]

In its closing salvo, *Of Angels' Song* sets the search for truth (*sothfastnes*) against troth (*trouth*). The distinction that Hilton makes in this final section is telling. Whereas "sothfastness" can be translated into modern English relatively straightforwardly as "truth," the Middle English meaning of the word "troth" has a far more complex and ambiguous set of connotations. Although perhaps in some instances it might carry the resonance of its cognate "truth" or "conformation with reality," its actual semantic force also includes "fidelity or obligation to a specific cause, formally pledged."[90]

*Of Angels' Song* plays on these connotative commitments, ultimately sacrificing the pursuit of "truth" for the safety of "troth"—in this case, fidelity to orthodox religious praxis. Hilton admits that the verifiability (*"sothnes/sothfastnes"*) of his description of angelic song cannot be ascertained. Moreover, the (in)capability of coming to *"soth"* is a result of the *"felyng"* itself. While *felyng* here refers to sensation and perception, there is a resonance in this passage between the word *felyng* as a form of sensation and its emotional connotations, as the previous sections of this chapter have shown. Hilton's move here will be familiar to many, for whom the illogic of *felyng* is deployed to denigrate revolutionary personal experience at odds with the "logic" of hegemonic orthodoxy. In the place of *soth* then, with all of its requirements of feeling, perception, and judgment, Hilton supplies *trouth,* whose equivocal meanings make "truth" and "allegiance to authority" one and the same. The causal elision of *soth* with *trouth* is a sort of pragmatic behavior-policing that reinforces hegemonic authority, and Hilton subsequently suggests that a safe alternative to the excessive and unbridled outbursts symptomatic of angelic song are the "psalmes and ympnes and antymps of haly kyrk."[91] Hilton is satisfied with the sufficiency of the meaning-making capacity of authoritative religious frameworks, which for him are more trustworthy than the epistemological relationship of individual sense-perception (*felyng*) as it accords with "reality" (*soth*). Angelic song, and Hilton's ability to describe it, do not *suffys*. But this does not matter. Hilton's allegiance to *trouth* over *soth* is not simply a question of diction—that is, the words a believer chooses to use to attend to devotional practice—but of how language structures devotional experience, and how ideological frameworks—in this case, late medieval Western Christianity in a moment of increasingly ungovernable popular private devotion—authorized certain types of language-experience as more sufficient than others.

In the medicalizing, suspicious turn that he makes at the end of his treatise, Hilton decouples a long-held relationship in Western Christianity between sensation and the knowledge of spiritual truth. Even though most medieval theologians understood that bodily sensation might err, they were inclined to believe that human intellect and reason were enlightened by God and served to check and balance sensation. Judgments about physical sensations were therefore ultimately relatively reliable.[92] "Far be it from us to doubt the truths that we have learned through the bodily senses!" Augustine says in the *De trinitate.* "Through them we learn about the heaven and earth, and the things in them that are known to us, insofar as He who fashioned both us and them wanted us to know them."[93] But as vernacular reading, devotion, and individual religious experience unmoored from traditional Church hierarchical structures became more common in the thirteenth and fourteenth centuries, the ability to discipline the interpretation of sensory phenomena became vital for the containment of heteropraxy (especially when the practitioners were the uneducated, the mentally ill, or women—the more body-bound, lascivious, and less intellectual of the sexes—who necessarily experienced divinity directly through sight, sound, touch, taste, and smell rather than through the powers of the mind).[94]

In its late medieval English context, *Of Angels' Song* is not so much a critique of angelic being as it is a critique of the structures by which the human body—in both a metaphysical and a physical sense—might be compelled to adjudicate his or her spiritual sensations. Hilton is satisfied with the sufficiency of the meaning-making capacity of authoritative religious frameworks (*trouth*). For him, these are more trustworthy and more worthwhile than epistemological inquiries into the relationship of sense-perception (*felyng*) to "truth" (*soth*). Hilton's allegiance to *trouth* over *soth* is not simply an election of one type of song over another—a privileging of liturgical song over angels' song—but also an explicit support of one structure of authorization (ritual language, liturgical chant, and political expediency) over another (individual sensation, perception, and discernment). Because angelic song manifests as ineffable, as a phenomenon that queries what language does not say, it prioritizes inchoate and nontransferable affects. Liturgical song, on the other hand, is about the regime of power inherent in the effable, in the power of the licit, of the law, of *logos,* and normative structures of representation that carry over from one body to another through speech acts. Liturgical song, Hilton argues, is more "sufficient" than other types of song because it defines, through religious law and the threat of violence, the boundary between what is normative and what is heretical. Hilton's treatise raises the possibility of angelic song in order to bring the body back into conformation with the institutional apparatus of credal performance.

Though Hilton appropriates an extant discourse of spiritual sensation to answer his "dere brother," he is obviously troubled with his description of the phenomenon and adopts the language of spiritual sensation in part in order to corral or curtail its power. It is for this reason that any investigation into spiritual audiation should consider the ramifications of the unfolding discourse around such a body: the spiritual body is in one sense contained by the physical body (through language that mimics the processes of physical sensation, and thereby dictates its operation) and in some sense explodes beyond it (through deconstructions of these analogies, via ineffability topoi). This is a conceptual difficulty, but one with wide-ranging ramifications: spiritual sensation provides the individual direct access to God, undermining orthodox connections to Church establishments; it is an inherently political sensation, and any investigation of how it operates must work against Hilton's conservative impulse. The body that emerges, albeit unwillingly, out of Hilton's text, is a revolutionary one.

In spite of the work he does to barricade the synaesthetic rowdiness of angelic song and the metaphysical body that both conjures it and is conjured by it, however, *Of Angels' Song* gives space to angelic song.[95] If in Keats's *Ode* nature and art are brought into tension with one another, and the claims of the poem are themselves deconstructed by poetics—the "silent music" of visual art both represented by and evading the possibilities of language to articulate it—so too, in *Of Angels' Song*, does the bizarre silence of metaphysical song both inhabit the treatise and evade it. The treatise *touches* upon angelic song; this touch cannot be shown, but it can be felt. From its sonorous haptics emerges a spiritual body that is noneidetic, that is not flesh, yet is distressingly real—so real that Hilton marshals the full disciplinary force of exteroceptive touch as a containment mechanism.

Chapter 3

# Attending to *The Boke of Margery Kempe*

It is said that music (*musica*) is named from "*muso, sas,*" that is,
"to doubt" (*dubitare*), or "to murmur in silence" (*cum silentio
murmurare*), or more appropriately, "to inquire about something
by thinking" (*cogitando aliquid inquirere*), which pertains to
theoretical music.

—Jacobus, *Speculum musicae*

## Music as Murmuring Silence

In the first book of his *Speculum musicae*, Jacobus defines the word *musica*
through a series of spurious etymologies taken from medieval authorities on
music. A common rhetorical maneuver in speculative treatises, Jacobus's *Speculum* uses these etymologies to reveal hidden significations not only of the
word itself, but also of the human practice of *musica*. For instance, when describing performed music, Jacobus primarily draws from Isidore of Seville's
*Etymologiae*, saying that *musica* comes from the Greek word for "seeking"
(*muson*), or, alternatively from the Muses, who number nine after the nine
parts of the body that articulate the voice (two lips, four teeth, the tongue,
the throat, and lungs). Other etymologies in this passage provide other answers: *musica* might also come from the Greek for "water" (*mois*), because the
first instrument was the water-organ, and because water (along with air) is
the material of sound.[1] In each of these cases, performed music's body is the
medium through which it travels: in the first instance, the human body gives
it form; in the second, water does the work of incorporation.

For Jacobus, *musica speculativa*, too, has its etymological basis; and, as he goes on to describe, this sort of music comes from a phrase (*muso, sas*) that means, according to Jacobus, "to doubt" (*dubitare*), or "to murmur in silence" (*cum silentio murmurare*). Unlike the first of the two etymologies, which describes *musica practica* in quotidian if poetic terms, this second definition employs the language of paradox to stress just how strange it is that music might be silent: in Quintilian's (d. ca. 100) *Institutio Oratoria,* the word *murmurare* is given as a prime example of an onomatopoeia, a word formed from the sounds it mimics, but Jacobus uses *murmurare* to describe a sound without sound.[2] What does a murmur sound like if it is silent? To what does the word "murmur" refer if an onomatopoeia lacks its noise? Jacobus's brief word-associative exercise suggests that medieval regimes of sound—the ideological frameworks that structured sonic experience—positioned music, which is a highly organized, culturally overdetermined form of sound, at the intersection of silence and noise. Music is a contradiction.

In his critical work on noise in society, the twentieth-century theorist Jacques Attali echoes Jacobus when he argues that music is "inscribed between noise and silence, in the space of the social codification it reveals."[3] As music emerges out of sound, it reveals the larger ideological forces that dictate which sounds have meaning, which are meaningless, and what sounds are refused access to the system at all (that is, what is silenced). In other words, music is socially and situationally contingent. For Jacobus, music arises out of particular discursive contexts, and it is the mental labor carried out upon sound—and not sound itself—that makes sound musical. Attali's political economy of music and Jacobus's etymological etiology of it are not identical in their broader political critiques, but they nonetheless suggest something similar about the nature of music. Music is not (or is not only) an a priori thing made of vibrating matter, mathematical ratios, or water-organs. Rather, music arises out of a specific type of metacognitive act: when a listener orients herself to listening, and ruminates upon that act, music emerges, even amid silence and noise. Music is an orientation toward the sound-object that recognizes the relationship that always already exists between sound, the listener, and the social structure as a whole.[4] This is what Lisbeth Lipari calls an "ethics of attunement."

I will discuss sound-objects in more detail in Chapter 5, but for now, we can imagine them simply as the phenomenal things that emerge out of acts of attentive listening. In an ethics of attunement, neither sound nor hearing in the simple sense of "perceiving or apprehending by the ear" is meaningful in and of itself. Instead, an ethics of attunement is concerned with listening—with noticing, holding and being held accountable—and with making sound matter within a system of signification. As Isidore says in the *Etymologiae*, "unless sounds are held by the memory of man, they perish, because they cannot be written down."[5] For Isidore, music is not a fleeting sensory object, but rather an obligation to attend. Because music requires not only the production of sound but also a willing *listener*, music—and the bodies between which it resonates—emerges out of the intersubjective play between performer and audience, between the maker of sound and the ears that make the sound make sense.

This chapter argues that music as "murmuring silence" is a primary force at work in *The Boke of Margery Kempe*, particularly as considered in terms of Lipari's ethics of attunement and Attali's social inscription of musicality as a midway point between silence and noise. In the *Boke,* Margery creates obligatory listening scenarios again and again, using what rhetorical theory calls "rhetorics of silence": the ways in which language accrues meaning through its delays, its interstitial spaces, and through socially negotiated acts of listening.[6] This chapter is not interested in silence or the inchoate absence of sound per se, but rather in a series of attunements and socially determined auditory interdependencies between Margery and her audience(s)—both diagetic and extradiagetic—that emerge out of the relatedness of silence and noise. That is, it is interested in Jacobus's murmuring silence and in Attali's notion of noise. Here, the sonic body is opened up to the listening other, where it arises out of an obligatory rhetoric of silence.

What does it mean to attend to *The Boke of Margery Kempe*, or, in Attali's formulation, to find meaning in the middle point between silence and noise? First, it means taking seriously the moments in the *Boke* when Margery is silent, or when silence serves as a structuring principle of the text. Second, it means recognizing how Margery's raucous noisemaking in the *Boke* is given meaning by acts of attunement, that is, by her listeners' or readers' engagement with her rambunctious body/text, and by the larger structural conditions—like repetition, dissonance, cadence, and return—through which noise becomes meaningful. And so, while this chapter will not address music in *The Boke of Margery Kempe* in the traditional or normative meaning of the word, it will consider silence, noise, the spoken word, and music as part of a continuous spectrum of meaningful sonority.

There are many instances in the *Boke* where Margery explicitly states that not only her weeping, but also (and crucially for a rhetoric of silence) the moments where she finds herself *unable to cry*, are gifts of God. Repeatedly, Margery emphasizes that the givenness and seemingly aleatory nature of both her tears and her silences are what make them meaningful. There are, in addition to these involuntary silences, a number of occasions when Margery is in control of her vocal expression and intentionally holds silence. These are often moments when Margery is in real physical danger, and when silence, as a rhetorical stratagem, works by forcing her hostile interlocutors to wait—to, quite literally, *attend* to her—even though she is a subject with less political, social, or religious power than her interrogators. This form of silence is related, in turn, to the silence of many years between the events described in Margery's book and the time she chooses to commit her life story to paper; the opening declaration that Margery "was comawndyd in hir sowle that s che schuld not wrytyn so soone" is the same sort of maneuver as her taciturn response to the Archbishop and his men while under interrogation: it is a means of wresting feminine control away from the patriarchy's demand to be answered on its time.[7]

What connects each of these types of silence is their self-reflexive, explicit awareness of their utility as persuasive techniques. When Margery or her *Boke* make a conscious shift from noise, speech, or song to silence (or from silence back to sound), this draws her listeners' attention and gives meaning to her phatic, raucous, and unruly moments of weeping. Margery's auditors and her readers actively participate in her noisemaking when they are forced to recognize its eruption from the boundaries of silence; it is the curious rhythm of her voice that causes them to question when, why, and how she has a voice.

## Finding Silence in the Hubbub: Reconsidering "the Voice" in Margery's *Boke*

Since its rediscovery by Hope Emily Allen in 1934, *The Boke of Margery Kempe* has been read as a book of voices: voices in conversation, dialogue, and debate, of "authentic" voices and performative ones, of the competing voices and concerns of the book's "author" and her "character," of the role of the amanuensis's voice in voicing Margery, and of the role of feminist critique in finding women's voices in the medieval past. One critical nexus of scholarship on the *Boke*, for instance, centers on the recovery of Margery's voice: after four hundred years in which Margery had been nothing but a name appended to a boilerplate devotional tract, Allen's discovery provided readers with a rare, triumphal text, a moment in which the archive opened itself, assuring readers that there was a real, noisy, flesh-and-blood woman in the medieval period who not only had written about her boisterousness, her sociality, and gregariousness, but, perhaps even more amazingly, whose ineluctable voice had survived the stridently heteropatriarchal and hegemonic forgetting the archive tends to do.[8] Critical studies of the late twentieth century often attempted to tease apart just whose voice was at work in the *Boke*—Margery's, her amanuensis's, or some amalgamation of the two.[9] More recent studies by Liz Herbert McAvoy, Felicity Riddy, and Nicholas Watson have suggested that the varied voices and potential *auctores* of her *Boke* are fictions created by Margery herself.[10] Even now, the role of voices in the *Boke* is not a settled issue: in a striking study, Julie Orlemanski interprets Margery's noises as "distributed expressivity," the idea that the concept of the voice is itself a product of communal agreement and coming-into-discourse, an argument on which this chapter builds its discussion of silence.[11] P. R. Robins uses the failure—or success—of voicing in gaining ecclesiastical approval to juxtapose the written lives of Margery Kempe and Joan of Arc, arguing that the impossibility of disentangling "blended . . . clerical, lay, male, female, visionary, learned, colloquial, formal, vernacular, [and] Latin" voices of Margery's (and Joan's) texts is precisely what makes them both interesting and powerful.[12] Rhetoric scholar Julia Marie Smith leverages the notion of the "rhetorical chorus" to think about the *Boke*, suggesting that a "polyphonic relationship" exists between Margery and the other voices that infiltrate her text, from scribes to annotators.[13] Kathy Lavezzo explores Margery's weeping as a vocal practice that bonds women to each other in an erotics of empowerment.[14] "Voicing" is also used to describe the role of Margery's thoughts and her spiritual conversations with God throughout the text. In his 2004 edition of the *Boke*, Barry Windeatt calls on readers to focus on Margery's internal voices; Corinne Saunders and Charles Fernyhough's ongoing project on the *Boke* considers how Margery Kempe's "inner voices" might be approached using contemporary biopsychological frameworks, such as theories of mind, auditory hallucinations, or dialogic thinking.[15] The varied, consistent, and sustained interest in the role of voicing for the meaning of Margery's life narrative—even as feminist discourse itself has grown, shifted, and changed, and the role of the voice in expressing agency has mutated—suggests that readers of the *Boke* implicitly recognize the voice's formal and thematic centrality to the text. Even for readers skeptical about the degree of freedom Margery had in writing the *Boke* and for those who might argue that discourses of the authenticity of the voice are always problematic, the *Boke* is imbued with the potency of a feminist history that might be reclaimed through acts of voicing.

Of course, there is good reason for this focus on the voice. The *Boke* is full of the sounds Margery makes, whether disorganized or organized, *vox inarticulata* or *confusa* and *vox articulata*. "Cry" and its variants, both grammatical and orthographical, appear 228 times in the *Boke*; "weep" 260 times, "sob" seventy-two times, "roar" seventeen; the words "lowde" or "lowdely" describe Margery's voice fifty-six times, and "boisterous" or "boisterously" thirty-three. The *Boke* is also built on dialogue: around 600 times in the text, the word *seyd* introduces direct speech, both internal and external; there is music, too, though not with anything like the same frequency of the spoken word: "sing(ing)," "melody," "music," and "melodious" appear a total of twenty times. With all of these noises, vocal performance is one of the *Boke*'s most important qualities (on a number of occasions in the last twenty years, the *Boke* has successfully been adapted as a play in a nod to this tendency toward the performative).[16] Margery's vocal virtuosity dismantles heteropatriarchal authority; her noisiness is the fifteenth-century eruption of a punk aesthetic.

The stories Margery tells about herself, too, often equate voicing with presence and participation in the social ecosystem, and silence with social—and actual—death. Just such an exchange happens between Margery and a particularly hostile monk in Canterbury. "What kanst thow seyn of God?" the monk asks Margery, challenging her when she speaks publicly about her mystical conversations.

> "Ser," sche seyth, "I wyl bothe speke of hym and heryn of hym," rehersyng the monk a story of scriptur.
> The munke seyd, "I wold thow wer closyd in an hows of ston, that ther schuld no man speke wyth the."[17]

Here, the monk might be wishing immurement on Margery, or perhaps he is merely wishing her the figurative death of the anchor-hold. In either case, the text equates silence with juridical or ritual demise. Margery's ability to speak ad libitum is vitally important to her.

Margery's book is indeed one of noises, but these noises acquire meaning from their positionality relative to the silences that surround them, and from the push-and-pull of speaker and listener in acts of mutual recognition. Take, for instance, the *Boke*'s many chapters that focus on Margery's internal mental landscape, which Windeatt, Saunders, and Fernyhough argue are central to Margery's project. This space and these chapters are raucous and congenial, full of mental sounds and conversations: conversations occur in Margery's "mind" 140 times; in her "sowle" 260, her "thowt" 192, and her "undirstondyng" seventy-one times; she feels things in her "herte," "sowle," "mende," "consciens," "wyttys," "reson," "revelacyons," "self," "wyl," and "contemplacyon." In total, words denoting an interior resonant space tally to 1,024. There is no disputing that these inner spaces themselves exist in a sort of noisiness, or that readers have easy access to their vociferousness. However, for a citizen of King's Lynn or for one of Margery's fellow travelers on the road to Jerusalem, these moments of inner speech would have manifested as silence—not the silence of absence, but instead a silence preconditioned by and understood as part of a cyclical pattern of silence and noise. Her fellow pilgrims would recognize this pattern: first Margery would sit in silence, and then she would break out into weeping and wailing, after which she would return back to the outward silence of mental dalliance. The *Boke* explicitly outlines this intervallic nature of her weeping during her pilgrimage to Jerusalem:

> Fyrst whan sche had hir cryingys at Jerusalem, sche had hem oftyn tymes, and in Rome also. And, whan sche come hom into Inglonde, fyrst at hir comyng hom it comyn but seldom as it wer onys in a moneth, sythen onys in the weke, aftyrward cotidianly, and onys sche had fourteen on o day, and an other day sche had seven, and so as God wolde visiten hir, sumtyme in the cherch, sumtyme in the strete, sumtym in the chawmbre, sumtyme in the felde whan God wold sendyn hem, for sche knew nevyr tyme ne owyr whan thei schulde come. And thei come nevyr wythowtyn passyng gret swetnesse of devocyon and hey contemplacyon. And, as sone as sche parceyvyd that sche schulde crye, sche wolde kepyn it in as mech as sche myth that the pepyl schulde not an herd it for noyng of hem. For summe seyd it was a wikkyd spiryt vexid hir; sum seyd it was a sekenes; sum seyd sche had dronkyn to mech wyn; sum bannyd hir; sum wisshed sche had ben in the havyn; sum wolde sche had ben in the se in a bottumles boyt; and so ich man as hym thowte. Other gostly men lovyd hir and favowrd hir the mor. Sum gret clerkys

seyden owyr Lady cryed nevyr so ne no seynt in hevyn, but thei knewyn ful lytyl what sche felt, ne thei wolde not belevyn but that sche myth an absteynd hir fro crying yf sche had wold. And therfor, whan sche knew that sche schulde cryen, sche kept it in as long as sche mygth and dede al that sche cowde to withstond it er ellys to put it awey til sche wex as blo as any leed, and evyr it schuld labowryn in hir mende mor and mor into the tyme that it broke owte. And, whan the body myth ne lengar enduryn the gostly labowr but was ovyr come wyth the unspekabyl lofe that wrowt so fervently in the sowle, than fel sche down and cryed wondyr lowde. And the mor that sche wolde labowryn to kepe it in er to put it awey, mech the mor schulde sche cryen and the mor lowder.[18]

Here, Margery directly connects the iterability of her tears (which first happen once a month, and then increase in frequency to as many as fourteen times a day) with the public's ability to make ethical or moral judgments about those tears. Note that her weeping occurs in discrete instances—she does not talk about her tears in terms of their continuity; rather, she describes each weeping episode as a unique, articulated *event* separate in number but connected in kind to the tears that precede and follow it. In the moments between her tears she experiences relief, but this relief in turn is marked by a prodromal perception of another imminent crying episode in which she feels either shame or social culpability. Margery's affective relationship to the onslaught of her tears—even more than the weeping itself—causes her to consider what these spells look like to those around her. "Sche wolde kepyn it in," she says, because she does not want to "noy" them. This, in turn, results in a social response. Some people say she has a "wicked spirit that vexes her," others that she is sick or drunk; some wish her removed from town and drowned; but others love her, support her, and recognize Margery's desire to *not cry*—to remain silent—if it were within her capacity to do so.

These moments reveal the importance of listening as a locus of power and authority. The word "heard" appears ninety-three times in the *Boke*; each of these are instances when Margery or one of the other figures in her book are invested not in the production of noise, but in the reflective reception of it. When God names his intent to marry her and show her His "prevyteys" and His "cownselys," Margery listens in utter silence: "The creatur kept sylens in her sowle and answeryd not therto, for sche was ful sor aferd of the Godhed and sche cowde no skylle of the dalyawns of the Godhede, for al hir lofe and al hir affeccyon was set in the manhode of Crist."[19] Margery's most important spiritual development—the one that shifts the text from imagination-based modes of devotion and the "manhode of Crist" toward an intellective affection for the "dalyawns of the Godhede"—takes place in quietude.

The *Boke* attempts to show just how important the anticipation of sound in moments of silence was not only for Margery, but also for her listeners and readers. The text alternates between noise and silence in specific, tactical ways, showing how private, mystical experience gains social meaning thereby.

## Rhythms of Weeping, Rhythms of Listening

Both in Margery's life and in her *Boke*—to the extent that her lived experience and the record of that experience can be disentangled—Margery's goal is to make an aural mystical experience that is internal, private, and phenomenally silent audible to her audiences, both lived and textual. By doing so, she hopes to authorize her experience as well.

Perhaps most importantly, Margery must prove that her tears have been granted to her as a particular favor of God. For readers of her *Boke*, who have access to the interiorizing language of justification the *Boke* provides, it is patently obvious that the rhythmic alternation between silence and tears is the means through which this favor is expressed. "Thu schuldyst knowyn wele," God says to Margery early in the text, that "thow mayst not han terys ne swych dalyawns but whan God wyl send hem the, for it arn the fre yyftys of God wythowtyn thi meryte, and he may yeve hem whom he wyl and don the no wrong. And therfor take hem mekely and thankyngly whan I wyl send hem, and suffyr pacyently whan I wythdrawe hem, and seke besyly tyl thow mayst getyn hem, for terys of compunccyon, devocyon, and compassyon arn the heyest and sekerest yyftys that I yeve in erde."[20] While "tears of compunction, devotion, and compassion" are the "highest and surest gifts" that might be given by God, without the capacity to be withdrawn, they lose their status as particular and exemplary favors. For Margery to "suffer paciently" when God withdraws them is just as important as for her to cry when God grants her episodes of weeping. Later in the same exchange, God specifically connects this pulsating rhythm of presence and absence to the particular grace granted the mystic. "I far sumytme wyth my grace to the as I do wyth the sunne," he says. "Sumtyme thow wetyst wel the sunne schynyth al abrod that many man may se it, and sumtyme it is hyd undyr a clowde that men may not se it, and yet is the sunne nevyr the lesse in hys hete ne in hys brytnesse. And rygth so far I be the and be my chosyn sowlys."[21] To be chosen is not to dwell always in the immediate experience of God's presence, but to recognize His absence itself as part of the cadence of exceptional grace.

Margery's spiritual maturation involves building the capacity to be silent: God tells her that she will have until a certain time to speak—to "sey what thow wylt"—and, thereafter, she must be quiet: "I schal yevyn the leve to byddyn tyl sex of the cloke to sey what thow wyld. Than schalt thow ly stylle and speke to me be thowt, and I schal yefe to the hey medytacyon and very contemplacyon."[22] This is not a type of meditation that comes naturally to Margery, but rather one that requires its own type of guidance and training, as the *Boke* makes clear:

> Another day this creatur schuld yeve hir to medytacyon, as sche was bodyn befor, and sche lay stylle, nowt knowyng what sche mygth best thynke. Than sche seyd to ower Lord Jhesu Crist:
> 'Jhesu, what schal I thynk?'
> Ower Lord Jhesu answeryd to hir mende . . . [23]

Here, Margery lies down and is quiet, but sits uneasily until God gives her specific meditational tasks to do; Margery must be taught how to be silent, and learning this skill is part of what shows her spiritual development.

When, near the end of the first book, God calls himself "an hyd God in thi sowle" and draws attention to the periodic nature of Margery's tears, he draws a direct connection between her involuntary silences, anticipation, and her tears:

> I wythdrawe sumtyme thi teerys and thi devocyon that thu schuldist thynkyn in thyself that thu hast no goodnes of thiself but al goodnes comyth of me, and also thu schuldist verily wetyn what peyn it is for to forbere me, and how swet it is for to fele me, and that thu schuldist be the mor besy for to sekyn me agen, also, dowtyr, for thu schuldist knowyn what peyne other men han that wolde felyn me and may not. For ther is many a man in erth that, yyf he had but oo day in al hys lyve tyme of swech as thu hast many days, he wolde evyr lovyn me the bettyr and thankyn me for that

oo day. And thu maist not, dowtyr, forberyn me oo day wythowtyn gret peyne.[24]

This moment makes it clear to Margery that silence, like weeping, is a gift of God, especially when it is in the context of her tears; but it also makes that link startlingly explicit to her readers, who have immediate access to God's justification for an anticipatory rhetoric of silence.

So much for Margery's readers. The *Boke* must also accomplish a different, more difficult task: it must portray how this rhythm of silence and internal noise makes itself palpable to those within Margery's lived, aural community (and not just her readers). The people of Lynn initially experience this rhythmic presence and absence, the push-and-pull of noise and silence, as a form of artificiality or compositionality, because, at least in the minds of the people, "normal" forms of crying have an observable cause and are marked by discrete, often singular, outbursts, rather than sustained and repetitive cycles of weeping followed by silence. For Margery, a concern throughout the book is proving the nonvolitional nature of these outbursts as well as her pauses between them; she must show that they are not part of a calculated performative strategy of self-sanctification, but instead that the cries are beyond her control. In addition, Margery must prove her cries' divine etiology to those around her. When people who have known her for much of her life first comment on her crying, it is to express their inability to understand the cause of her outbursts, and therefore whether they are divine or demonic: "And thei that knew hir governawnce befortyme and now herd hir spekyn so mech of the blysse of hevyn seyd unto hir: 'Why speke ye so of the myrth that is in hevyn? Ye know it not and ye have not be ther no mor than we.'"[25] And so, the *Boke* spends quite a bit of time depicting the ways in which her friends, acquaintances, and enemies come to understand her noisiness as given by God.

The *Boke* charts this passage of coming-into-scrutability. Originally, her tears are nonsensical to those around her because they cannot hear into her brain—the melodies are private and internal, phenomenally silent to everyone but Margery—and so it is Margery's goal, first through the pattern of her living and then, much later in her life, through the writing of her *Boke*, to help others hear into her internal experience and to make, in some ghostly, attenuated sense, her sonic or aural experience available to others. The *Boke* must show, then, how those around Margery become convinced of the divine origins of her experience. It does this through a series of scenes depicting attentive listening.

In one such instance, the *Boke* uses a member of the clergy as an authority on the discernment of spirits in order to prove Margery's saintliness
to those around her. The relationship between the intervallic nature of Margery's tears and the public perception of Margery's sanctity is highlighted
when Master Alan, her confessor, directly connects the gaps between her
tears to their givenness by God:

> Sithyn a worshepful doctowr of divinité, a White Frer, a solem clerk
> and elde doctowr, and a wel aprevyd, whech had knowyn the sayd
> creatur many yerys of hir lyfe and belevyd the grace that God wrowt
> in hir, toke wyth hym a worthy man, a bacheler of lawe, a wel grown-
> dyd man in scriptur and long exercisyd, whech was confessowr to
> the sayd creatur, and wentyn to the sayd frer as the good preystys
> dedyn beforn and sentyn for wyne to cheryn hym wyth, preyng hym
> of hys charité to favyr the werkys of owr Lord in the sayd creatur
> and grawntyn hir hys benevolens in supportyng of hir yyf it happyd
> hir to cryen er sobbyn whyl he wer in hys sermown. And thes wor-
> thy clerkys telde hym that it was a gyft of God and that sche cowde
> not have it but whan God wolde geve it, ne sche myth not wyth-
> stande it whan God wolde send it, and God schulde wythdrawe it
> whan he wilde, for that had sche be revelacyon, and that was un-
> knowyn to the frer.[26]

Through Margery's confessor, the *Boke* makes it clear that the withdrawal
of her tears is part of her spiritual process and directly indicates their givenness by God in a rhythm that is beyond Margery's control and that Master
Alan makes explicit to those around her. In this instance, Margery's community not only hears her make noise; they also *attend,* through the discrete moments of crying between which there are gaps in her voice, to silences
that are pregnant with the possibility of sonic eruption. This rhythmic os-
cillation between quietude and sound is murmuring silence, moments when
those watching would have been waiting, breath held, for Margery to cry,
thinking about the meaning of her sounds.

A similar occurrence takes place in chapter 58, which opens with Margery at prayer, requesting that God fulfill her desire that a good priest read
her "every day a sermown" and "Holy Scriptur." This prayer is answered as
the chapter continues, when a new priest, traveling with his mother, arrives in Lynn. The priest and his mother invite Margery to their shared

dwelling, where the three of them spend the evening in holy reading and conversation:

> Than the preyste toke a boke and red therin how owr Lord, seyng the cité of Jerusalem, wept therupon, rehersyng the myschevys and sorwys that schulde comyn therto, for sche knew not the tyme of hyr visitacyon. Whan the sayd creatur herd redyn how owr Lord wept, than wept sche sor and cryed lowde, the preyste ne hys modyr knowyng no cawse of hyr wepyng. Whan hir crying and hir wepyng was cesyd, thei joyyd and wer ryth mery in owr Lord. Sithyn sche toke hir leve and partyd fro hem at that tyme. Whan sche was gon, the preste seyd to hys modyr, "Me merveylyth mech of this woman why sche wepith and cryith so. Nevyrtheles me thynkyth sche is a good woman, and I desyre gretly to spekyn mor wyth hir."[27]

As she so often does in her *Boke*, Margery's expressed intent here is to spend as much time as possible listening to the Word of God; she does not begin her evening with the roars or cries that she is, by this time in her life, known for. But Margery's attentive listening soon turns into active, mimetic, and noisy participation in the reading. "Whan . . . [she] herd redyn how owr Lord wept," she, too, begins to weep; the story of Jesus's tears explicitly trigger her own; it is only when she hears about Jesus's tears that she herself cries—not before. Her noisemaking in turn calls those around her to attention: both the priest and his mother sit in Margery's presence, marveling because they "know no cawse of her wepyng," a form of rupture from the more straightforward semantic register of the biblical lesson that is, to them, inscrutable. When Margery's tearful episode ends, all three "joy and are right merry"; and the priest is so moved by her performance that, after she leaves, still in awe, he tells his mother that "sche is a good woman" and he "desyre[s] gretly to spekyn mor wyth her." This intimate scene at the priest's house illustrates the relationship the *Boke* builds between attentive listening, noise, and the emergence of meaning out of noisemaking. First, Margery's initial act of attentiveness to the priest's lection causes her to burst out in an empathetic response to the text; her sudden phatic vocalization— one that the priest cannot quite comprehend—brings him and his mother to attention themselves, and, in the specific context of an oral-textual environment of collaborative reading, ultimately allows the priest to assign value and purpose to her noise. Regardless of what her cries "mean" in a strictly semantic sense, the priest and his mother are able to make a judgment about the quality of her character because of them. In short, this is a scene of coming-into-attunement, where Margery's interlocutors discover that her weeping holds devotional potential. Because Margery listened, they listen.

Sometimes, too, the *Boke* recounts situations where those around Margery create laboratories for the discernment of spirits, thereby empirically determining the source of her weeping by juxtaposing it to her silences. The longest such account, though not the only one, is outlined at the end of Book I, in part of a series of concluding chapters meant to enumerate Margery's increasing spiritual *auctoritas* as she ages:

Tweyn preistys whech had gret trost in hir maner of crying and wepyng, nevyrthelesse thei wer sumtyme in gret dowte whedyr it wer deceyvabyl er not. Forasmeche as sche cryid and wept in the syght of the pepil, thei had a prevy conseyt, hir unwetyng, that thei wolde prevyn whedyr sche cryid for the pepil schulde heryn hir er not. And on a day the preistys cam to hir and askyd yyf sche wolde gon too myle fro then sche dwellyd on pilgrimage to a cherch stod in the feld, a good party distawnce fro any other hows, whech was dedicate in the honowr of God and Seynt Michael Archawngyl. And sche seyd sche wolde gon wyth hem wyth good wil. Thei toke wyth hem a childe er tweyn and went to the seyd place al in fere. Whan thei had a while mad her preyerys, the sayd creatur had so mech swetnes and devocyon that sche myth not kepyn it prevy but brast owt in boistows wepyng and sobbyng and cryid as lowde er ellys lowder as sche dede whan sche was amongys the pepil at hom, and sche cowde not restreyn hirselfe therfro, ne no personys beyng ther present than the tweyn preistys and a childe er tweyn wyth hem. And than, as thei cam homward ageyn, thei mett women wyth childeryn in her armys, and the forseyd creatur askyd yyf ther wer any man childe amongys hem, and the women seyd, "Nay." Than was the mende so raveschyd into the childhod of Crist for desir that sche had for to see hym that sche myth not beryn it but fel downe and wept and cryid so sor that it was merveyl to her it. Than the preistys haddyn the mor trust that it was ryth wel wyth hir whan thei herd hir cryin in prevy place as wel as in opyn place and in the feld as in the town.[28]

In this scene, two priests carry out an analysis meant to determine the veracity of Margery's tears. Like all good experiments, this one is carried out by relatively impartial observers (while they have "gret trost" in Margery's "maner of crying and weping," the priests nonetheless are unsure whether it is "deceyvable," that is, intended to deceive) who test their hypothesis by pitting Margery's social weeping against a blind control. With Margery removed from "the pepil at hom" and placing her in the relative isolation of a country church, her worship practice begins in silence, but soon erupts into sobs "as lowde er ellys lowder" than those she weeps in front of others, thus proving, to the men's satisfaction, the "truth" of her tears. The priests' scenario of "privy" or occult attendance is thus leveraged to authorize the many open, social moments of attendant listening elsewhere the *Boke*; this experiment would be a failure were it not for Margery's silence.

These moments show that the movement between silence and sound is legible not only to Margery, and not only to readers of her *Boke,* who are privy to Margery's own interior monologues and written interpretations of these oscillations. Indeed, Margery's "murmuring silence" is legible to those around her, and, in becoming legible, is interpreted as a sign of extraordinary heavenly favor.

There are other types of silence in the *Boke* as well. On a number of occasions, it is Margery's silence—her own, volitional repression of her voice—that proves rhetorically effective, granting her access to social spaces from which she might otherwise be rejected because of her voice, or where silence saves her from physical violence through the tactical maneuvers of rhetorical delay. Margery repeatedly uses silence amid noise as a form of rhetorical persuasion that allows her to maneuver deftly through dangerous sociopolitical environments. Murmuring silence positions Margery as authoritative by engaging even her most animous interlocutors as attendants on her voice.

One of the most striking examples of such silence occurs before Margery's pilgrimage to Jerusalem, where a condition of her acceptance into the group of pilgrims is that she curtail her weeping, wailing, and constant talk. "Yif ye wyl go in owyr felwashep," her fellow travelers bargain with Margery, "ye must makyn a new comnawnt, and that is this: ye schal not [speke] of the Gospel wher we come, but ye schal syttyn stylle and makyn mery, as we don, bothin at mete and at soper." To the requirement that she "sit still," Margery "consenty[s]" and is thereafter "receyvyd ageyn into hir felawshep."[29] Likewise, during the interrogation in which Margery is asked to gloss the meaning *crescite et multiplicami,* her response is not only to defend herself on the merits, but to beg the right to travel "in peace and quiet," as other, less problematic women do:

> "Hast thu any lettyr of recorde?"
> "Sir," sche seyd, "myn husbond gaf me leve wyth hys owyn mowthe. Why fare ye thus wyth me mor than ye don wyth other pilgrimys that ben her, wheche han no lettyr no mor than I have? Syr, hem ye latyn gon in peys and qwyet and in reste, and I may no rest have amongys yow."[30]

In this exchange Margery leverages traditional expectations of feminine comportment—that she be unobtrusive—in order to demand her right to move about the countryside unmolested.

At punctuated intervals in the *Boke,* this stereotypically feminine do-cility is also directed at her interactions with God. Although her audiation of heaven often results in loud exclamations, at times, her response to these visitations is a profound silence. Early on, the *Boke* recounts that she "lost hir bodyly strength and lay stylle a gret whyle, desyryng to put [the noise] away."[31] Conversely, much later, near the end of the first book, when these auditory experiences have taken on a quotidian cast, it is their *absence,* rather than their presence, that causes Margery to be silent. After a series of particularly abhorrent satanic visions that follow a withdrawal of heavenly presence, Margery becomes quiet:

> "I wold not, Lord, for al this world suffryn swech an other peyne as I have suffryd thes xii days, for me thowt I was in helle, blyssed mote thu be that it is passyd. Therfor, Lord, now wyl I lyn stille and be buxom to thi wille; I pray the, Lord, speke in me what that is most plesawns to the."[32]

Margery's silences are a bargaining chip with God, where Margery promises to be silent and submissive in return for a return to their frequent mystical dalliance. This is an important reminder that, for Margery, complicity, com-pliance, and silence are part of the "buxomness" of a normative feminine spirituality that Margery deploys tactically *amid* her cries and tears in order to eventuate her own spiritual desires. The *Boke* depicts murmuring silence not only as Margery tuning in to God, but also shows that murmuring silence might tune God Himself.

## Music, Prudence, and Politics: Rhetorics of Silence

What do Margery's silences have to tell us? If the *Boke* has traditionally been read as powerful—even optimistic—because of its voicing, it might at first seem pessimistic to investigate its silences, or to assert silence as central to Margery's project of self-authorization as a mystic as well as self-defense in the face of real-world threats of violence. Certainly, voicing, presence, and political action go hand in hand in Western thought. "Your vote is your voice," runs a popular election-season exhortation; victims of violence are encouraged to speak out; whistle-blowers make noise; practical action is defined as vocal action. However, there is a dark underside to the equation of voicing with power that implicitly equates silence to absence or to failure: when a subject fails to speak, these arguments imply, she also fails to be present in a way that is meaningful. There are a number of related issues with this equivalence. First, it requires oppressed or silenced people to become advocates within and against superstructures that actively devalue, refuse to listen to, or do not recognize as "voices" the very voices that are speaking; often, as it is with Margery's female body, the voices of oppressed communities are interpreted, by structural power, as no more than "roryng." As Gayatri Spivak notes, those denied forms of political representation also lack access to mimetic representation.[33] By equating voicing and presence, current critical tropes suggest that those in positions of power are willful listeners and that they attend to the subjects who are speaking. But "the voice" does not exist on its own; it emerges within interpersonal and intersubjective structures of belonging. There can be no voice, no speaking, without an active listener. Equating voicing with political action without addressing the necessity that those with privilege listen—or to speak on behalf of those whose voices do not code as voices—ultimately only reproduces techniques and structures of oppression. In essence, the issue of "voicing" is not simply about the literal voice, but about political representation, structural power, and entrenched advocacies that crystallize around the language of voicing as a tool of oppression. This is a formulation that further entrenches these systems by neglecting the strategies of those in power, which is, often, to retreat into silence as a means of maintaining control even as the disenabled are labeled as noisemakers.

Medieval saints' lives in particular serve as veritable formularies for this type of silent retreat of power and the concomitant physical and emotional violence that women who speak truth to such power structures should not only expect, but embrace.[34] For instance, the virgin martyr tales of the Katherine Group—Saint Catherine of Alexandria, Saint Margaret, and Saint Juliana—each portray a woman who boldly speaks and is then violently killed.[35] John Capgrave's extended *Life of Saint Katherine*'s eponymous heroine speaks "lowde" in defense of her virginity, and converts fifty pagan philosophers to Christianity through persuasive oral argumentation, only to be tortured on a wheel and beheaded.[36] Chaucer's tale of Saint Cecilia encourages women to speak out against abuse while simultaneously engaging in a violent fantasy of martyrdom against those very same women.[37] Medieval heroines are encouraged to be both vocally expressive in speaking out against their oppressors, and subsequently docile in the face of the repetitive and extreme violence that follows such expressions. By transposing violent physical injustice onto martyrdom, these texts entrench an ideological framework in which speech and retributive subjugation are not only causally linked, but normalized and valorized. Under such a system, holding silence is not necessarily an expression of pessimism; or, if it is, it is a pessimism that must be recognized before it can be rectified.[38] Like the forms of oppression and power maintenance that obtain in contemporary systems of voicing and silence, medieval martyr tales participate in a similar play of vocal expressiveness that is luxuriously—even wantonly—instrumentalized for the purposes of its own containment.

While acts of silencing work inarguable violence, silence itself might nevertheless structure forms of possibility. Although Quintilian considered "stopping abruptly and courting applause by silence" an oratorical fault, there is nevertheless rhetorical power in holding silence, in both its premodern and its modern manifestations, whether that silence is imagined as a collective or an individual expression—the "moment of silence" to memorialize a tragic event; the silence of monastic rumination; in the Black Lives Matter movement, the sublimation of the deaths of innocent black and brown people at the hands of a extrajudicial policing in the bodies of protesters with taped mouths, the pause that precedes a flippant response to a stupid question, or the outright refusal to speak when spoken to, to refuse to be hailed by structures of interpellation.[39] These are silences of self-preservation, of community formation, and of rebellion. A critique that invokes rhetorics of silence is fundamentally indebted to an intersectional matrix of contemporary social critique.[40]

We are right to query the political utility of applying a theory developed out of the generational trauma inflicted on BIPOC to the entirely self-conscious deployment of that same technique by a bourgeois white woman who, in spite of the "shame and scorn" she suffered, was nevertheless almost never in real peril of being burned at the stake. Nevertheless, finding resonances in medieval sources—places in which silence serves as a tactic of resistance—is not difficult, and might also help to inform more contemporary accounts as well. For instance, during her heresy trial of 1310, Marguerite Porete "contumaciously refused to appear" before her inquisitor, William of Paris, and, when forced to do so, "refused to undergo an oath" to renounce her *Mirror of Simple Souls*; for the next year and half, she declined to "swear and respond" to his questions.[41] Similarly, Joan of Arc refused to answer questions posed to her during her heresy trial in 1431. Under the canonical rules of due process, defendants had the right not to answer questions before being charged; because Joan was never formally charged, rather than answer and incriminate herself, she called for her interrogators to "pass on."[42] In these instances, Marguerite and Joan employ silence as a form of radical resistance to juridical frameworks that would encode any type of utterance as inculpatory.

With Marguerite's and Joan's defiant silences in mind, it is possible to turn to a pivotal moment in Margery's *Boke* with an eye to how she orchestrates silence and the timing or spacing of her speech: "The seyd creatur, lying in hir bed the next nyth folwyng, herd wyth hir bodily erys a lowde voys clepyng: 'Margery.' Wyth that voys sche woke, gretly aferyd, and, lying stille in sylens, sche mad hir preyerys as devotwly as sche cowde for the tyme."[43] This is the opening of the chapter in Book 1 that eventually finds Margery under interrogation at the palace of the Archbishop of York. The chapter thus begins with a divine rehearsal of the interpellation that awaits her in the coming days. God calls to her "bodily erys," and she responds by lying "stille in sylens."

Margery does not break her external silence until the next day, when her hearing before the Archbishop and his retinue begins.

> Than seyde the suffragan to the seyde creatur, "Damsel, thu wer at my Lady Westmorlond."
> "Whan, sir?" sayde sche.
> "At Estern," seyd the suffragan.
> Sche, not replying, seyd. "Wel ser?"[44]

Just as she does in her response to God, Margery does not reply immediately. Instead, like Marguerite Porete and Joan of Arc, she delicately diffuses the clerical inquiry with a parsimonious set of questions of her own, after which she stands in silence, refusing to respond directly to their accusations, in response to which the suffragan "multiplye[s] many schrewyd wordys before the Erchebischop" so that "it is not expedient to rehersyn hem."[45] The *Boke* tallies the accounting of words here in a balance of power: the "multiplied" words from the Archbishop and his aide are impotent to the extent that they might be passed over in silence, "unrehersyed," whereas Margery's placid countenance betrays the location of her agency. Margery suffers their "noyful wordys" while remaining prudently laconic.[46] Her delayed speech gives her time to gather her thoughts and to contemplate her best strategies for response. It also has juridical effects: by being silent, Margery requires her interlocutors to engage in acts of attentive listening themselves.

All of this reads like a bit of theater, and that is precisely the point. Deploying what in one context would be a principled survival tactic and a final act of defiance in order to orchestrate a type of musical resonance in her readers is exactly the reason these theories *work* on Margery: because they lay bare her performativity for what it is, an aesthetic engagement that emerges out of political and social environments and that, in turn, has political ramifications. Like Marguerite and Joan, Margery takes time to respond to questions directed at her when they might involve injurious legal consequences; she allows meaning to accrue in the quiet spaces between question and response.

A better understanding of the power of this moment in the *Boke* can be gained from looking in detail at medieval accounts of silence as a rhetorical maneuver. Here there is fruitful overlap between rhetorical and music-theoretical treatises, particularly those written up to and through the twelfth century, where prosody and song were not separate arts so much as overlapping ones, and where short pauses in speech or chant, called by various names—*suspensio vocis* (suspension of the voice), *respirandum* (breath), *distinctio* (distinction), *mora/morula* (delay, little delay), *pausa* (pause), or *vox amissa* (lost voice)—were understood to carry a meaning-making capacity. While polyphonic musical compositions of the late medieval period deployed the *pausa* or *vox amissa* within significantly more complex rhythmic modes than plainchant, here, too, they provide fruitful ways to think about the power of silence, albeit in a manner discrete from its rhetorical function.[47] And, while medieval rhetorics generally follow Quintilian's definition of rhetoric as the *ars bene dicendi* or the *bene dicendi scientia*, prioritizing sound over silence, there is a tradition in medieval rhetoric, following Albertanus of Brescia's *Ars loquendi et tacendi*, that explicitly recognizes the value of keeping silent.[48] For Albertanus and those who borrowed from him, including Brunetto Latini and Chaucer, knowing how, when, and what to speak well necessitated knowing how, when, and what not to say. "He who does not know how to keep silent does not know how to speak," Albertanus avers before going on to list the many types of things a prudent speaker—someone who wants to win goodwill, influence, and success—should avoid: inane, empty, irrational, profane, hard, rude, nasty, and bad things.[49] Medieval rhetorical treatises, then, make explicit the implicit tactics and performed resistances of Marguerite, Joan, and Margery: silence, sometimes, is a powerful way to affect, and to effect political change on, one's audiences. "Sweet words multiply friends and soothe enemies," he says, quoting Ecclesiasticus.[50] Because rhetoric is in large part about persuasion and specifically persuasive speech directed at political ends, silence, as an integral element of rhetoric, is a political act.

In Albertanus's mind, the point of silence—which was part of prudent speech, not separate from it—was to create a specific emotional state in listeners, and, through the sweet musicality of well-timed words, to placate listeners. "Pipes and psaltery make a sweet melody, but a sweet tongue surpasses both," he says.[51] Of course, not even the most superficial reader of Margery's *Boke* would qualify her words as "sweet"; rather, the interplay of silence and speech that she performs itself has mollifying effects.

The fourteenth-century grammarian Nicolaus Dybinus gives an account of silence in rhetoric that asserts the power of well-timed silence:

Boethius says in his *De consolatione philosophiae* that Rhetoric teaches how to make sweet and mellifluous speeches, but also to be silent at the appropriate time and occasion. This the philosopher especially commended, because rhetoric was a quality of those great men, Socrates, Solon, and Xenocrates, who knew, because of rhetoric, both the best kind of speaking and of being quiet. Socrates was once at a council of princes, and hearing some useless talk, he did not want to speak; but the prince was irritated and asked him why he kept quiet. Socrates said: "I have often regretted that I spoke, but never that I was silent." At another time, Solon [was] asked why he was quiet as if he were a fool or a mute. Then he answered, "To talk a lot is the business of fools." Xenocrates was asked why he stopped speaking, whether he had some speech defect. He said, "Nature allotted

me one mouth and I have two ears, on account of which it is more
useful to me to listen than to speak." When philosophers and rhet-
oricians gave responses like these, the anger [*ira*] and melancholy
[*dolor*] of princes was assuaged, and rhetoric made the philosophers
themselves the beloved counselors of princes. Thus we can see how
rhetoric drives away anger and melancholy.[52]

Here, both Socrates and Xenocrates leverage silence to earn the loyalty of
their patrons, where it operates more persuasively than speech in forging interpersonal connections. Isidore of Seville says that the point of rhetoric is to
"render the listener benevolent, docile, or attentive."[53]

It is likewise a commonplace of music theory treatises to call the rest
(*pausa*) a "refreshment, as in punctuation, for the fatigued spirit" (*recreatio
spiritus fatigati sicut punctuatio*).[54] That is, the pauses in music are what allow
listeners to delight in sound itself. Georgius Anselmus (fourteenth century)
says in his *De musica*: "Just as the orator often soothes the weary listener
(*defatigatum auditorem*) with some joke and makes him well disposed, so the
trained singer mixes some delays (*moras*) with the melody and makes the
listener more eager (*avidum*) and attentive (*intentum*) to the rest of the phrases
of the song."[55] Anselmus's text makes clear that pauses are specifically gen-
erated to interpellate the listener within the ambit of music's rhetorical power.
Silence changes listener attitudes in ways that speech or sound cannot. The
pause is the space in which the auditor is made eager and attentive, and, in
doing so, becomes an active participant in his own persuasion. Together,
then, rhetoric and music theory carve out a place of primary importance for
pauses, delays, rests, and silences through their ability to make meaning
through their affective influence on both the performer and her audience.
This is the ability, as the music theorist Engelbert of Admont (d. 1331) describes in his *De musica*, to make meaning out of undifferentiated sound.
"Just as in the other senses the delight in what is perceived proceeds from
perception and perception from observing distinctions," he says, "so in the
hearing of song there will be no pleasure unless the song is clearly perceived,
nor can it be clearly perceived unless correctly parsed."[56]

By the fifteenth century and the *Practica musice*, Franchino Gaffurio
would treat the rest not only as a basic element of constructed song, but as
a vital element of consonance and delight: "The rest was invented to give a
necessary relief to the voice, and a sweetness to the melody; for as a preacher

of the divine word, or an orator in his discourse, finds it necessary often-
times to relieve his auditors by the recital of some pleasantry, thereby to make
them more favorable and attentive, so a singer, intermixing certain pauses
with his notes, engages the attention of his hearers to the remaining parts
of the song."[57] Silences allow the simple undifferentiated acts of hearing to
become musical listening, acts which, like Jacobus's murmuring silence, in-
cur delight. The *pause* (in its many guises both inside and outside of music)
is explicitly designed to capture goodwill.

The first role of rhetoric is *captatio benevolentiae*, and it is a careful attentiveness to silence's place in speaking—to timing, and to the rhetorical
effects of the pause—that allows Margery to influence the Archbishop's assessment of her. Whether Margery's speech is *delightful* to her audience or
not, it has its desired rhetorical effect: she receives a letter from the
Archbishop—first of York, and then, in the next chapter, of Canterbury—
granting her the right to travel freely throughout the country. The *Boke's*
account of this encounter is, like so many of its passages, attenuated, its wit
borne out of its brevity, as the imagined, multiple, and cacophonous sounds
of Margery's accusers are thrown into stark relief by her own laconic retorts.
A rhetoric of silence might help tease apart the way that Margery's power as
a speaker is dependent on the pauses she takes. Margery is a compelling
speaker in part because she understands how silence makes her listeners
complicit in their own persuasion. But this is not the only time in the *Boke*
when Margery deliberately silences herself, sometimes in an effort to quell
physical violence against her person. When a mob in Canterbury threatens
to burn her under suspicion of Lollardy, Margery responds with silence.
"Than seyd the pepyl: 'Tak and bren hir!'" the *Boke* recounts.

And the creatur stod stille, tremelyng and whakyng ful sor in hir
flesch, wythowtyn ony erdly comfort, and wyst not wher hyr husbond was become. Than prayd sche in hir hert to owyr Lord. . . .
And anon, aftry sche had mad hir prayers in hir hert to owyr Lord,
ther komyn tweyn fayr yong men and seyd to hir, "Damsel, art
thow non eretyke ne no loller?" And sche seyd, "No, serys, I am
neythyr eretyke ne loller." Than thei askyd hir wher was hir in.
Sche seyd sche wyst nevyr in what strete, nevyrthelesse it schuld be
at a Dewchmannys hows. Than this tweyn yong men browgt hir
hom to hir ostel and mede gret cher, preyng hir to pray for hem.[58]

Margery's silence in this passage enables the disarticulation of the roiling mob into individual speakers, ultimately diffusing the tension of this scene. As is clear from the question they ask Margery upon meeting her in the street—"Art thow non eretyke ne no loller?"—the two men who rescue Margery from the mob by escorting her back to her lodgings are not initially believers in her orthodoxy; at most, they are open-minded skeptics who, intrigued by her silence, query her about her true intentions.

Much later in the *Boke*, Margery's strategy of rhetorical delay results in the textual, if not literal, disappearance of those who verbally challenge her. Outside of York Minster, Margery is accosted by a priest who, taking umbrage at her white clothes, demands that she explain the validity of her *habitus*:

> And in that tyme many good men and women preyd hir to mete and madyn hir ryth good cher and weryn ryth glad to heryn hyr dalyawns, havyng gret merveyle of hir speche for it was fruteful. And also sche had many enmyis whech slawndryd hir, scornyd hir, and despysed hir, of whech o prest cam to hir whil sche was in the seyd Mynstyr and, takyng hir be the coler of the gowne, seyd:
>
> "Thu wolf, what is this cloth that thu hast on?"
>
> Sche stod stylle and not wolde answeryn in hir owyn cawse. Childer of the monastery goyng besyde seyd to the preste:
>
> "Ser, it is wulle!"
>
> The preste was anoyed for sche wolde not answer and gan to sweryn many gret othis. Than sche gan to spekyn for Goddys cawse; sche was not aferd. Sche seyd:
>
> "Ser, ye schulde kepe the comawndmentys of God and not sweryn so necgligently as ye do."
>
> The preste askyd hir hoo kept the comawndmentys.
>
> Sche seyd: "Ser, thei that kepyn hem."
>
> Than seyd he: "Kepyst thu hem?"
>
> Sche seyd ageyn: "Syr, it is my wille to kepyn hem, for I am bownde therto, and so ar ye and every man that wil be savyd at the last." Whan he had long jangelyd wyth hir, he went awey prevyly er sche was war, that sche wist not wher he becam.[59]

In *Medieval Identity Machines*, Jeffrey Jerome Cohen explores this passage in some detail as part of his argument that the *Boke* understands the voice to be a "physical, nonlinguistic force"; this passage, according to Cohen, is one in which the "sound of her voice in its exteriority, by forming a dispersive alliance with her own sonority" enables Margery "to silence criticism, to transform into an instantly comprehensible aural purity any threatened unintelligibility, to precipitate community even as language failed."[60] Cohen's general argument about the force of Margery's presence is strong, but he wrongly notes sound as the central element of Margery's interpersonal relationships at this moment: when the priest demands that Margery tell him what sort of garment she's wearing, he says, "Kempe answers meekly that it is wool," an answer that in turn allows her to respond to his curses with righteous indignation.[61] The misreading here is small but meaningful: in the *Boke*, it is Margery's *silence* that has power, that unmasks the priest, drawing him into the hypocritical swearing that in turn allows Margery to take the moral and spiritual high ground. Margery's rhetorical tour de force is not only enabled, but set in motion, by her willingness *not* to speak.[62]

If Margery's self-silencing is a response to coerced speech that transforms her own disempowerment and marginalization into an active strategy of persuasion and *captatio benevolentiae*, we might understand, too, the moments in the text when Margery explicitly defers the writing of the *Boke* to the future as similarly strategic. "Sum proferyd hir to wrytyn her felyngys wyth her owne handys, and sche wold not consentyn in no wey, for sche was comawndyd in hir sowle that sche schuld not wrytyn so soone," she says in the prologue, and, later, "And sche seyd that it was not Goddes wyl that thei schuld be wretyn so soon, ne thei wer wretyn xx yer aftyr and mor."[63] In scholarship, this delay is usually contextualized within the "wondrous and humorous" multilayered drama of authorization that follows Margery's account of her life from feminized oral performance to the masculinized inscription of the text within literate systems of authority.[64] But for Margery, the delay *itself* is powerful, a means of building anticipation and persuasion into her life story in its own right. For readers of Margery's *Boke*, who always already come to the text after this period of delay, her life story arrives on the scene with her conscious construction of her life story as a retrospective and reflective act central to its poignancy as a life narrative. Although the text often jars and jumps, and the *Boke*'s structure itself seems governed by a chronology dislocated by the text's associative mnemonics, by insisting on delay as a central element of its coming-to-being, Margery imbues even this chaos with a sense of purposefulness and intentional, if hidden, organization. By refusing to "wretyn so soon," Margery draws her readers—even twenty-first-century readers—into critical engagement with her text not in spite of, but because of, its formal and structural vigor, confusion, and complexity.

## Roaring Silence

Next to an account of one of Margery's raucous crying outbursts in the sole surviving manuscript of *The Boke of Margery Kempe,* British Library, Additional MS 61823, an annotator writing in a small brown hand has written the short phrase *nota de clamor* in the margin.[65] In Middle English, the word *clamor* typically refers to the noisiness of shouting, as it seems to in Margery's *Boke,* but for a medieval audience, the word *clamor* would have also connoted legal situations in which the rowdy body was restrained and regulated.[66] By the late fourteenth century, excessive clamor was a reason to bring someone before a law court.[67] "Sound words" like *clamor* and *roaring* were used in texts to indicate public dissent to official policy, as well as listed as legal reasons to bring someone before the court. As Emily Steiner notes, "Clamour . . . is just one of many characteristics with which a dominant group might stigmatize a subordinate one as rebellious, irrational, insensitive, or abject."[68] In Chaucer's *Wife of Bath's Tale,* it is the "clamour and . . . pursute" that the ladies make to King Arthur that force the rapist-Knight to face the repercussion of his crime.[69] Even today, the use of *clamor* as a legal term continues: in 2018, a woman in Guernsey halted roadworks near her house by invoking the Norman right of *clameur de haro.*[70] Similarly, much like being issued a public disturbance charge or an antisocial behavior order today, being charged as a "roarer" was to enter the class of the social criminal. In 1311, for instance, Edmund and Richard de Pelham were indicted in the Ward of Walebroke as night-walkers and "rorers" for defrauding strangers.[71] That same year, Simon Braban, Richard le Pastemakere, Thomas de Bery, and others were "indicted in the Ward of Walebroke as a night-walker[s] and rorer[s]" for a variety of crimes.[72] Three hundred years later, the term was still in everyday parlance, as Thomas Middleton and Thomas Dekker's socially transgressive Moll Cutpurse makes clear in *The Roaring Girl.* When Margery talks about herself as "rorying" and when her readers refer to her tears as "clamor," they are not simply describing an inarticulate and an illiterate sound, but a social and legal category. How Margery is understood—and whether her cries have meaning or not—is dependent not merely on the sounds she makes, but also on how her listeners categorized her as a person worthy of attendance.

The word *clamor* has musical connotations as well. In an anonymous music treatise of the fifteenth century, *clamor* takes on a specific technical meaning where it refers to music in which the voice sings in a register that takes it outside its normal tessitura, producing a high-pitched, painful wail. These sounds "exceed human voices, so that they are not sung, but make a great noise (*clamor*), . . . no song of any rational mode ascends" to these notes, the treatise states.[73] Clamor of this sort is *vox literata*—the treatise identifies it with the highest notes of the scale, or the *excellentes*—and therefore, even as it surpasses musicality, it is nevertheless encapsulated within the very framework of musical meaning it ruptures. This high-pitched *clamor* anticipates musical resolution in the fall of the notes back to the cadence and then to musical rest. In other words, *clamor* is not pure noise, but rather a form of dissonance seeking resolution: it is unharmonious sound that becomes musical given its context.

The brown-ink annotator of Additional MS 61823 understood Margery's project as one not of pure noise, but as a murmuring silence that became meaningful as her many "listeners"—from those who people her *Boke* itself to her copyist, her readers, and her commentators—forged an intersubjective sonic body that relied on listening not just to noise, but also into silence. The monastic reader of Margery's *Boke*, conditioned by prior exposure to *clamor*, anticipates her sonic production as organized rather than disorganized sound because repeated exposure has allowed for ruminative practice upon the sonic environment under scrutiny. Those who have access to the portentous silence that precedes and follows Margery's outbursts attend to these moments in a collaborative and complicit performance. Because attending into silence is what allows the notion of "murmuring silence" to have meaning, one must go searching, in the *Boke*, for moments of silence.

In short, if we are to take Margery at her word, this means taking her at her silences, too, understanding that not only her noise but also her silence encourages forms of attentive listening and intersubjectival meaning-making. Margery's silences should be taken seriously precisely because Margery takes them seriously, as she is dragged into speech, unwilling to participate in the optimism of the voice for which contemporary critique has made her a champion. "Sche had levar a wept softly and prevyly than opynly yyf it had ben in hyr power," the *Boke* reminds us.[74] This reticence may be a fiction, but if it is, it is an overwhelmingly powerful one, because it presents

Margery's weeping as a type of murmuring silence. This is not a contradiction in fact—Margery cried, and she cried loudly—but of intent or mood; her subjunctive silence surrounds the *clamor* of her book, orienting it within a regime of sound in which even noise makes sense.

In much the same way, around five hundred years later, during a lecture at Vassar College in 1948, the composer John Cage outlined his idea for a new piece of music. The piece, he said, would be composed of "uninterrupted silence . . . three or four-and-a-half minutes long—those being the standard lengths of 'canned' music—and its title will be *Silent Prayer*." Cage planned to sell a recording of the piece to the Muzak Corporation.[75] Four years later, pianist David Tudor performed *Silent Prayer,* now renamed *4′33″*, at the Maverick Concert Hall just outside of Woodstock, New York. As a storm passed overhead, Tudor signaled the beginning and end of three "movements" (30″, 2′23″, and 1′40″) by closing and then opening the keyboard cover on his piano. He played nothing. The audience rebelled even before the piece was over, whispering, and then walking out in frustration. Those who remained to the end engaged in a heated question-and-answer session following the program, during which a local artist reportedly called on his fellow concertgoers to mutiny. "Good people of Woodstock, let's drive these people out of town!"[76] he cried. The audience felt cheated, as if they had been made the butt of an elitist, theory-minded musical joke. "They missed the point," Cage would later remark of the audience at the premier. "There's no such thing as silence. What they thought was silence, because they didn't know how to listen, was full of accidental sounds."[77] In the second performance of *4′33″*, this time in a concert hall, there was no riot.

Cage's original intent with *Silent Prayer* had been in part to thumb his nose at a recording industry committed to the psychological manipulation of human capital by corporate interests, to deconstruct ideology through nonsound; it was also an attempt to use silence as a tool to generate randomness: the piece actually performed during a thunderstorm the evening of August 1952, in a barnlike auditorium that opened out onto the forests of upstate New York, said something positive: *music* is noise, it is an act of transformation in which the ears are tuned to hear the unmediated world. For Cage, silence is about randomness, a deconstruction of silence that proves that there is no such thing as silence. Cage's silence is, then, somewhat different from Margery's understanding of silence. Nevertheless, in both instances, silence shifts the burden of music-making onto the audience. That done, music, silence, and noise become facets of the same object: the resonant space between that audience's expectation and the actual sonic environment.[78] They demand that the listener be aware of their role in their own persuasion.

Like Cage, like Attali, and like Jacobus's etymology of *musica* as murmuring silence, *The Boke of Margery Kempe* argues that there is a continuous movement between noise, silence, and musical expression in mystical experience, a shuffling from silence to euphoric dissonance and to a tuneful ruminative sequela that is intimately tied to the acts of attunement and listening.

Early in her *Boke*, the text "The cryeng was so lowde and so wondyerful," she says, "that it made the pepyl astoynd, les than thei had herd it beforn and er ellys that thei knew the cawse of the crying."[79] It is easy to overlook the importance of silence in this passage, given that the subject of the sentence is "the cryeng," which is loud and wonderful; it shocks the fellow pilgrims, who have already ostracized her. But note what is really being said in this passage: that they were astonished *unless they had heard the crying before* or *knew its cause*. In other words, Margery's crying ceases to be noise the moment that it becomes a recurrent activity; when crying outbursts are broken up by moments of silence, the outbursts themselves begin to acquire a sort of meaning. Her listeners also become accustomed to her cries if they have been preconditioned to understand their cause. That is, rather than ask her audience to simply *hear* her crying and sobbing, the *Boke* instead stresses attendance, or listening, to the interplay of silence and noise, of consonance and dissonance. Margery's sobbing and "roryng" are not antithetical to silence, but, rather, of a piece with it, centering the work of auditory attunement as the goal of its project. If music is defined by the *habitus* with which one listens, then Margery's outbursts are not noise per se; instead, like musical dissonances, they are forms of sonic tension that, in emerging from and resolving into silence, have musical meaning. The *Boke* expects something from its audiences: attentiveness, and an understanding of when to be silent and when to respond to Margery's cries with cries in turn.

Margery's complex structures of silence and voicing broaden the acceptable possibilities for what is classified as "organized" or "meaningful" sound. Through organized repetition, she forces the socially legible or biopolitical (normative, and normalizing) to conform to her own sonic/unsonic practice. In other words, rather than structure her practice of sound around that which is already considered salutary for society (by excising both excessive silence and what might be considered noise) Margery champions silence and noise, initially causing discomfort in order to grant her fellow townspeople, pilgrims, and readers the opportunity to come to pleasure and to develop into sense through careful attendance.

That Margery's attunement to moments of silence has been overlooked in scholarship is itself a product, then, of entrenched patriarchal readings of the text. Throughout history, nonnormative members of society are categorized as rowdy or noisy. The fact that institutional power can *afford to be silent* in the face of such disruption should tell us all we need to know about the relationship of silence and noise: that noise is the coded domain of those without power, and silence of those who hold it. However, if we notice Margery's silences as well as her noises, we see that the *Boke* seeks to create a type of silence-amid-noise that the oppressed might use in their struggles against the powerful.

Reading Margery as rebellious because of her voice is useful, in part because it is a construction of contemporary desires to read voicing as dissent and as power. But this impulse leaves out the potential for silence to form meaning as a type of dissent as well as a profound form of speaking. The *Boke* is about an authoritative lineage of unwillingness of which Margery is a member. Silence, frustration, and exhaustion are, like speaking out, all valid reactions to oppressive regimes, and for Margery, regimes with which Margery was wrestling in order to write her book. If for Margery noise is an involuntary act, then silence is the performance of the will, and therefore out of the silences of the *Boke* emerges a radical feminist politics. In those times when Margery is not raucous or roaring, but instead silent, she becomes a body that is not meant to be *heard,* but rather to be *attended* to, whose delays, like Georgius Anselmus says in the *De musica*, entrain the listener in an affective engagement.

Chapter 4

# Music, *Amicitia*, and Carthusian Mystical Diaries

so fa RM & f Norton of Wakenes & of the passyon
—*The Boke of Margery Kempe,* marginal annotation

## Richard Methley, John Norton, and Textual Entanglement

In 1476, Richard Methley entered the Carthusian Charterhouse of Mount Grace, deep in the Yorkshire wilderness.[1] Six years later, in 1482, John Norton joined the Carthusian order, and moved to Mount Grace soon thereafter.[2] From then until their deaths in the early sixteenth century, Methley and Norton lived and worshipped in the same charterhouse. In becoming Carthusians, Methley and Norton were joining a community that was, in some important respects, more like a collection of anchor-holds than a cenobitic monastery: the founding documents of the Carthusian order, the *Consuetudines Guigones*, required that monks be alone for much of the day. Whereas in cenobitic monastic orders, the collaborative work of singing the liturgy together eight times every day was a central element of the religious life, Carthusian monks celebrated many of their liturgical hours alone, for the most part singing the divine office, meditating, and reading in individual cells.[3] The architectural layout of Carthusian charterhouses highlights this form of living: unlike the Benedictines, whose monasteries were generally built around large communal buildings (a church, with its quire, a dormitory, a refectory, and so forth), charterhouses were comprised of a series of single-resident cells built around a central cloister and a more modest church. As William of St. Thierry observed, these private cells lead the Carthusian "to angelic purity . . . and the perfection of all sanctity" and made him worthy to "savour [God], to understand him, to apprehend him, [and] to enjoy him."[4] While there were opportunities for collective worship—communal services were held on feast days, the monks sang vespers and matins together, and conversation was allowed in the refectory—when they did meet, they were still to do so as quietly as possible and without impropriety; were not to "twist their fingers together, nor swing their legs, nor play with their books while singing, and . . . obtain a pardon if they let a book fall."[5]

Because a comparatively large portion of the labor of the Carthusian monk was done both in silence and in a solitary cell, the rules of the order gave special devotional import not to the musical performance of a collectively sung liturgy, but instead to private manuscript reading and copying.[6] "We desire," the *Consuetudines* says, "that books be made with the greatest attention and kept very carefully, like perpetual food for our souls, so that because we cannot preach the word of God by our mouths, we may do so with our hands.[7] In her trenchant study of one of the most famous Carthusian manuscripts of the late medieval period, British Library, Additional MS 37049, Jessica Brantley notes the capacity for such texts themselves to be performative. The delightful, colorful images of this miscellany "indicate the fundamental role of performance in devotional reading more generally," Brantley argues.[8] While her study is built on the operatic grandeur of just one Carthusian "imagetext," Brantley's claims imply a performative capacity for Carthusian manuscripts more generally. That is, even less visually stunning books copied, housed, and read in Carthusian cloisters—from Margery's *Boke* to Marguerite Porete's *Mirror* to the two manuscripts written by Methley and Norton, which are the heart of this chapter—have a performative devotional capacity *because of* the constraints Carthusians placed on other, louder forms of religious performance. Carthusian textual projects—the writing, copying, binding, and reading of books—were the choirs in which Carthusian voices and communal belonging were, in a sense, performed to their fullest extent.

Over the decade of the 1480s, while living in Mount Grace, both Richard Methley and John Norton engaged in the same sort of collaborative reading and writing practice that the marginal annotation in *The Boke of Margery Kempe* hints at. Both men had mystical experiences of heavenly song and wrote about them; those texts are now contained in two manuscripts. Methley's manuscript—now Cambridge, Trinity College MS O.2.56—includes

Table 1. A Brief Comparison of the Manuscripts

| *Methley, Trinity MS O.2.56* | *Norton, Lincoln Cathedral MS 57* |
| --- | --- |
| *Scola amoris languidi* (1r–22v) | *Musica monachorum* (1r–27r) |
| refrain: *amore langueo* | refrain: *pura obediencia* |
| form: dialogue | form: dialogue |
| content: a "schooltext" on mystical love | content: importance of obedience to the Carthusian rule |
| ends: effusive poem of love-longing | ends: ascent through celestial hierarchies |
| *Dormitorium dilecti dilecti* (25r–48r) | *Thesaurus cordium vere amantium* (28r–76v) |
| refrain: *ego dormio, et cor meum vigilat* | refrain: *venite ad me* |
| form: single-perspective treatise | form: dialogue |
| content: "sleep" as a fundamental element mystical practice | content: mystical vision of a holy mountain |
| *Refectorium salutis* (49r–70v) | *Devota lamentatio* (77r–95v) |
| refrain: *ego dormio* and *amore langueo* | refrain: *ego dormio* |
| form: mystical diary | form: mystical diary |
| content: account of mystical revelations over the course of the liturgical year | content: account of mystical revelations on a single day |
| "A!" and "Oh!" repeated | "A!" and "O!" repeated |

three treatises: the *Scola amoris languidi* (fols. 1r–22v), the *Dormitorium dilecti dilecti* (fols. 25r–48r), and the *Refectorium salutis* (fols. 49r–70v). Norton's manuscript—now Lincoln, Cathedral Library MS 57—also contains three treatises: the *Musica monachorum* (fols. 1r–27r), the *Thesaurus cordium vere amantium* (fols. 28r–76v), and the *Devota lamentatio* (fols. 77r–95v). And, as their books make clear, both men were writing not only for themselves as contemplatives, but also for and with each other—and for their wider Carthusian readership—in an act of performative textual entanglement. Table 1 summarizes the most salient structural, formal, and content-based similarities between the manuscripts.

In their tripartite structure, Methley's and Norton's manuscripts share something very basic in common. But the similarities between the two men's experiences—and their manuscripts—run much deeper. For instance, the first treatises in both manuscripts are written as dialogues between a teacher and a student (Methley's *Scola amoris languidi* and Norton's *Musica monachorum*); the second treatise of each manuscript traces a single vision dealing

with a mystical ascent (Methley's *Dormitorium dilecti dilecti* and Norton's
*Thesaurus cordium vere amantium*); and the third and final treatise is structured like a diary: both Methley's *Refectorium salutis* and Norton's *Devota
lamentatio* record a series of visions in the first person; and both give dates
for these visions, locating them in a specific day of the Church year and place
in the charterhouse. Perhaps most tellingly, all six treatises employ refrains
that serve as a jumping-off point for devotion or contemplation, and that,
through the work of repetition, gain the status of a type of object, albeit an
object made of imagined sound—a sound-object.[9] In the next chapter, I develop the notion of a sound-object more fully, but for now, suffice it to say
that these are textual tags that, through iteration, hold an ephemeral spoken or sung phrase before the mind in attenuated form.[10] These refrains are,
respectively, *amore langueo* (Methley's *Scola amoris languidi* and *Refectorium
salutis* and Norton's *Devota lamentatio*), *ego dormio cor meum vigilat* (Methley's *Dormitorium dilecti dilecti*), *pura obediencia* (Norton's *Musica monachorum*), and *venite ad me omnes qui laboratis et onerati estis et ego reficiam vos*
(Norton's *Thesaurus cordium vere amantium*, whose source is Matthew 11:28).
Two of these phrases are borrowed from Rollean mysticism (*amore langueo*,
which has its ultimate source in *Canticum canticorum* 2:5 and which both
Methley and Norton use, and Methley's *ego dormio*, from *Canticum canticorum* 5:2), highlighting the affective kinship that both Methley and Norton
felt for the fourteenth-century mystic and the type of written musicality
that they performed.[11] These refrains show that both Methley and Norton
used Rollean *canor* as a means of articulating their experience of mystical
song, not only claiming to have actually *had* an experience of *canor*, but also
appropriating Rolle as an authority on how to write about that same experience, quoting him and mimicking his alliterative Latin style in some places,
and lapsing into and out of the prosopoetics that typifies his writing in others.
    Nevertheless, had Methley and Norton not been living and writing in the
same charterhouse at the same time, these formal and generic similarities
alone would be enough to conclude that their texts, at the very least, influenced each other. But because these two very similar manuscripts were composed by two writers living at the same time in the same monastery and by
men who belonged to a monastic order known for careful reading and copying
of manuscripts as a form of communal belonging, we can conclude that their
shared experiences of *canor* and their shared manuscriptival projects went
hand in hand. We can imagine Norton and Methley passing their fascicles off
to each other in the supposed silence of Mount Grace, a silence that was, if

their manuscripts and the red-ink annotator's marginalia are to be believed, at least a partial fiction. "I heard the angels singing last night!" one might have whispered; and the other, who had heard his confrere's voice echoing through the walls of the charterhouse, might have nodded in silent understanding. Although this scenario is romantic, an imaginative fancy that takes liberties with the archival evidence, it is not entirely fantastical. The Lincoln and Trinity manuscripts present a form of collaboration performed by and structured within a distributed textual corpus—a sort of "sonic" textual intersubjectivity. The two manuscripts are, to appropriate a quotation from Aristotle on friendship, one book in two manuscripts, one textual soul in two bodies.

Although Richard Methley has received a fair amount of scholarly attention—primarily as the translator of the *Cloud of Unknowing* and Marguerite Porete's *Mirror of Simple Souls*—Methley's three treatises contained in the Trinity manuscript have, until recently, gone largely unstudied, with important exceptions being James Hogg's editions of the Latin treatises in Trinity MS O.2.56 in *Analecta Cartusiana*.[12] But if Methley is frequently overlooked in scholarship, Norton is almost always ignored. Norton's archive, small as it is, has to my knowledge never been studied in detail, dismissed by scholars as "primarily visionary in nature" and therefore not worth individual attention.[13] The following sections of this chapter, then, do two things simultaneously: first, they argue that intersubjectival textuality is the sonic embodiment of Methley's and Norton's mystical experience; and, second, they argue that to fully appreciate *either* Norton's *or* Methley's role in late medieval mysticism, their texts must be read together, as productions of intimate friendship and amicable intersubjectivity. An attentiveness to mystical song lies at the heart of these entangled manuscripts.

In addition to the similarities between Norton's and Methley's texts charted in Table 1 and discussed in the pages to follow, I have also included an appendix that summarizes each manuscript; while my focus in this chapter is on mystical song or *canor*, there are contiguities between the two manuscripts that exist beyond the scope of this sonorous study.[14]

## Textual Entanglement and Carthusian *Canor*

Norton's and Methley's mysticism borrows *canor* from Rolle and modifies it for the monastic—and specifically, the Carthusian—life. Both manuscripts adapt Rolle's extraliturgical and expansive musical devotion to the demands placed on the Carthusian hermit to perform the monastic office quietly, and largely in private. This is a surprising adaptation of Rollean mysticism, because Rolle himself argued that the private experience of *canor* and monastic liturgical responsibilities were at odds with each other. But Methley and Norton demonstrate how Rolle's euphoric sonic experience, far from being contradictory to the responsibilities of a monk, might actually align with them. Carthusian mystical song is solitary because it is written and read, and communal because the manuscripts that contain it are collaborative projects.

Moreover, Norton's *Musica monachorum* and *Thesaurus cordium vere amantium* explicitly discuss what it means to be a monk with liturgical responsibilities and a penchant for long contemplative sessions that culminate in *canor*. Both the *Musica* and the *Thesaurus* posit that mystical song is performed through obedience to the Carthusian rule: the first treatise is a dialogue that teaches the Carthusian novitiate that the "music of the monks" (*musica monachorum*) is monastic obedience, and in the *Thesaurus* Norton elaborates on this idea at length. "The heart," Norton says, "sings continuously in chaste love . . . and makes a noise of the taste of heaven and sweetly speaks of divine delights" when it performs the duties of the Carthusian rule.[15] Later in the same treatise, Norton voices Christ, who encourages the Carthusian to understand solitary contemplation as a sort of sonorousness: "Therefore I say, O sweet son, labor resolutely in the confinement of the silence of the cell and of your senses, by my mellifluous (*mellifluo*) love alone. And sing of me from the heart (*cane me cordialiter*)—in chaste love, with a pleasant song (*cantu ameno*), without the influence of sorrow, in all of your actions both of the soul and of the body, and not in respect of any creature— captured in your heart by meditating in many ways upon my passion."[16] As the Carthusian performs his liturgical observations, his body merges with his cell to become a place for music—for "mellifluous love"—and his heart is the center of that sonic production. While singing is generally construed as an act of engaging the voice, an outward trajectory from the singer to the world, Norton's *Musica* and *Thesaurus* reverse the directionality of singing, making it part of interior spaces. Here, sense-perception is a type of melody; listening is a form of song. The liquefaction of the self and the synaesthetic gestures of this passage are reminiscent of Hilton's *Of Angels' Song* even as they borrow from Rollean mysticism. The Carthusian monk is a resonant object set ringing as he tunes his sensorium to the silence of the cloister.

A similar attentiveness to the role of liturgical obligation as an integral part of mystical experience can be found in Methley's manuscript. In the *Refectorium salutis*, the final section of the Trinity manuscript and a mystical diary, each entry begins with Methley at prayer or celebrating Mass and ends with *canor*: "Today, that is, the day after the Feast of Saint Dionysius, the great contemplative, just after the eighth hour (according to the English way of reckoning the hours), I began to say Terce alone in choir, with my bodily eyes closed, but my spiritual eyes open. Then jubilant melody (*canor iubilens*) descended upon me with melodious jubilation (*iubilus canorus*), together with the amorous langour that can heal all things—and they have not yet departed from me. Rather, my heart is perceptibly dancing in my chest even as I write; and it is now after ten in the morning on the same day."[17] Liturgy is the instigating event of *canor* as well as the means by which Methley makes his experience legible to his monastic audience; liturgical observation places *canor* in time and space. Obedience to the work of *canor* within the liturgical hours "makes a man perfect," says Methley; although it "is practiced in community among regular monks," it is performed "in singularity between God and his highest anchorite."[18] *Canor* exists as part of the liturgical *habitus*.

*Canor* is concomitant with the Carthusian liturgy. In addition, the manuscriptival nature of Carthusian contemplative practice means that Methley's and Norton's texts formally echo and encapsulate musical performance, shifting between poetry and prose to suggest the presence of *canor*. In doing so, Methley and Norton are indicating *canor* in the same way Rolle had done a century and a half earlier. Over the course of his career, Rolle experimented with form, as the prose of his early commentaries gradually developed into the poetics of the *Melos amoris* and then finally into the delicate interplay of prose and poetry in his later works (the *Emendatio vitae* and the *Super lectiones mortuorum*).[19] *Canor*, itself ineffable, thus plays through the Rollean corpus as a form of stylistic experimentation; the quotidian rhythms of prose shift into the rhythmic, repetitive, alliterative, and allusive—that is, the heightened—register of poetic incantation. While this interplay is not what Rolle considered *canor* itself, it does suggest the intent to mark textual effects, to limn the noumena of mystical song in textual phenomenon.

Throughout their manuscripts, both Methley and Norton fall into the Rollean tendency to inscribe *canor* as prosopoetics. In the *Scola*, Methley asks how one is able to know what the languor of love is if he has not been taught to love.[20] His answer, which is that he learns in a moment (*discit in momento*), in an experience given by God (*experiencia a deo datur*), employs the same sort of prosopoetic shift that Rolle employs in his own textual performances of *canor*:

> *Languet autem christus dilacione quia expectat pacienter ut coronet dili-gentem se in tempore suo haud dubium optimo. Quomodo potest aliquis intelligere quomodo languor amoris est in dilacione nisi didicerit diligere? Multa signa multum esse alicuius amorem erga aliquem ostendunt. Sed procul dubio qui expertus est amoris dilacionem plus discit in momento quam aliquis per signa in toto vite sue tempore. Quid igitur? Numquid quia inscius es discere diligere non potes? Aut quia expertus non es discere erubesces? Experiencia a deo datur sed cum ei per insciciam via paratur, disce ergo per signa* **quomodo deus languet amore ut coronet gloria et honore quem diligit in multo et mirifico dulcore immo aliquando angelico canore.**[21]

Methley's Latin prose switches into a semipoetic register within its discussion of the sudden exhilarating revelation of *languor amoris*:

> *Quomodo deus languet amore,*
> *Ut coronet gloria et honore,*
> *Quem diliget in multo et mirifico dulcore,*
> *Immo aliquando angelico canore.*[22]

The discussion of the ineffable and unteachable immediacy of learning to love affects the formal structure of Methley's prose; it shifts the relationship words have with each other from one of signification (a Socratic, pedagogical dialogue) to a relationship dictated primarily by sonority: rhyme breaks the sentence into shorter *clausulae*, each of which ends with the same rhythm. Though the poem above is inchoate, incomplete, even bad—it does not follow a particular metrical scheme, and its feminine rhyme is not typical of late Latin poetics—it is nonetheless a gesture toward poetic language.[23] Whether or not the initial experience of *canor* comes about through passive or active mental exertion, the production of musical poetics pursuant upon this experience is the proof of that experience.

This rudimentary poem is a sign of things to come in the manuscript. In the final chapter of the *Scola*, the soul and the flesh engage in an increasingly staccato dialogue until, finally, the text breaks into song, tracing the body of a crucified Christ as it does so:

*Iesu bone rector morum*
*Et salvator seculorum*
*iubilus merencium*
*Manus dextre vulnus sanctum*
*Cordis nostri fugat planctum*
*more diligencium.*

*Eterne rex altissime*
*Atque panis dulcissime*
*esus te fruentium*
*Vulnus nos sinistre manus*
*Benedicat ne vulcanus*
*urat cor credentium.*

*Salue Jesu Salue Jesu*
*Melos auri mel in esu*
*sanitas amantium*
*Dextri pedi vulnus latum*
*nostrum expurget reatum*
*salus infirmantium.*

*Ure igni sancti flatus*
*Renes noster aduocatus*
*vita te videntium*
*Pedis levi vulnus patens*
*cordis pandat vulnus latens*
*more confitentium.*

*Salve iesu iesu bone*
*In amoris unione*
*sanctitas viventium*
*Vulnus cordis lanceati*
*Sanet vulnus desperati*
*cordaque canentium.*[24]

The soul traces Christ's body, mapping divine hands and feet onto the heart. This is what music sounds like outside of the *corpus*, when flesh dissolves to synthesize itself with the mystical body of Christ, itself pierced, perforated, and wearing away. As the lover's body dissolves into song, the body of Christ dissolves alongside it and into it in a heartfelt song (*vulnus cordis lanceati . . . cordaque canentium*). This production, however, is not completely idiosyncratic, but, in a nod to the textual basis of Carthusian spirituality, has precursors in the Latin liturgical tradition: its leonine verse invokes the rhymed votive offices in vogue in the late medieval period, its references to *iubilus* recall the poetics of Richard Rolle, and its repeated *salves* are well known from the poetics of the Cult of the Holy Name.[25]

Norton, for his part, is not invested so much in rhyming poetics as he is in the type of alliteration found in Rolle's *Melos amoris* and *Emendatio vitae*. Throughout his manuscript, he deploys strings of alliteration to perform the idea of inspired speech: in the *Thesaurus* alliteration describes the path to a heavenly castle (*ad uias ducentes perfectos peregrinos ad portam predicti castelli*);[26] in the *Musica* he weaves the sound of a hard initial *c* [k] into his discussion of the choir of heavenly angels (*gloriosos choros angelorum in unitate ueri amoris et conspectu summi conditoris in purissima et castissima obediencia gloriose curie celestis*).[27] Both of these alliterative moments occur in the middle of sentences and are not semantically independent in their own right, but this is part of the point: tunefulness, expressed as alliteration, takes over from sense not when grammatical sense dictates (at the end of sentences), but instead when emotional force compels him.

Perhaps the most stunning display of alliteration in the *Thesaurus* comes in the middle of a series of chapters describing heaven. Here, Norton's treatment of continual, chaste love includes a chain of sustained alliteration reminiscent of Richard Rolle's Latin style: **Quia quociens cordialiter cantatur** **continue in cordibus caste amancium demones contristat, purgandos letificat et** **multos a penis liberat, angelis & sanctis in celis cum omnium beatorum spirituum** **agminibus magnum et mirabile gaudium prestat. Et facit matrem meam dulcissimam mariam cum tota celesti curia melliflue orare per orbibus amantibus meis** **multifarie meditantibus in mee passionis memoria. et sic facit eos celico sapore sonare suas peticiones, et dulciter diliciis diuinis ditari, et in deo durantur sine diminucione.**[28] The Latin here takes part in a mimetic tunefulness, as the passage itself describes the unending song of the saints and angels in heaven. Music, as theorists remind us, is structured out of repetition, and through the repetition of chains of common initial sounds, Norton creates a playful text that asks the reader to anticipate, and listen for, such repetition.[29]

Finally, both Methley and Norton also attempt to encapsulate mystical song through pious exclamations, repeated *A! A! A!* or sighs that work like the *iubilus* of medieval music theory, a kind of melody sung without words. Jerome calls a *iubilus* "rough sounds" of praise, and Augustine defines a *iubilus* as "a sound of joy without words."[30] Methley's and Norton's *A*s break down the tidy categorization of voice as rational or irrational (*confusa/articulata*) and legible or illegible (*literata/illiterata*), because while these *A*s fundamentally refer to a form of experience that is illegible (incapable of being written down), and while they also simultaneously refer to an experience beyond rationality (*canor* disrupts human cognition, making its production a form of *vox confusa*), these *A*s are not only written down, but also acquire meaning beyond simple groans or purely affective movements of air. They are an experience beyond human rationality rather than below it.

Both Methley's and Norton's texts explore and provide interpretations of the possible meanings of this mystical *A*. In Methley's *Scola*, where many of these outbursts occur, marginal glosses aid the reader in their interpretation; Methley foregrounds the exclamatory *A* with a descriptive configuration that grants these "cryptic" outbursts linguistic meaning:

When people are alarmed by a dangerous fire, they do not shout, "Fire has attacked my house, come and help me!" In their anguish, not to say agony, they can hardly utter a word. So they just shout "Fire, fire, fire!" Or if the spirit moves them even more powerfully, they scream "A! A! A!" (*a a a*)—and they mean that sound to express their danger. So it was with me, in my small way. At first I kept commending my spirit to God by saying "Into your hands," either vocally or (as I suspect) mentally. But as the languor of love grew more intense, I could hardly think and I only formed in my spirit the word *Amor, Amor, Amor!* Love, love, love! Finally, as I fell away from even that formula, I waited for the moment when I could totally breathe forth my spirit. Then I could only sing (rather than shout) *A! A! A!*, or something like that, in my spiritual joy.[31]

*A! A! A!* is a sigh as well as signifier for *amor*, love, a word that is sung in such a way that its tunefulness breaks down into sighs. What might it mean to shorten the language of love to a single syllable? Methley's equivocal *a* is simultaneously a sung tone, a nonrepresentational sigh, and the word *amor*.

And what about Norton? At the beginning of his *Lamentatio*, the diary that ends the Lincoln manuscript, Norton talks about being "seized in the spirit to a place truly delightful, a place enriched indescribably with celestial sweetness."[32] What follows is a long prayer to the Virgin Mary interspersed with the same sort of repetitive exclamations that Methley employed:

> O virgin and mother and most powerful lady, wisest and kindest. Listen, Listen, Listen, Listen, Listen, Listen, Listen, and Attend (*Audi. Audi. Audi. Audi. Audi. Audi. et Exaudi*). And hear me, cry-ing to you in lament and from the heart, and lead me away from this body.[33]

Norton, too, sighs. A few pages later, he, like Methley, shortens *Audi* to *A*, and then, for the rest of the *Lamentatio*, uses this shortened form. Thus, while the *word* signified by the *iubilus* differs from Methley's (*audi* as op-posed to *amor*), the spoken sound remains the same, an equivocal signifier of spiritual excitement:

> Therefore, like an infant, I say, A! A! A! Receive me, my mother most merciful.[34]
>
> For I know that you are loving. And truly I confess that you are loving. A! A! A! O sweetest lady, what more am I capable of saying?[35]
>
> A! A! A! what more can I say?[36]

Both Norton's and Methley's *A*s are simultaneously performative and deictic. On the one hand, the *iubilus* as represented by the *A* is an act of pure music: lacking words, it is nonrepresentational, and a movement of affect or emotion. The *A* is the smallest possible unit of sound, and the articulation of these *A*s condense what Bruce R. Smith calls the "physical facts of time and space [and] the psychological experience of time and space" into their smallest quanta.[37] On the other hand, the vocalic *A* can be distending in time as long as human breath allows. At the same time, the *A* has literal meanings; it points to *audi* and *amor*, two words of great importance to both Methley's and Norton's mystical process. In these two cries of *A*, which are perhaps the purest moments of individualized and hyperenclosed, per-sonal experience in both manuscripts, Methley's and Norton's texts reach out to each other and to their reading audience, making legible the occult sighing of the *A*.

## Spiritual Friendship, Intersubjectivity, and the Monastic Other

Mysticism as a written genre has long been defined by its interest in, attachment to, and calling-into-presence of an absent other; it is, as Amy Hollywood says, a play on "the relationship between the absence of God and the contingency of the self."[38] For this reason, all mystical writing uses the text to take the place of the absent love-object; the text, in turn, is more than a mere site of transference, but instead actually becomes for the reader the very absence that arouses the desire-for-the-absent that defines mystical affect as well as selfhood. This absence-in-presence is poignant in a Carthusian context, where the reality of daily life meant that each monk spent hours at a time reading in solitary silence. Whereas, as Mikko Lagerspetz argues, cenobitic monastic liturgical observations created a "shared time" that produces musical intersubjectivity, for Methley and Norton, for whom communal worship was less frequent, their texts—and not the charterhouse choir—would have been the primary "shared time" of their choral sonic body.[39]

The sonic body that Norton and Methley perform is textual and intersubjective, a form of voicing that arises out of a self that is always already other *through* the work of writing and textual production. That is, Methley and Norton take Rollean *canor,* with its investment in actual physical heard sound, and mutate it into something that is not only textual, but absolutely reliant on friendly acts of textual borrowing and exchange. Methley and Norton experience Rollean *canor* by means of an epistolary friendship. Their sonic body emerges in their intertwined manuscripts, which embrace and perform their deeply collaborative musical expression.[40]

Norton's and Methley's manuscripts, taken together, work as an intersubjective sonic body, one that implicitly engages an ethics of obligation and friendship through shared themes, expressions, and formal properties. However, this sociality is only legible to the reader who has access to and engages with both manuscripts in parallel. Were Methley and Norton the only people to read their manuscripts in this way, or did others in Mount Grace have access to both texts? Who, exactly, could participate in their intersubjective body?

While we cannot know for sure how many of Methley's and Norton's confreres at Mount Grace read their manuscripts side by side, both manuscripts address a wider Carthusian readership, and both show a sense of friendship, fraternal care, and responsibility to the Carthusian community as a whole.[41]

On the first folio of the Trinity manuscript, at the beginning of Methley's *Scola*, likely the first of all six of Methley's and Norton's treatises to be written, Methley stresses the importance of friendship for the work to follow. "The highest aim of all creatures is to love and be loved (*amare et amari*)," he writes.[42] This is the opening salvo of the Carthusian epistolary intertexts that follow, and its effect on the *Scola, Dormitorium, Refectorium, Musica, Thesaurus,* and *Lamentatio* is highly important. Understanding the claims on the subject that the phrase *amare et amari* makes in the context of Carthusian spirituality means investigating the history and usage of this phrase. What is Methley claiming when he states, at the beginning of his (and Norton's) project, that the most important thing to learn is mutual, reciprocal love?

In a medieval context, the phrase *amare et amari* would have immediately conjured a centuries-old discourse on friendship that began with Aristotle. The source of this passage, ultimately, is Aristotle's *Rhetoric,* where the philosopher says that "a friend (*philos*) is one who loves (*ho philōn*) and is loved in return (*antiphiloumenos*)."[43] While this statement seems plain enough, for Aristotle, friendship is far from simple, as he makes clear in Books 8 and 9 of the *Nichomachean Ethics.* There are three types of friendship, Aristotle says: friendships based on utility, on pleasure, and around mutual love and an interest in the Good. In other words, friendship has an implicit politics; differences in social status, ethical or moral training, or identity played a large part in determining whether two men (and in these discussions, the subjects are always assumed to be male) might be friends or not. When, some three centuries later, Cicero penned his *Laelius de amicitia,* he echoed many of Aristotle's sentiments. But for Cicero, writing in the tumult of the Late Roman Republic rather than for the Athenian *demos,* friendship was explicitly, rather than implicitly, political. People of unequal status could never be perfect friends, he argues, for one would always be in the others' debt in some way.[44] In addition, perfect friendship, restricted as it was only to the mutual love of ethical men of equal (specifically patrician) status, could only be experienced in pairs, any other arrangement leading to potential conflicts of interest, time, and affection.[45] In other words, the model of ideal friendship in the Greco-Roman world was exclusive and decidedly rigid: friends were exemplary pairs of men who shared their lives, and who, by epitomizing the appropriate relationship not only between men but between men and the state, become suitable subjects of historical discourse.[46] As Jacques Derrida argues in *The Politics of Friendship*, in a historical sense, "the question of friendship is the question of the political."[47] According to this reading, no friendship can escape the political.

The meaning of friendship shifted in the medieval period. Even as Christian writers took classical texts as their models for friendship, they sought to decenter these texts' secular friend-structures—with their potential for homoerotic desire—and replace them with religious ones. In his *Confessions*, Augustine appropriates and critiques the classical tradition of friendship constituted by ethical obligations both toward the state and toward the bodies of his peers. "What delighted me," Augustine says of his childhood, "if not to love and be loved (*amare et amari*)?" he says, quoting Aristotle while simultaneously denigrating the worldly behavior of his youth.[48] For Augustine, childhood friendships were not to be celebrated but rather viewed with pity and shame, lost, as they were, in "clouds of libidinal desire."[49] The spectral fear of potential queer affect and attachment is central to Augustine's reconfigured notion of Christian friendship as distinct from its classicizing models. At this moment in the *Confessions,* Augustine argues that true friends—that is, Christian friends—should locate their love for each other not in the body, the mind, or the social status of their friends, but instead in their mutual recognition of each other as believers.

In the *De spirituali amicitia,* Aelred of Rievaulx (d. 1167) refines Augustine's definition of perfect Christian friendship for a specifically monastic context. How could, Aelred asks, a cloistered monk form friendships without disrupting the social order of the monastery, or worse, falling into "unnatural" carnal desire for his friends? Here again is the simultaneous fear and foregrounding of queer desire at the heart of medieval discourses of friendship; in contemporary scholarship, Aelred of Rievaulx has become synonymous with veiled, closeted, or otherwise sublimated homoerotic desire.[50] A Cistercian abbot, Aelred understood that natural human desire to form close interpersonal bonds was at odds with the Benedictine rule's injunction against just such particular friendships, and *De spirituali amicitia* was Aelred's attempt to resolve this paradox.[51] Here Aelred not only subordinates fraternal love to the overarching love of God, but also defines friendship between humans as an anthropomorphic version of the love between God and mankind. "Was it not a foretaste of blessedness thus to love and be loved (*sic amare et sic amari*)," says Aelred of his friendships, "to help and thus to be helped; and in this way from the sweetness of fraternal charity to wing one's flight aloft to that more sublime splendor of divine love, and by the ladder of charity now to mount to the embrace of Christ Himself; and again to descend to the love of the neighbor, there pleasantly to rest?"[52] Aelred imagines spiritual friendship as the functional operation of theophany; centering God at the heart of friendship guards against the sorts of binaristic affections whose presence in a monastery might cause upheaval of the social order. By transposing the human friend onto God, Aelred broadens the notion of friendship from its original binaristic parameters. In effect, Aelred argues that the interpersonal desire of Christian friendship is, first and foremost, friendship with God; because each friend becomes an image of God, friendship can be extended beyond the dyad to the entire community of Christian believers concurrently. Where Cicero only knew of four pairs of true friends, Aelred argues, Christian friendships exist in the thousands. All martyrs, he says, are "of one heart and one soul."[53] *De spirituali amicitia* finds the self not through dyadic pairing, but in polyamorous friendships.

Nevertheless, there is a tension at the heart of Aelred's treatise, which is written as a series of conversations between the character of Aelred and the younger monks Ivo, Walter, and Gratian. In Book 1, Aelred and Ivo engage in a heartfelt discussion about the Christian supersession of the Ciceronian model of friendship. In Book 2, which takes place some years after Book 1, Ivo has died, and the conversation continues, but not without reflection on his loss. "He is always with me," Aelred says, "his devout countenance beams upon me and his gentle eyes smile. There his joyful words have so much flavor for me that it seems that either I have passed over with him to a better life or he still shares this humbler one with me."[54] In light of this heartfelt, intimate nostalgia, it appears that the spiritual love championed by Aelred does not eliminate their dyadic relationship, but instead coexists with it in a paradoxical tension. Aelred and Ivo's particular friendship, with its queer affect, potentially destabilizes the hierophanic spiritual friendships even as spiritual friendships seek to contain its queer potential.

There are, then, important similarities between classical models of friendship and the Augustinian or Aelredian ideal, in spite of their supposed differences. In both, although friendship masquerades as personal, it is just as much about creating standards for civic engagement and reinforcing existing structures of belonging as it is about personal attachment. In the classical world, this is toward the state; in the Christian world, this is toward God and religious hegemony. In both, the importance of particular intimacy is fundamental. In the classical model, this is relatively uncomplicated; but for Aelred—and to a lesser extent, Augustine—Christian friends, in spite of the primacy of their relationship to God, are not interchangeable because of this mutual friendship, but always retain some sense of particularity.

It is in this light that we should read Richard Methley's and John Norton's manuscripts, which are intensely focused on textual exchange, entanglement, and an intimate dyadic relationship with each other's work, all while simultaneously espousing the importance of spiritual friendship. When Richard Methley opens his *Scola* with a quotation about mutual love, he is explicitly and specifically placing his manuscript within the paradoxical discourses of spiritual friendship that would have inflected a monastic reading context. "No one who languishes for love can possibly envy his brother,"[55] Methley says. "O lovers (*amatores*), now you must know how I languish for love and truly desire to be dissolved (*dissolui*) and be with Christ. Glory to him forever! He has given me the gift of humility and brotherly love (*fraterne charitatis*); and so I languish for love."[56] Methley situates God at the center of a complex set of relationships and obligations. First, his addressees are grammatically plural lovers (*amatores*); Methley, as a brother of these lovers, wishes to be dissolved (*dissolui*) into Christ, which is a central characteristic of spiritual friendship. Second, Methley describes his writing as a product of "fraternal charity" (*fraterna caritas*), which he aligns with love-longing. Situating God at the center of friendship makes friendship a crucial part of the monastic ethos.

Similarly, the first treatise in the Lincoln manuscript, Norton's *Musica monachorum*, is concerned with communal belonging and dedication to the Carthusian rule as a form of perfect friendship.[57] As prior of Mount Grace, Norton would have been concerned not with public affairs, as the abbot of another order might have been, but instead with the internal affairs of the charterhouse and of the men under his care. In the *Musica,* Norton identifies with his readership, serving as a guide to navigating the strict obedience the *Consuetudines Guigones* demanded. The *pura obediencia* refrain that repeats through the treatise plays on this investment. "Charity (*caritas*) is the material of all salvation and all good works," Norton says, but "wisdom is the effector of that material and the instrument of operating and manifesting the works of the same. And gracious love, burning, is the excellence, the agreement, and the perfection of all the works of the beforementioned material."[58]

For Norton, charity and love manifest in the proper regulation of behavior, where *caritas* forms bonds of perfect friendship through obedience.[59] "Without doubt, if both persevere, they will be gloriously crowned in heaven, and they will rejoice without end in my benediction with the angels and saints of heaven, forever and ever. Amen."[60] This obedience will ultimately lead to the formation of a spiritual community as the Carthusian becomes an *amicus spiritualis* of the angels.

Methley, like Norton, is attentive to the social demands of the charterhouse. Throughout the Trinity manuscript, Methley makes references to being "among the brothers" when he is visited by mystical experiences and wishing that, in writing to the other monks in the charterhouse, he might share in a part of this experience: "After dining at table in the refectory with my brothers (in the literal sense), I came to my cell and another sensation came upon me, in yet another new way";[61] "For my heart is almost completely torn apart and mangled because I languish for great love, even now as I write to you, dearest brothers";[62] "As I felt myself stirred this way in the spirit, I did not want to willfully abandon the reading and the brothers on account of that sensation, unless the spirit and the fervor of love and pain were to work even more strongly on me"; and so on.[63] In the *Dormitorium*, he reflects on his responsibility to teach his brothers how to reach the thalamal space of the bedroom of the beloved: "Step by step, my brothers, is, I say, how one must ascend to this bedroom."[64] The manuscript ends, in the final page of the *Refectorium*, with an appeal to collective editing practice by the very group of brothers Methley was seeking to inspire: "See, dearest brothers, I have written this *Refectory of Salvation* for you. Correct it if necessary, give thanks to God, and pray for me. If you have written well, correct what you have written; otherwise, I ask you not to write. Praise and honor to God!"[65] Here, Methley asks his brothers to "write well" specifically by being attentive to the practice of copying his manuscript, a practice that he links to the work of brotherly care. Methley's call for careful emendation of his manuscript may be a stock gesture in medieval manuscripts, but it gains particular salience here, in light of the stress Methley places on friendship, fraternal responsibility, and intertextuality.

In his *Refectorium salutis*, Methley comes to an awareness of himself through his responsibility to his monastic brothers. On a certain evening, Methley says, he was reading a text aloud to his brothers in the refectory. Suddenly he felt as if his heart was "being beaten with a sword," during which he had one of the many crying outbursts described throughout the *Refecto-*

*rium*'s diaristic account.[66] However, despite this very public, affective experience, Methley continues to read, fulfilling his monastic obligation: "As I felt myself thus stirred this way in the spirit, I did not want to willfully abandon the reading and the brothers on account of that sensation, unless the spirit and the fervor of love and pain were to work even more strongly on me."[67] Although Methley suggests that there might come a time when his mystical experience becomes too strong to fulfill his spiritual vocation, his overriding wish is to remain with his brothers. Methley finds himself, in the moment of mystical ecstasy, outside of himself, concerned for the devotional experience of the other monks in the refectory even as his sense of self is dissolving into the divine. In this moment Methley recognizes the peculiarity of his experience because of his positionality vis-à-vis his listening confreres. What brings Methley into an awareness of himself is the fraternal responsibility he feels to keep reading. Methley recognizes himself as an intersubjective sonic body.

Norton's manuscript engages in the same concern about being overheard. In the *Musica,* he gestures to the places and spaces of Carthusian contemplative practice; while sometimes he refers to himself as being alone in his cell, at other times he is in the oratory or other communal spaces.[68] By situating his mystical audiations—ones that would have resulted in the weeping and crying outlined above—in places where others can hear him, Norton encourages his Carthusian readers to participate in these moments with him. These claustral performative spaces tie Norton's visions to an exclusively Carthusian version of *excessus mentis*, but they also raise the intriguing possibility that he might be overheard; the text is at once deeply personal and private, while also being a performative work of stagecraft, suggesting that the sound of the *musica monachorum* echoes through the spaces of the charterhouse.

Carthusian monasteries, as noted above, were essentially a conglomeration of hermit cells. As Glynn Coppack notes, the Carthusian cell is "a two-story house, with an entry passage, living room, study, bedroom, oratory on the ground floor and with a work room above. The cell is set in the corner of a garden and is surrounded by walls about 10 feet tall. Monks typically threw their garbage out of their second-story window, and in excavations of Mount Grace, we can tell from the garden detritus just which cells were responsible for which parts of book production: Cell 8 was a bookbinder, Cell 10 and 11 produced pen nibs, Cells 12 and 13 colored pigment."[69] With this evidence at hand, it is impossible to imagine the book production of Mount Grace, and its attendant mystical expression, as anything other than a product of an entire community humming with an audible, material rhythm. And yet, as Katherine Zieman points out, two of Methley's treatises—the *Scola* and the *Dormitorium*—refer to communal spaces that did not even exist in a Carthusian charterhouse (the schoolhouse and the dormitory, respectively).[70] And so, both Methley and Norton engage in a sort of sociality that is as much imaginative—and enacted by the text—as it is real. The manuscriptival exchange represented in Lincoln and Trinity is about friendship in its many paradoxical and self-contradicting forms, and in a polyamory of queer desire it performs these multivalent friendships through epistolary exchange.

Beyond the charterhouse, the Lincoln manuscript itself imagines a broader circle of readers, though in a much more systematic way. Appended to the beginning of each of Norton's treatises in the manuscript is a short introductory epistle by William Melton (d. 1528), humanist, mathematician, priest, and chancellor of York.[71] These letters are repeatedly addressed to an audience that is not presumed to be Carthusian, suggesting that, in the forty or so years after Norton completed his tripartite manuscript, the work had been copied and circulated to interested readers of devotional and mystical experience beyond the walls of the charterhouse. Furthermore, the manuscript's copyist, one John Flecher—about whom nothing more than his name is known—recognizes the importance of fraternal charity, friendship, and the relations of obligation that Norton's manuscript engender. "I, Brother Flecher, have written out these things," he says at the opening of the manuscript, "so that you may know that I have read through your treatise, not carelessly, but with grateful goodwill and fraternal charity, which for us, in turn, may our God and Lord, our Savior Jesus Christ, preserve for eternity. Amen."[72] In this short note, Flecher reflects upon a responsibility to Norton that is friendly, that is textual, and that is simultaneously nostalgic and futural. He identifies the most perfect form of friendship—*fraterna caritas*, or *spiritualis amicitia*—with the copying of the manuscript.[73] Norton himself recognizes the importance of the responsibility to absent, deceased, or missing friends at the end of his *Thesaurus*: "Therefore they are called most blessed," he says, "who had, in this work unto death, together scaled the holy mountain in chaste love. And at their time of death they were pure for contemplation, without any sinfulness."[74] Thus the Trinity manuscript recognizes its obligation to the other in multiple ways: from Norton to Methley and to his Carthusian community, as well as the obligation of copyists and readers to comment on and disseminate the treatise to a non-Carthusian audience.

There is a productive tension between the intimate dyadic relationality of Methley's and Norton's manuscript production, which charts a writerly friendship between individuals, and their manuscripts' more general fraternal responsibility, which spreads itself to cover the entirety of the Christian community. At the beginning of the *Scola*, Methley refers to his reader as a singular *tu*, potentially directly addressing it to Norton—although Norton is never named in the treatise itself: "And you, my sluggish brother—you are seeking a remedy against the devil's temptations. Do not be cast down in despair—for I, your brother (*frater tuus*), was once tempted as you (*tu*) are, but never vanquished by it, if I remember well."[75] At the end of the *Scola*, Methley once more addresses his reader, who has now mutated to the plural *vos*: "My orthodox and catholic brothers, correct this work if there is need, and if it pleases you (*si vobis placuerit*), copy it. Praise God with me forever, I beg you, for I languish for love."[76] Norton takes him up on the offer in the *Lamentatio*, responding with a series of repeated *amore langueo*'s; we might imagine the red-ink annotator, pen and book in hand, responding similarly.

Near the end of his *Refectorium salutis*, the final text in the Trinity manuscript, Methley recalls an important paratext for his project:[77] "When I had finished Mass, I fainted again and again, having become utterly languid. For my life consists of love, languor, sweetness, warmth, and song, yet perceptible warmth is the rarest. The Beloved has promised me that I would experience love more often in languor, just as the kindly Richard of Hampole experienced it more often in warmth. I have not read that he experienced such frequent languor."[78] This explicit reference to Rolle ends a series of mystical experiences patterned after Rolle's. For Methley, as for Rolle, *excessus mentis* was about lived experience, and, as the previous discussion has shown, his narration often lapses into the alliterative prosopoetics familiar to all students of the Latin Rollean canon. Methley allows Rolle into his work only after articulating, both for himself and for his readership, what *canor* means in a specifically Carthusian context: it is a textual object, defined by collaborative writing and reading practice, a practice that always keeps one's dear friends in mind. Unlike Rolle, for whom *canor* is fleshly and produces a *real* sound in the ears—no matter what its effects are on the mind and spirit and how it gets beyond the body—Carthusian *canor* is textual. More importantly, this intertextuality opens it up to an ever-widening circle of potential readers as the site of its completion.

The dyadic and the multiplicitous relationships of the Trinity and Lincoln manuscripts carefully configure polyvalent networks of responsibility and care, not only articulating the intimate writing partnership between Norton and Methley, but also forging and depicting communal friendships in the wider monastic family as potentially intimate as well. The "open" journals of Norton and Methley depict a contemplative communion of saints as an ever-expanding sonic body, one that includes their fellow monks, future readers, and their "kindly" brother, Richard of Hampole.[79]

## Opening the Book

In his posthumously published study of premodern queer kinship, *The Friend*, Alan Bray traces the deeply loving—and, as of the early 2000s, the historically overlooked—friendships men had with other men in the premodern era in England. However, *The Friend*'s investment in queer friendship and fraternal obligation does not exist only in the body of the book; it begins with its paratext. When Bray died in 2001, he left behind him a near-complete draft of *The Friend* in manuscript form. It was only through the editorial labor of his close friend and colleague the professor of religion Mark Jordan that the book was published in 2003. As Jordan writes in his prefatory note to the text, in preparing the manuscript for the press after Bray's death, he felt a dual sense of responsibility: first and foremost to Bray as a friend, and secondarily, to the reader of the published book, who deserved to own a text that hewed as close to Bray's original authorial intentions as possible. The friendly obligations articulated in the book's introduction do not end there, however. In Bray's own introduction, he articulates his inspiration for his work: the research of his own deceased friend Michel Rey. "In 1987 I heard Michel give a lecture in Amsterdam, entitled 'The Body of My Friend.' The lecture," Bray says, "was only an outline, and his early death left his doctoral thesis uncompleted and his loss keenly felt by many. . . . In the years that followed that lecture Michel and I often discussed the history of friendship, and after his death the sense that I should follow his work began to grow on me."[80] In a multilayered sense, *The Friend* is a text that operates as a site of ethical obligation to the absent other. This includes not only the historical friendships that are the basis of Bray's study, but also the friendships in the text's margins, each cut short by untimely deaths: the friendship between the young doctoral student Michel Rey and Alan Bray, and that between Alan Bray and his editor-friend Mark Jordan. In *The Friend*, acts of editing, commenting, and dedication are forms of remembrance that provide affective force to the book's central arguments. Both *The Friend*'s subject matter and its conditions of production rely on amicable responsibility and nostalgia.

Methley's and Norton's entangled manuscripts are produced, like *The Friend*, through networks of kinship and obligation, out of the work of textual exchange, mutual reading practice, and love. In this way, they are like another such book, British Library, Additional MS 61823, the sole surviving manuscript of *The Boke of Margery Kempe*, which also was a product of attending, of silence, and collaborative nostalgia. In the twenty-eighth chapter of the first book, on an occasion where its author, Margery, in the self-othering fiction of her third-person narration, recalls the first instance of her devotional weeping in Jerusalem. "The cryeng was so lowde and so wondyrful that it made the pepyl astoynd," she says.[81] At first Margery's tears happen only rarely, but, over time, they increase in frequency until they occur up to fourteen times a day. "Sumtyme," she says, she cried "in the cherch, sumtyme in the strete, sumtym in the chawmbre, sumtyme in the felde whan God wold sendyn hem, for sche knew nevyr tyme ne owyr whan thei schulde come."[82] The tears' aleatory nature impresses upon Margery their divine origin, and she interprets their givenness as a symptom of her close friendship with God, who, through them, calls her to account for herself. But this is not the only relationship the *Boke* offers at this moment in the manuscript. In the margin next to Margery's account, the so-called red-ink annotator of the *Boke*—probably a Carthusian monk, a man whose attentive marginal comments run throughout the manuscript—sees fit to make a note. "So fa RM & f Norton of Wakenes & of the passyon," he says. This marginal annotation, which has garnered more than a little attention, refers to Richard Methley and John Norton.[83] Just as Margery develops a sense of self through her tearful relationship to God, so too did the red-ink annotator of her *Boke*, through those same tears, recognize his weeping brothers in the charterhouse. Along with the prologue of the *Boke*, with its origin story of double amanuenses and its *evel*, or poor, writing, the *Boke* arrives on the desk as multiply collaborative, an open text whose many readers put their hands and pens to it with sympathy, care, and self-identification. It is of a type with Methley's and Norton's own manuscripts.

By making the future of a text the site of its fulfilment, *The Boke of Margery Kempe*, Alan Bray's *The Friend*, and Methley's and Norton's entangled manuscripts foreground the importance of readership, commentary, and friendship in the textual process. Each of these books recounts its origin as a retelling and expects, in turn, to be retold or added on to, longing for a completion that never occurs because the text always accommodates—even desires—more readers and further commentary. "All work," John Garrison says in a tribute written to Bray almost two decades after *The Friend*'s publication, "so often begins as something else, rhizomatically connecting casual conversations, love affairs, scholarly roundtables, published essays just as people are so often connected by shared friends."[84] For Garrison (and for Mark Jordan, Alan Bray, and Michel Rey), and for Margery Kempe (and John Norton, Richard Methley, the unknown Carthusian who overheard them weeping as she did, Brother Flecher, and William Melton), incompletion makes intersubjectivity happen. The text opens up the possibility of the future as the always-deferred place of friendship.[85]

Just as importantly, in all three situations—Methley and Norton, Bray, and Kempe—the text begins as a series of conversations or as aural experiences: Margery recounts her life—and her tears—to her first amanuensis in a series of face-to-face encounters, and the red-ink annotator of the manuscript in turn adds his own aural experiences to the *Boke*'s clamor. "So fa RM & f Norton," he says, recalling the sound of his confreres' tears as they echoed through the halls of the Charterhouse of Mount Grace, responsories to Margery's cries. In the same way, an incomplete dissertation begun by Michel Rey becomes Bray's own text through a spoken exchange between Rey and Bray, and Methley and Norton hear the angels singing and begin to record their experiences. In each of these cases, the other of the text is initially an aural-oral one, a close friend and confidant, but, once inscribed in text, the circle of intersubjective others gradually widens to include the entire universe of possible readers. The intersubjective ethics of these books arises first out of overheardness, and then out of the textual inscription of a sonic experience that captures the intimacy of the face-to-face encounter, turning aurality into textuality, remaining incomplete to the extent that any given reader might, in reading the text, respond with their own aural experience. Thus sound, overheardness, and the intimacy of friendship give way to a textual intersubjectivity that fissures the binarized sense of Self and Other, of friendship and intersubjectivity, broadening it out to a wider community.

The *Scola, Refectorium, Dormitorium, Musica, Thesaurus,* and *Lamentatio* display an epistolarity in which *canor* and desire for the other are performed through textual exchange and mutual influence. The epistolary form places an indeterminate reader in the center of an intimate exchange; this is a relationship that is unstable, nonbinary, and where desire is oriented not only to the known Other (that is, to Methley and Norton as monastic brothers), but toward a circle of readers that, from Mount Grace, expanded outward to an undisclosed and variable audience. This indeterminacy is only amplified by the fact that their diaries do not announce themselves as an epistolary exchange, but instead require the reader with access to both texts to deduce the intimate relationship of influence and affection out of which they were produced. The Trinity and Lincoln manuscripts show that sonic bodies exist in texts passed between individuals, as well as between those texts and their circle of readers.

# Chapter 5

# Piers Plowman, the Sound-Object, and the Singing Community

"Wait, wait!," said Pantagruel. "See? There are more that still haven't thawed out." Then he threw on the deck in front of us handfuls of frozen words, which might have been sugared almonds, like so many pearls of different colors. . . . And after they had been warmed for a bit, between our hands, they melted like snow and we actually heard them, but without understanding a word, for they were in a barbarous language. . . . And when they'd melted, we heard: hin, hin, hin, hin, his, tick, tock, whizz gibber, jabber, frr, frrr, frrr, boo, boo, boo, boo, boo, boo, boo, boo, crack, track, trr, trr, trr, trrr, trrrrrr, on, on, on, on, on, wooawooawooon, gog, magog, and God only knows what other barbarian words. The pilot explained that these were the sounds of combat, and the whinnying of horses as the armies met.
—François Rabelais, *Gargantua and Pantagruel*

But when this calfe of our lordes praysinge is offered, yt must be cut in gobettes, for all the wordes and syllables oughte to be sayd dystynctely from the begynnynge vnto the ende, in eche member and eche parte therof. For lyke as clyppers or falsers of the kynges money are punysshed by deth-ryght so they that clyppe away from the money of goddes seruyce eny wordes or letters or syllables & so false yt from the trew sentence.
—Thomas Gascoigne, *The Myroure of Oure Ladye*

# Sound-Objects

The famous "paroles gelées" passage of Rabelais's *Gargantua and Pantagruel*
begins when Pantagruel, sailing the Frozen Sea, hears disembodied sounds
around him, invisible shouts and cries from a maritime battle months earlier,
in the cold of winter. As the noise of war rang out, they were frozen, and
remained in stasis until, melting in the warm spring air, their now fluid
forms—unmoored from the bodies that originally produced them—hit the
ears of the sailors on Pantagruel's ship. Attempting to make sense of these
noises, Pantagruel likens them to a series of loci classici that attribute agency
and objecthood to sound; as Pantagruel recounts, Antiphanes once called
Plato's writing words that "freeze as you send them out into the frigid air";
Aristotle described Homer's poetry as if it could "flutter and fly, alive and
moving"; and, as Ovid tells it, Orpheus's head, torn off its body by the Thra-
cian women, continued to sing while his lyre, unmanned, was plucked by
the wind.[1] By literalizing the metaphors of Antiphanes, Aristotle, and Ovid,
Rabelais turns sounds from events into objects, a metamorphosis that is as
provocative as it is seemingly preposterous. Interpreted variously as a satiric
literalization of Renaissance commonplace tradition, a materialist embodiment of language theory in Renaissance humanism, and a prophetic paean
to the sound-recording technologies of modernity, Pantagruel's "paroles
gelées" also pose serious—and fundamental—questions about the relationship between sounds and their sources, their listeners, and the material world
more generally.[2] Why, it asks, is it so odd to hear sounds divorced from their
sources? Is the voice really a marker of presence? Rabelais's frozen words reify the gap between sounds and the things that produce them and the ears
that hear them, portraying them with stunning clarity and wit. But this separation, Rabelais seems to say, occurs in any act of voicing: no matter how
close one stands to a musician, there is always a momentary lag between the
sound of an instrument and the time that sound takes to travel through the
air to the listener; there is always a gap between a speaker's intent and the oral
expression of that intent; there is, as Mladen Dolar argues, an echo-space
between the mind and the vocal chords and between the mouth and the
ear.[3] "Sound," Michel Chion says, "is always lagging . . . we are always late in
coming to it."[4] Dolar's argument recalls Derrida's discussion of the voice,
which he argues does not represent presence any more than writing does; in
both, presence is always impossible, always deferred. If sound, Rabelais

seems to say, is a thing that can float free of its source—as it does on Pantagruel's journey on the Frozen Sea—it might also be an object.

Rabelais was not the first writer to think of sounds in this way. In addition to the famous Aristotelian passage on sound as "broken air" and the whirling, cacophonous House of Rumor in Chaucer's *House of Fame* ("Soun ys air ybroke," says the Chaucer's narrator, following Aristotle), other medieval accounts also consider the potential objecthood of sound.[5] In *The Myroure of Oure Ladye,* Thomas Gascoigne draws from folk accounts of the demon Titivillus, who waits in the eaves of churches for clumsily said prayers and sung liturgies, gathering "ydell woordys," as well as "sylablys & woordys, overskypped and synkopyd, & verse & psalmyes the whiche these clerkys han stolyn in the queere, & haue fayled in here seruyse" into his "gret sacchell."[6] Here, not only misspoken words, but also words that are *not* spoken have a materiality, as Titivillus collects "overskipped" and "syncopied" words as well as idle speech. Gascoigne's text encourages his readers to be attentive to what they say: their syllables and words should be carefully parsed, cut into "gobettes," "members," and "parts"—pieces of flesh, as if they had bodies of their own. Here, the objectivity of words is a useful tool for enjoining correct prayer, but it is also a source of concern. If words can be treated like objects and removed from their original site of utterance—if a word can be chopped up—it might also be "severed" from its semantic intent; Titivillus makes it clear that there is a gap between the sound of the voice and the thoughts in the mind. The popularity of the Titivillus myth in medieval and early modern art, architecture, and folklore—where he sometimes collects spoken words, and sometimes written ones—suggests a medieval fascination with the materiality of language, and the slippage between speech and writing itself indicates a preoccupation with the possibility of sonic embodiment.[7] Sound is a type of body.

It is the thesis of this chapter that William Langland's *Piers Plowman,* like the "paroles gelées" of Rabelais's *Gargantua and Pantagruel* and the demon Titivillus with his satchel, is an experiment in reifying sound, and in making music—literally—matter, both through the formal properties of alliterative poetry and through the poem's narrative construction. Not only does the aural resonance of its alliterative long-lines attenuate sounds before the ear, but so do the poems' personae, which are rarely described in visual terms (or if they are, those descriptions are terse, far short of the long blazons common to other personification allegories whose modus operandi is primarily ekphrastic or visual). *Piers's* personae are, rather, made of the speeches they give. In addition, the poems' final passus portray the Christian commune as a type of sonic object wherein the performance of the liturgy renders the *corpus mysticum* in song, as the poem enacts personae that are methexic—profoundly incorporative and participative—rather than simply mimetic. While each of these forms of sonic objecthood can be addressed discretely, they are interrelated: *Piers Plowman*'s sounds are the source of its ethics, assimilatio, and protreptics.[8]

As can be seen from the examples Pantagruel cites, the idea of sonic embodiment goes back to the beginning of the written word in the West, and probably further. But "sound-objects" as such received their first sustained analytical treatment in philosophy and music theory beginning in the mid-twentieth century, as sound-recording technologies made possible a form of sonic capture, reproduction, remixing, and distortion that sound studies historians mark as an originary moment in the history of sound.[9] We might argue over whether this originary moment actually exists—whether the extreme fidelity of mechanically reproducible recordings in the form of the wax cylinder mark a *rupture from* or an *intensification of* sound-recording technologies that began with the first notated music in the fifth century B.C. and continued with the development of notational systems in the millennia to follow—but sustained philosophical and theoretical studies of sound as an *object* emerge with the advent of modern audio-recording technologies, and specifically with Pierre Schaeffer, the composer and early electronic musician who developed the notion of the *objet sonore* in the mid-twentieth century.[10]

Schaeffer's project exploratory and experimental, developing over a period of about twenty-five years, and his critical focus and the way he manufactured and manipulated sound changed over that time.[11] But at the heart of Schaeffer's investigation into sound-objects was the following question: What properties must a sound have in order for it to be apprehended as an object analogous to the visio-tactile objects that one encounters in everyday experience? In what ways would a sound—no matter what was done to it—always differ from those same, visually apprehended objects? In constructing his answer to these questions, Schaeffer borrowed heavily from Husserl's notion of adumbration, that is, the idea that objects gain their objectivity through the observer's ability to see and interact with them in multiple iterations and from multiple directions over time. For instance, as a viewer looks at a table from multiple perspectives, they are able to build an awareness of the table as an independent object due to its perduration in space and time. What, Schaeffer asked, was the sonic equivalent of adumbration?

For Schaeffer, the answer lay in masking a source's sound through the distortion of the sound itself. By distorting sounds, Schaeffer hoped to get beyond normal ways of listening. In normative listening, Schaeffer argued, sounds are either indicators of a speaker's intent (that is, sound carries linguistic meaning) or point to a particular source that a listener attempts to identify (Schaeffer suggests that, in a piece of orchestral music, the listener spends their time attempting to identify the musical instruments being played rather than listening to the qualities of the sound itself). Whether or not his assessment is correct—and one might take issue with both of his characterizations of normative listening—is not the issue here; rather, the effects of this assessment are. They led Schaeffer to develop a practice that he called "reduced listening," or *entendre*. In reduced listening, the listener engaged in an "act of attending to sound apart from its source," that is, a form of listening that actively attempted to avoid identifying the object that made the sound or the intention behind its production. By occluding the source of the sound through manipulation (recording, editing, sampling, distorting, and looping sounds until etiological judgments about their sources were difficult if not impossible to make), Schaeffer hoped to direct attention away from the source of a sound, to compel listeners to stop looking *behind* a sound for intent, and to focus instead on the sonic qualities of a sound for its own sake. Reduced listening, according to Schaeffer, categorizes seven qualities that a sound might have: mass (the "intensity" of a sound), harmonic timbre (harmonics), grain (the subjective "roughness" or "smoothness" of a sound), bearing (the presence or absence of vibrato), dynamic criterion (attack and how intensity varies over time), melodic profile (range of pitches or a single pitch), and mass profile (the change, or lack of change, in the intensity of a sound).[12]

Schaeffer called the etiologically veiled sounds of reduced listening *acousmatic* sounds, after the myth of Pythagoras and his students. As the story goes, novitiates to the cult of Pythagoras were—for a period of time—blocked from seeing the famous teacher by a curtain. Without access to Pythagoras's visual demonstrations, the *akousmatikoi* (as they were called) would have received his teachings not as verifiable theorems, but rather as gnostic mantras in which sonic ephemera themselves became the objects of religious belief and devotion. "The underdetermination of source and cause motivate[d] a reification of the sonic effect," says Brian Kane in his study of Schaefferian sound-objects. "By bracketing an effect from its source and cause," he goes on, Pythagoras and his students "transform[ed] a sound from an event into an object."[13] As Kane suggests, acousmatic sounds "flicker into being only with spacing, with the simultaneous difference and relation of auditory effect, cause, and source"; when the source of a sound is unknowable, that sound relates to itself, and to other sounds, rather than to the objects that might have produced it.[14] In his appropriation of the myth of Pythagoras, Schaeffer hoped to challenge the preeminence of visio-tactile embodiment and objecthood, opening spaces for intentional acts of hearing sound as sound. Listeners, he hoped, would retune themselves to their sonic environments in a radical new way.[15]

What is perhaps most interesting about Schaeffer's acousmatic listening and the notion of the sound-object are the degree to which they fail even as they succeed: in listening to Schaeffer's musical compositions, for instance, one *can* attend to the sound for its own sake, but their looped and distorted samples of human voices, instruments, and everyday objects actually *invite* etiological investigation rather than forbidding it. In this sense, acousmatic sound and sound-objects do not do away with visuality or the prospect of normative forms of embodiment, but instead exist in constant and concurrent tension with them.

## The Visual Fields of *Piers Plowman*, Acousmata, and Sound-Objects

How does the Schaefferian sound-object apply to allegory in general, and to *Piers Plowman* in particular? Although allegory is massive, inchoate, and impossible to define as a whole, one might think of allegory, in a broad sense, as a sort of Schaefferian acousmatic veil. In a very broad sense, allegory works through occultation.[16] It is a discursive mode whereby the "truth" of the text is always receding from the stratum of the written word. As a call to attend to the ways meaning is encoded as well as decoded, allegory requires attentiveness to the folding and unfolding relationship between signifier and signified, language and concept. In allegory, these two things are always at a remove from each other, in a semiotic play of the sort of gap or lag that Chion argues is always present in systems of the voice.

Furthermore, the interplay between "hiddenness" and "tonality" is central to the etymology of the word allegory itself. *Allegorein* comes from the Greek *allos* (other) and *agoreuein* (to speak), that is, to "speak other(wise)," and both this term and the Latinized *alieniloquium* were in use in the medieval period. In the seven subtypes of *alieniloquium* that are listed and defined in Isidore of Seville's *Etymologiae*, each has to do with a different type of tension between the denotative meaning of a word and its voicing or performed intent. Isidore defines the first subtype, *irony*, as a "tone of voice" by which "the contrary [of what is said] is understood."[17] The second subtype, *antiphrasis*, is irony, except in this case "only words"—that is, written words—are used. While irony, strictly defined, requires a present speaker and a sonic performance, in antiphrasis, the appropriate "tone"—one that runs orthogonal to the denotative semantic content of an utterance—is conjured by the text itself, without the aid of a present speaker; the reader must imagine the text itself taking on the capacity for *tone*. In antiphrasis, the text takes on the form of the embodied speaker and carries the capacity not only of semantic weight, but also the force of affect understood as tonality or voicing.

Of the five remaining subtypes of allegory, three concern other forms of tonality: *charientismos* (or hostility) makes harsh sentiments "seem pleasant"; *sarcasm* is "bitter"; and *astysmos* (or the backhanded compliment) is derisive pleasantry lacking anger. With the exception of the last two types, *riddle* and *paroemia* (proverb), Isidore defines *alieniloquium* by the way in which tone changes the meaning of an utterance, that is, how imagining the role that sound plays in language—even if that utterance is textual—is integral to interpreting intent. The definitions of each of these categories conjure a speaker whose tone speaks words askew, creating an antagonistic relationship between words and their meanings. As Hugh of St. Victor says, *alieniloquium* is a rhetorical technique by which "one thing is said and another thing is signified."[18]

Medieval writers had at their disposal any number of image-based terms to refer to what we today call allegory—*hyponoia, symbolon, figura, signum, imago, eikon,* and *aenigma*—but Langland imagines his project primarily as one not of showing other, but of speaking or sounding other, with all of the tonal properties the term *alieniloquium* conjures.[19] The text has interjections that mark castigation, chastisement, praise, and heightened emotions, like "Lo!" "Harrow!" "Help!" "Alarme!"—speech is qualified (the lunatic speaks "clergially"; the unlearned do not know how to "jangle," and Reson "rouneth"); voices are "loude" and "crie"; rubricated tags in Latin often provide ironizing commentary on the vernacular text; and there are any number of musical or quasi-musical performances, moments in which speech is heightened and extended into song, such as quoted snippets of songs and *crieries*.[20] In addition to these moments, the poem also repeatedly refers to itself as a work of speech that transforms visual experience into sonic experience, sensorially, "speaking other."

In the opening lines of the B-text, the narrator dons the cloak of a shepherd—or perhaps a sheep—and steps out into the rolling hills of the Malvern countryside in order to "hear" the wonders of the world, and sits down by a "bourne" that burbles so merrily it puts him to sleep.[21] It is telling that Will sits here. If sounds attain their objectivity by, in part, repeating themselves over time in the absence of visually defined forms, what resonant object could be more useful than a stream? "The constant flowing noises that we perceive when we find ourselves next to a brook or a stream," Michel Chion suggests, come from an object that "has no bounds. . . . The flow of water constantly renews itself; the sound that we hear is the sum of myriad local displacements."[22] The stream, as an object, arrives at the ear already "spatially diluted."[23] It is this proleptic brook—the stream that presages the dream to come—that gives a nod to the capaciousness of the text's sound-objects.

Later in the Prologue, Will notes that even though his experience is visual, his account is oral and aural: "Barons and burgeis and bondemen alse / I *seigh* in this assemblee, as ye shul *here* after."[24] And throughout the poem, audiation serves as a means of mediating visual experience. Later, in Passus B.5, Will again refers to the poem as an act that turns sight into speech: "Of this matere I myghte mamelen ful longe, / Ac I shal *seye* as I *saugh*, so me God helpe."[25] In literate societies, which inscribe aural-oral language onto material objects in visual semiotic systems, the oral/aural/visual are always embedded in each other, and Langland's poem calls attention to itself as a literary product— as literature—by reiterating its relationship to the synaesthetic combination of sight and sound. These moments in the poem do not privilege the visual, but instead recognize both the visual and the sonic registers as significant.

*Piers Plowman* is not alone in the way that it plays with the relationship between visual experience and oral narrative; medieval romance in particular also calls attention to itself as a spoken genre that refers to visual and physical marvels. But *Piers Plowman* explicitly theorizes the relationship between sight and sound through the personifications scattered throughout its narrative. In his sermon on the human ability to make sense of experience in Passus 12, for instance, Ymaginatif instructs Will about the difference between Kynde Wit and Clergie: *Quod scimus loquimur, quod vidimus testamur*, Ymaginatif says, and then goes on to gloss this Latin quotation as part of a lengthy sermon on the salvific potential of experiential learning.[26] Clergie (*quod scimus*), as Nicolette Zeeman notes, are truths that must be taught rather than those things that can be deduced from experience; *clergie* requires aural instruction, the presence of a teacher and a student in the same room with each other. Kynde Wit (*quod vidimus*), on the other hand, is an innate capacity that turns visual objects and the natural world at large into knowledge through reason.[27]

Of course, visual experience is important: in the C-text, Will's intent is not just to *hear* wonders, but to *see* them as well; when he sees the "feld ful of folk" in Passus 1, he promises to "shewe" his readers, rather than to tell them, about his vision.[28] Later, Will recognizes that visual experience is key to *kynde knowing.* "If I may lyve and loke, I shal go lerne bettre," he says.[29] And when Fortune hands Will the mirror of Middle-earth in Passus 9, she too encourages him to "se wondres."[30] However, when Ymaginatif states "that we speak about what we know, and we testify to what we see," *both* visual and innate forms of knowledge are ultimately expressed as oral-aural forms. Ymaginatif's methods of knowledge acquisition (*quod scimus* and *quod vidimus*) are grammatically meaningless without the deponent verbs, the acts of voicing that speak them into being: "we speak (*loquimur*) what we know, and we testify (*testamur*) what we see." If we take the definition of allegory literally—that it is *speaking other*—then *Piers Plowman* itself is this act of voicing.[31] *Piers Plowman* suggests that an allegorical form without the power of speech is a voiceless effigy, a mnemonic lacking the sound that gives it life beyond the imagination.[32]

In his history of ventriloquism, Stephen Connor rehearses the distinction that historians of orality and literacy make between oral cultures and literate ones: "For literate or, so to speak, 'sighted' cultures, words are thought of as forms of record, signs capable of capturing bits of the world and of experience and holding them in place. In aural-oral cultures, words are events; in visual-literate cultures, they are mnemonic objects."[33] While this heuristic is poignant, it creates a false cultural dichotomy. The late medieval period, for instance, is a moment in which characteristics and impulses of "aural-oral culture" and "literate culture" exist side by side, at times comfortably, and at times in tension with each other: the spoken *hoc est corpus meum* of a parish priest, heard by a parishioner, is an event that transubstantiates bread into the body of Christ and wine into his blood, while, simultaneously, the missal the priest holds contains the authorizing visual and written fragments of the Scripture and its authoritative historic-mnemonic function. This is also the case with *Piers Plowman*, which uses both textual and sonic registers. *Piers Plowman* records, loops, and distorts sounds; it presents personifications that are acousmatic, or reified sound; the entire poem allows its reader to practice identifying and articulating its sonic bodies, and its final passus perform the ramifications these sonic bodies have on the Christian commune. *Piers's* sound-objects, in their reifying of aural events, effectively mingle these two ways of approaching the word.

## Personifications as Sound-Objects

As what Suzanne Conklin Akbari and others have called a "rhetorical allegory," *Piers Plowman* performs an uncomfortable relationship between language and language's ability to express reality, constantly shifting and reconfiguring its relationship to itself through the tensions it creates between voice, text, and meaning.[34] "Langland's personifications are constantly coming to be and passing away," says Jill Mann in her thought-provoking overview of *Piers Plowman's* allegorical techniques.[35]

But if *Piers Plowman* is a rhetorical allegory, it is so first and foremost because it is built on a ground that enchants both its readers and its narrator through sound. Both the poem's mutability and its intangibility arise not only out of an allegorical *rhetoric* of polysemy, punning, and verbal play, but more specifically out of the text's *sonority*. As David Lawton says, *Piers Plowman* is "possessed by voice [. . . , it is the] sum of its myriad voices."[36] Throughout the poem, Will meets a series of interlocutors face-to-face. But of what do each of these faces consist? Will himself is a visual absence. Dressed in a cloak like a "sheep," his body and visage are shielded from view; we find out very little about what he truly looks like: in Passus B.15.152 Will describes himself as "longe" or tall, and, in Passus B.20.190 we learn that he has been "hit under the ere"—that is, deafened—by age; apart from this, however, we know nothing. Will's body is a sort of cipher. So, too, are most of the interlocutors he meets on his journey: *Piers Plowman* rarely describes its personifications in visual detail. Will's journey is therefore formulated around acts of listening; the personifications he meets—which are rarely described in detail—are instead constructed of sounds.

This is not to say that *Piers Plowman* entirely eschews imagery or visual metaphors. The landscape upon which Langland's personifications walk is detailed in vibrant, imaginative ekphrases, from the scrupulously catalogued "fair feeld ful of folk" of the Prologue (B.P.17) to the Tree of Charity outlined in detail in B.16.4–74 and the Barn of Unitee of B.19.320–30. Will's dialogues with the poem's underdescribed personifications take place upon a well-dressed visual stage. Furthermore, not all of *Piers*'s personifications pass by without visual description. Lady Mede is a "womman wonderliche yclothed" in fur and a crown, with fingers "fetisliche . . . fretted with gold wyr" and rubies, diamonds, multicolored sapphires, and a robe of red scarlet with "ribanes of reed gold" (B.2.8–16) draped around her. Passus B.5's descriptions of the Seven Deadly Sins are some of the most evocative physical language of the poem: Wrathe has "two white eighen," with a runny nose and a hanging neck (B.5.133–34), Coveitise is "bitelbrowed and baberlipped, with two blered eighen" and cheeks like a leather purse (B.5.189–94), and Envye is "pale as a pelet, . . . as a leek that hade yleye longe in the sonne." (B.5.77–84). These descriptions are evocative enough that one fifteenth-century copy of the C-text, Bodleian Library MS Douce 104, contains fifty-two marginal illustrations of figures from the poem, among them Lady Mede, Conscience, and Hunger.[37] However, such detailed descriptions dwindle as the poem continues; laconic yet memorable, Langland's epithets more often than not stress verbal efficiency rather than visual *copia*: Anima is, simply, "wihtouten tonge and teeth," Pacience wears "pilgrymes clothes," Piers is "peynted al blody," and Elde is "hevy of chere."[38] While these visual tags are potent, providing mnemonic hooks upon which to hang the speeches that ultimately animate their forms, they are not visual allegories. Some personifications, like Ymaginatif and Conscience, are never described in visual detail at all. Furthermore, the Douce manuscript is the only manuscript of *Piers Plowman* to have been decorated, and with illustrations described as "unambitious" and "utility-grade" or, in a more charitable vein, as "immediate, localized, and politicized": images are not the focal point of *Piers*'s personifications in either the textual or the material record.[39]

   Whether evocative or not, however, the lack of verbal space and time Langland devotes to the visual *qualia* of his personifications becomes abundantly clear when compared to other late medieval allegorical texts. The beast allegories that make up the bulk of *Richard the Redeless* are described in detail, and never open their mouths.[40] In *Wynnere and Wastoure*, the king and the baron, the poem's primary figures, receive thirteen and twelve lines of physical description, respectively, as the narrator traces their form from head to toe.[41] The similarly hearty blazons of Youthe, Medill Ylde, and Elde in *The Parlement of the Thre Ages* make up fifty-four lines of the 665-line poem. If *Piers Plowman* were to devote the same depth of description to each of its personifications as the *Parlement* (of course, making a determination on the exact number of personifications in *Piers Plowman* is impossible, an impossibility that arises in part out of its flouting of the conventional ekphrastic configurations of allegory), these descriptions would, taken together, comprise the longest passus in Langland's poem.[42]

Unlike its cousin poems, *Piers* operates according to a logic of iconographic parsimony, where curt epithets provide a highly selective, often diffuse visual impression rather than a sustained, totalizing portrait. The translucency of expression functions like an acousmatic veil, not because (as with Pythagoras or Schaeffer's sound-objects) the text is *entirely opaque*, but because, by providing a bare minimum of description, the paucity of its ekphrasis becomes palpable. Like the monster in a horror film who is seen only in shadow, the glimpses of *Piers'* underdetermined bodies provide what theorists of the gaze refer to as "stains," amorphous shapes that are given form by imaginative desire. Non-totalizing by their very nature, such figures recruit not only the capacity to see, but also the entire array of sensory perception as the viewing and reading subject strains their attention toward the shapeless cipher of the text.[43] What gives these figures form, is not each epithet's visual *qualia*, but instead the desire on the part of the reader for the unseen that visual thrift elicits; the *horror vacui* of reading practice mobilizes attentiveness to speech and sound in order to fill the holes in the visual field. The blurriness of *Piers'* sounding personifications have ramifications for the way that they operate in the poem. In a literal sense, they do not hold or offer per*spect*ives (which might, through a focus on the visual field, provide a sense of static reality and continuity), but instead per*son*tives: permeable, reworkable, and ever-vanishing interlocutors that are always making way for the next. *Piers's* personifications are complex plays of ventriloquism.

By shuttling the animating force of personification allegory away from vision and onto sound, *Piers Plowman* activates a paideia of mutability wherein any number of shifts and changes might resound throughout the text. Because, in Isidore's terms, sound "vanishes as the moment passes and is imprinted on the memory," when the speech of any given personification stops, it makes itself available both to errors of memorial encoding, or recall, and to opportunities for reorientation and reassessment.[44] This is particularly true of *Piers Plowman's* waking moments, where Will often recalls the conversations that have just taken place.[45] In the opening lines of B.13, for instance, Will summarizes what he has experienced in the four preceding passus:

And of this metyng many tymes muche thought I hadde:
First how Fortune me failed at my mooste nede,
And how that Elde manaced me, myghte we evere mete;

And how that freres folwede folk that was riche,
And peple that was povere at litel pris thei sette,
And no corps in hir kirkyerd ne in hir kirk was buryed
But quik he biquethe hem aught or sholde helpe quyte hir dettes;
And how this coveitise overcom clerkes and preestes;
And how that lewed men ben lad, but Oure Lord hem helpe,
Thorugh unkonnynge curatours to incurable peynes;
And how that Ymaginatif in dremels me tolde
Of Kynde and of his konnynge, and how curteis he is to bestes,
And how lovynge he is to bestes on londe and on watre:
Leneth he no lif lasse ne moore;
The creatures that crepen of Kynde ben engendred;
And sithen how Ymaginatif seid, '*Vix iustus salvabitur*,'
And whan he hadde seid so, how sodeynliche he passed.[46]

If this is meant to be a literal summary of the preceding passus, it is a fail-ure. Instead of recounting the whole of Passus 8–12, the dream sequence in which Will converses with Thought, Wit, Dame Studie, Clergie, Scripture, Fortune, Elde, Holynesse, Coveitise, Lewtee, Trajan, Reson, and Ymagina-tif in highly complex and contradictory ways, Will recounts in detail only the final portion of Ymaginatif's speech, even going so far as to directly quote Ymaginatif: *vix iustus salvabitur*.[47] If *Piers Plowman* operated according to tex-tual logic, we might expect a better, more complete summary or recension of the preceding passus here. But this is a moment in which Langland is revealing his investment in the sonority of the poem. If Will's experience were readerly, he could summarize the preceding passus just like he might a didactic text. While complicated and nuanced, such a task would be possi-ble. But instead, Will's summary not only privileges recency, but elides com-plexity in a manner more akin to recounting a snippet of overheard conversation or piece of music. Sonic meaning and acoustic memory allow only for repetition, not summary; and, as the echoic trace of Ymaginatif's speech lingers in Will's mind, this is exactly the performance he supplies: *vix iustus salvabitur*.[48] Because Will has encountered the previous passus as sonorous—as sound-objects—he is able to describe their general sound, per-haps their shifts in "rhythm" or "tempo," but to summarize them in the way one might a text is impossible.[49] The impossibility of summation occurs dur-ing the poem's waking moments again and again throughout the book, which ends with the echoic memory of its final dream-lines: Will wakes,

Conscience's speech still ringing in his ears. "And sende me hap and heele, til I have Piers the Plowman!" Conscience cries. *Piers Plowman* does not attempt a summary of the text, but instead, like a musical rondeau, returns to the poem's beginning in order to replay itself in toto. The sonic (in)capacity of the poem to sustain summarization serves a useful function, allowing *Piers Plowman* to present both complexity (in the initial performance) and simplicity, confusion, or inaccuracy (which drives the narrative forward and opens it up to further verbal exchanges) in turn.

Voice in the absence of a physical body also allows the very bodies of the poems' personifications themselves to be mutate, shift, and change.[50] Ymaginatif arrives in the text as a mystery, a persona about which we know nothing until he opens his mouth to speak. He is not a figure—that is, he is not present at hand—until he speaks; his voice literally calls him into being, and he vanishes as soon as he stops talking, his presence in the poem and his availability to Will absolutely contingent on his actively sounding voice. "I have folwed the, in feith, these fyve and fourty wynter," he says, unnoticed unless he is moving Will to "mynne on thyn ende" (B.12.1–4), that is, actively engaging with Will. Ymaginatif has a body, but, as an acousmatic form, this body does not *exist* until he speaks himself into being. In much the same way that the working memory can hold only one thing in the mind at a time, so too does Ymaginatif, as an embodiment of the medieval theory of the mind, perform the inchoate transition between the active and passive intellect, extant only as an unnoticed shadow until called into dialogue with Will. After a lengthy discussion, he vanishes as quickly as he appeared:

> 'And wit and wisdom,' quod that wye, 'was som tyme tresor
> To kepe with a commune—no catel was holde bettre—
> And muche murthe and manhod'—and right myd that he
>    vanysshed.[51]

Will, who has grown accustomed to speakers who arise and then fall back into the fabric of the text's unconscious, seems amazed at Ymaginatif's vocal corporeation; Ymaginatif is not a figure, but a *voice,* an organized sound that dies even as it is born. Nevertheless, Will has always been in the presence of Ymaginatif.

Scenarios like this—where voices *are* the bodies of personifications— occur elsewhere in the text. Trajan's speech precedes him into the text in B.11, where he interrupts the action with a stirring interjection. "Ye, baw for bokes!"

he barks (B.11.140). In B.6, Piers makes his entrance into the text in the form of a sudden interjection. "This were a wikkede wey but whoso hadde a gyde," he says, "that myghte folwen us ech a foot" (B.6.1–2). While Piers effectively thrusts his head into the text at this point, reconfiguring its focus away from Mede's marriage and onto the quest for Dowel, Dobet, and Dobest, it is not a visual body that structures this metanoia, but his voice. And, again in C.15, Piers disappears just as suddenly, immediately after delivering a long speech on patience: 'And whan he hadde yworded thus, wiste no man aftur / Where Peres the plogman bycam, so priueyliche he wente (C.15.150–51). In each of these cases, personification works like a reverse apostrophe in which an invisible body calls out from the text of the poem in order to reify itself.[52]

There are also the personifications for whom the timbre of the voice is at the center of an identity that is shifting and mutable: Anima and Pees (Peace). Anima, for instance, presents a fascinating locus for teasing apart the relative operations of sight and sound in the poem's construction of personifications. Masha Raskolnikov notes that the "challengingly open" body of Anima as she metamorphoses from the female lover of Kynde (B.9) into a male representation of the higher mental faculties later in the poem (B.15).[53] This is part of a larger program in *Piers Plowman*, Raskolnikov argues, of eliminating the expectation of female-gendered instructional personae as the poem turns inward to show the poet in intellectual communication with himself. But of course, in *Piers Plowman,* Anima was never "female-bodied" in the visual-spatial sense: Anima is not described in physical terms that might code as "female" under visual observation. Instead, Anima's gender relies on two things: first, on a medieval allegorical tradition that marks abstract qualities as feminine in allegory, and second, out of a voice that shifts between the masculine and feminine register as the pronouns used to refer to her shift between Passus 9 and 15. This pronomial-vocal change draws attention not to Anima's visual body (Anima is never described in visual terms), but instead to a linguistic-sonic one. When Anima is a "she," in B.9, she never opens her mouth. But when Anima shifts to the pronomial "he," Anima not only speaks readily, but has specific things to say about the qualities and power of his voice. "My vois is so yknowe," he says, "that ech a creature of his court welcometh me faire." (B.15.20–21). The reader is called to imagine the voice of one known well in "Cristes court" (B.15.17)—that is, a masculine voice whose legal speech is legitimated not because his body is visibly male (in fact, the only physical description of Anima is one of *lack:* he is "withouten tonge and teeth," B.15.13), but rather because the timbre of this toothless, tongueless voice manifests postpubertal masculine identity, marking him, in turn, as an agential legal subject.

Similarly, in B.4, Pees appears in Parliament to present a bill of indictment against Wrong. The reader is given no description of Pees save that "he" has a "panne blody."[54] When Pees appears later in the poem, first in B.5.622 and later in B.18, he has become a she, one of the Four Daughters of God, "in pacience yclothed."[55] Pees's gender fluidity is central to his/her specific role as speaker at each point in the text: in B.4, Pees, as "he," is testifying in court, a space where masculine speakers attempt to dominate Lady Mede through a series of performative legal utterances legitimated by their male-gendered voices. Later, when Pees appears as she, her speech is in the feminine, Marian role as an intercessor (as well as a dancer). She is also speaking, but this time it is not in court, but rather praying, an intercessor. In the cases of both Anima and Pees, the mutability of gender is housed not in physical bodies, but rather in the specific and local performative qualities of public speech and performance.[56]

If Ymaginatif exists because he gives voice to his own presence, and if Anima and Pees speak in registers that embody them as gendered subjects, there are other figures in the text that we never hear from at all and yet retain the powerful imprint of sound as a constitutive of their existence in the poem.[57] These are the many names—of people, places, and things—that Langland playfully constructs of multiply hyphenated words: Cortyes-of-speche (C.4.17); Thomme Trewe-tonge-telle-me-no-talles-Ne-lesynges-to-lauhe-of-for-Y-louede-hit-neuere (C.4.17–19); Soffre-tyl-Y-se-my-tyme (C.4.20); Auyseth-the-byfore (C.4.20). Yeuan-yelde-ayeyn-yf-Y-so-moche-haue-Al-that-Y-wikkedly-wan-sithen-Y-witte-hadde (this name stretches across two different patterns of alliteration) (C.6.309–10); Beth-buxom-of-speche (B.5.567); Youre-fadres-honoureth (B.5.568); Swere-noght-but-if-it-be-for-nede-and-nameliche-on-ydel-the-name-of-God-almyghty (B.5.570–71); Coveite-noght-mennes-catel-ne-hire-wyves-ne-noon-of-hire-servaunts-that-noyen-hem-myghte (B.5.573–74); Bere-no-fals-witnesse (B.5.580); Sey-sooth-so-it-be-to-doone-in-no-manere-ellis-noght-for-no-mannes-biddynge (B.5.583–84); Bileef-so-or-thow-beest-noght-saved (B.5.589); Bidde-wel-the-bet-may-thow-spede (B.5.592); Werch-whan-tyme-is (B.6.78); Do-right-so-or-thi-dame-shal-thee-bete (B.6.79); Suffre-thi-Sovereyns-have-their-will: deme-hem-noght-for-if-thow-doost-thow-shalt-it-deere-abugge; Lat-God-yworthe-with-al-for-so-His-word-techeth (B.6.80–82). These characters never speak. And yet they maintain a durable presence on the stage of the poem for as long as their names take say or read, occupying not only visual space on the manuscript page, but also, simultaneously, distending time and holding the aural equivalent of space.[58] In holding these sonic bodies in front of our ears for as long as possible, the text makes the indexical value of these names readily apparent. *Piers's* persona-formation is concerned with the furrows that are made in the air, the resonant sound waves that cause sonic bodies to emerge from the text and then die away as these sounds die.

From the creation of the world (*Dixit et facta sunt*, B.9.32a) to the resurrection of Lazarus (B.15.592–94) and from the many waking moments in the text brought about by the end or climax of a speech to the characters literally constituted by the speeches they give, *Piers Plowman* is a work of sonic figuralism and allegory. Music in the poem is about making connections: the *crieries* of workers in acts of commerce define these bodies as mercantile subjects; so, too, do the lethargic singers, Jakke the Jogelour and Robyn the Ribaudour, who refuse to work for the commune.[59] Beggars, Activa Vita, and Haukyn are all called minstrels; priests and parsons hunt souls with their liturgical *Placebo*.[60] Charity sings; Hope plays a trumpet; song is played for Mede's wedding; when readers finally hear a bit about Will's life beyond the poem, in C.5, he tells us he is a chantry priest (a not unconflicted one, but one nonetheless). Moreover, it is in part because of their construction as sound-objects that *Piers Plowman* is able to so beautifully or convincingly depict "interior" states of being. Sight distinguishes the objects of perception from the viewer, creating, in the act of seeing, a notion of the self in which separate and discrete boundaries can be drawn between inner and outer, between self and nonself. On the other hand, sounds embed themselves in the ears, and, if identity is forged in the act of hearing, the subject that arises is always already entangled, its boundaries softened. *Piers Plowman's* personifications are sound-objects.

## Alliteration, Anticipation, and the Sound-Object

I would like to return now, more explicitly, to Schaeffer's sound-objects and how they resound through Langland's poem. *Piers Plowman's* dedication to sonority does not stop with allegory and personification. Form follows function, and the alliterative long-line itself approaches the asymptote of musicality, thereby constructing a sound-object. Rabelais's "paroles gelées" and Gascoigne's "gobettes" are helpful in understanding how alliteration might work like Pierre Schaeffer's sound-objects, where sounds become objects through repetition and distortion and severance from their original bodies: in the case of Titivillus, disarticulated phonemes are gathered up into a sack because they have been severed from intent; for the mariners on Pantagruel's ship, the frozen words are nothing but "barbarous gibberish" represented in the text as repeating alliterative syllables ("hin, hin, hin, hin, his, tick, tock, whizz gibber, jabber, frr, frrr, frrr, boo, boo, boo, boo, boo, boo, boo, boo, crack, track, trr, trr, trr, trrr, trrrrrr, on, on, on, on, on, wooawooawoooon, gog, magog"); in *Piers Plowman*, the repeated phonemes of the alliterative line attain an affective meaning that works with, but is not identical to, the literal meaning of its poetry.

That *Piers Plowman* (and the myth of Titivillus) consider sound *as* sound is unsurprising in a medieval context, and in fact has a basis in medieval theories of Latin literacy and education. In Priscian's *Institutiones grammaticae*, basic grammatical knowledge is framed as the capacity to discern distinct phonemes within the fabric of larger semantic and phonological units. "The letter is the smallest part of a compound sound," Priscian writes. "It may be called 'smallest' because, of all the things that can be divided, the shortest is that which cannot be divided."[61] Letters are the atoms of language, and discerning their existence by "dividing" them from surrounding sounds is the basis of literacy. Letters lack the semantic meaning that words, clauses, or sentences have; nevertheless, they form meaning as an emergent property of organization, pattern, and combination. Book II of the *Institutiones,* on syllables, demonstrates this property of language. Book II is filled with semantically nonsensical lists of felicitous and infelicitous phonemes that teach the reader what syllables sound like, how they work, and how they ought to be written down: *Sabbura, sabbata, gibbus, gibberosus, gibber, obba* is just one of the many examples contained in this book.[62] "Sabbura Sabbath bulging humpbacked hump decanter" is gibberish, but through repetition outside of quotidian states of referential meaning, the sound [bb] can be heard in its own right and for its own sake, identified as an object, and then inscribed in written language. The focus here is not on the *meaning* of these words and certainly not on these words in relation to each other, but purely on holding their sounds before the ear long enough to make them discernible and therefore legible. In each of these cases, literal nonsense makes *sonic* sense, as repetition of the same sound (in this case, the [bb] slowly builds expectations of grammatical or phonetic legitimacy). As a central text of Latin pedagogy and literacy training, Priscian's *Institutiones* would have had a large role in encoding a medieval reading *habitus* that, in turn, would affect the way a medieval reader approached *Piers Plowman.*

The examples from Rabelais, Gascoigne, and Priscian look quite a bit like Schaeffer's sound-objects, and they suggest that the medieval and early modern periods imagined the concept of sound-objects well before Schaeffer formulated them explicitly. In each of these examples, the repetition of "nonsense" sounds allows them to be severed from their sources and imagined as distinct entities. But if sounds can be objects, they are necessarily fraught and complex ones, ones that operate unlike the more normative objects that present themselves to us through quotidian visio-tactile means. Sound, Aristotle says in Book II of the *De anima*, is "a movement of air";[63] and, as Isidore says in the *Etymologies*, "sound vanishes as the moment passes and is imprinted on the memory."[64] If normative objects are defined as matter, suspended in space and delimited by boundaries such that repeated viewings are possible, sound becomes an object by allowing itself to be suspended in time; the "space" of that suspension need not always be iterated performance, but can also be an imagined or remembered performance. As Isidore says in this same section, "Unless sounds are held by the memory of man, they perish, because they cannot be written down."[65]

If Schaeffer's musical compositions, which he called *musique concrete*, centered on reduced listening and used looping, repetition, and distortion to induce listeners to focus on the texture, weight, and shape of sounds, divorcing them from compositional intent in the process, the same process can be seen in the localized examples of Rabelais, Gascoigne, and Priscian. In a very general and abstract way, poetry—particularly medieval poetic forms in both Latin and the vernacular—encourages this sort of listening as well, as the constraints poetry places on the organization and selection of words place emphasis not only on their semantic function but also on their rhythm, meter, alliteration, assonance, and tone (that is, on their sonic characteristics).[66] And although reduced listening to poetry cannot be compelled (and poetry can never be fully severed from intentional or discursive frameworks; there is no such thing as pure Schaefferian *entendre* or "purely musical" listening when it comes to the written word), verse is a sort of ameliorated or attenuated form of *musique concrete,* as meaning is created not only out of the deictic force of words, but also out of the sonic aspects of language detached from its signifying capacity. For medieval writers, the connection between poetry and music was clear, as Martianus Capella's *Marriage of Philology and Mercury* and many other poetic handbooks suggest, and contemporary theorists of verse similarly liken poetry to a form of music. One definition of verse is that it is "low-grade musical material"; while poetry lacks a tonal compositionality unique to music, it has a percussive quality that encourages musical forms of listening.[67] This universalizing claim carries a heightened import in light of Schaefferian sound-objects, particularly as they appear in alliterative poetry. How, in a poem dedicated to conversations—that is, to voices that decay—does Langland's verse manage anything like the solidity of the physical form? The alliterative long-line organizes sounds in order to create the very "tonal" properties of language that Justice claims poetry lacks. In *Piers Plowman*, the objectivity of sound develops as the repeated initial sounds of each alliterative long-line forge an anticipatory orientation to the text, rehearing and remembering and giving sounds bodies, literally re-membering them.[68]

With Schaeffer's sound-object in mind, a section from the Prologue that repeats the same alliterative sound becomes particularly interesting. At this point in the poem, Will has already enumerated the many social estates that mill about in the "far feeld ful of folk" (B.P.17), and is beginning to construct a more nuanced picture of the ways in which each of these estates—from the commune to the clergy and the ruling class—is both reliant upon and responsible for the others. The alliterative line itself mirrors the interdependent structure of these estates, repeating an initial /k/- phoneme across these twenty-seven lines while delicately introducing other alliterative patterns:

I parceyved of the power that Peter hadde to kepe—
To bynden and to unbynden, as the Book telleth—
How he it lefte with love as Oure Lorde highte
Amonges foure virtues, most vertuous of alle vertues,
That cardinales ben cald and closyng-yates
Thare Crist is in kyngdom to close and to shette,
Ac of the cardinales at court that caught of that name
And power presumed in hem a Pope to make,
To han the power that Peter hadde, inpugne I nelle,
For in loue and in lettrure the eleccion bilongeth;
Forthi I kan and kan naught of court speke moore.
Thanne kam ther a Kyng: Knyghthod hym ladde;
Might of the communes made hym to regne.
And thanne cam Kynde Wit and clerkes he made,

For to counseillen the Kyng and the Commune save.
The Kyng and Knyghthod and Clergie bothe
Casten that the Commune sholde hem [communes] fynde.
The Commune contreved of Kynde Wit craftes,
And for profit of al the peple plowmen ordeyned
To tilie and to travaille as trewe lif asketh.
The Kyng and the Commune and Kynde Wit the thridde
Shopen lawe and leaute—eeh lif to knowe his owene.
Thanne loked up a lunatik, a leene thyng withalle,
And knelynge to the Kyng clergially he seide,
"Crist kepe thee, sire Kyng, and thi kyngryche,
And lene thee lede thi lond so leaute thee lovye,
And for thi rightful rulyng be rewarded in hevene."⁶⁹

As Macklin Smith notes, this twenty-seven-line segment of the Prologue exhibits a series of what he calls "adjunctive groups," that is, a construction wherein two or more lines alliterating on the same sound "frame or inter-lace" other alliterative groupings.⁷⁰ The most plentiful, sonically dominant alliterative phoneme here is /k/, with thirteen lines in total, initially in a group of three lines (ll. 104–6), then in two (ll. 111–12), followed by an anticipatory line in which the alliterative stress is on /m/ but which includes a /k/ (in *communes*) typifying what Smith calls a "prominent isolate" (l. 113). This is followed immediately by a five-line section alliterating on /k/ (ll. 114–18). Three more lines on /k/ follow in close succession, one singly (l. 121) and the next in a pair (ll. 124–25). While /k/ dominates these lines, there are also significant running alliterations on /p/ (three lines: ll. 108–9, 119) and /l/ (four lines: 110. 122–23, 126). The resonance of this /k/ is like an echo, and, if the semantic content of this passage is ignored, like an echo, the /k/ keeps recurring throughout the passage.

The abundance of running alliteration in this passage is due to the word-play and the rhetorical game that Langland is playing in these lines, as he triangulates the various powers and social responsibilities of Conscience, Kynde Wit, the Kyng, and the Commune. Certainly, the gravitational pull of these four major personifications lend these lines the revenant body of the /k/. But even prior to the arrival of Conscience, Kynde Wit, the Kyng, and the Commune in this passage, the /k/ was anticipated by the cardinal virtues, Church cardinals, and Christ (ll. 104–7) earlier in the passage. While the heaviest concentration of alliteration on /k/ ends with Lunatik's speech on line 127 (it is interrupted by the gnomic nonalliterative Latin leonine hexa-metric passage of ll. 128–45), the lines that follow this Latinate interjection, the text returns once more to its heavy-handed reliance on verses alliterat-ing on /k/ through line 207:[71]

> Comen to a counseil for the commune profit;
> For a cat of a court cam whan hym liked . . . (ll. 148–49)
> . . .
> Cracchen us or clawen us and in hise clouches holde (l. 154)
> . . .
> And some colers of crafty work; uncoupled they wenden. (l. 162)
> . . .
> And knytten it on a coler for oure commune profit. (l. 169)
> . . .
> "Though we hadde ykilled the cat, yet sholde ther come another
> To cracchen us and al oure kyne, though we cropen under
>     benches.
> Forthi I counseille al the commune to late the cat worthe . . ."
>     (ll. 185–87)
> . . .
> "Ther the cat is a kitoun, the court is ful elenge." (l. 194)
> . . .
> "Shal never the cat ne the kiton by my counseil by greved,
> Ne carpynge of this coler that costed me nevere.
> And though it costned me catel, biknowen it I nolde,
> But suffren as hymself wolde so doon as hym liketh—
> Coupled and uncoupled to cacche what thei mowe." (ll. 203–7)

The density of /k/-alliterating lines is lower here (21 percent) than in the earlier, shorter section (48 percent), but the text relentlessly reinvokes the /k/ that returns the poem to the patterns of the preceding section as if in an echo. Unmoored from semantic signification, the hundred or so lines that comprise this section repeat the sonic force of the /k/ not only over the space of the text on the manuscript page, but also over the temporal landscape in which it takes to read or recite the poem out loud.

While this section is the longest, most obvious example of sound rep-etition in the poem, a line-by-line analysis of *Piers Plowman* shows that Lang-land is invested in alliterative repetition—what we might call, following

Schaeffer, sonic adumbration—throughout the text. Over the length of the poem, adjunctive groups and double-, triple-, or quadruple-line alliterative groupings occur in every passus, such that anywhere from 25–40 percent of any given passus's lines belong to part of a larger alliterative grouping. For comparison's sake, had each line's alliterative sound been chosen at random, the percentage of adjunctive lines in the poem would hover around 8 percent, even if we exclude from the possible options for alliteration the five least frequently used phonemes (/z/, /v/, /sh/, /ch/, /j/).

In *Piers Plowman,* then, as in other alliterative poetry, repetition of initial phonemes works as a type of temporal distension, stretching sound until it can be held before the ear over time much the same way an apple, table, or book might be held before the eye. The alliterative long-line creates "go-bettes" of words, meting out sounds, the way Priscian does, in books 1 and 2 of his *Institutiones.* There is an obvious difference though, of course: where Priscian's lists are nonsense and Titivillus collects words because, though sensical, they lack rational intent, the poetry carries semantic meaning as well.

This temporal distension—this capacity to "hold before the ear," as music does—has musical effects on alliterative verse that are often underplayed by metrists, who have long shown an attentiveness to and respect for the musicality of prosody, but nevertheless explicitly privilege the semantic force of language over its affective musical qualities. George Kane's exploration of *Piers Plowman*'s meter exemplifies these metrical critiques: "In the simultaneous apprehension of the whole we impute to the semantically empty constituents of the pattern, here to the initial sounds organized as pattern by their recurrence, the meaningfulnesses of the expressions where they occur, so that their a-logicality is not merely subsumed into, but greatly enhances, the entire significance."[72] For Kane and other scholars of alliterative meter, sound is substrate, "semantically empty," matter given form by the "meaningfulness of expressions"; repeated phonemes and stress patterns are "a-logical," existing to enhance the significance of "meaningful" text but without any meaning in their own right.[73] While scholars of alliterative meter are deeply respectful of the sonic aspect of the alliterative long-line, their readings still tend to reproduce a rhetorical hierarchy that understands the rational utterance or *vox articulata* as the goal of poetics, and sonic patterns, meters, or rhythms as a decorative "enhancement."

Here music theory might help us to speak more holistically to prosody as meaningful in its own right, where iterability is fundamental to meaning-making apart from the semantic content of the words. "Composing," says an anonymous musical treatise from the fifteenth century, "is defined in this way: it is the proportionate and necessary putting [together] of the diverse species or concordances, ascending and descending, according to perfection and imperfection; or in this way: a composition is a construction regulated by harmony according to the perfection and imperfection of the diversity of several notes."[74] Arising out of the thoughtful placement of rhythms and tones in relation to each other, iterability is central to medieval music's understanding of itself as a subject, and music theorists were intent on the validity of compositional iteration. This can be seen not only in the many medieval musical *formes fixes* structured around strophic patterns, rondels, and refrains, but in more granular elements of compositional style, such as the repeating rhythmic modes of the *ars antiqua* (typified by Pérotin and Leonin), as well as in the later medieval and early Renaissance isorhythmic motet, in which a rhythmic pattern would repeat throughout a piece. Isorhythmic motets are far more complicated than can be discussed here, as they involve complex metrical games of diminution and augmentation, as well as layering rhythmic repetition over melodic repetition and variance; for the purposes of this discussion, all that needs to be said is that medieval polyphony was particularly attuned to iterability.[75] Repetition is how music makes meaning, not just in the medieval period, but as a more general principle of the art form.[76]

Most surviving medieval music has lyrics, and medieval composers were focused on good word setting (*bona cadentia dictaminium*)—meaning that words and music ought to comport both rhythmically and affectively.[77] For instance, Elizabeth Eva Leach argues that the pleasure of hearing Machaut's motets arises not simply from their sound, but from the simultaneous, careful textual and musical organization that is united in the musical form: "Polytextuality in music has a specific effect, which seems at first listening to militate against semantics in favor of the pleasures of pure sound. However, the effect of three people 'speaking' (in song) at once is not chaotic in musical terms but highly ordered and organized both rhythmically and harmonically."[78] In spite of the near ubiquity of texts in surviving songs of the medieval period, musical "meaning" is still differentiated from textual meaning: text is representational, music is gestural; text is semantic, music is affective. Boethius notes that "when we hear what is properly and harmoniously united in sound in conjunction with that which is harmoniously coupled and joined together within us and are delighted by it, then we recognize that we ourselves are put together in its likeness"; it is this quality of music that led Augustine to famously decry the dangerous power of music, differentiating it from the power of language, to move him to ecstasy in the *Confessions*.[79] In the *Speculum musicae*, Jacobus notes the capacity for well-composed music to instill delight: "Although sense delights in some consonances and is saddened by others, the cognition of all of them is pleasing to the intellect."[80] That music might impart joy through the expression of sadness is a commonplace of medieval musical treatises, and, in the fourteenth century, the ability to perform artful—even joyful—music while experiencing sadness became one mark of a professional musician or lyric maker; in the late medieval period, then, music was seen as a machine for leveraging affective effects distinct from those of the composer's own.[81] In music, song texts impart one type of meaning, and the notes another; when Augustine feels threatened by the emotive power of music or when Jacobus argues for music's ability to delight not the emotions, but the intellect, it becomes apparent that, for medieval listeners, sentiment and *sententia* are not arranged in a hierarchical system of meaning-making, but instead infinitely refer to each other in a resonant, iterable timespace that is both deictic and phatic.

Modern critical interpretations of the alliterative verse use a similar vocabulary and chart similar effects that critical readings of music do. Although Kane argues that the musical force of alliterative poetry is subordinate to the deictic force of its words, when metrists argue for the centrality of alliterative variety to verse—patterns of lifts and dips, modulations of alliteration and accent, accentual-syllabic meter, and rhyme—their descriptive vocabulary not only returns invariably to the affective argot of music, but also suggests that it is the emotional register of musicality that provides the poetic line with its capacity to hold emotional meaning. They make, in essence, the same argument for the affective force of meter that medieval writers made about music. For instance, after a thorough and mathematical accounting of the formal variations of alliteration in *Piers Plowman*, Macklin Smith attends to the effects of the alliterative technique: alliteration creates "fluid momentum," suggests "loss," "thinness" (180), "freshness," "freedom" (190); it is "emphatic" or "balanced" (190), "playful" (192), "tricky," "dark," "portentious" (194), "manic" (198), "intensifying" (204); it provides a sense of "urgency" (212). Most tellingly, "what the syntax indirectly states the /s/-echo lets us experience viscerally" (205). Smith's explicit conclusion of his argument is that "alliteration [is] a supra-metrical, stylistic device . . . serv[ing] not only to introduce the dream-vision allegory" but also to "exhibit and forefront its poetics" through "overlaid ironies, reminders of spiritual contexts in the midst of social criticism, allegorical figurations, or representations of theological paradox."[82] Smith's own evocative rhetoric here suggests that the voiced, performative, emotional, and musical force of alliterative poetry does more than "forefront" its poetics; it makes the reader *feel* something about the words that are spoken through the tonal qualities of language.

Affective musical critiques are, of course, not the sole purview of *Piers Plowman*. In a particularly "prosodic" article on prosody in *Pearl,* Alan Gaylord notes the emotional or sensual quotient of the *Pearl* poet's combined alliterative-accentual-syllabic form. The Dreamer "howls in pain," the maiden is "blunt, stark, yet not without bracing humour" (195); the meter gives the reader a "rough ride" (197); passages are "saffroned with alliteration" (200).[83] Nor is this language unique to alliterative verse. In his studies of Chaucerian meter, Gaylord discusses his intent to show "how Chaucer moves, and in moving, moves us."[84] As Adin Lears argues, sound is the somatic ground upon which sense is based in Langland's poem, to playful effects, manipulating "poetic language to stress sound over meaning."[85] The architectural properties of poetry—meter, end rhyme, alliteration—stir emotions. Meaning emerges from metrical sound as musical meaning does: it is emotive. When Langland knits his adjunct alliterations into line after line, passus after passus, of his text, he is creating an affective landscape for the poem. What, one might ask, is the semantic content of the line "semynge to synneward, and somtyme he gan taste / About the mouth or bynethe bigynneth to grope" (13.347–48) *without* what Smith calls its "sleazy, slow-accelerating movements?"[86] Meter and alliteration are integral, not ancillary, to poetic meaning.

## The Ethics of the Sound-Object: Liturgy and the Commune in *Piers Plowman* B.18–20

The formal and alliterative properties of *Piers Plowman* are not the only ways in which the poem performs sound-objecthood; sound-objects also appear in the poem's narrative. Acousmatic listening is, as Brian Kane says, a "shared, intersubjective practice of attending" in which the community comes to formulate itself in response to the shared suspension of the visual field; and, as *acousmata* birth sound-objects, we can find in the veiled singing faces of B.18–20 a way of thinking about the call to fraternity and community that the aural experiences of these passus enact. That is, even as the figures and personifications Will meets on his journey give him access to a space within himself, these same sense-objects also blur the very self that would otherwise serve as the locus of inquiry in a traditional psychomachia, turning it into a communal, intersubjective site of ethical inquiry. Passus B.18–19 describe a series of liturgical performances that briefly bring the commune together around the figure of Christ's death and resurrection during the *triduum* before the chaos of the eschaton in Passus 20 violently destroys this temporary peace. The liturgy itself is a type of sound-object. Its iterability performs a sort of permanence, and the ways that the liturgy manifests in these final passus show the ethical ties that the liturgy, as a sound-object, might form. Here, the sound-object turns away from the single questing subject of Will, actively constructing a collective subject for its ethics around the sound-object of liturgical performance. Acousmatic sound forms a Christian community before destroying it in the Passus 20.[87]

When Will falls asleep at the opening of Passus 18, his dream begins with a performance of the Palm Sunday liturgy. "Of gerlis and of *Gloria, laus* gretly me dremed / And how *osanna* by orgen olde folk songen. . . . Olde Jewes of Jerusalem for joye thei songen," Will says.[88] In having Will's dream occur on Palm Sunday, Langland simultaneously activates both the historical specificity of a particular liturgical performance and the universalizing notion of "the liturgy" to which each specific performance points. Here, both the historical and the spatial specificity of the Palm Sunday liturgy and its broader, more general meaning for the "Christian body" is important, and so a bit of historical framing is warranted. If a sound-object is, as Brian Kane suggests, a "practice," it must—as all practices are—be historically situated and located, and medieval Palm Sunday liturgies in western Europe typically had specific characteristics that made them uniquely poised to perform the community-forming and methexic power of the sound-object.

First, on Palm Sunday, the laity had multiple opportunities to take part in the sung performance of Mass alongside the clergy, a practice that was relatively rare. The laity's role on this particular day was not a passive one, nor was it one that encouraged silence or sotto voce devotion (such as the forms of participation described in *The Lay Folks' Mass Book*). Instead, lay citizens actively participated in Mass, processing around the town and becoming part of the antiphonal choir, singing in response to the clergy.[89] *Piers Plowman* gestures to lay sung involvement when the text recalls the "gerlis" and the "olde folke" as well as the "Olde Jewes of Jerusalem" singing the *Gloria* and the *Osanna*, portions of Mass usually reserved for priests. During what were often extended processions—in some graduals and missals, upward of twenty antiphons would have been sung—the priests and the congregation would sing in a call and response to each other, bridging, through their vocal performance, the gap between the clergy and the laity.[90] These processions also served to reorient physical and temporal space. At Chartres, where the Palm Sunday procession left the cathedral and worked its way around town, the French cityscape would be sonically carved with the places central to the story of Holy Week (Golgotha, the Mount of Olives, the Garden of Gethsemane); a similar inscription would have occurred at the Wells, Salisbury, and York Cathedrals, the visual cues of towns giving way to an imaginative reconstruction—through absence—of the city of Jerusalem. In some cases, the Palm Sunday service concluded with a series of carols sung by the laity in English, and performances like this are portrayed in *The Entry into Jerusalem* of the York Cycle; the citizens announce their intent to sing in "unysoune / with myghtfull songes" (ll. 262–63) while their children "schall / go synge before" (ll. 264–65) to announce the coming procession.[91] Thus the church, its yard, and the town were, through the performance of the chants, turned into a form of the historical Jerusalem. York remained York, and yet somehow ceased to be York; the laity were both the laity and the citizens of Jerusalem; and the priests became Christ and his disciples. Antiphonal processions serve as a sort of containment that asserts the validity of the social order; like carnivals, they strengthen the boundaries of normative religious behavior by temporarily overturning these very norms.

Perhaps the most compelling instance of sonic objectivity in the poem—and one that *Piers Plowman* intentionally invokes in B.18.8—arises from a liturgical practice that Langland likely knew and drew upon to paint his portrait of this moment: the use of "angel choirs" at the end of the Palm Sunday procession. In some cathedrals in England, specifically Yorkminster, Wells Cathedral, and Salisbury Cathedral, small balconies that could only be reached from the inside of the church spanned an interior space above the main doors of the cathedral. A series of small apertures ran along this balcony in the exterior wall. Stone or cement carvings—at Wells, these were carvings of angels—surrounded these holes, simultaneously adorning and obscuring them.[92] Made specifically for the feast of Palm Sunday, these balconies, which were known as "angel choirs," held the young singers who chanted the *Gloria, laus*, and completely hid them from view in the process. In manuscripts of the rites of Sarum and York, rubricated directions call for a number of choristers to stand *in eminenti loco* and to sing the *Gloria, laus* as the community entered the main doors of the church at the end of the Palm Sunday procession. While architectural evidence of permanent structures remains at Wells, Yorkminster, and Salisbury, we can infer from this direction that, where permanent structures did not exist, temporary ones might be erected specifically for the occasion. To the lay community below, who would have just completed a procession in which the sounds of their antiphons would have overlaid an imagined Jerusalem on the spatiotemporality of Wells's churchyard, the "gerlis" *Gloria, laus* would have been truly and thoroughly hidden, the human bodies of the singers ensconced behind the angelic stonework of the church facade. There would have been a necessary severance between the voices singing and their physical forms; the cathedral's physical structure imposed the production of acousmatic sound within the liturgical rite.

When Will says that he dreams "Of gerlis and of *Gloria, laus*," he is nodding to the acousmatic separation between sound and physical form that a lay parishoner might have experienced on Palm Sunday, whether through the processional palimpsesting of timespace or the hidden bodies chanting the *Gloria*. Will does not say, for instance, that he heard the "gerlis" specifically *singing* the *Gloria*; instead, the syntax of this line uses the coordinating conjunction "and" to distinguish two separate things: on the one hand, the "gerlis," and on the other, the *Gloria*s, betraying the immanent incongruity or rupture that exists between the invisible singers who produce the chant and the sound that floats free of those very bodies. It is Will who unites these two terms, joining aural cause and sonic effect, reconstructing, through the "lag" and the "gap" between sound and body that Michel Chion, Rabelais, Gascoigne, and Pierre Schaeffer recognize at the heart of all utterance. The *Gloria* and *Osanna* of B.18 portray the ritual performance of a sound-object that, through repetition, continuously constitutes and reconstitutes the Christian commune. From the young to the old, from the living Christians of medieval Europe to the "Old Jewes" of Jerusalem, there is a uniformity in variety that emerges out of the *Gloria, laus* and the *Osanna*. Through an attentive act of listening, these ventriloquial voices are overlaid with a millennium of belonging-meaning: the "gerlis" might be both the children of Jerusalem and the young choristers in the country church simultaneously.[93] Langland leverages the mutability and iterability of the sound-object to disrupt the normative, forward-flowing chronological conception of time; but he does this, ironically enough, through the liturgy itself, which is specific, spatially, and historically situated. That is, we might imagine other versions of the Palm Sunday liturgy in which the sound is not treated or does not manifest in this way. The ethical demands of *Piers Plowman* and acousmatic sound do not take *Piers Plowman* out of history, but instead locate it in a liturgical space that is definitive and specific, one in which musical sound is not, by being disconnected from its source, made universal, but instead made highly particular and historical. This practice is the result of scaled, multiple, and hybridized forms of acousmatic sound that produce sound-objects, from the alliterative long-line to the personifications in the text to the acousmatic performance of the Palm Sunday liturgy.[94]

Even as the eschaton of B.18–20 seeks to encompass the "Christian commune," the true boundaries of this acousmatic, amorphous object are impossible to determine, and, ultimately, they collapse under their own weight. The repetition at the heart of the sound-object operates as a "stand-in for a process of structuration," but it is always incomplete, falling away as soon as the repetition stops. And so, the types of figures (personifications, selves, and communes) that *Piers* creates are always already absent in their presence, fragmented. In spite of the *Veni Creator Spiritus* that is sung in B.19.211 by the "many hundred" people gathered around the cross on Easter morning, and even though Conscience calls everyone to come into the Barn of Unitee, this is not enough to concretize the sound-objects, to make them visio-tactile. The Barn fails, and the poem dissolves.

In the place of real closure, the only option available to the sound-object is repetition. Conscience's goal, at the end of the poem, is to "seken Piers the Plowman"—that is, an infinite regression, or, better, an infinite ingression— into the heart of Being, into the part of Being that recognizes the lack at its negative center.[95] The perpetual repetition of the self is the sound-object and the liturgical manifestation of the subject. There is no such thing as stability, but only performance and reperformance, and so the notion of the commune must be continually reperformed (liturgically, musically, narratively, vocally) even as it is its own advent. In other words, the poem ends with an incipit; *Piers Plowman* operates according to the repetitive logic of the sound-object. Conscience's performative utterance (to seek Piers, and to bring the poem to an end) forecloses the possibility of closure. The poem is stuck, it would seem, in one of Pierre Schaeffer's loops. *Piers Plowman*'s ending rejects the traditional mimetic narrative closure in which a story is told to readers who remain separate from the text, instead inviting its readers to participate in the continuing search for the poem's eponymous cipher.[96]

Chapter 6

# Disability, Music, and Chaucer's Advental Bodies

He sayd a lay, a maner song,
Withoute noote, withoute song.
—Geoffrey Chaucer, *The Book of the Duchess*

## Disabling Music and the Advental Body

The preceding chapters of this book have set forth a series of scenarios where the dominant frameworks of medieval music theory and performance—that flesh and mind are distinct loci of musical experience—are, at least momentarily, deactivated, held in suspension, or disabled. I use the term "disabled" intentionally here, as it is a useful one when thinking about sonic embodiment. First, in the broader sense of "to be rendered incapable of action or use; incapacitated; taken out of service," musical embodiment constantly disrupts normative definitional praxis. Second, in the more specific, theoretical sense of the term as defined by disability studies and critical disability theory as "having limits to activity, movement, and sensation that arise out of the body's political and social interaction with the affordances of its environment," sonic bodies are also, often, disabled ones.[1] Geoffrey Chaucer, this chapter argues, experiments with the body-disabling power of music as a site of poetic potential. For Chaucer, music is devastating to the body, but it also makes poetry happen. In Chaucer, sonic embodiment functions as a disabled body because it is presented as a constant site of delay and disjointed temporality.

In *Telling Flesh*, the contemporary feminist social theorist Vicki Kirby provides an account of the percussionist Evelyn Glennie, who has been deaf since the age of twelve. In spite of her deafness, Glennie perceives the world as sounding; her method of hearing sound involves her whole body, as she feels the orchestra playing through vibrations in her head, hands, and feet. "Sound," says Kirby, "is thus intricately scored and played through the staff of her body, recorded and performed in the very tissue of skin, blood, and bone."[2] Kirby argues that touch "impersonates sound because both [touch and sound] are underscored by the rhythm of a *différance* in which the body is never not musical."[3] "We have to listen to ourselves, first of all," Glennie herself has said of musical performance, linking the grip she has on her drumsticks—her embodied connection to her instrument—to the fluidity and precision of the sound she makes.[4] Kirby's language does not equate touch with sound, but instead uses the rhetorical figure of *impersonation*, recalling in turn the *persona*, and *personification* (*per* + *sona*) to describe the act of touching. Simultaneously performative and rhetorical, both material and textual, impersonation defines the body as an incantatory scene of its own inscription. "The body is the spacing of this game, the ma(r)king of an uncanny interlude," Kirby says.[5] From the Anglo-Latin *interludium* and *ludus* (play, game), the Middle English word *interlude* denotes a light or humorous dramatic, often musical, performance acted in between the longer scenes of medieval mystery plays or other somber performances.[6] The *interlude* is a space of time that is nonidentical to its own time, a time in which time is waiting to happen. When Glennie experiences the sounds of the orchestra through her own instrument-body-persona, she is always in a state of attention to the coming moment. The ludic, musical body is a disabled body, but it is also an anticipatory body, a body of postponement and delay. Similarly, Alison Kafer's *Feminist, Queer, Crip* argues that the disabled body is always temporally "out of joint," and that disabled bodies exist in "crip time," the delayed or extra time that it takes such bodies to travel or to accomplish tasks because of the insufficient affordances of the environment, as well as the promissory time in which curative medical treatments might allow the disabled subject "triumph over the mind or the body."[7] These curative futures are "endless deferral[s] that hold that body in thrall," simultaneously optimistic and insidious.[8] As with Kirby and Kafer, in Chaucer's work, the sonic body is an *advental* body: one that is always arriving but never arrives, a body that is promised but always in a state of deferral.

Speculative music treatises of the medieval period mark bodies, minds, and affects as normative and nonnormative, as orderly or disorderly—in short, as abled or disabled—based on the type of music they perform. Beginning with Boethius, academic writers on music differentiated between the *musicus* and the *cantor* based on the intellectual capacity of both. On the one hand, the *musicus,* who was a true musician, knew music theory and the abstract mathematical principles behind music; on the other, the *cantor,* was simply a rote singer of songs, someone whose intellect was too weak or unreliable to learn the philosophical basis of his songs.[9] This view held throughout the medieval period. As Marchettus of Padua says in his *Lucidarium* (1318–19),

> "The musician (*musicus*)," according to Boethius, "is he who possesses the faculty of judging modes, rhythms, and the genera of songs by reflection, according to the system of music theory." . . . The musician knows the power and nature of the musical proportions; he judges according to them, not according to sound alone. The singer (*cantor*) is, as it were, the tool (*instrumentum*) of that musician—who is an artisan in that he is occupied with a tool, but a musician inasmuch as he puts into practice what he has previously investigated through rational process. Thus the musician is to the singer as the judge to the herald. The judge sets things in order and commands the herald to proclaim them. So it is with the musician and the singer: the musician investigates, perceives, discerns, selects, orders, and disposes all things that touch on this science, and he commands the singer, who serves as his messenger, to put them into practice.[10]

For Marchettus, the musicality of a sound is dependent on the rational intentionality of the performing subject and the capacity of that individual to "investigate, perceive, discern, select, order, and dispose" according to a particular science. The *musicus* is fully human, while the *cantor,* the rote singer, is deanimated, demoted from the ranks of humanity to that of a mere instrument (*instrumentum*) of the *musicus,* serving as his tool and vessel.[11] Notably, then, it is not just the mind of the *cantor* that is disabled, but also his body: as an instrument played by the *musicus,* the *cantor*'s body assumes the subject-position of an inert object made passive by the definitional terms of music theory itself.[12]

Similar demotions of personhood are seen throughout music theory. In an often-quoted passage from Aelred of Rievaulx's *Speculum caritatis* (ca. 1150), "bad" music actively dehumanizes its singers: "Sometimes, and this is shameful to say, the voice is distorted into horses neighing, sometimes manly strength is set aside and it is sharpened into the high pitch of the female voice."[13] The wrong sort of music turns men into animals, or worse, into women. While this might initially seem nothing more than a derogatory statement, in a medieval philosophical and medical framework that understood the female body to be a deficient male body, medieval hierarchies of being mobilize this metaphor of gender and animality not only to insult, but to demarcate these singers as functionally disabled. Aelred's misogynistic, queer-phobic assessment yokes the fragility of masculinity to the potentiality of an able body to be read as incapacitated—that is, female—when it performs music incorrectly.[14] As medieval music theory demarcates itself as a subject, it simultaneously invokes what Alison Kafer terms a "compulsory able-bodiedness and able-mindedness."[15]

When Jacobus wrote his *Speculum musicae* in the early fourteenth century, he would echo these claims: "Some of [the *moderni*] apply hocket (*hoketant*) too much, they break consonant (*consonantiis*) notes too often, run up and divide up, they leap in unsuitable places, they clash, they bellow (*saltant, hurcant, iupant*), and they yelp and bark in the manner of dogs (*ad modum canis hawant, latrant*), and like insane people (*amentes*), they take nourishment from a disorganized and convoluted ruckus, they use a harmony that is far removed from nature."[16] Jacobus, like Aelred, dehumanizes singers he thinks are bad, calling them *amentes* or fools—literally, people with mental deficiencies—and describing their songs in animalistic terms. Here, musical performance and embodiment are contingent upon each other: the body is disabled because it performs bad music; the music is bad because it is sung by bodies dispossessed of legitimacy. As these examples illustrate, medieval music theory's definition of itself is formulated on an ableist dichotomy of *capability* and *inability*, aligning musicality with able or normative embodiment, neurotypicality, and intellectual achievement, and noise or bad music with bodies that are disorderly or illegitimate.

If the normative definition of "music" in speculative music treatises emerges out of a framework of ability-disability, then, in order to challenge this framework, it is appropriate to look to moments in medieval literature where singers and songs go awry, where music-makers are made by the narrative or understand themselves to be instrumentalized and agentially demoted, or where the music they sing is insufficient, incomplete, or bad. Such examples are frequent in Chaucer's poetry, primarily in the *Canterbury Tales*, where musical performance nearly always causes narrative tension (that is, where the performance of music is an instrument or tool of the narrative). The disabling of singing bodies is central to the *Tales'* thematics, its narrative structure, its social critique, and the ways that it creates convincing narrative subjects for its fiction. Examples are manifold, and have already been noted by scholars, particularly by Bruce Holsinger and Carolyn Dinshaw: for instance, in the General Prologue, the queer bodies of the Pardoner and Summoner are performed in songs that leave them vulnerable to ridicule and ostracization, but also serve as potential threats to the cohesion of the Canterbury group as a whole.[17] In the *Knight's Tale,* Arcita prays to Mars for help in his battle against his cousin, but the jangling music that answers his prayers portends his death, rather than his victory.[18] In the *Prioress' Tale, musica humana* has, in Holsinger's words, "gone awry," as acts of singing coalesce into scenes of violence directed first at the clergeon's body and then on the Jewish community as a whole.[19] In the *Second Nun's Tale,* Saint Cecilia "sings to God allone in [her] heart"; and this moment of silent, interior song heightens the spiritual force of her violent beheading.[20] In the *Nun's Priest's Tale,* the rooster Chaunticleer closes his eyes and stretches out his neck to sing, only to have a wily fox grab him in his rapacious mouth.[21] Singing bodies are a driving force of the *Tales'* satire, but they are also meticulously and consistently subjected to physical and emotional violence that leaves them vulnerable, incapacitated, and otherwise demoted as subjects. The disabling, disfiguring, or disorderly rhetorics of sonic embodiment in Chaucer's poetry serve the function of what David T. Mitchell and Sharon L. Snyder call narrative or figurative prosthesis: that is, his poems deploy musical disability in order to further plot or to stress the moral, ethical, or allegorical valences of a text without necessarily dwelling upon the social constructions by which disability is coded, entrenched, or erased.[22] Chaucer's use of music in the *Canterbury Tales* prosthetizes disability.

At the same time that these acts of violence and marginalization serve to instrumentalize the narrative subjects doing the singing, the fabric out of which these characters are created—the way that they become the *tools* and *elements* or the *cogs* in the narrative machinery of the *Tales* themselves—is through their formal and narratological shift from active singing bodies to the passive subjects of violence. Chaucer's use of music in the *Tales* does more than simply prosthetize disability. It formalizes it, yoking it to poesis and to narratology, shedding light on human difference even as it instrumentalizes it. In a compelling study of Chaucer's *Monk's Tale,* for instance, Jonathan Hsy argues that poetic form—and not just narrative—allows the contemplation of disability by subverting audience expectations; "attending to the complexity of literary form," he says, "goes hand-in-hand with an ongoing appreciation for the range of human variance across time."[23] If bodies are, in Hsy's terms, depicted as "disorderly" in textual narratives, then a textual form might also—as form both reflects and determines content—similarly and simultaneously depict, structure, and call attention to such disorder. In this way, the formal imperfections of a piece of literature not only stand witness to, but actually textually embody, human variance. Similarly, both Julie Avril Minich and Sami Schalk discuss at length how disability theory, as a methodology, "involves scrutinizing not bodily or mental impairments but the social norms that define particular attributes as impairments, as well as the social conditions that concentrate stigmatized attributes in particular populations."[24] The body is both real and a text; and, as the body becomes textual, texts, too, through genre, form, narrative, and rhetorical tropes, become bodies. Often, as Hsy argues, in medieval narratives, the disabled body appears in a text in order to be "rehabilitated, fixed, cured, or offered as an exemplum"; but in Chaucer's poetry, as Hsy notes, the sonic body does not seek a cure; instead, it dwells in the insistent, never-to-come future in which it will be made whole.[25] Chaucer's investment in music, violence, disabling rhetorics, and the development of character is sustained and central to the collusion and complicity that Chaucer builds between his texts and his readers that allow them to be read as fiction.[26] As Jonathan Hsy and Julie Orlemanski argue, it is this specific function of disability theory to "reframe the relationship between embodiment and literary form," as Hsy puts it, or, as Orlemanski does, to understand how character might itself arise out of forms of disability, that Chaucer explores in his poetry, where disability structures narrative possibility as well as forms of reading.[27] Chaucer's singers, and the *Tales*, are comprised of the difference between the able body and the disenabled, "disorderly" one.

Finally, if asynchrony and the deferral of music are important to Chaucer's poetry, they are also important to his conception of himself as a poet, and part of a rhetoric of disability linked to musical performance in his work more generally. In the retraction to the *Canterbury Tales* at the end of the *Parson's Tale,* Chaucer begs forgiveness for composing "many a song and many a lecherous lay"; certainly, in addition to the many singers of the *Tales* and his other poems, Chaucer's poetry appropriates and adapts French and Italian songs and the *metra* of Boethius.[28] But, if he ever composed such songs, none are definitively known to survive.[29]

Nevertheless, although Eustache Deschamps refers to Chaucer's *noble plant* and *douce melodie* in his famous *ballade* to Chaucer, unlike his Italian contemporary the poet-musician Francesco Landini, or his French contemporary Guillaume de Machaut, who left a long trail of *dits* with intercalated and notated lyrics as well as individual pieces of notated ballades, complaints, and rondeaux, Chaucer never appears to have gathered notated musical work in an authorial collection, and none of his notated music—if there ever was any—survives.[30] Nevertheless, we do have poetry that records the traces of absent music. Musical disability, deferral, and delay—to borrow loosely from both Kirby and Kafer—are what gives Chaucer's poetry space to play.

There are a number of moments in Chaucer's poetry in which sonic bodies inhabit crip asynchronies for the purposes of poesis: the body of Echo in the *Franklin's Tale*, the lyric *I* in the triple ballad *Fortune*, with its resonances for the formal structure of Chaucer's dream poetry, and Troilus's body in *Troilus and Criseyde*.[31] By casting the body of music into the elsewhen, Chaucer authorizes his poetic project.

## The *Franklin's Tale*, Adventality, and the Voice That Remains

The *Franklin's Tale,* Shawn Normandin argues, is about the iterability of language and about the consequences that words have beyond and outside their original contexts. Although its meaning might change, a speech or a piece of writing retains meaning, and therefore ethical force. When Dorigen promises to sleep with Aurelius if he can remove the "grisly feendly rokkes blake" around the Brittany coast, her utterance triggers a moral paradox that cannot be solved by casuistry, but only by mercy.[32] "Dorigen's playful promise morphs into a serious one," Normandin says. "She does not pretend that her intentions can arrest her language's iterability."[33] This is also why Aurelius is described as Echo longing for Narcissus: as Aurelius repeats Dorigen's promise back to her, he performs the tale's—and Ovid's myth's—"dramatization of the necessarily repetitive and citable nature of language."[34]

But Chaucer's use of the myth of Echo and Narcissus does more than refer to the semantics of language. If able-bodiedness and able-mindedness are normally requirements for meaningful or musical utterances, the mythical figure of Echo (who is without a body and without a voice of her own) allows Chaucer to explore the role of sound and meaning-making beyond restrictive ableist discourse. In the Ovidian myth and its medieval retellings, Echo's body is not simply disabled; it is entirely absent. This is a limit case of the embodied subject and its capacity to make meaningful sound as necessarily able-bodied. When the Franklin describes Aurelius not only as a sorrowing "Ekko" who "langwissheth as a furye dooth in helle / and dye he most . . . For Narcisus," but also, in the same breath, as a musician composing "in his songes . . . manye layes / songes, compleintes, roundels, [and] virelayes," this provides a tantalizing opportunity to watch a sonic body perform in spite of limitations that would otherwise render it amusical.[35] In casting Aurelius in the role of Echo, the *Franklin's Tale* places an advental body at the thematic heart of its narrative. It specifically uses the body—and its ability to be present, to speak for itself, and to be taken seriously—as a means of considering meaning.

In medieval discourse, the term "echo" always implies the voice of an advental body. The ultimate source for definitions of "echo" is Aristotle's *De anima*, which serves as the dominant paradigm for physical descriptions of an echo, where an echo is described as a "rebounding of noise."[36] Thus John Trevisa, in his translation of Ranulph of Higden's *Polychronicon,* quotes Aristotle verbatim: "Ecco is the reboundynge of noyse."[37] However, while Aristotle and Ranulph/Trevisa understand an echo as *noise*—that is, *vox inarticulata*—when echo is defined in literature, religious texts, and music theory, it is not so spuriously denigrated. For Jacobus, for instance, an echo is a "new sound": "If a sound, after it has been produced, runs up against an obstacle, the air is beat back and, just as if it were [a] new [sound] (*quasi novus . . . sonus*), a sound is produced that is very similar to the first, which is called 'echo.'"[38] Similarly, the Wycliffite Bible hears echoes "sownynge aȝen fro hiȝeste hillis."[39] *Jacob's Well,* a fourteenth-century sermon collection, goes so far as to give an echo the potency of articulate speech, defining echo as "a *voys* that reboundyth aȝen, whan a man spektyh aȝen a wode."[40] Where does the capacity of echoes to produce legitimate sound originate?

A closer look at Ranulph's and Trevisa's description of the echo in its context in the *Polychronicon* makes the origins of echo-as-voice clear: medieval definitions of an echo are imbued with the rhetorical force of prosopoeia; echo is always already Echo. While the most concise, technical definition of "echo" understands it as "noise," the fuller context of Ranulph's treatise makes it clear that echo arises out of a classicizing mythopoesis:

Thessalia ioyneth in the south side to Macedonia, and was somtyme Achilles contray, and there bygonne Lapithe; thilke men chastisede and temede hors firste with bridels, and sette on hire bakkes; therfore the lewed people wende that it were alle on body, man and hors that they sitte on. And therfore an hondred horsmen of Thessalia were i-cleped *centaury*. That name is i-gadered of tweyne, of *centum*, that is, *an hondred*, and of *aura*, that is, *the wynde*. And so that name was to hem i-schappe *Centauri*, as it were an hundred wynde waggers: for they wagged wel the wynde faste in hir ridynge. In this prouince is the hille Parnassus; (poetis accounteth that hil noble and famous;) and hongeth with tweie copped stones. In the cop therof is the temple of Delphicus Apollo; and in the wyndynge of the myddel playn is a pitte, oute of that pitte philosofres were enspired; and dyuers answeres were i-yeue out of that pitte. Therfore yif noyse of men other of trompes sowneth in the valey, the stones answereth euerich other, and dyuers ecco sowneth. Ecco is the reboundynge of noyse.[41]

Even this impersonal, naturalized, and technical Echo is aligned with a world that exoticizes and impersonates the resonant space of echoic sound; Echo arises concomitant with the origin of the monstrous centaur and adjacent to the pit of Delphic inspiration.

In other words, Echo is more than its scientific definition; it is—she is—a figure born of mythopoeia and prosopopoiea, out of Ovid's *Metamorphoses* and the many moralizing and thematizing allegorical renderings of Ovid found in the *Ovide moralise* and texts like the *Polychronicon*. In the original Ovidian tale, Echo, a handmaid to Juno, spends her days chatting to her mistress, distracting her from Jupiter's chain of sexual escapades, liaisons, rapes, and general infidelity. As a result, Juno curses Echo so that Echo can "only repeat the last of what is spoken and returns the words she hears." Echo leaves the court of Juno, falls in love with Narcissus, and in one of the most beautiful tricks of language in Ovid's playful Latin, woos him and is rejected by him in his own words. Sick with unrequited love, Echo's body wastes away until she is nothing but bones and a voice and until those bones, in turn, are turned to stone. "Her voice remains (*vox manet*). She hides in the woods, no longer to be seen on the hills, but to be heard by everyone. It is sound that lives in her (*sonus est, qui vivit in illa*)."[42]

Echo exists in a paradoxical crossing point in animacy hierarchies that ascribe meaning to the voice. Echo is rock (pure matter, moved by sound but unable to make her own sound), like the "rokkes blake" upon which the narrative of the *Franklin's Tale* turns; by making Aurelius Echo, the tale aligns Aurelius with the very rocks he causes to disappear, in a double removal of self and a demotion of agency. By making him Echo, the *Franklin's Tale* raises the level of pathos through an act of associative dehumanization. But in making Aurelius Echo, that tale is, also literally, giving him the status of pure voice: *vox manet*. On the one hand, it would be wrong to deny Echo intentionality: although the *form* of her responses to Narcissus can only repeat the falling cadences of his speech, she nevertheless *deploys* those sounds as a carrier of her own volitional intention. But Echo cannot speak for herself. As a voice, Echo is not the "investigator, perceptor, discerner, selector, orderer, and disposer" (*cognoscit, sentit, discernti, religit, ordinat et disponit*) of Marchettus of Padua's *Lucidarium*. She is entirely and completely relational.

How does the medieval period account for Echo? As Elizabeth Dobbs notes, medieval moralizing adaptations like the *Ovide moralise*, Pierre Bersuires' *Ovideius moralizatus*, John of Garland's *Integumenta,* and others variously ascribe to Echo the role of back-biter, chatterbox, scold, complaining servant, or manipulator.[43] In the *Ayenbite of Inwit*, Echo is a flatterer, someone who eschews truth for preferment: "The uerthe zenne is. that huanne alle zingeth 'Placebo.' thet is to zigge: 'mi lhord zayth zoth. mi lhord deth wel.' and wendeth to guode al thet the guodeman deth other zayth. by hit guod by hit kuead. And theruore hy byeth ycleped ine the writinge: ecko. thet is the rearde thet ine the heye helles comth ayen and acordeth to al thet men him zayth. by hit guod by hit kuead. by hit zoth by hi uals."[44] In each of these cases, Echo's speech, far from being emptied of meaning, actually has *malicious intent*; it is language that reflects the speech back to itself to do damage. Moreover, Echo is to be feared because she exists to turn Narcissus into Narcissus/a narcissist, to manipulate others, to lure them into self-gratulatory and unreflective thinking. Echo brings the myth of Narcissus into being.[45]

This is what makes Chaucer's use of the Echo-Narcissus myth in the *Franklin's Tale* so interesting. Chaucer first worked through Echo in his translation of Guillaume de Lorris's portion of the *Roman de la rose*, where Echo crosses genders, playing the role not of the love-object of the *Roman*, but instead serving as a representation of the figure of Amant. When Echo dies in this retelling of the myth, she (now a he, Amant) curses Narcissus (now cast as the female love-object) to die, thus giving both Chaucer and Guillaume the opportunity to engage in a form of misogynist moralizing: ladies who reject the advances of desiring lovers come to bad ends, they say. It is this version of the myth that serves as the source for Aurelius in the *Franklin's Tale*, who, as Echo, uses her tale as a strategy for seduction and coercion:

> Withouten coppe he drank al his penaunce.
> He was despeyred; no thyng dorste he seye,
> Save in his songes somwhat wolde he wreye
> His wo, as in a general compleynyng;
> He seyde he lovede and was biloved no thyng.
> Of swich matere made he manye layes,
> Songes, compleintes, roundels, virelayes,
> How that he dorste nat his sorwe telle,
> But langwissheth as a furye dooth in helle;
> And dye he most, he seyde, as did Ekko
> For Narcisus, that dorste nat telle hir wo.[46]

Echo, who is allegorized as a manipulator when her body is female, becomes the object of pathos and redemption when the desiring echo is male.[47] In this moment, too, Aurelius's identity as a musician is particularly important: it is through his performance as a singer that his very specific feelings are turned into "general compleynyng," the songs serving as a form of occultatio. If a characteristic of musicianship in the late medieval period was to sever the composer's or musician's affects from the emotion latent in a particular song—to, as Machaut did, compose sad tunes while in a happy state of mind, or vice versa—then Aurelius uses this artistic and performative convention to conceal the fact that, indeed, his song's affects and his own are intimately aligned. *Ars adeo latet arte sua*, says Ovid in the *Metamorphoses*, fittingly, in the tale of Pygmalion, one of Orpheus's songs: "Thus art hides itself in art."[48] For Aurelius, now Echo, the gap between the self and the song is measured, strangely enough, in terms of the alignment of his "songes, compleintes, roundels, [and] virelayes" with his emotional state; through song he creates a lag or gap—a ludic space.

If Gayatri Spivak argues that Echo doesn't "own" herself, that she is a subaltern subject whose meaning is alienated from herself, what is happening in Chaucer's narrative of Aurelius-as-Echo is a telling, if disturbing, recuperation of Echo's agency. Chaucer appoints Echo to the role of subject by transmuting her into a figure of a young man whose undesired advances threaten to overwhelm the equal marriage contracted between Dorigen and Arveragus; and, while Aurelius begins the tale as the narrative's heel, he ends it—ostensibly—as its hero. The *Franklin's Tale* turns Echo into a narrative subject by making her masculine; the tale also makes women complicit in their own seduction by asking them to empathize with (female) Echo for the benefit of the (male) lover. This text furthermore forms the preconditions in which narcissism as a "female" disease would later become possible: Echo becomes man so that Narcissus might become woman, transmuting the youthful masculine body of the Ovidian narrative into the cold and distant female object of courtly love. Echo is always iterable, always rematerializing, always taking shape, not only as a voice within her narrative, but as a myth appropriated and adapted for particular discursive and political ends.

As Echo and her—or his—accounts in medieval metaphor and allegory show, disembodiment and nonintentionality are really not barriers to meaningful voicing. Rather, it is precisely the inchoate nature of Echo and the disabled, dematerialized, or disembodied source of the echo's sound that provides Echo with its force; this force is *relational*, bound up in a history of sexual coercion that is prior to semantics. That is, Echo is caught in an intersecting fabric of dispossession and disembodiment: on the one hand, between Juno and Jupiter, to whom she is a servant, and to Jupiter and Narcissus, for whom she is a female love-object, and it is these sets of relationalities that cause her both to lose her body and to gain her—echoic— voice. Echo's disembodiment, her lack of place, and her shifting body make her appropriable into systems of narrative meaning. Through prosopopoeia, she/he/it might be deployed to invest Aurelius's song with affective, seductive intent, where the "echo" is a reservoir of meaning. Echo's deferred voice is both disabled and, in the *Franklin's Tale*, enabled to sing for the purposes of patriarchy and male desire. In Chaucer's retelling of the myth of Echo and Narcissus, the relationship between sound and the voice is advental: always on the horizon, but never appearing. The voice remains, but the body is absent, delayed, or deferred, a body that, like Glennie's body, participates in this work of sonority at a remove. The endless deferral of sonic embodiment is a type of crip asynchrony, a hiccup in time that allows poesis to occur.

## The Advental Body and Palpable Absence
## in the *Ballade de Fortune* and *The Book of the Duchess*

In Chaucer's *Ballade de Fortune* and *The Book of the Duchess*, the invocation of music has formal and structural repercussions for advental bodies. In each of these poems—one a French *forme fixe* lyric and the other a narrative poem drawing heavily from French dream poetry—disability, musicality, and delay are overlaid upon each other in the construction of the subject. If, as Hsy argues, "the complexity of literary form goes hand-in-hand with an ongoing appreciation for the range of human variance across time," then these two poems in particular textually embody human variance through their performance of cyclicality and endless deferral.[49]

In the *Ballade de Fortune*, Chaucer constructs a musical body that, through the process of temporal deferral, never arrives at the scene of its own inscription. *Fortune* is a triple ballade in which voicing alternates between a human *pleintif* and the personification of Fortune. The first ballade, which is voiced by the *pleintif*, bewails the speaker's betrayal by and continued reliance upon Fortune: each stanza ends with the refrain "For fynally, Fortune, I thee defye!" in a particularly unconvincing proclamation of independence.[50] In the second ballade, Fortune defends herself, saying that not only is every person subject to her vicissitudes, but also that, by teaching *pleintif* both joy and sorrow, she has provided him with pragmatic and experiential knowledge. The final ballade alternates between the two speakers: a single stanza in which the *pleintif* rejects Fortune before giving way, in the final two stanzas and the closing *envoy*, to Fortune, who defends herself by pointing to the eternal, "resteles travayle" of the world; her actions are not cruel, but normal.[51]

*Fortune* is given the title *Balades de Visages sanz Peinture* (Ballades on a Face Without Painting) in a number of manuscripts. This ambiguous name heightens the palpability of the absent bodies at play in the text of the poem: in the context of lyric, what does it mean for a "face" to be "without painting"? Is this meant to be a poem that reveals its lyric speakers or singers in their naked states, unmasked? Or does the title refer to the work of personification, to prosopopoeia, where faces are not painted, but rather framed with words?[52] Of course, even words might "paint" a picture, but, in the case of *Fortune*, the ballade lacks visual metaphors; both Fortune and the *pleintif* are unfigured, their bodies not visualizable, the personification hinging on the sound object rather than on ekphrasis. The poem forges selves that are always of the moment, arising and passing away as the exigencies of affect, argument, or dialectic require; the speaking subjects constructed in this exchange "fix the plan and the modalities of discourse," as Paul Zumthor argues.[53] These are bodies made of words. Lyric challenges what it means to exist; the lyric *I* is the product of dianoia, of the emergence of a "self" out of discursive thought, a self whose ontological position does not proceed from any metaphysical a priori, but instead emanates from the act of voicing. Personification and lyric embodiment hinge on the voice. For the *plein-tif*, this is a body that exists in a state of subjunctive and contradictory un-singing, calling the refrain into the text for the sake of the lyric subject even as that same refrain is rejected. "Fynally, Fortune, I thee defye," repeats the lyric self in the refrain of the first ballade.[54] The *pleintif*'s defiance occurs in some final moment, some moment yet to come but never arriving, as the ballade structure simply repeats in cyclical form the refrain from stanza to stanza. Most importantly, this act of defiance occurs in an act of *not-singing*, of not allowing the music to burst into the poetic line in order to rupture the amusicality of the ballade. The lack of Fortune's favor, the *pleintif* says,

> Nay may not don me singen though I die
> *Jay tout perdu mon temps et mon labour.*[55]

In spite of Fortune's fickleness, the narrator refuses to lament, but in refus-ing to sing the song, the narrator calls the song into being through its own negation. The landscape of this poem is a dissolved body that exists in other-space.[56]

The ballade form of the poem itself recalls music in the absence of music, as the unnotated French *form fixe* stands in for the French song the narrator leaves unsung. In the narrator's final defiance of Fortune (a mo-ment of rejection that never arrives), he addresses her and is woven into the fabric of her mutability. The future, the contrafactual, and the subjunctive play a central role in framing corporeality and subjectivity, as the narrator imagines himself as a subject invested in what has not yet occurred: in the possibility of things being better than they are, of a time that he does not need to sing *jay tout perdu mon temps et mon labour*. Lyric play is deferral, a deferral that is drawn out over the three connected ballades and *envoy* that make up *Fortune*'s triple-ballad structure. But this deferral does not end in the narrator's reinscription into good fortune and thus the assumption of a singing body that might, in all truth, *refuse* to sing *jay tout perdu*. Instead, it ends with the disintegration of the narrator's lyric body as his complaint is dismissed and Fortune, the more persuasive of the two legal subjects, wins the case, and silences the *pleintif* once and for all: "Lat nat this man on me thus crye and pleyne," she says.[57] His lyric body disintegrated, Fortune denies the *pleintif* his body in denying him the right to sing. *Fortune* contemplates a body that is always not-bringing-itself-into-presence, always coming and never arriving.

The missing song of Chaucer's *Fortune* is a microcosm of the work music does in Chaucer's poetry, especially in his dream poetry, where songs are simultaneously sung and held in abeyance, both present and absent, and where they articulate bodies that are always about-to-be but are never realized. In the dream poems, bodies and music play off each other as sites of impossibility, implicating narratorial and confessional acts that deny, lose, or deconstruct song, disabling their singers in the process.

In *The Book of the Duchess,* the silencing of music is further complicated by Chaucer's adaptation of French narrative *dits* that include intercalated lyrics (and would have included notated music in the case of Machaut's manuscripts). By removing lyric variation and experimentation—flattening the wide variety of French *formes fixes* into a single running iambic tetrameter—Chaucer actively and intentionally de-musics his French sources.

The silencing of music, and its concomitant effects on the body of the knight, also appears in the poem's narrative. When the narrator stumbles upon the Black Knight in the forest, he is sitting, Orpheus-like, bewailing the loss of his beloved White, and singing a song without music. Chaucer borrowed the Knight's complaint in large part from Machaut's third motet (*Quare non sum mortuus*—Why did I not die?).[58] Here, however, Machaut's musical polyphony has been silenced:

> He sayd a lay, a maner song,
> Withoute noote, withoute song.[59]

Chaucer's invocation of Machaut's motet refuses the musical form even as it accepts his text; rather than incorporating music into his poem, Chaucer strips the Knight, and his complaint, of song. While "sayd" here has the potential to mean "sing"—as it of course often does in the many references in medieval romance and elsewhere to the "saying of masses"—the specifically spoken nature of the "sayd" lay here is reinforced by the following line, where the song is described as being "withoute noote, withoute song." In addition, not only does the lay lack the musical notes of its Machautian subtext, but it also lacks the formal or rhythmic and rhymed variety of *formes fixes* intercalated in the longer, narrative *dits* of fourteenth-century French poetry, as evidenced by the metrical qualities of this spoken song:

"Allas, deth, what ayleth the,
That thou noldest have taken me,
Whan thou toke my lady swete,
That was so fair, so fresh so fre,
So good that men may wel se
Of al goodnesse she had no mete!"[60]

The song is without "noote" (a word that gestures to the type of notated music seen throughout Machaut's works); it is also without "song" (the *son,* the sound, or rhythm).[61] The only remnant of musicality here occurs in the final lines of the song, where the narrative's couplets give way to a unique *aabaab* rhyming pattern. However, this *aabaab* scheme was troubling to early modern editors; Thynne's edition of 1536 rearranges the lines and adds a new one at line 479, a line that most modern editions omit while numbering the lines as if it were included. In other words, even if the poem's shift in the final six lines of the lay was intended to mime musicality, its change is small enough to be read as unintentional; the English reading audience—at least by the early sixteenth century—was not primed to look to Chaucer for formal variation in embedded lyric. Nevertheless, the variable rhyme remains a call to consider the Knight's embodied and affective dissonance, cueing a formal manifestation of the melancholia that characterizes his *plaint*'s thematics. The ambiguity of musical sonority here actively breaks down neat delineations between poetry and music, granting poetry the ability to invoke musicality even in the absence of "noote" or "song."

That the Black Knight suffers from debilitating melancholia has often been noted in scholarship.[62] For a medieval audience, melancholia was not simply sadness, but instead, a complex physiological, psycho-embodied way of being that affected mind and body as a *gestalt* as a result of a humoral imbalance, a disabling condition often aligned with and understood as a form of *accidia* or *acedia*, that is, the deadly sin of Sloth.[63] By interpreting melancholianot only as disabling—and medieval accounts often do, either making melancholics out to be incapacitated (as, for instance, Hoccleve does of himself in the *Complaint*) or (as in the case of Gaspar Ofhuys's account of Hugo van der Goes's melancholia) as moral exempla—but also sinful, these discourses marginalize the sufferer without considering the sort of environmental affordances that might allow melancholia legitimacy as a way of being in the world.[64]

Through the figure of the Black Knight, *The Book of the Duchess* portrays a musician-artist suffering from a form of both mental and physical disability that manifests as affective as well as compositional and formal, its music stripped bare and its meter compromised.[65]

If it is a truism that, in the fourteenth century, there is an "implied musical setting" for all poetry, even when no musical notation exists, this lyric moment is still explicitly distanced from musicality through its insistence on flattening formal variation, which conjures an absence, both of bodies and of music itself, in order to entrench the capacity of the poetic line itself as musical. The unsinging of the Knight, and the identification of the lack of song with White, recognize the present as a moment of silence, even though the poem's own past is marked by song. Not only is White identified with song—in his first encounter with White, the Black Knight "sawgh hyr daunce so comlily, carole and synge so swetely"; her voice is described as being truer than a mass sung by the pope—but the Knight also once positioned himself as the ideal composer-poet-lover, going so far as to recount his "firste song" to the narrator.[66] However, within the context of the poem's present, both White, and musicality, are lost. In its place is a recurring textual refrain that the Knight says three times in the poem:

"Thou wost ful lytel what thou menest;
I have lost more than thow wenest."[67]

The repeated refrain of the Black Knight "I have lost more than thow wenest" injects the narrative with its own, blatantly amusical refrain, calling attention both to the Knight's inability to overcome his sorrow *and* the Dreamer's capacity for structured composition with attention to musical *formes fixes*.

In a sense, the final lines of the poem call to mind the carefully structured narrative that is the dream, encapsulated as it is by the asymmetrical waking frames. By devoicing the Knight, Chaucer calls attention to the structure of the poem and the Dreamer as the creator of the poem. Along with this comes the "play" of reading, which, as the narrator remarks in the opening, is "better play / Then playe either at ches or tables."[68] Furthermore, a comparative reading of this opening fragment shows that Chaucer privileges the text over the song from the beginning; the written book provides consolation for sorrows that a sung lament can only re-perform. Text takes the place of song; the poem takes over the intercalated lyric.[69]

The "play" of reading becomes, therefore, in the final lines of the poem, the narrator's response to the musical play of the Machautian *dits*. As the narrator "wol, be processe of tyme, fonde to put this sweven in ryme," so Chaucer creates a polyphony of reading, first when the dream is remembered, then again when it is set in rhyme, again upon a first reading by the audience, and, once more, given a final reading as the strange self-reflexive *envoy* programs a final rereading into the poem itself, not to mention the comparative reading that would occur in any English text based on the French courtly lyric. The necessary obligation to both recall and imaginatively reconstruct—the cyclic structure of the poem as a whole—brings to mind the structure of Machaut's *Ma fin est mon commencement*: a sort of narrative rondeau. In a sense, these different types of reading serve as the tenor, duplum, triplum, and quadruplum of the poem, a more appropriate way of thinking Chaucer's appropriation (and the Dreamer's recasting) of Machaut than that of "source" and "adaptation" or even of "hypotext" and "hypertext," as it implies both separate lines of music and the harmonic interplay between the French and English texts.

As Chaucer translates the poems of Machaut, so he also translates the world of the dream, turning the French *songe* into his own sort of song. Instead of listening to *l'Amant's complainte* that will lull him to sleep, Chaucer's narrator falls into a dream through the use of his own, already-written narrative poem. The "song" then becomes the dream and the dream is the text of the narrative constructed by the poet, which Chaucer makes very clear at the end that he has had under construction all along. When he says, then, that "there is physicien but oone / That may me hele, but it is don,"[70] these words take on a new power. In the rereading, in attending to *The Book of the Duchess* as a multivoiced text, crying at the end for a second reading with the narrator's intentions in mind, we see Chaucer's narrator *already* retelling us the story the *first* time in a medicinal recollection-composition that is his "physicien." Through the text-as-song, the narrator )and Chaucer through him) heals *himself* through the creation of text, a further appropriation of the Grocheian palliative understanding of music, although here the lyric is specifically amusical. Even as the narrator dreams an irrevocable loss for the Black Knight, constructing the Knight himself as a sort of absence, his black dress a sign both of mourning and of negative presence, out of this absence the narrator constructs, through obsessive repetition and cyclicality, a textual whole. Both Blanche's and the Black Knight's bodies are advental; *The Book of the Duchess* is a textual whole constructed out of this physical and musical lack. This, in essence, is Chaucer's "song": a text that deprives the Knight of music while simultaneously healing himself as a poet through the articulation of this narrative's florid amusicality. It is this unvoiced and then resung version of Machaut that allows Chaucer, as an author, to present John of Gaunt with an ameliorative text, a piece that, performed under the aegis of the court, simultaneously heals and makes claims for the power of Chaucer as physician.

In a thoughtful study of idleness, melancholia, and homosociality in *The Book of the Duchess*, Adin Lears argues that "the paradoxical figures" that people the poem perform a "poetics of idling" that "marvelously render[s] passive into active, idle into creative, and, finally suggest a queer way to make something from nothing."[71] This is a compelling reading, but I would like to suggest that the form of *The Book of the Duchess*, in its return to its opening and to the scene of its own inscription in the final lines of the frame narrative, presents us with a formal performance of an eternal deferral of this "making"—the Knight is never healed; he remains melancholic, and the text provides for no resolution of his disability; and the poem echoes these narrative elements through its resistance to closure. It is fitting that both at the center of the *Ballade de Fortune* and in *The Book of the Duchess* sits a body that is somehow incapacitated, or disabled, by this futurity. Both poems perform their own adventality.

## Troilus and Criseyde

The ending of *Troilus and Criseyde* has troubled scholarship of the poem for years; it has been called an "illogical solution of the philosophical problem[s]" outlined in the poem's narrative, where classical historiography, Boethian philosophy, and a Dantean cosmos are expected to exist side by side.[72] But if we interpret Chaucerian poetry as creating sites of advental sonic embodiment, this can help us to understand what is happening when Troilus takes leave of the earth—and of his body—in his laughing, musical apotheosis. Here, the object of redemption in *Troilus* is not Troilus; this is not the promise of a maimed body that might be left behind for a better one (the type of body promised to the chronically disabled as a means of triggering the sorts of cruel optimism that hold the disabled body against itself).[73] Instead, Troilus's laughter amid his apotheosis performs the healing and restitution of the work of poesis, which serves as a supplement for the absent, advental, or impossible body.

*Troilus and Criseyde* is a poem interwoven with music. These musical moments are times when the narrative halts its forward progress to mourn the problems of being an embodied singer. In the *Canticus Troili*, for instance, Troilus recites an English translation of Petrarch's Sonnet 88 (*S'amore non è*), where Troilus weeps for Criseyde's absence, for her physical separation from him. But while Troilus's complaint is called a song, the narrator makes sure to note that Troilus does not actually sing for us:

> I dar wel seyen, in al, that Troilus
> Seyde in his song, loo, every word right thus
> As I shal seyn; and whoso list it here,
> Loo, next this vers he may it fynden here.[74]

Like the Black Knight in *The Book of the Duchess*, Troilus's song is missing a melody; the text gestures to an idea of song, but it, like Criseyde, is absent.[75] Throughout the poem, songs and singing mark deferral and loss: Criseyde's friend Antigone sings a song of love; Troilus sings three songs; when he and Criseyde are together (briefly), Troilus spends all his day "in blisse and in singynges" (III.1716); when Criseyde is forced to leave Troy she sings a "pleinte" because she must leave the man she calls "her Orpheus" (IV.791).

For the most part, *Troilus and Criseyde*'s musical moments are like music elsewhere in Chaucer's poems: they portray bodies trying, and failing, to sing effectively; Troilus's songs and letters will not bring Criseyde back, and they cannot save him from his eventual death. Like the Black Knight in *The Book of the Duchess*, Troilus and *Troilus* are—as David Aers has noted—a rumination on melancholia and "perpetual anxiety," thus linking the production of music with chronic mental and physical disability.[76]

But the final scene in *Troilus* reimagines the relationship of music to the body, and therefore is also able to reimagine the power of song. Here, at the very end of the text, Troilus has been abandoned by Criseyde, has been killed, and is ascending into heaven:

> And whan that he was slayn in this manere,
> His lighte goost ful blisfully is went
> Up to the holughnesse of the eigththe spere,
> In convers letyng everich element;
> And ther he saugh with ful avysement
> The erratik sterres, herkenyng armonye
> With sownes ful of hevenyssh melodie.
> . . .

And in himself he lough right at the wo
Of hem that wepten for his deth so faste.[77]

Troilus's laugh to himself is a facsimile of medieval music: the "ha-ha-ha" of his silent laughter is actually very similar to the rearticulated "a-a-a" found throughout medieval song: from the perpetual angelic *Hosanna* sung by the angelic choirs to the *iubilus* of medieval *Alleluias*, which allow for a distension of the fabric of song, as the rearticulation of the monosyllabic "a" pushes the musical line forward while holding the text in abeyance, like the broken air of the hocket, or like the repeated gasps and invocations performed by the mystic as he or she experiences the rapture of the spirit. Laughter, like all of these other examples, is a form of extended, rearticulated breath, and Troilus's "haha!" is also a celestial inversion of the "Ah, ah!" of his earlier complaint, his tragic song that is the expression of a body in pain. This final section of the poem suggests that the poetic line and not its sonic effects have been the proper "body" of music in Chaucer's poetry all along. In the proem to Book I, *Troilus* describes itself, as a text, as a "sorwful instrument"; the poem's final lines return once more to musicality, with the "erratik sterres, herkenyng armonye" that cause Troilus to "lough." Poetry is the prosthesis of the advental body.[78] A disembodied Troilus sees the truth, and laughs. What is left of Troilus's body at this point is nothing, there is no rehabilitated body to be reconciled with itself, his laugh does not make a noise, and it is not heard by anyone on earth. *Troilus* ends in literal nothingness, in absence, and yet the poetic line allows this nothingness existence: this is the absolute minimum of music, but it is music.

## Natural Music, Poetry, and the Advental Body

Less than ten years after Chaucer wrote *Troilus and Criseyde*, Eustache Deschamps dramatically reframed the relationship between poetry and music in a famous passage of his *L'art de dictier*, calling *musica mundana, humana,* and *instrumentalis* "artificial" music, and defining poetry, in contrast, as "natural" music.[79] In Deschamps's mind, the ratios and proportions behind harmony and *contrapunctus* are part of a hyperperformative techne, less authentic than poetry because they can be taught. Poetry, on the other hand, Deschamps argued, is innate, natural, a form of "oral music" that produces "words in meter, sometimes in *lais*, sometimes in *balades*, sometimes in single and double *rondeaux*, and in *chansons baladees*."[80] Of course, Deschamps is creating a fiction. Not all people are capable of writing poetry, and in Deschamps's own estimation, the practice of poesis is limited to those "whose own noble ability will have endowed him for natural music," a statement that directly links poetic composition to hierarchies of social prestige.[81] Moreover, Deschamps includes a long series of examples of different verse forms and instruction in how to create them within the *Art* itself; the very act that Deschamps is touting as "natural" is, in fact, supremely artificial, its own sort of techne.

However, whether the terms "artificial" and "natural" are appropriate appellations of music and poetry or not, Deschamps's treatise argues that the writing of poetry has musical legitimacy, even if it does not include music (as normatively understood). "Those who make natural music generally don't know artificial music or how to give their lyrics an artful melody," Deschamps asserts, "nevertheless, this natural science is always called music because the *diz*, *chancons*, and *livres metrifiez* that they compose are read out loud and produced by a voice *that can't sing* in such a way that the sweet words thus composed, recited aloud, are pleasing to those who hear them.[82] In other words, it is not the presence or absence of an underlying melody that, combined with text, produces pleasure, but rather the creation of pleasure that determines whether acts of speech are musical. Although it would be wrong to suggest that Deschamps wants *musique naturelle* to be something that all people can compose—as is adduced by his comment on "noble natures" above—he nevertheless understands poetry as a form of accessibility, a way of turning the disabling structures and regimes of older forms of musical ability around on themselves, refiguring the affordances of music so that it is *affect* that determines *music*, and not the other way around. Even more importantly, artificial music "can be sung by voice and by art without any words," Deschamps claims, and "the lyrics of the songs can often be recited in places where they are most willingly heard—even where artificial music would not always be performed, as among lords and ladies in private and in secret."[83] Poetry, Deschamps argues, is more mobile, more able, than music, because the conditions of its performance are simpler. In the *Art*, then, Deschamps makes explicit claims about poetry that Chaucer implies again and again throughout his work: that poesis is a valid site of musical performance.

Throughout his poetry, Chaucer crips medieval music theory's definition of itself as mental and physical capability, doing so in order to imagine how not-having, lack, and delay allow his verse to inhabit the potency of music tout court. If music is important to Chaucer, it is important because it works differently than many of his contemporaries' expectations of music, performing not its own presence, but a type of musical presence-in-absence, just as, when his characters sing, their bodies perform their own fragmentation and dissolution. As a result, Chaucer's deployment of music does more than enact violence on bodies; it actively constructs a type of body that is interludic, a body always in a state of *différal*: bodies that simply are not there but that one waits for; bodies that are postponed or delayed; bodies that lack something; bodies that pulse over distances; bodies made of lag time and reverberation. For Chaucer, the musical body is always in the *moment before*, the *moment after*, or *elsewhere* or *elsewhen*, what Derrida would call an eschatological body, a body that is always expected but never arrives; or perhaps, as Agamben imagines it, a body that exists as a prosthesis for the body to come.[84] Moreover, these bodies are not physical or material in the colloquial sense, but instead are literary figurations where what the body imagines itself to be negotiates the site of its own absence. Chaucer's poetry itself is a form of song, albeit a type of song in which musicality and the singer are never quite in the same place at the same time. These bodies are what poetry does to sound, a way of imagining the sonic body not as voice—as presence—but instead, as in the previous chapter's discussion of voice and the sound-object, as an ineluctable gap.

# Coda

I began my research for *Sonic Bodies* ten years ago as a dissertation on the processional and antiphonal chants of the nuns of Syon Abbey, the fifteenth-century double monastery dedicated by Henry V and perhaps the most stunning example of late medieval women's song in England and of English nation-building propaganda. While the songs of the sisters of Syon create sonic bodies in interesting ways, they are not a part of this book because, as my dissertation developed I realized I wanted the book project's scope to be wider, its claims on musical practice more broad, and also, if possible, its focus to be not on texts that understand themselves as musical performance texts (processionals, hymnaries, ordinals, and the devotional texts that explicitly instructed the nuns on their liturgical duties), but instead on texts that did *not* explicitly label themselves (or had not been explicitly labeled by modern critics) as musical. If, in the most general sense, I thought, discerning what something is means defining what it is not, then defining the sonic body meant looking in the places where it did not seem to be. For a project on sonic embodiment this meant dwelling in and tiptoeing through mysticism, devotional writing, and narrative poetry rather than manuscripts that anyone might agree were musical on their face. What I found were forms of musical embodiment that had been understudied or even ignored. As a result, this book explores the liminal and relational spaces where the musical and the amusical meet and where song, poetry, plain speech, noise, and silence are entangled.

This is another way of saying that this book often refuses to take the medieval period at its own word about what is, strictly defined, music or not, because these definitions arrive on the scene always already politicized and embodied; sonic embodiment is not only an aesthetic or formal definition, but an ethical, political, and historical one. As Boethius stressed in the *Institutione musica,* music is related not only to speculation but also to morality.[1] Jacobus makes this clear in the *Speculum,* as he demotes the songs of the *moderni* to the braying of asses, the hissing of vipers, and the barking of dogs. But this notion was not at all unique to Jacobus. Marchettus of Padua says in his *Lucidarium* (1318–19) that the musician (*musicus*) "knows the power and nature (*rationem*) of the musical proportions; he judges according to them, not according to sound alone. The singer (*cantor*) is, as it were, a kind of tool (*instrumentum*) of this musician."[2] Marchettus categorically defines musicality not only by consonances in sound or by a particular formal construction of sounds, but instead by the capacity of a musician to make aesthetic and rational judgments about such sounds. In a medieval philosophical framework where certain bodies—adult white men—were considered more capable of rational judgment than others, "the body" as socially and historically constructed emerges as central to the appellation "music." Even intellected music, then, is contingent on the politics of the very body it attempts to eschew.

When I set out to write this book, it was with the general feeling that the ways in which we as medievalists were writing about the body and music, or, conversely, music and the body, were lacking an attentiveness to the productivity of a more fragmented, less wholesale conception of embodiment. As the central arguments and objects of critique for the chapters of this book crystallized, however, new avenues opened in front of me in an inexhaustible, fractal potency. If sonic embodiment is catastrophic to the hegemony of visual embodiment, what other forms might it imagine?

This book provides a few scenarios in answer to this question. But there are many avenues this book might have taken but did not. I would like to briefly suggest some potential areas for work that might done on sonic embodiment in other textual and critical environments.

First, Geraldine Heng notes that the "rich tonal qualities" of Christian martyrs are contrasted with the cacophony of Jewish prayer in *The Prioress' Tale*; how is the sonic body raced in medieval literature, and how do the logics of "musicality" and "noise" constitute the body of the foreigner?[3]

Second, we might think about sonic embodiment's generative impact on sex, gender, and sexuality. Bruce Holsinger sees in late medieval clerical responses to the polyphony of the *ars nova* a queerphobia that "provides a discursive vocabulary for locating musical practice within and among the bodily acts, performance and representations that constitute the sexual universe of Middle English literature"; these critiques shed light on the Chaucer's Pardoner and his threat to the heteronormative order.[4] The Pardoner's carnal acts have ramifications for his—and his fellow pilgrims'—spiritual lives, thus mingling the "music of the flesh" and the "song of the spirit." I absolutely agree with the blurred boundary between *carne* and *anima* in medieval song, but wonder whether it is not so much that clerical responses to polyphony deride a homoerotics that was extant as a pre-extant ontological category, but whether, rather, the sonic body that emerges out of performance and critiques of performance created a space in which the category of heteronormativity (and thus homophobia) was itself created. For instance, in the *Roman de silence,* the central character Silentia/Silentius's quest for gender- and self-determination aligns with their desire to become a minstrel; as Silentia/Silentius sings their way into a particular gender identity (with all of the registers of the voice that this might make one imagine), sound literally embodies them, determining whether they are seen as male or female, queer or straight. While the tension between Nature and Nurture in *Silence* gestures to the desire that there be some sort of biological imperative around gender, sex, and sexuality, the play of the poem reminds us that this very imperative is itself bound up in discursive arenas and in performance. The sonic body also has a role to play in the racing of the medieval world.[5]

Third, medieval texts imagine the perdurance of sound, or embed affect in sound's ephemerality; how does the sonic body force us to rethink the notion of temporality? The *Towneley Scourging,* for instance, repeatedly insists that its viewers identify with Mary's weeping at the foot of the cross, asking them to distend her tears through time, granting them a presence that the passing of sound always denies.[6] Dante builds his critique of the *canzone* form out of—in part—an observation of linguistic sound-changes over time; how does the notion of phonetic change and the concept of "vernacular eloquence" depend on the temporality of sound?[7]

Fourth, Elizabeth Eva Leach writes a dazzling account of birdsong in the medieval period, arguing that because it was the product of irrational singers, it was judged to be *vox inarticulata*, and therefore amusical.[8] How would New Materialist critiques of embodiment and animacy hierarchies challenge these medieval theories of the voice and reinvigorate the potentiality of avian musicality?

Finally, in the *Regiment of Princes*, Thomas Hoccleve takes the notion of sonic embodiment out of the frame of mystical ascents, instead charting it according to notions of subjectivity and communal belonging:

A wryter moot thre thynges to him knytte,
And in tho may be no disseverance:

> Mynde, ye, and hand—noon may from othir flitte,
> But in hem moot be joynt continuance . . .
> Thise artificers see I day by day,
> In the hootteste of al hir bysynesse,
> Talken and synge and make game and play,
> And foorth hir labour passith with gladnesse;
> But we laboure in travaillous stilnesse;
> We stowpe and stare upon the sheepes skyn,
> And keepe moot our song and wordes yn.[9]

Here, acts of writing and of singing constitute the self. On the one hand, he says, are the manual laborers of London, whose days are filled with exterior songs, with talking and singing; on the other, are the writers and copyists in the Office of the Privy Seal, who must "hold their song and words in."[10] While this passage juxtaposes physical work and intellectual labor, the metaphors of industry that distinguish them are also that which unify them. Hoccleve understands himself as a craftsman, where stooping, staring at parchment, and being silent are forms of physical exertion unlike that of London's carpenters, ironworkers, and masons not in kind, but in directionality. Manual laborers' work is communal, and their song directed outward; Hoccleve's labor is solitary, his song introverted. Moreover, this labor—the maintenance and containment of body, mind, hand, and song in scenes of writing—holds Hoccleve himself in "joynt continuance," that is, it provides him with the continuity of subjectivity that allows him to understand himself as a self. For Hoccleve, whose wits famously "wente to pleie" during the melancholia of his *Compleinte,* song, the body, and written systems of signification—music, the self, and the text—are what constitute him as a subject.[11] How do class and power construct sonic bodies?[12]

Each of these questions follows naturally from the discourse on sonic embodiment that this book has begun, and offers productive new areas for future research. In short, this book is an argument for broadening the acceptable boundaries for *music* and *the body* in medieval literature, stretching these terms almost to their breaking point, and then loosening our grip on them in order to see what sort of useful political, ethical, or social meaning emerges from the distended language in our hands.

# A Short Exposition of the Manuscripts in Chapter 4

## Richard Methley: Cambridge, Trinity College MS O.2.56

### *Scola amoris languidi* (fols. 1r–22v)

The *Scola* is constructed as a dialogue between a teacher and a student, where Christ (the teacher) instructs the lover (the student) on an aspect of spiritual desire through a series of questions and answers. After each exchange, Christ grants the student a revelation whose visual and sonic matter aid in resolving whatever point had been in question or doubt. These revelations occur in specific rooms of the charterhouse and during specific church festivals, a technique that serves a mnemonic and pedagogic function.[1] The manuscript includes copious marginal glosses and explanatory notes that look like the shorthand a student might use while listening to a lecture or reading carefully for the first time.[2] The *Scola* closes with an effusive poem of love-longing for God in which the mystic ascends into the angelic choir. Throughout the treatise, the phrase *amore langueo*—borrowed from Rolle's *Form of Living*—is subjected to repeated interpretation and redefinition, where some aspects of *amore langueo* are understood to be beneficial (such as the Christian who repeats the Holy Name out of love), whereas others stem from an imperfect faith (languor can be a product of spiritual torpor).

### *Dormitorium dilecti dilecti* (fols. 25r–48r)

The *Dormitorium* reinterprets a quotation from one of Rolle's English epistles: *Ego dormio, et cor meum vigilat*.[3] However, unlike the *Scola*, the *Dormitorium* presents the narrator as a teacher, an authority who expounds on mental liquescence and the spiritual benefits of sleep and sitting.[4] Though Rolle is never mentioned, he is not far from the text's mind: as in Rolle's own work, Methley suggests that sleep, far from being a sign of spiritual torpor, instead provides a test case for the rejection of the flesh all true contemplatives should seek, providing freedom from the affairs of the world, and freeing the obedient mind to think of God.[5] By using the Rollean *Ego dormio* as a mantra, the *Dormitorium* ponders the meaning of corporeality in relation to mystical ascent, while operating as a bridge between the *Scola* and the last text in the manuscript, the *Refectorium salutis*.

### *Refectorium salutis* (fols. 49r–70v)

The *Refectorium* is a mystical diary that cycles through the liturgical year twice, and experientializes the mnemonic framework of liturgical place and time encoded in the first treatise, the *Scola*: each chapter opens with a note about the specific Church feast and location in the charterhouse where each vision occurs. A capstone to Methley's project, the *Refectorium* performs the thematic elements of the *Scola* and the *Dormitorium*: mystical song, liquefied corporeality, dialogues with Mary, Christ, and the angels, temptation by the devil, the sustained repetition of the name of Jesus, the tension between the body and soul, and the virtues of sleep and of sitting in the contemplative life are all expressed in first-person narration. Whereas the preceding treatises fixated on a single phrase and glossed it, the *Refectorium* combines both *amore langueo* and *Ego dormio* along with a series of mystical sighs, a *iubilus* of *As* and *Os*. It is both a record of mystical experience and a performance of that experience.

## John Norton: Lincoln, Cathedral Library MS 57

Lincoln Cathedral MS 57 contains three treatises written by John Norton for which the mathematician and humanist William Melton (d. 1528) provided brief introductory epistles. The entire manuscript was copied by a monk who calls himself "Frater Flecher" at some point in the first half of the sixteenth century. There is quite a bit of rubrication, by both Flecher and a second hand, which also made interlinear corrections and wrote the text on fols. 75r–76v. Flecher often writes *maria*, *ihc*, and, rarely, more extensive pious ejaculations in the margins; there are also a number of small marginal pen-drawings.[6]

## *Musica monachorum* (fols. 1–27)

The *Musica monachorum*'s main focus is praise of the Carthusian life, and is structured as a dialogue between the narrator and a number of interlocutors. The repeated phrase in this treatise, *pura obediencia* (pure obedience), structures a discussion of the ways Carthusian obedience draws the mystic away from temptation toward love; the narrator is visited by devils, Christ, and Mary; the devils tempt him to sin, and Christ and Mary espouse the apotropaic virtues of obedience to the Carthusian rule, "called by the angels the most excellent."[7] A central section listing specific examples of obedience from the Bible comprises the majority of the text. The final section of the *Musica monachorum* is a recension of Pseudo-Dionsyius's *Celestial Hierarchies* and the *Ecclesiastical Hierarchies*, where Norton outlines his ascent to the Trinity through the ranks of priests, prophets, apostles, and angels on account of his monastic obedience.

## *Thesaurus cordium vere amantium* (fols. 28r–76v)

The *Thesaurus* is an extended explication of Matthew 11:28, *Venite ad me omnes qui laboratis et onerati estis et ego reficiam vos* ("Come to me all who labor, and I shall refresh you"). Each chapter begins with a word from this quotation and teases out its hidden meaning—*O* (What does it mean to call?) *vos omnes* (Who is "everyone?"), *laboratis* (What does it mean to work?), *onerati* (What is a spiritual burden?) *venite ad me* (How does one come to Christ?), *ego reficiam vos* (What sort of refreshment should the devout person expect?). This treatise is structured as a series of dialogues that aid in a mystical ascent: in a vision, the narrator is carried out of his flesh and to the top of a mountain, where he sees a golden castle full of singing men, women, saints, and angels. Christ appears and promises to manifest himself to the monk with a "miraculous melody of [his] heart."[8] The remainder of the *Thesaurus* is devoted to constructing a simulacrum of this castle within the narrator's heart, a project accomplished through a second series of dialogues in which Christ himself glosses the meaning of the vision. The *Thesaurus* elaborates on the musicality of the *Musica*: where the *Musica* quite literally argues that monastic music is about obedience to the Carthusian rule, the *Thesaurus* performs that music.

## *Devota lamentatio* (fols. 77r–95v)

Like Methley's *Refectorium*, the final treatise in the Lincoln manuscript is a
mystical diary; it records a series of visions beginning in Norton's cell after
Mass on the Friday before Whitsunday in 1485.[9] Norton is visited by the Virgin Mary, who appears to him along with a choir of angels; the Virgin is on
a mission to grant him the gifts promised to the obedient of the *Musica monachorum* and *Thesaurus*.[10] The *Lamentatio* includes an excursus on the angelic order, and instruction on how Carthusians use silence to reject
corporeality and enter the sonic space of angelic music.[11] In repeating *amore
langueo*, Norton echoes both Methley's *Scola* and Rolle's *Form of Perfect Living*. The treatise also includes a long series of repeated "O! O! O!" and "A! A!
A!" and a lyric prayer that echoes the prayer at the end of Methley's *Scola*
and many of Rolle's lyrics.[12] Like Methley's *Refectorium*, the structure of the
text is based on the liturgical calendar; unlike Methley's diary, Norton's includes only one entry, and only one long revelation. The form of the *Lamentatio* itself is musical, with repeated *O*s and calls to the other to listen.

*     *     *

Norton's and Methley's manuscripts have much in common and appear to
have influenced each other. But in which direction did this influence travel?
Using internal evidence, it is possible to make some educated guesses, but
hard to say with any certainty. For instance, all three of Methley's treatises
can be dated using internal evidence. The second two treatises are fairly
straightforward: like the *Scola*, it is possible to date the other two treatises
in the Trinity manuscript through internal evidence from Methley himself.
The *Dormitorium dilecti dilecti*, Methley says, was written "in 1485, . . . nine
years after my entry into the Carthusian Order."[13] The *Refectorium salutis*,
which was written over approximately two years, begins "on the Feast of the
Translation of St Hugh of Lincoln [October 6]" in 1487, "when suddenly, an
angelic song with a holy melody came upon me."[14]

However, the first treatise, Methley's *Scola amoris languidi*, which dates
to 1483/4, describes the conditions that prompted the composition of the text,
and put it in strikingly communal terms. "I was once tempted by boredom,"
Methley says, "as if I remembered nothing of the way of life when I first
entered this monastery." However, writing the *Scola* has served to renew his
spiritual fervor, as he continues: "I have completed seven years and am in my

eighth as I write this to you on the day before the feast of St Oswald the King [August 5] in the monastery of Mount Grace; and, because I am a Carthusian, I invite you to the same calling."[15] "I am in Mount Grace writing to you," Methley says, summoning his reader to "the same calling," that is, to the Carthusian life in general as well as to mystical experience that includes *canor.* While the "you" Methley is addressing here is unspecified and universal, he employs the singular form (*te/tibi*) rather than the plural (*vos/vobis*), thus indicating a highly personal, if not singular, form of address. Is Methley here writing directly to Norton, who would have joined the charterhouse of Mount Grace sometime after his entry into the order in 1482? Is it possible that the *Scola* coincided with Norton's move to the charterhouse in York, and that this indefinite *te* is the much more particular Norton? We do know, for instance, that Methley's other treatises are written for specific men: *The Epistle of Hew Hermite* to a young hermit living near Mount Grace, and Methley's Latin translations of *The Cloud of Unknowing* and Marguerite Porete's *Mirror* to Thurston Watson, another confrere at Mount Grace who eventually transferred to the Charterhouse in Hull, where he died in 1505.[16] If this is the case, from the very beginning of Methley's and Norton's writing project, the *Scola* addresses its readers with the intent of fashioning the very exchange that would entangle both writers over the next decade. Whether the addressee is Norton or not, however, what is most important is that the *Scola* imagines itself as a production for a single reader of intimate acquaintance, someone whom Methley envisions drawing into the circle of his own experience of *canor.*

Norton's treatises cannot be dated as specifically as Methley's, but, in his introduction to the manuscript, William Melton says that Norton's first two treatises (the *Musica monachorum* and the *Thesaurus cordium vere amantium*) were written in Mount Grace; Melton dates the vision that would become his final treatise, the *Devota lamentatio,* to 1485, and Norton himself tells us this as well.[17] Thus, we know that Methley wrote the *Scola* in 1483/4, his *Dormitorium* in 1485, and his *Refectorium* in 1487. We also know that Norton had the vision that would become his *Devota lamentatio* in 1485 (though we do not know for sure when he transcribed this experience). It is likely that Methley's *Scola*—with its repeated Rollean quotation of *amore langueo,* and its call to its readers to engage in heightened displays of affective religious expression—influenced Norton's *Lamentatio* of 1485 (which also repeats a Rollean *amore langueo*); if this is the case, then, Norton's *Lamentatio,* with its mystical, *iubilus*-like sighing and its single, diary-like entry, appears to have influenced the structure of Methley's *Refectorium* (1487) and its series of diaristic accounts in turn.

While this educated assessment relies on the dating and stylistic evidence of the treatises, this narrative relies on the assumption that Norton experienced the events of 1485 and then wrote about them soon thereafter, which he of course may not have done. And, whereas it seems likely that the order of composition is Methley's *Scola* (1483/4), Methley's *Dormitorium* and Norton's *Lamentatio* (both 1485), Methley's *Refectorium* (1487), and then Norton's *Musica* and *Thesaurus* (at some point after 1485), other theories might be proposed. For instance, perhaps Norton wrote all three of his treatises in 1485—the year of his *Lamentatio*—whereas Methley's were written in a serial manner. Or perhaps Norton had the vision that would become his *Lamentatio* in 1485, but he did not write any of his treatises until after Methley had completed his manuscript in 1487. It is also possible that Norton wrote his *Musica* and *Thesaurus* prior to 1485, and that these texts directly influenced Methley's *Scola* (which is, like the *Musica*, about obedience), and his *Thesaurus* influenced the *Dormitorium* (with its interest in mystical ascents). Because of the paucity of datable information for Norton's first two treatises, it is simply impossible to state anything with full confidence, and the array of options is truly dizzying, and it is not my intent, here, to chart ironclad routes of transmission or influence.

# Notes

1. There has been much debate about Jacobus's identity. The *Speculum musicae* was originally attributed to Johannes de Muris by Edmond de Coussemaker in the late nineteenth century, but this attribution was revised by Heinrich Besseler, who noticed that the initial letter of each book of the *Speculum* spelled out IACOBUS in an acrostic. Recent scholarship by Rob Wegman identifies Jacobus as Jacobus Leodiensis. See Edmond de Coussemaker, ed., *Scriptorum de musica medii aevi nova series a Gerbertina altera*, 4 vols. (Paris: A. Durand, 1864–76); Heinrich Besseler, "Studien zur Musik des Mittelalters I," *Archiv für Musikwissenschaft* 7 (1925): 180–81; Karen Desmond, "New Light on Jacobus, Author of *Speculum Musicae*," *Plainsong and Medieval Music* 9:1 (2000): 19–40; Margaret Bent, *Magister Jacobus de Ispania, Author of the* Speculum Musicae (Farnham: Ashgate, 2015); Rob C. Wegman, "Jacobus de Ispania and Liège," *Journal of the Alamire Foundation* 8:2 (2016): 254–76; Karen Desmond, *Music and the Moderni, 1300–1500: The* Ars Nova *in Theory and Practice* (Cambridge: Cambridge University Press, 2018), 10ff.

2. Theodor Adorno, "On Jazz," tr. Jamie Owen Daniel, *Discourse* 12:1 (1989–90): 45–69. See also Robert W. Witkin, "Why Did Adorno 'Hate' Jazz?," *Sociological Theory* 18:1 (2000): 145–70.

3. *O magnus abusus, magna ruditas, magna bestialitas, ut asinus sumatur pro homine, capra pro leone, ovis pro pisce, serpens pro salmone! Sic enim concordiae a discordiis distinctae sunt ut nullatenus una sit alia . . . Sunt autem aliqui qui, etsi aliqualiter discantare noverint per usum, modum tamen non observant bonum. Nimis lascive discantant, voces superflue multiplicant. Horum aliqui nimis hoketant, nimis voces suas in consonantiis frangunt, scandunt et dividunt, et in locis inopportunis saltant, hurcant, iupant et, ad modum canis, hawant, latrant et, quasi amentes, incompositis et anfractis pascuntur vexationibus, harmonia utuntur a natura remota.* Jacobus Leodiensis, *Speculum musicae, Liber primus: Jacobi Leodiensis Speculum musicae*, ed. Roger Bragard, Corpus scriptorum de musica, vol. 3/7 ([Rome]: American Institute of Musicology, 1973), VII.9, 23. Rob C. Wegman, *The Mirror of Music: Book the Seventh* (N.p.: Lamotte, 2017), 20. Translated by Andrew Hicks.

4. For targeted studies of Jacobus and embodiment, see George Harne, "Unstable Embodiments of Musical Theory and Practice in the *Speculum musicae*," *Plainsong and Medieval Music* 21:2 (2012): 113–36; Harne, "The Ends of Theory and Practice in the *Speculum Musicae*," *Musica Disciplina* 55 (2010): 5–31.

5. The corporeality of medieval musical forms affects medieval reading practices, as Seeta Chaganti argues in *Strange Footing: Poetic Form and Dance in the Late Middle Ages* (Chicago: University of Chicago Press, 2018), 227–76. On the zoomorphic and anthropomorphic

qualities of song, see Anna Zayaruznaya, *The Monstrous New Art* (Cambridge: Cambridge University Press, 2015), 21–69.

6. Mel Y. Chen, *Animacies* (Durham, NC: Duke University Press, 2012), 40ff.

7. Elizabeth Eva Leach argues that some animal sounds might be considered musical (for instance, birdsong), but the animals listed here in Jacobus are not melodious in the sense that their avian counterparts might be. See Elizabeth Eva Leach, *Sung Birds: Music, Nature, and Poetry in the Later Middle Ages* (Ithaca, NY: Cornell University Press, 2007).

8. For a summary of these assessments, see Bruce Holsinger, *Music, Body, and Desire in Medieval Culture: Hildegard of Bingen to Chaucer* (Stanford, CA: Stanford University Press, 2001), 5.

9. Holsinger, *Music, Body, and Desire*, 12.

10. For a historical narrative of twentieth-century "recovery" efforts of medieval musicology, see Daniel Leech-Wilkinson, *The Modern Invention of Medieval Music: Scholarship, Ideology, Performance* (Cambridge: Cambridge University Press, 2002).

11. Emma Dillon, *The Sense of Sound: Musical Meaning in France, 1260–1330* (Oxford: Oxford University Press, 2012).

12. Andrew Hicks, *Composing the World: Harmony in the Medieval Platonic Cosmos* (Oxford: Oxford University Press, 2017), 3.

13. Zayaruznaya, *The Monstrous New Art*, 24.

14. A full bibliography of new materialism and object-oriented ontology is neither possible nor warranted here. The following texts have been helpful in framing my thinking. Karen Barad, *Meeting the Universe Halfway: Quantum Physics and the Entanglement of Matter and Meaning* (Durham, NC: Duke University Press, 2017); Vicki Kirby, *Telling Flesh: The Substance of the Corporeal* (London: Routledge, 2014); Timothy Morton, *Hyperobjects: Philosophy and Ecology After the End of the World* (Minneapolis: University of Minnesota Press, 2013); Jane Bennett, *Vibrant Matter* (Durham, NC: Duke University Press, 2009); Stacey Alaimo and Susan Hekman, eds., *Material Feminisms* (Bloomington: Indiana University Press, 2008); Graham Harman, *Guerrilla Metaphysics: Phenomenology and the Carpentry of Things* (Chicago: Open Court, 2005).

15. Sarah Kay and Miri Rubin, *Framing Medieval Bodies* (Manchester: Manchester University Press, 1994), 5.

16. For an exploration of the meanings and resonances of "matter" for the medieval reader, especially as that which informs text, see Kellie Robertson, "Medieval Materialism: A Manifesto," *Exemplaria* 22:2 (2010): 99–118.

17. Ernst Kantorowicz, *The King's Two Bodies: A Study in Medieval Political Theology* (Princeton, NJ: Princeton University Press, 2016).

18. Caroline Walker Bynum, *The Resurrection of the Body in Western Christianity, 200–1336* (New York: Columbia University Press, 1994), 26ff.

19. Patricia Dailey, *Promised Bodies: Time, Language, and Corporeality in Medieval Women's Mystical Texts* (New York: Columbia University Press, 2013), 1–26.

20. Angelology is a deep field, and no bibliography will be exhaustive. See in particular Meredith Gill, *Angels and the Order of Heaven in Medieval and Renaissance Italy* (Cambridge: Cambridge University Press, 2014), especially "Bodies and Voices: Annunciation and Heavenly Harmonies," 100–150; Beth Williamson, "Sensory Experience in Medieval Devotion: Invisibility and Silence," *Speculum* 88:1 (2013): 1–43; David Keck, *Angels and Angelology in the Middle Ages* (Oxford: Oxford University Press, 1998).

21. See Reinhold Hammerstein, *Die Musik der Engel: Untersuchungen zur Musikanschauung des Mittelalters* (Bern: Francke, 1962) for a study of angelic song.

22. *Res scilicet transcendentes ad metaphysicam vel divinam scientiam pertinentes.* Jacobus Leodiensis, *Speculum musicae*, 37.

23. Walter Hilton, *Of Angels' Song*, in *English Mystics of the Middle Ages*, ed. Barry Windeatt (Cambridge: Cambridge University Press, 1994), 131–36, 133.

24. See the discussion below, and for a fuller treatment, see Ruth DeFord, *Tactus, Mensuration, and Rhythm in Renaissance Music* (Cambridge: Cambridge University Press, 2015), especially 51ff.

25. Cheryl Glenn and Krista Ratcliffe, eds., *Silence and Listening as Rhetorical Arts* (Carbondale and Edwardsville: Southern Illinois University Press, 2011).

26. A historical connection might be drawn here between Margery's silence and radical critiques of voicing and power in postcolonial studies, Afro-pessimism, and immigrants' rights movements as renunciatory politics. I'm thinking here specifically of Fred Moten's *The Undercommons: Fugitive Planning and Black Study* (New York: Minor Compositions, 2013); Homi Bhabha's *The Location of Culture* (New York: Routledge, 1994); and of course Gayatri Spivak's *Can the Subaltern Speak?*, in *Colonial Discourse and Post-Colonial Theory: A Reader*, ed. Patrick Williams and Laura Chrisman (New York: Columbia University Press, 1993), 66–111.

27. Julie Orlemanski, "Margery's 'Noyse' and Distributed Expressivity," in *Voice and Voicelessness in Medieval Europe*, ed. Irit Ruth Kleiman (New York: Palgrave Macmillan, 2015), 123–38.

28. Barbara Newman's recent edition of Methley's works is forthcoming as of the writing of this book. Barbara Newman, ed. and tr., *The Works of Richard Methley* (Collegeville, MN: Liturgical Press, 2021).

29. Both Cambridge, Trinity College MS O.2.56 and Lincoln, Cathedral Library MS 57 contain three treatises. The first treatises in both manuscripts are written as dialogues between a teacher and a student, the second treatise of each manuscript traces a single vision dealing with a mystical ascent, and the third and final treatise is structured like a diary. All six treatises employ a verbal refrain, a repeated phrase that serves as a jumping-off point for devotion or contemplation, and Methley and Norton share one of them, which is borrowed from Rollean mysticism: *amore langueo*. Both also share similarities in Latin style.

30. Pierre Schaeffer, *Treatise on Musical Objects: An Essay Across Disciplines* (Oakland: University of California Press, 2017); Michel Chion, *Sound: An Acoulogical Treatise*, tr. James A. Steintrager (Durham, NC: Duke University Press, 2016); Brian Kane, *Sound Unseen: Acousmatic Sound in Theory and Practice* (Oxford: Oxford University Press, 2014); Mladan Dolar, *A Voice and Nothing More* (Cambridge, MA: MIT Press, 2006); Rey Chow, "Listening after 'Acousmaticity': Notes on a Transdisciplinary Problematic," in *Sound Objects*, ed. James A. Steintrager and Rey Chow (Durham, NC: Duke University Press, 2019), 113–29.

CHAPTER I

Note to epigraph: *Potest autem et alia musicae species, ut videtur, his adiungi, quae coelestis vel divina dici potest. Haec res intuetur a motu et sensibili materia separatas et secundum esse et secundum intellectum, res scilicet transcendentes ad metaphysicam vel divinam scientiam pertinentes.* Jacobus Leodiensis, *Speculum musicae*, 37.

1. See "Music, Odd Bodies, and Sonic Embodiment: Thinking About This Book" in the Introduction.

2. *Res scilicet transcendentes ad metaphysicam vel divinam scientiam pertinentes.* Jacobus Leodiensis, *Speculum musicae*, 37.

3. As Jerome of Moravia explains in the *Tractatus de musica* (thirteenth century), borrowing from Aquinas (who in turn borrowed the idea from Aristotle's *De caelo*), humans are not able to hear *musica mundana* or *musica humana* because "as soon as we are born, this sound coexists with us. And for that reason, it is not able to be made evident through its opposite, which is silence. For each of these two, that is, voice and silence, are themselves decided and discerned reciprocally. Whence this happens to everyone with respect to the sound of the celestial bodies, just as it happens to coppersmiths, who on account of their habituation, do not, as it were, perceive the difference between sound and silence because their ears are completely filled with this sound." *Dicebant enim hanc esse causam, quare hanc vocem non audimus, quia statim cum nascimur, coexistit nobis iste sonus, et ideo non potest nobis manifestari propter suum oppositum, quod est silentium. Haec enim duo, scilicet vox et silentium, se invicem dijudicantur et discernuntur. Unde accidit hoc omnibus de sono caelestium corporum sicut accidit de malleatoribus aeris, qui propter consuetudinem quasi non sentiunt differentiam soni et silentii, eo quod aures eorum sunt impletae nimis hujusmodi sono.* Jerome of Moravia, *Tractatus de musica*, ed. S. M. Cserba, Freiburger Studien zur Musikwissenschaft, vol. 2 (Regensburg: Pustet, 1935), 3–179, 28, www.chmtl.indiana.edu/tml. My thanks to Andrew Hicks for pointing out the ultimate source of Jerome's comment in Aristotle.

4. At Paris, for example, lectures on the quadrivium took place only on festival days—about sixty days in the year. See Joseph Dyer, "Speculative *Musica* and the Medieval University of Paris," *Music & Letters* 90:2 (2009): 177–204; Dorit Tanay, *Noting Music, Marking Culture: The Intellectual Context of Rhythmic Notation, 1240–1400* (Holzgerlingen: Hänssler, 1999); Jeremy Yudkin, "The Influence of Aristotle on French University Music Texts," in *Music Theory and Its Sources: Antiquity and the Middle Ages*, ed. André Barbera (South Bend, IN: Notre Dame University Press, 1990), 173–89.

5. *Musica est de numero relato ad sonos ex qua relatione fiunt consonantie musicales et ideo musica est de consonantiis.* Anonymous, *Quaedam communia* (after 1250), quoted in Gilles Rico, "Music in the Arts Faculty of Paris in Thirteenth and Early Fourteenth Centuries" (PhD diss., Oxford University, 2005), 45.

6. Pseudo-Dionysius, *The Complete Works*, tr. Colm Luibheid (New York: Paulist Press, 1987); Barbara Newman discusses the monastic tradition of *musica celestis* in the introduction to her edition of Hildegard von Bingen's *Symphonia*. See Barbara Newman, *Symphonia: A Critical Edition of the* Symphonia armonie celestium revelationum, tr. Barbara Newman (Ithaca, NY: Cornell University Press, 1988), 20–21. For a discussion of Richard Rolle and his inherited angelology, see Claire Elizabeth McIlroy, *English Prose Treatises of Richard Rolle* (Cambridge: D. S. Brewer, 2004), 77–79; the twenty-one daily matins lessons used by the Bridgettines were known as the *Sermo angelicus*, as they were supposedly dictated to Bridget "from the lips of the angel himself." Bridget of Sweden, *The Revelations of St Birgitta of Sweden*, vol. 4, *The Heavenly Emperor's Book to Kings, The Rule, and Minor Works* ed. and tr. Bridget Morris (Oxford: Oxford University Press, 2015), 159.

7. Isaiah 6:3; Luke 2:14; Revelation 5:11 and 7:11. Dante, *Paradiso*, *Sanctus* in Canto VII.1–3; *Hosanna* in Canto VIII.29; *Io sono amore angelico* in Canto XXIII.103–8; *Te Deum* in Canto XXIV.113; *Sperent in te* in Canto XXV.98; *Sanctus* in Canto XXVI.69; *Osanna* in Canto XXVIII.94; *Ave Maria* in Canto XXII.95. Dante Alighieri, *The Divine Comedy* (Richmond: Alma

Classics, 2012). Angels feature heavily in *Corpus Christi* plays, singing in the York *Creation of the Angels and the Fall of Lucifer* (l. 40), *The Annunciation to Mary and the Visitation* (l. 165), and *The Resurrection* (l. 186), among others. See Clifford Davidson, ed., *The York Corpus Christi Plays* (Kalamazoo: Medieval Institute Publications, 2011).

8. Augustine, "Sermon 194.2," in *The Works of St Augustine: Sermons* III/6, tr. Edmund Hill, ed. John E. Rotelle (New York: New City Press, 1993), 54.

9. In medieval culture, rocks' lack of *anima* does not make them pure substrate; instead, they engage with and work in the world in meaningful ways. See Jeffrey Jerome Cohen, ed., *Animal, Vegetable, Mineral: Ethics and Objects* (Washington, DC: Oliphaunt Books, 2012).

10. Mary Carruthers, *The Book of Memory: A Study of Memory in Medieval Culture* (Cambridge: Cambridge University Press, 2008), 56–98; Thomas Aquinas, *Commentary on Aristotle's De anima*, ed. and tr. Kenelm Foster, Silvester Humphries, and Ralph McInerny (New Haven, CT: Yale University Press, 1994), 139–50; Aristotle, *De Anima*, ed. and tr. Robert Drew Hicks (Cambridge: Cambridge University Press, 1907), 83–89, 419a35–421a6.

11. Quoted in James Steven Byrne, "Angels and the Physics of Place in the Early Fourteenth Century," in *Conversations with Angels: Essays Towards a History of Spiritual Communication, 1100–1700*, ed. Joad Raymond (New York: Palgrave Macmillan, 2011), 52.

12. *Angelus igitur est substantia intellectualis, semper mobilis, arbitrio libera, incorporea, deo ministrans, secundum gratiam, non natura, immortalitatem suscipiens; cuius substantiae speciem et terminum solus creator noscit.* John Damascene, *De Fide Orthodoxa*, ed. Eligius M. Buytaert (St. Bonaventure, NY: The Franciscan Institute, 1955), II.3, 69; for a longer treatment of angels as "separate substances," see Thomas Aquinas, *Treatise on Separate Substances*, tr. Francis J. Lescoe (West Hartford: St. Joseph College, 1959). *Deus autem creaturam producit per intellectum et voluntatem, ut supra ostensum est. Unde ad perfectionem universi requiritur quod sint aliquae creaturae intellectuales*: Thomas Aquinas, *Summa Theologiae: Latin Text and English Translation, Introductions, Notes, Appendices, and Glossaries* (New York: McGraw-Hill, 1964), I.50.1.

13. Thomas Aquinas, *Summa Theologiae* I.50.1: *Angeli, Deo comparati, sunt materiales et corporei, non quod in eis sit aliquid de natura corporea.*

14. Thomas Aquinas, *The Power of God*, tr. Richard J. Regan (Oxford: Oxford University Press, 2012), VI.8.185: *Non tamen erit vere naturalis actio, sed similitudo talis actionis . . . locutio quae attribuitur Angelis in corporibus assumptis, non est vere naturalis locutio, sed quaedam similitudinaria per similitudinem effectus.* Thomas Aquinas, *Quaestiones Disputatae de Potentia Dei* (Westminster: The Newman Press, 1952).

15. In addition to early treatments by Pseudo-Dionysius and others, a spate of twelfth-, thirteenth-, and fourteenth-century writers dedicated effort to solving the problem of angelic substance and communication. The most important of these were Peter Lombard's (d. 1160) *Sententiae*, Bk. II, and *distinctiones* 3–12 in particular. See Peter Lombard, *The Sentences, Book 2: On Creation*, tr. Giulio Silano (Toronto: Pontifical Institute of Medieval Studies, 2008), 12–53; Aquinas's treatise *On Separate Substances* and his *Summa Theologiae* I.q.50–64, 105–14. For contemporary discussions of theories of angelic communication in the medieval period, see Isabel Iribarren and Martin Lenz, eds., *Angels in Medieval Philosophical Inquiry: Their Function and Significance* (New York: Routledge, 2016), especially Martin Lenz, "Why Can't Angels Think Properly? Ockham Against Chatton and Aquinas," 155–70; Ghislain Casas, "Language Without Voice: *Locutio angelica* as a Political Issue," in *Voice and Voicelessness in Medieval Europe*, ed. Irit Ruth Kleiman (New York: Palgrave Macmillan, 2015), 13–28;

Meredith J. Gill, *Angels and the Order of Heaven in Medieval and Renaissance Italy* (Cambridge: Cambridge University Press, 2014); Joad Raymond, *Conversations with Angels: Essays Towards a History of Spiritual Communication, 1100–1700* (New York: Palgrave MacMillan, 2011); Bern Rolling, "Angelic Language and Communication," in *A Companion to Angels in Medieval Philosophy*, ed. Tobias Hoffmann (Leiden: Brill, 2011), 223–60; David Keck, *Angels and Angelology* (Oxford: Oxford University Press, 1998).

16. Bernard of Clairvaux, "Sermon 5: On the Four Kinds of Spirits," in *Commentary on the Song of Songs*, ed. and tr. Killian J. Walsh and Irene M. Edmonds (Spencer: Cistercian Publications, 1971), 29. *Ceterum angelica corpora, utrum nam ipsis spiritibus naturalia sint, sicut hominibus sua: et sint animalia, sicut homines, immortalia tamen, quod nondum sunt homines: porro ipsa corpora mutent, et versent in forma et specia qua volunt quando apparere volunt, densantes et solidantes ea quantum volunt, eum tamen in sui veritate prae subtilitate naturae atque substantiae suae impalpabilia sint, et nostris omnino intangibilia visibus; an vero simplici spirituali substantia subsistentes, corpora cum opus est sumant, rursumque explete opere, ponant in eandem, de qua sumpta sunt, materiam dissolvenda: nolo ut a me requiratis. Videntus patres de hujusmodi diversa snesisse; nec mihi perspicuum est, unde alterutrum doceam: et nescire me fateor. Sed et vestris profectibus non multum conferre arbitror harum rerum notitiam.* (Bernard of Clairvaux, *Sermones in Cantica canticorum* (Paris: Libraria Academica Wagneriana, 1888), 29.

17. Perhaps this is a direct response to Book II, Distinctions II–XI of Peter Lombard's *Sententiae*, which dealt with angelic being and substance; Bernard of Clairvaux was one of Peter's patrons, and because the *Sententiae* served as a primary topic of commentary for those pursuing a doctorate of theology in the medieval university, this in large part explains the massive concentration of debates about angelic embodiment in the thirteenth and fourteenth centuries.

18. Even the notable exception to the view of angelic embodiment, Bonaventure, believed that though angels were material in quantity, they were not material in extension. John F. Wippel, "Metaphysical Composition of Angels in Bonaventure, Aquinas, and Godfrey of Fontaines," in Hoffman, *A Companion to Angels in Medieval Philosophy*, 45–78.

19. Medieval mechanical models of sound propagation were taken from Aristotle's *De anima* II.8, where sound is described as an impact of two bodies that then reverberates through some medium, like air or water. However, the type of bodies being struck determines whether any real sound is produced. As Aristotle says, "As we stated above, it is not concussion of any two things taken at random which constitutes sound. Wool, when struck, emits no sound at all, but bronze does, and so do all smooth and hollow things; bronze emits sound because it is smooth, while hollow things by reverberation produce a series of concussions after the first, that which is set in motion being unable to escape. . . . It is not the air or the water which chiefly determine the production of sound: on the contrary, there must be solid bodies colliding with one another and with the air: and this happens when the air after being struck resists the impact and is not dispersed." Aristotle, *De anima*, 419.b.10. One of the most famous articulations of medieval sound science is the Eagle's Aristotelian discourse in Chaucer's *House of Fame*: "Thou wost wel this, that spech is soun / . . . soun ys noght but eyr ybroken / . . . Throwe water now a stoon, / Wel sot thou hyt wol make anoon / A litell roundell as a sercle / . . . Every sercle causynge other / Wydder than hymselve was." Geoffrey Chaucer, "The House of Fame," in *The Riverside Chaucer*, ed. Larry D. Benson (New York: Houghton Mifflin, 1987), ll. 762–822; ll. 762, 765, 789–91, 797–98.

20. His *Speculum* credits the initial formulation to the *De musicae commendacione* of Louise of Toulouse (d. 1297), now lost. This lost treatise is attributed to Lodewijk Heyligen

(d. 1361). See Andreas Giger, "Ludovicus Sanctus," in *Grove Music Online*, ed. Deane L. Root (Oxford: Oxford University Press, 2001), https://doi.org/10.1093/gmo/9781561592630.article .45460.

21. *Haec res intuetur a motu et sensibili materia separatas et secundum esse et secundum intellectum, res scilicet transcendentes ad metaphysicam vel divinam scientiam pertinentes.* Jacobus Leodiensis, *Speculum musicae*, 37.

22. *Haec enim fuit Aristoteli via, per motum in cognitionem devenire substantiarum separatarum. Quid igitur inconveniens, si harmonicam modulationem generaliter sumptam extendamus,* [39] *non solum ad res corporales, naturales et substantiales numeratas, sed etiam ad metaphysicales, inter quas invicem numeratas et collatas attenditur quaedam habitudo cuiusdam connexionis, ordinis, concordiae vel proportionis, ut contineatur non solum sub duabus partibus philosophiae theoricae, sed sub tribus, ut est prius dictum?* ("This was Aristotle's method: to arrive through the analysis of motion at the cognition of separate substances. Why would it be contradictory if we extend harmonic melody (taken generally) not only to corporeal, natural, and substantial numbered things, but even to metaphysical things? Among these, when numbered and compared against each other, we note a certain disposition of connection, order, concord and proportion, such that music can be included not only under two parts of philosophy, but under three [physics, mathematics, and theology/metaphysics], as was said above.") Jacobus Leodiensis, *Speculum musicae*, 38–39, I.XI, www.chmtl.indiana.edu/tml. Thank you to Andrew Hicks for his translation of this passage.

23. *Supra dictum est musicam a "Musis," quibus sapientia quaerebatur, nuncupari. Res autem ad habitum sapientiae pertinentes sunt res metaphysicales, inter quas praecipue sunt divinae res et intelligentiae. Ad has igitur musica se extendit. Adhuc dicta est musica a "muso, sas", quod est "cogitando aliquid inquirere.* ("It is said above that 'music' is so called from *musis* ['the Muses'], by whom wisdom was sought. However, the things that pertain to the habit (or disposition) of wisdom are metaphysical things, among which especially are divine things and things of the intelligence, to which things therefore, music extends itself. Furthermore, 'music' is said to be from *muso sas*, that is, to inquire by thinking.") Jacobus Leodiensis, *Speculum musicae*, 39, I.XI, www.chmtl.indiana.edu/tml.

24. *Musica extendit se ad omnia, quia nihil sine illa.* Jacobus Leodiensis, *Speculum Musicae*, 37, I.X.

25. Jerome of Moravia, *Tractatus*, 28, www.chmtl.indiana.edu/tml.

26. *Nam cum sint novem coeli materiales et mobiles, ut coelum excludatur empyreum, sunt etiam novem coeli spirituales, ut novem angelorum ordines, cum quibus sociabuntur boni homines. Adhuc ab illis coeli civibus haec musicae species coelestis nuncupatur, non tantum quia de illis est obiective, sed quia in eis est subiective; ipsi enim perfectissime hanc habent musicam, qui iam non in speculo et in aenigmate per aliquod extrinsecum repraesentatum Deum contemplantur, sed immediate facie ad faciem Deum intuentur.* ("For since there are nine material and mobile heavens, as the empyrean heaven is excluded [from these nine], there are also nine spiritual heavens, as there are nine orders of angels, with whom good men will keep company. Furthermore, this species of celestial music is [so] named by these citizens of heaven, not only because it concerns them objectively, but because it is in them subjectively, for they possess this music most perfectly who contemplate God not in a mirror and in an enigma, through some extrinsic representation, but they see God face to face.") Jacobus Leodiensis, *Speculum musicae*, 41.

27. The single complete manuscript is Paris, BnF lat. 7207; Paris, BnF lat. 7207A (Books I–V and fragments of the table of contents of Book VI) and Florence, Biblioteca Medicea Laurentiana, Plut XXIX.16 (excerpts) are partial manuscripts. See Margaret Bent, *Magister Jacobus*

*de Ispania, Author of the* Speculum Musicae (New York: Routledge, 2016), 4; Dorit Tanay argues that while medieval music theory generally followed practice, operating descriptively rather than prescriptively, theoretical systems might also subtly condition and shape performance practice. See Tanay, *Noting Music, Marking Culture*; see also Karen Desmond, *Music and the Moderni, 1300–1500: The Ars Nova in Theory and Practice* (Cambridge: Cambridge University Press, 2018).

28. *Cum itaque inter omnia a deo creata homo post angelum magis recipiat, quod est intellegere et ratiocinari, debet ipsi per bonas operationes applaudere et eum nocte dieque laudare. In isto autem officio angeli sunt potentes propter nobilitatem suae naturae et quoniam organis sensitivis et fatigabilibus non utuntur. Homo vero istam operationem diu continuare non potest, eo quod in materia corporali formam habet et cum organis corporalibus operatur, sed et alias operationes oportet eum frequentare, ut est comedere et bibere et dormire et multas alias operationes has sequentes.* Johannes de Grocheio, *Die Quellenhandschriften zum Musiktraktat des Johannes de Grocheio: Im Faks. hrsg. nebst Übertr. d. Textes u. Übers. ins Dt., dazu Bericht, Literaturschau, Tab. u. Indices,* ed. Ernst Rohloff (Leipzig: Deutscher Verl. f. Musik, 1972), 58–59. This translation, and all other translations of Latin musicological sources not attributed to published material, are by Elizabeth Lyon.

29. *Musica igitur est quam sancti angeli cum thronis et dominacionibus cumque omni milicia celestis exercitus ad laudem et gloriam omnipotenti deo canunt sine fine dicentes. Sanctus Sanctus Sanctus dominus deus et cetera.* ("Music, then, is how the holy angels, with thrones and dominations and with all the assembled hosts of heaven sing the praise and glory of omnipotent God without end, saying, *Sanctus, sanctus, sanctus, dominus deus* et cetera.) Anonymous, *Musica compendium* (fifteenth century), transcribed by Oliver B. Ellsworth (*Thesaurus Musicarum Latinarum,* 2002), Salzburg, St. Peter's Abbey, a.VI.44, ff. 23r–41r, fol. 24r, www.chmtl.indiana.edu/tml.

30. *Ut sicut ille supernus et supercelestis chorus celestis Iherusalem incessanter et ineffabiliter sua musica in supercelestibus Ierarchijs deum et dominum omnipotentem collaudant.* ("Just as that superior and supercelestial choir of the heavenly Jerusalem incessantly and ineffably praise God the Lord Almighty with their music in the supercelestial hierarchy.") Anonymous, *Speculum cantancium siue psallencium* (fourteenth century), transcribed by Peter M. Lefferts (*Thesaurus Musicarum Latinarum,* 1996), www.chmtl.indiana.edu/tml.

31. *Quoniam sancti in celis cum angelis et archangelis thronis et dominationibus cumque omni milicia celestis exercitus non cessant hympnum canere quotidie: Sanctus sanctus et cetera. Et in terra ab angelis cantabatur: Gloria in excelsis Deo, a quibus nec de literatura queritur nec de logica disputatur.* ("Because the saints in heaven with the angels and archangels, thrones and dominions, with the entire host of the heavenly army do not cease to sing the daily hymn: *Sanctus sanctus* et cetera. And on earth, *Gloria in excelsis Deo,* was sung by the angels, who neither quarrel about the discipline of grammar, nor engage in disputations about logic.") Amerus, *Practica artis musice,* ed. Cesarino Ruini, Corpus scriptorum de musica, vol. 25 (N.p.: American Institute of Musicology, 1977), 19–112, 20. The same sentiment is quoted almost verbatim in Johannes Velendrinum's (d. 1375) *Opusculum de musica,* in *Opusculum de musica ex traditione Iohannis Hollandrini. A Commentary, Critical Edition and Translation,* ed. Alexander Rausch, Musical Theorists in Translation, vol. 15 (Ottawa: Institute of Mediaeval Music, 1997), 26–80, 26; and in Anonymous, *Commendacio artis musicae secundum quendam Gregorium,* in *Commentum Oxoniense in musicam Boethii: Eine Quelle zur Musiktheorie an der spätmittelalterlichen Universität,* ed. Matthias Hochadel, Bayerische Akademie der Wissenschaften, Veröffentlichungen der Musikhistorischen Kommission, vol. 16 (Munich: Bayerische Akademie der Wissenschaften; C. H. Beck, 2002), 414–32 (even pages only), 418.

32. *Ancora: lo Cielo empireo per la sua pace simiglia la Divina Scienza, che piena è di tutta pace; la quale non soffera lite alcuna d'oppinioni o di sofistici argomenti, per la eccellentissima certezza del suo subietto, lo quale è Dio.* ("Furthermore, the Empyrean Heaven on account of its peace resembles the Science of Divinity, which is filled with perfect peace; this science does not at all permit the strife that comes from differences in opinion or from sophistical arguments.") *Convivio* II.xiv, quoted in Massimo Verdicchio, *The Poetics of Dante's* Paradiso (Toronto: University of Toronto Press, 2010), 161.

33. *Supercelestis est que in angelorum et sanctorum iubilo ac deduccione optima.* ("Supercelestial music is what exists in the *iubilus* and the best *deductio* [notes/musical range] of the angels and saints.") Henricus Helene, *Summula*, transcribed by Peter M. Lefferts (*Thesaurus Musicarum Latinarum*, 2008), fol. 12r. The same term is found in the contemporary anonymous *Speculum cantancium siue psallencium* (fourteenth century), transcribed by Lefferts. See above, note 30. Tr. Andrew Hicks.

34. *Musica angelica est illa quae ab angelis ante conspectum dei semper administratur.* Quoted in Willem Elders, *Symbolic Scores: Studies in the Music of the Renaissance* (Leiden: Brill, 1994), 214.

35. Scholastic views of angelic embodiment would have repercussions for later artistic and literary descriptions of angelic music too; the angels of Milton's *Paradise Lost*, with their famously soft, metaphysical bodies of "essence pure" spend their "happy hours in joy and hymning," and the narrator takes their enduring song as the model for his own unending act of poetic composition. "Thy name / Shall be the copious matter of my song / Henceforth, and never shall my harp thy praise / Forget, nor from thy Father's praise disjoin!" Milton's understanding of angelic song echoes the medieval descriptions outlined above. See John Milton, *Paradise Lost*, ed. Barbara K. Lewalski (Oxford: Blackwell, 2007), I.425, III.417; III.412–15.

36. Stefano Mengozzi, *The Renaissance Reform of Medieval Music Theory: Guido of Arezzo Between Myth and History* (Cambridge: Cambridge University Press, 2010), 123.

37. *Armoniam celestem sancti patres concentum angelorum dixerunt esse, quam in celi patria in laude creatoris sine fine decantant. Nam cum quis beatus illuc producitur tristitiam et gemitum ulterius non habebit, quia videndo Deum in eternum cum eo gaudebit. Ad te igitur, o prudens lector, meus sermo fiat. Quamquam armoniam terrenam queras, quam tibi donare promictimus, tamen ne obliviscaris querere a Deo armoniam illam celestem, que tanto est ista suavior, quanto celum terra videtur esse excelsius.* Johannes Ciconia, *Nova musica, liber primus de consonantiis,* in Johannes Ciconia, *Nova musica and De proportionibus,* ed. and tr. Oliver B. Ellsworth, Greek and Latin Music Theory, vol. 9 (Lincoln: University of Nebraska Press, 1993), 42–232, 54.

38. Alastair Minnis, *Medieval Theory of Authorship: Scholastic Literary Attitudes in the Later Middle Ages* (Philadelphia: University of Pennsylvania Press, 1988).

39. Nicholas Watson, *Richard Rolle and the Invention of Authority* (Cambridge: Cambridge University Press, 1991), 273–94.

40. See Nicholas Watson, "The Middle English Mystics," in *The Cambridge History of Medieval English Literature,* ed. David Wallace (Cambridge: Cambridge University Press, 1999), 539–65, 548.

41. Reginald Maxwell Woolley, ed., *The Officium et Miracula of Richard Rolle of Hampole* (New York: Macmillan, 1919).

42. Katherine Zieman, "The Perils of *Canor*: Mystical Authority, Alliteration, and Extragrammatical Meaning in Rolle, the *Cloud*-Author, and Hilton," *Yearbook of Langland Studies,* no. 22 (2008): 133–66. See also Robert Boenig, "St Augustine's *Jubilus* and Richard Rolle's *Canor,*" in *Vox Mystica: Essays in Honor of Valerie M. Lagorio,* ed. Anne Clark Bartlett (Cambridge: D. S. Brewer, 1995), 75–86.

43. Watson, *Invention of Authority*, 66.

44. See, for instance, Andrew Albin, *Richard Rolle's* Melody of Love: *A Study and Translation with Manuscript and Musical Contexts* (Toronto: Pontifical Institute of Medieval Studies, 2018); Christopher Michael Roman, *Queering Richard Rolle: Mystical Theology and the Hermit in Fourteenth-Century England* (New York: Palgrave Macmillan, 2017); Adin Lears, *World of Echo: Noise and Knowing in Late-Medieval England* (Ithaca, NY: Cornell University Press, 2020).

45. Richard Rolle, *The* Incendium Amoris *of Richard Rolle of Hampole*, ed. Margaret Deanesly (Manchester: Manchester University Press, 1915), 237.

46. Richard Rolle, *The* Melos Amoris *of Richard Rolle of Hampole*, ed. E. J. F. Arnould (Oxford: Blackwell, 1957), 12. Albin, *Richard Rolle's* Melody of Love, 142.

47. *Verus namque et ardens amator Dei quietem mentis et corporis continuam esse appetit, quia maxime tribulatur quando discurrit. Sessio solatur sanctos. Contemplativi capiunt canticum quiescentes, canorum gaudium gerunt; nam fatigato corpore cor iam in canore non calet quietum.* Richard Rolle, *The* Melos Amoris *of Richard Rolle of Hampole*, ed. E. J. F., Arnould, (Oxford: Blackwell, 1957), 12. Albin, *Richard Rolle's* Melody of Love, 142.

48. Richard Rolle, *Ego Dormio*, in *Richard Rolle, Prose and Verse Edited from MS Longleat 29 and Related Manuscripts*, ed. S. J. Ogilvie-Thomson, EETS no. 293 (Oxford: Oxford University Press, 1988), 26–27.

49. *Activi vero in exterioribus gaudent canticis, nos contemplacione divina succensi in sono epulantis terrena transvolamus . . . nemo unquam in amore Dei gaudere potuit, qui prius vana istius mundi solacia non dereliquit.* Richard Rolle, *The* Contra amatores mundi *of Richard Rolle of Hampole*, ed. Paul F. Theiner (Los Angeles: University of California Press, 1968), 80.

50. *Omnis melodia mundialis, omnisque corporalis musica instrumentis organicis machinata, quantumcumque activis seu secularibus viris negociis implicatis placuerint, contemplativis vero desiderabilia non erunt. Immo fugiunt corporalem audire sonitum, quia in se contemplativi viri iam sonum susceperunt celestem.* Rolle, *The* Contra amatores mundi, 80.

51. In the next chapter, I will explore how Rolle's *canor* was critiqued by Walter Hilton (d. 1396) using the framework of the spiritual sensorium; but the spiritual senses are complex and cannot be addressed thoroughly here. See "Spiritual Sensation, the Internal Senses, and the Synaesthetic Body" in Chapter 2.

52. *Ecce eternus iubilus ingeritur. Melos mirabile manet in mente; aures ascultant angelicum amenum ac carmen canorum concipitur in corde.* Rolle, *The* Melos Amoris, 49. Albin, *Richard Rolle's* Melody of Love, 184.

53. *Mens moderata in melodiam mutetur ne metuat molestantem et cor in charitate cremans convertitur in cantum ut canat quotidie carmen Conditori.* Rolle, *The* Melos Amoris, 43. Albin, *Richard Rolle's* Melody of Love, 176.

54. My thanks to Elizabeth Lyon for pointing out this clever use of terminology.

55. *Silere non scio: sic charitas me cogit, ut cuncti cognoscant quia capax consisto cantabilis clamoris et sonum suscipio celicum insignem, dum discedere dilexa a divitum dolore et sancte subsistere solitarie sedendo, canens et calidus ac iubilans ingenter.* Rolle, *The* Melos Amoris, 4–5. Albin, *Richard Rolle's* Melody of Love, 136.

56. *Quamobrem clarissime coronabuntur inter choros concinencium cantica canticorum coram Creatore, atque honorifice assumentur ad equalitatem angelorum quia sine corrupcione carnis tam ardenter amaverunt.* Rolle, *The* Melos Amoris, 28. Albin, *Richard Rolle's* Melody of Love, 160.

57. Jessica Brantley, *Reading in the Wilderness: Private Devotion and Public Performance in Late Medieval England* (Chicago: University of Chicago Press, 2007), 8.

58. Quoted in Steven Rozenski Jr., "Authority and Exemplarity in Henry Suso and Richard Rolle," in *The Medieval Mystical Tradition in England, Exeter Symposium VIII*, ed. E. A. Jones (Cambridge: D. S. Brewer: 2013), 93–108, 103.

59. Rozenski, "Authority and Exemplarity," 100; Andrew Albin, "Auralities: Sound Cultures and the Experience of Hearing in Late Medieval England" (PhD diss., Brandeis University, 2010), 171.

60. This is not the only example of intentionally missing notes in musical transcription when the emotional content is plaintive. The three-voice motet *Ex corruptis / In principibus* from the *Roman de Fauvel* is also intentionally noteless, as the "emotional excess" registers on the manuscript page as "expressive deficiency." See Anna Zayaruznaya, "'*Sanz Note*' and '*Sanz Mesure*': Toward a Premodern Aesthetics of the Dirige," in Kleiman, *Voice and Voicelessness in Medieval Europe*, 155–75, 158.

CHAPTER 2

Note to epigraphs: John Keats, *Ode on a Grecian Urn*, in *The Broadview Anthology of British Literature: Concise Edition*, vol. B, ed. Joseph Black et al. (Buffalo: Broadview Press, 2013), 453–54; Hilton, *Of Angels' Song*, 131.

1. In medieval accounts of sensation, the organ of touch was the heart. Aquinas, commenting on Aristotle's *De sensu et sensato*, at 439a1, says: "Then, when he says 'And so the sensitive part,' he shows where the organ of taste and touch is based. He says that it is 'near the heart,' and he gives the reason, namely that 'the heart is opposite the brain' with respect to position and quality. As the brain is the coolest part of the body, the heart is 'the warmest of' all 'the parts' of the body. For this reason they are placed in opposition to one another in order for the heart's heat to be moderated by the brain's coolness. . . . Since the organ of touch is made of earth, it must be in the body's warmest place as in its principle, so that by the heart's heat the coolness of the earth can be brought to a moderate temperature. This does not prevent an animal from perceiving by means of touch through the whole of its body, because as other senses perceive through an external medium, touch and taste perceive through an internal medium, namely flesh. And just as the principle of sight is not on the surface of the eye, but within, the principle of touch is also within, near the heart, a sign of which is that the most painful wounds are those around the heart. But it cannot be said that there are two sensitive principles in an animal, one near the brain, where the visual, olfactory, auditory principle is established, and one near the heart, where the tactile and gustatory principle is established. The sensitive principle is primarily in the heart, which is also where the source of heat is located in the body of an animal, because nothing is sensitive without heat, as is said in *On the Soul*. The sensitive power flows from the heart to the brain, and from there it proceeds to the organs of three senses, sight, hearing, and smell. But touch and taste are relayed to the heart itself through a medium united to the body, as was said." Thomas Aquinas, "On Sense and What Is Sensed," in *Commentaries on Aristotle's "On Sense and What Is Sensed" and "On Memory and Recollection,"* tr. Edward M. Macierowski and Kevin White (Washington, DC: Catholic University of America Press, 2005), 51–52. *Ostendit 'ubi sit organum tactus et gustus constitutum;' et dicit quod est juxta cor, et assignat hujus rationem, quia cor est oppositum cerebro secundum situm et qualitatem: et sicut cerebrum est frigidissimum omnium, quae in corpore sunt, ita et cor est calidissimum inter omnes corporis partes: et propter hoc sibi invicem opponuntur secundum situm, ut per frigitatem cerebri temperetur caliditas cordis. Et*

*inde est quod illi, qui habent parvum caput secundum proportionem ceterorum membrorum, impetuosi sunt, tamquam calore cordis non sufficienter reflexo per cerebrum. Et e converso illi, qui excedunt immoderate in magnitudine capitis sunt bimis humorosi et pinguiores per magnitudinem cerebri calorem cordis impedientem: propter quod oportet organum tactus, quod terreum est, esse principaliter in loco calidissimo corporis, ut per caliditatem cordis ad temperiem terrae frigiditas reducatur. Nec obstat quod per totum corpus animal sentit sensu tactus: quia sicut alii sensus fiunt per medium extrinsecum, ita tactus et gustus per medium intrinsecum, quod est caro. Et sicut visivum principium non est in superficie oculi, sed intrinsecus; ita etiam principium tactivum est intrinsecus circa cor. Cujus signum est quod laesio, si accidat in locis circa cor, est maxime dolorosa.* Thomas Aquinas, *In Aristoteles Libros: De Sensu et Sensato, De Memoria et Reminiscentia, Commentarium,* ed. Angeli M. Pirotta (Turin: Libraria Marietta, 1820), 28–29.

2. Hearing becomes what Sara Ahmed and Jackie Stacey would call a sensation of "contingency, locatedness, the irreducibility of difference, [and] the passage of emotions and desire." Sara Ahmed and Jackie Stacey, eds., *Thinking Through Skin* (London: Routledge, 2001), 3. See also Claudia Benthien, who argues that touch, as a proximal sense, marks a place of encounter in which the object of the sense and its medium collide. Claudia Benthien, *Skin: On the Cultural Border Between Self and the World,* tr. Thomas Dunlap (New York: Columbia University Press, 2002), 2.

3. Keats's *Ode* and his investment—and Romantic investments more generally—in synaesthesia have often been critiqued and complicated. See Ronald Carter, Malcolm MacRae, and John McRae, eds., *The Routledge History of Literature in English: Britain and Ireland* (New York: Routledge, 1997), 235–39; Yeshayahu Shen and Ravid Aisenman, "'Heard melodies are sweet, but those unheard are sweeter': Synaesthetic Metaphors and Cognition," *Language and Literature* 17:2 (2008): 107–21. For a recent challenge to synaesthetic ways of reading Keats, see Elizabeth Oldfather, "'Ode to a Nightingale': Poetry and the Particularity of Sense," *European Romantic Review* 30 (2019): 557–72.

4. What angelic song is, how it is heard, and who hears it are the sort of *quaestiones* that would later be pilloried in early modern Protestant accounts of medieval Scholasticism, its debates about how many angels could dance on the head of a pin, and its stultifying "syllogisms, majors, minors, conclusions, corollaries, [and] conversions." Desiderius Erasmus, *The Praise of Folly,* tr. Hoyt Hopewell Hudson (Princeton, NJ: Princeton University Press, 2015), 91. For examples of Renaissance referrals of angelic pin-dancing, see William Sclater (d. 1626), *An exposition with notes vpon the first Epistle to the Thessalonians* (Printed by William Sclater for John Parker, 1619), 385; William Chillingsworth, *Religion of Protestants* (Printed by Leonard Lichfield, sold by John Clarke, 1638), 2.

5. The most frequently cited manuscripts of *Of Angels' Song* are Oxford, Bodley MS 576; British Library Add. MS 27592; Lincoln, Cathedral Library MS 91 (the Thornton manuscript); and Cambridge, University Library MS Dd.5.55. There is also a print edition by Pepwell from 1521. The manuscripts that contain *Of Angels' Song* tend to contain devotional material by Rolle and Bonaventure. For some years, *Of Angels' Song* was thought to have been written by Rolle, in spite of its obvious skepticism about angelic song. As with Hilton's other works (like the *Scale of Perfection,* the *Treatise on the Mixed Life,* and his Latin Epistles *Epistola de Leccione, Intencione, Oracione, Meditacione et Allis,* the *Epistola ad Quemdam Seculo Renunciare Volentem* and *Firmissime crede*), *Of Angels' Song* is a treatise of pastoral care and is critical of Rollean mysticism; while not unreceptive to embodied forms of spirituality, it asks its reader to be discerning when engaging in them.

6. Diana Deutsch, "The Speech-to-Song Illusion: Crossing the Borderline Between Speech and Song," in *Musical Illusions and Phantom Words: How Music and Speech Unlock Mysteries of the Brain* (Oxford: Oxford University Press, 2019), 151–69.

7. Windeatt, *Mystics*,133.

8. Windeatt, *Mystics*, 136, 135.

9. Windeatt, *Mystics*, 135.

10. See Chapter 4.

11. For more reading on the transmission and circulation of Rolle's work, see Tamas Karáth, *Richard Rolle: The Fifteenth-Century Translations* (Leiden: Brepols, 2018); Andrew Albin, "Canorous Soundstuff: Hearing the *Officium* of Richard Rolle of Hampole," *Speculum* 91:4 (2016): 1026–39; Ralph Hanna, "The Transmission of Richard Rolle's Latin Works," *Library: The Transactions of the Bibliographical Society* 14:3 (2013): 313–33; Elizabeth Freeman, "The Priory of Hampole and Its Literary Culture: English Religious Women and Books in the Age of Richard Rolle," *Parergon: Journal of the Australian and New Zealand Association for Medieval and Early Modern Studies* 29:1 (2012): 1–25; McIlroy, *English Prose Treatises of Richard Rolle*; Kevin Gustafson, "Richard Rolle's English Psalter and the Making of a Lollard Text," *Viator: Medieval and Renaissance Studies* 33 (2002): 294–309; Carl Horstmann, *Yorkshire Writers: Richard Rolle of Hampole and His Followers* (Cambridge: Brewer, 1999); A. I. Doyle, "Carthusian Participation in the Movement of Works of Richard Rolle Between England and Other Parts of Europe in the 14th and 15th Centuries," in *Kartausermystik und -mystiker*, Analecta Cartusiana 55 (Salzburg: Institut for Anglistik und Amerikanistik, University of Salzburg, 1981).

12. On Rolle and *canor*, see the Introduction. See also Andrew Albin's discussion of *canor* in his introduction to his edition of the *Melos amoris* as well as Nicholas Watson's in his monograph on Rolle. Albin, *Richard Rolle's Melody of Love*, 35–36, 105–17; Watson, *Invention of Authority*, in particular 8–9.

13. For a discussion of the importance of these fourteenth-century movements, skepticism, and embodiment, see Julie Orlemanski, *Symptomatic Subjects: Bodies, Medicine, and Causation in the Literature of Late Medieval England* (Philadelphia: University of Pennsylvania Press, 2019), especially "From Noise to Narration in the *Book of Margery Kempe*," 249–77.

14. See in particular Nancy Caciola's thoughtful discussion of the role of skepticism in policing women's spirituality. Nancy Caciola, *Discerning Spirits: Divine and Demonic Possession in the Middle Ages* (Ithaca, NY: Cornell University Press, 2003), 274–320.

15. Steven Justice, "Did the Middle Ages Believe in Their Miracles?," *Representations* 103:1 (2008): 1–29.

16. Windeatt, *Mystics*, 133.

17. Furthermore, the ability of language to accurately represent reality is not unique to mystical experience but is universal to the narration of experience in general. See, for instance, Elaine Scarry, *The Body in Pain: The Making and Unmaking of the World* (Oxford: Oxford University Press, 1987).

18. For a discussion of touch in medieval philosophical frameworks, see Dag Nikolaus Hesse, "The Soul's Faculties," in *The Cambridge History of Medieval Philosophy*, ed. Robert Pasnau (Cambridge: Cambridge University Press, 2014), 305–19; Katie L. Walter, ed., *Reading Skin in Medieval Literature and Culture* (New York: Palgrave Macmillan, 2013).

19. This is not only an Aristotelian or Avicennan understanding of touch, but a mystical one: for earlier writers like Bonaventure and Bernard of Clairvaux touch implies proximity,

intimacy, and immediate awareness. Paul L. Gavrilyuk and Sarah Coakley, eds., *The Spiritual Senses: Perceiving God in Western Christianity* (Cambridge: Cambridge University Press, 2012), 9.

20. Walter Hilton, *The Scale of Perfection*, tr. John P. H. Clark and Rosemary Dorward (New York: Paulist Press, 1991), 13.

21. For more complete historical narratives of spiritual sensation, see Gavrilyuk and Coakley, *The Spiritual Senses*; Gordon Rudy, *The Mystical Language of Sensation in the Later Middle Ages* (New York: Routledge, 2002); Augustin Poulain, *The Graces of Interior Prayer*, tr. L. L. Yorke Smith (London: Kegan Paul, Trench, Trübner, 1950); and Karl Rahner, "Le debut d'une doctrine des cinq sens spirituels chez Origène," *RAM* 13 (1932): 113–45. In *Promised Bodies*, Patricia Dailey discusses the trope of the "inner" and "outer" body in medieval religious literature and experience; throughout his six-volume *Presence of God: A History of Western Christian Mysticism* (New York: Crossroad, 1991–2016), Bernard McGinn discusses spiritual sensation in the works of specific medieval mystics, but more specifically, see Bernard McGinn, "The Language of Inner Experience in Christian Mysticism," *Spiritus: A Journal of Christian Spirituality* 1:2 (2001): 156–71.

22. "There are seven stages of this internal knowledge, the first of which is reached through illuminations relating purely to the sciences. The second consists in virtues. . . . The third stage consists in the seven gifts of the Holy Spirit, which Isaiah enumerates. The fourth consists in the beatitudes, which the Lord defines in the Gospels. The fifth consists in the spiritual senses. The sixth consists in fruits, of which is the peace of God which passes all understanding. The seventh consists in raptures and their states according to the different ways in which people are caught up to see many things of which it is not lawful for a man to speak." Roger Bacon, *Opus maius*, tr. Robert Belle Burke (New York: Russell and Russell, 1962), II.6.1:585, 586. *Et sunt septem gradus hujus scientiae interioris, unus per illuminationes pure scientiales. Alius gradus consistin in virtutibus. . . . tertius gradus est in septem donis Spiritus Sancti, quae enumerat Isaias. Quartus est in beatitudinibus, quas Dominus in evangeliis determinat. Quintus est in sensibus spiritualibus. Sextus est in fructibus, de quibus est pax Domini quae exsuperat omnem sensum. Septimus consistit in raptibus et modis eorum secundum quod diversi diversimode capiuntur, ut videant multa, quae non licet homini loqui.* Roger Bacon, *Opus maius*, ed. John Henry Bridges (Oxford: Clarendon Press, 1897), 2:170–71. For a fuller account of Albert the Great's contribution to spiritual sensation in the context of later medieval writing, see Rudy, *The Mystical Language of Sensation*, 42.

23. *Notre âme possède-t-elle des sens spirituels intellectuels, ayant une certaine ressemblance avec les sens corporels, de telle sorte qu'elle puisse connaitre d'une façon analogue, et de diverse manières, la présence des purs esprits, et, en parlieulier, la présence de Dieu?* Augustin Poulain, *Des grâces d'oraison: Traité de théologie mystique* (Paris: G. Beauchesne, 1922), 93. This translation is taken from Mark McInroy, *Balthasazar on the Interior Senses: Perceiving Splendor* (Oxford: Oxford University Press, 2014), 4 (emphasis mine). For another helpful history of the senses (primarily in the early Middle Ages), see Elizabeth Sears, "The Iconography of Auditory Perception in the Early Middle Ages: On Psalm Illustration and Psalm Exegesis," in *The Second Sense: Studies in Hearing and Musical Judgment from Antiquity to the Seventeenth Century*, ed. Charles Burnett, Michael Fend, and Penelope Gouk (London: The Warburg Institute, 1991), 19–38.

24. Nicholas of Cusa presents a different solution to the problem, suggesting that the spiritual senses are the "theological significance" of the internal senses, combining the Aristotelian doctrine of the common sense (*sensus communis*) and the inner senses (*sensus interi-*

*ores*) with the Origenist doctrine of the spiritual senses (*sensus spirituales*). See Garth W. Green, "Nicholas of Cusa," in Gavrilyuk and Coakley, *The Spiritual Senses*, 210–23.

25. Origen, *Contra Celsum*, tr. Henry Chadwick (Cambridge: Cambridge University Press, 1953), 44.

26. Pseudo-Dionysius, "The Celestial Hierarchy," in *Pseudo-Dionysius: The Complete Works*, tr. Colm Lubhéid (New York: Paulist Press, 1987), XV.3.332, 185.

27. *Ecce in hac auctoritate distinguuntur quinque sensus spirituales quibus fruimur Deo. Visu spirituali delectamur in plenitudine Dei, et auditu spirituali delectamur in simphonia Die . . . et odoratu spirituali in bono odore Dei, et tactu spirituali in suavitate Dei.* William of Auxerre, *Summa Aurea* 18.3.3.2.2, quoted in Boyd Taylor Coolman, *Knowing God by Experience: The Spiritual Senses in the Theology of William of Auxerre* (Washington, DC: Catholic University of America Press, 2004), 43–44.

28. "By desire not by hand, by wish not by eye, by faith not by senses. . . . you will touch with the hand of faith, the finger of desire, the embrace of devotion; you will touch with the eye of the mind." Bernard of Clairvaux, *Sermons on the Canticle of Canticles*, tr. a Priest of Mount Melleray (Dublin: Browne and Nolan, 1920), 331.

29. Coolman, *Knowing God by Experience*, 132.

30. *Haberes visum spiritualem acutum et perspicacem in contemplacione rerum spiritualium quibus pasceres cor tuum satis delicate. Audires eciam laudes Dei sine sono corporis, puro intellectu mentis, ab omni creatura dulci modulamine decantatas.* Walter Hilton, "De imagine peccati," in *Walter Hilton's Latin Writings*, vol. 1, ed. John P. H. Clark and Cheryl Taylor (Salzburg: Institut für Anglistik und Amerikanistik, 1987), 94–95.

31. *Mi ripingeva là dove il sol tace* ("pushed me back where the sun is silent"). Dante Alighieri, *The Divine Comedy* (Richmond: Alma Classics, 2012), *Inferno* I.60, 7.

32. Anonymous, "Pearl," in *The Poems of the Pearl Manuscript: Pearl, Cleanness, Patience, Sir Gawain and the Green Knight*, ed. Malcolm Andrew and Ronald Waldron (Exeter: University of Exeter Press, 2002), ll. 58–59, 57.

33. Josephine Machon, "Defining (Syn)aesthetics," in *(Syn)aesthetics: Redefining Visceral Performance*, ed. Josephine Machon (London: Palgrave Macmillan UK, 2009), 13–33, 13.

34. Glauco Cambon, "Synaesthesia in the *Divine Comedy*," in *Dante Studies, with the Annual Report of the Dante Society* 88 (1970): 1–16, 1, 4.

35. Jessica Wiskus, *The Rhythm of Thought: Art, Literature, and Music After Merleau-Ponty* (Chicago: University of Chicago Press, 2013), 98.

36. Reuven Tsur, *Playing by Ear and the Tip of the Tongue: Precategorical Information in Poetry* (Amsterdam: John Benjamins, 2012), 223.

37. Shane Butler and Alex C. Purves, "Introduction," in *Synaesthesia and the Ancient Senses*, ed. Shane Butler and Alex C. Purves (New York: Routledge, 2014), 1–8, 5, 6.

38. Machon, "Defining (Syn)aesthetics," 13, 16.

39. Alexander Luria, *The Mind of a Mnemonist: A Little Book About a Vast Memory*, tr. Lynn Solotaroff (Cambridge, MA: Harvard University Press, 1968), 77.

40. Wiskus, *The Rhythm of Thought*, 98.

41. Tsur, *Playing by Ear*, 227.

42. Gilles Deleuze and Félix Guattari, "How Do You Make Yourself a Body Without Organs?," in *A Thousand Plateaus*, tr. Brian Massumi (Minneapolis: University of Minnesota Press, 1987), 149–66.

43. Windeatt, *Mystics*, 133.

44. For contemporary neurobiological studies of interoception that are relevant to this chapter, see in particular Marina Kluchko and Elvira Brattico, "Interoception in the Sensory Sensitivities: Evidence from the Auditory Domain," in *Cognitive Neuroscience* 10:3 (2019): 166–68; Stefan Koelsch, Peter Vuust, and Karl Friston, "Predictive Processes and the Peculiar Case of Music," in *Trends in Cognitive Sciences* 23:1 (2019): 63–77; Norman Farb, Jennifer Daubenmier, et al., "Interoception, Contemplative Practice, and Health," *Frontiers in Psychology* 6 (2015): 1–26; J. Brendan Ritchie and Peter Carruthers, "The Bodily Senses," in *The Oxford Handbook of Philosophy of Perception*, ed. Mohan Matthen (Oxford: Oxford University Press, 2015), 353–70; Stefan Wiens, "Interoception in Emotional Experience," *Current Opinion in Neurology* 18:4 (2005): 442–47; A. D. Craig, "Interoception: The Sense of the Physiological Condition of the Body," *Current Opinion in Neurobiology* 13 (2003): 500–505; and A. D. Craig, "How Do You Feel? Interoception: The Sense of the Physiological Condition of the Body," *Neuroscience* 3 (2002): 655–66.

45. At the same time, the five exteroceptions themselves occur along a spectrum of distal or proximal effects, with sight and hearing teloreceptive relative to touch, smell, and taste.

46. Craig, "Interoception, 500–505; Craig, "How Do You Feel?," 655–66.

47. Craig, "How Do You Feel?," 662.

48. Medieval theories of the emotions largely followed Plato, who suggested that the emotions were literally motions of the soul, either toward what was desirable (concupiscible emotions) or away from what was fearful (irascible emotions). See Simo Knuutila, "Medieval Conceptions of Emotions from Abelard to Aquinas," in *Emotions in Ancient and Medieval Philosophy* (Oxford: Oxford University Press, 2004), 177–254.

49. Most recently, Katie Walter, *Middle English Mouths: Late Medieval Medical, Religious, and Literary Traditions* (Cambridge: Cambridge University Press, 2018); but also useful are Gabrielle Parkin, "Read with Your Hands and Not with Your Eyes: Touching Books of Hours," in *Later Middle English Literature, Materiality, and Culture: Essays in Honor of James M. Dean*, ed. Brian Gastle and Erick Kelemen (Newark: University of Delaware Press, 2018), 147–66; Carolyn Walker Bynum, *Christian Materiality: An Essay on Religion in Late Medieval Europe* (Brooklyn: Zone Books, 2015); Jennifer Borland, "Unruly Reading: The Consuming Role of Touch in the Experience of a Medieval Manuscript," in *Scraped, Stroked, and Bound: Materially Engaged Readings of Medieval Manuscripts*, ed. Jonathan Wilcox (Turnhout: Brepols, 2013), 97–114; Robyn Malo, *Relics and Writing in Late Medieval England* (Toronto: University of Toronto Press, 2013); Elizabeth Robertson, "*Noli Me Tangere:* The Enigma of Touch in Middle English Religious Literature and Art for and about Women," in Walter, *Reading Skin*, 29–55; Carroll Hilles, "The Sacred Image and the Healing Touch: The Veronica in Julian of Norwich's *Revelation of Divine Love*," *Journal of Medieval and Early Modern Studies* 28:3 (1998): 553–80.

50. Walter, *Middle English Mouths*, 15 and 12. Walter's book as a whole goes into more detail on the importance of touch for medieval writers than this book is able to.

51. Perhaps the closest contemporary interoceptive analogues are ASMR or frisson. ASMR, or autonomous sensory meridian response, is a tingling feeling that some people experience when they are exposed to soft, repetitive noises. The tingling—a sort of inner touch—radiates from back of the head throughout the body and is accompanied by feelings of relaxation and contentment. Frisson, which is related to ASMR though not identical to it, is the euphoria and excitement, accompanied by chills, that some people feel when listening to music. In both ASMR and frisson, the introduction of auditory stimuli causes a pleasurable

synaesthetic and autonomous response accompanied by an affective state. Both ASMR and frisson describe the sort of experience that Hilton would understand as angelic song. See Beverly Fredborg, Jim Clark, and Stephen D. Smith, "An Examination of Personality Traits Associated with Autonomous Sensory Meridian Response (ASMR)," in *Frontiers in Psychology* 8 (2017): 1–9; Marissa A. del Campo and Thomas J. Kehle, "Autonomous Sensory Meridian Response (ASMR) and Frisson: Mindfully Induced Sensory Phenomena That Promote Happiness," *International Journal of School and Educational Psychology* 4 (2016): 99–105; Joceline Anderson, "Now You've Got the Shivers: Affect, Intimacy, and the ASMR Whisper Community," *Television and New Media* 16 (2015): 683–700; Emma L. Barratt and Nick J. Davis, "Autonomous Sensory Meridian Response (ASMR): A Flow-Like Mental State," *PeerJ* 3:e851 (2015); Emily C. Nusbaum, Paul J. Silvia, et al., "Listening Between the Notes: Aesthetic Chills in Everyday Music Listening," *Psychology of Aesthetics, Creativity, and the Arts* 8:1 (2014): 104–9; Julie Beck, "How to Have a 'Brain Orgasm,'" *The Atlantic*, December 16, 2013, https://www.theatlantic.com/health/archive/2013/12/how-to-have-a-brain-orgasm/282356/; N. K. Ahuja, "It Feels Good to Be Measured: Clinical Role-Play, Walker Percy, and the Tingles," *Perspectives in Biology and Medicine* 56:3 (2013): 442–51.

52. This move is made partly under bibliographic duress as well: literary-critical work on synaesthesia is still in its nascent stage; other archives and other discourses have well-developed ways of talking about synaesthesia in comparison.

53. This is not the case for Byzantine manuscripts, where angels frequently interact with humans; this is due to theological differences regarding angelic being that are beyond the scope of this book. For more, see Amy Gillette, "The Music of Angels in Byzantine and Post-Byzantine Art," *Peregrinations: Journal of Medieval Art and Architecture* 6:4 (2018): 26–78. And, naturally, across the huge corpus of medieval art and iconography, there will be some exceptions. Nevertheless, the tendency is toward the lack of tactile interaction between human bodies and angelic ones in Western medieval art.

54. Gill, *Angels and the Order of Heaven*; Josephine von Henneberg, "Saint Francesca Romana and Guardian Angels in Baroque Art," *Religion and the Arts* 2 (1998): 467–87.

55. This is not manuscript bleed-through. BnF NAF 16251 is illustrated on only one side of each page, and so fol. 56v is blank, as is 57r. Folio 57v (the beheading of John the Baptist) does not correspond with the kneeling figure on folio 56r.

56. The roundels in the Church of St. Orso in Aosto are from the twelfth century. The paintings of Guariento di Arpa were originally made for the Reggia Chapel in the Palazzo Carrara in Padua. They are now housed in the Museo Civico at Padua.

57. British Library, Stowe MS 12, the Stowe Breviary, fol. 128r, depicts a sick man being touched on the forehead by an angel. This is Tobit, who is being cured of blindness. That is, the angelic touch occurs in the absence of visual experience.

58. British Library, Royal MS 2.B.xv, fol. 66v. Aberdeen, University Library MS 25, for instance, was created for Elizabeth Woodville, queen of Edward IV. This book has ties to Syon Abbey and the fraternity and hospital dedicated to the Virgin Mary and All Angels near Syon around 1446. A few other examples survive: Liverpool Cathedral, MS Radcliffe 6 was modeled after the Aberdeen manuscript; Jean Luyt commissioned Bodleian Library MS Lat liturg.e.17, a northern English Sarum prayer- and office-book with substantial "angelic" material; and two Books of Hours made for Thomas Butler, the seventh Earl of Ormond (d. 1515)—British Library, Royal MS 2.B.xv and Harley MS 2887—contain prayers to the Guardian Angel. See Anne Sutton and Livia Visser-Fuchs, "The Cult of Angels in Late Fifteenth-Century England:

An Hours of the Guardian Angel presented to Queen Elizabeth Woodville," in *Women and the Book: Assessing the Visual Evidence*, ed. Lesley Smith and Jane H. M. Taylor (London: The British Library; Toronto: University of Toronto Press, 1996), 230–65.

59. *Angele qui meus es custos pietate superna me tibi commissum: salva defende guberna. O tu dulcis angele qui mecum moraris, licet personaliter mecum non loquaris. Animam cum corpore procor tuearis. Tuum hoc est officium ad quod assignaris. O beate angele nunti dei nostri, cogitatus et actus meos regula: ad votum dei altissimi.* British Library, Royal MS 2.B.xv, fol. 66v.

60. British Library, Additional MS 37049, fol. 74v.

61. Thomas Hoccleve, "Honoured be Thous blissful Lord Jesu," in Brant Lee Doty, "An Edition of British Museum MS Additional 37049: A Religious Miscellany" (PhD diss., Michigan State University, 1969), 414–16.

62. See, for instance, David Cottington's assessment of cubism's pessimism that vision might adequately apprehend depth or tactility in *Cubism and Its Histories* (Manchester: Manchester University Press, 2004), 203–9.

63. Herbert L. Kessler, *Spiritual Seeing: Picturing God's Invisibility in Medieval Art* (Philadelphia: University of Pennsylvania Press, 2000).

64. Jeffrey Hamburger, *Nuns as Artists: The Visual Culture of a Medieval Convent* (Berkeley: University of California Press, 1997); Seth Lerer, "'Representyd Now in Yower Syght,' the Culture of Spectatorship in Late Fifteenth-Century England," in *Bodies and Disciplines*, ed. Barbara Hanawalt and David Wallace (Minneapolis: University of Minnestoa Press, 1996), 29–62.

65. Williamson, "Sensory Experience."

66. Modern physical models claim that we never really "touch" anything. Instead, the atoms that make up our bodies and the world around us are not only 99.9999999 percent empty space, but also repel each other through electromagnetic forces. Our nervous system produces the *illusion* of touch.

67. John Trevisa, *On the Properties of Things, John Trevisa's Translation of Bartholomaeus Anglicus* De Proprietatibus Rerum, *a Critical Text*, ed. M. C. Seymour et al. (Oxford: Clarendon Press, 1975), 1:186.

68. Anonymous, "A Treatise on the Mensuration of Heights and Distances," in *Rara mathematica; or, A Collection Of Treatises on the Mathematics and Subjects Connected with Them*, ed. James Orchard Halliwell-Phillipps (London: John William Parker, 1839), 56–71, 62.

69. Benthien, *Skin*, 2.

70. For instance, in *The Cloud of Unknowing*, "Ever the nere men touchen the trewth, more war men behoveth to be of errour," and elsewhere repeatedly in the text. See Anonymous, *The Cloud of Unknowing*, ed. Patrick J. Gallacher (Kalamazoo: Medieval Institute Publications, 1997), ll. 1275–76; Capgrave's *The Life of Saint Katherine* has the eponymous saint use this sense of the word: "I will touch anothir thing / I wole ye shull encline all youre entente / To herkyne my wordis and my talkyng." John Capgrave, *The Life of Saint Katherine*, ed. Karen A. Winstead (Kalamazoo: Medieval Institute Publications, 1999), ll. 911–13.

71. Julian of Norwich, "A Revelation of Love," in *The Writings of Julian of Norwich: A Vision Showed to a Devout Woman and A Revelation of Love*, ed. Nicholas Watson and Jacqueline Jenkins (State College: Pennsylvania State University Press, 2006), chap. 51, 281.

72. See Nancy G. Siraisi, "The Music of Pulse in the Writings of Italian Academic Physicians (Fourteenth and Fifteenth Centuries)," *Speculum* 1 (1975): 689–710, as well as Jane Hatter, "*Col tempo*: Musical Time, Aging, and Sexuality in 16th-Century Venetian Paintings," *Early Music* 39:1 (2011): 3–14.

73. *Et ego quidem miror quomodo proportiones iste per tactum discerni possunt: dico tamen quod ei est facile qui in gradu tangendi consueuit, et proportionatur sonos per artem, postquam erit ei potentia cognosciendi musicam acquisitam, et comparabit artificiose sensatum ad id quod intellectu est perceptum.* Avicenna, *Liber Canonis* (Basil: Johannes Heruagios, 1556), Book 1, Fen 2, Doctrina 3, Chapter 1, 89; Oskar Cameron Gruner, tr., *A Treatise on the Canon of Medicine of Avicenna* (New York: AMS Press, 1930), 293.

74. "The motions of the pulse are produced according to due proportions, which music uses, but the proportions there existing cannot be referred to hearing but only to touch, and therefore they are not part of the science of music." *Aliqui tamen motus alii habent consimiles proportiones, sed non possunt sono et gestui conformari in unam delectationem, ut sunt motus pulsus. Fiunt enim secundum debitas proportiones, quibus music utitur, sed ibi existentes non possunt referri ad auditum, sed respectu tactus tantum; et ideo non sunt de scientia musicae,* Latin and English quoted in Siraisi, "The Music of Pulse," 708.

75. Bacon is probably reflecting here the novel idea, introduced in the thirteenth century, that music is the science of *sonus numeratus* as opposed to *numerus ad aliquid.* See Gilles Rico, "'*Auctoritas Cereum habet Nasum*': Boethius, Aristotle, and the Music of the Spheres," in *Citation and Authority in Medieval and Renaissance Musical Culture: Learning from the Learned. Essays in Honour of Margaret Bent,* ed. Suzannah Clark and Elizabeth Eva Leach (Woodbridge: Boydell and Brewer, 2005), 20–28, 24.

76. English attestations of the word "pulse" are fairly late, with some of the first uses by John Trevisa in his translation of Ranulph Higden's *Polychronicon.* English medicine lacks the musical references to pulse found so frequently in Latin and Italian sources. See "pouse" in Robert E. Lewis et al., eds., *The Middle English Dictionary* (Ann Arbor: University of Michigan Press, 1952–2001).

77. For a discussion of meter and rhythm from a slightly later historical perspective, see the first chapter, "Beating Time," in Roger Grant, *Beating Time and Measuring Music in the Early Modern Era* (Oxford: Oxford University Press, 2014), 15–42.

78. Both the words *mensura* and *tactus* had vernacular equivalents as well, such as *tatto, tacte, Takt,* tact, *mensura, mesure, Mensur,* measure, *battuta, batue, Schlag,* beat, *compas, morula, ictus, praescriptus, dimentio,* and stroke. See DeFord, *Tactus,* 51.

79. There is some room for dissent about whether breathing or the heartbeat was more fundamentally important for the *tactus.* For instance, Howard Mayer Brown, in the *tactus* entry in the *New Grove Dictionary of Instruments* (Oxford: Oxford University Press, 1984), cites Gaffurius in support of this notion ("One tactus equals the pulse of a man breathing normally"), but Dale Bonge argues that both Gaffurius and his contemporary Ramos de Pareja were more interested in the beating of the heart (more specifically, diastole-systole, the long-short beats of the heart mapping on to the medieval propensity for ternary time) itself than in the pulmonary causes of the heartbeat. See Ephraim Segerman, "Tempo and Tactus After 1500," in *Companion to Medieval and Renaissance Music,* ed. Tess Knighton and David Fallows (Berkeley: University of California Press, 1992), 337–44, 340.

80. *Instar pulsus istius pedem aut manum sive digitum tangens in aliquem locum canendo moveat.* DeFord, *Tactus,* 56.

81. DeFord, *Tactus,* 58.

82. DeFord, *Tactus,* 3.

83. See Michelle Sauer's work on audiotactility: Michelle M. Sauer, "Audiotactility and the Medieval Soundscape of Parchment," *Sounding Out!* (October 2016), https://soundstudiesblog.com/author/ndanchoress/; and Sauer, "Touching Jesus: Christ's Side Wound

and Medieval Manuscript Tradition," *Women's Literary Culture and the Medieval Canon: An International Network Funded by the Leverhulme Trust* (January 2016), http://blogs.surrey.ac .uk/medievalwomen/2016/01/05/touching-jesus-christs-side-wound-medieval-manuscript -tradition/. One might compare the medieval practice of assaying manuscript side-wounds with the "little side holes" (*Seitenhölchen*) that appear on Moravian index cards of the eighteenth century that let the reader look *out* of the side-wound, giving the impression of having crawled into Jesus's side. See Craig Atwood, "Little Side Holes," *Journal of Moravian History* no. 6 (Spring 2009): 61–75.

84. DeFord, *Tactus*, 58.

85. Windeatt, *Mystics*, 134.

86. See both "Frenesie" and "Fantasie" in Lewis et al., *The Middle English Dictionary*; online edition, ed. Frances McSparra, et al. (Ann Arbor: University of Michigan Library, 2000–2018). *Modo cantant, modo rident, modo plorant se custodientem . . . raro silent, multum clamant. Hii periulosissime egrotant et tamen se egrotare nunc ignorant.* Bartholomeus Anglicus, *De proprietatibus rerum* (Nuremberg: Anton Koberger, 1483), Book 7, Cap. iv, n.p.

87. Knuutila, "Medieval Conceptions of Emotions," 205.

88. Windeatt, *Mystics*, 131.

89. Windeatt, *Mystics*, 136.

90. For more on "troth" versus "truth," see Richard Firth Green, *A Crisis of Truth: Literature and Law in Late Medieval England* (Philadelphia: University of Pennsylvania Press, 2002), 1–40.

91. Windeatt, *Mystics*, 135, 136.

92. Some of the most important treatments of skepticism of the medieval period are Augustine's *Against the Academicians* and *The Teacher*, but writing by Thomas of York, Siger of Brabant, Henry of Ghent, and John Duns Scotus provided Scholastic treatments of the issue. Medieval philosophy rejected the idea that knowledge from sensation was impossible. Most modern academic treatments of early skepticism focus on either the classical period or the Renaissance. For skepticism in the medieval period, see Henrik Lagerlund, ed., *Rethinking the History of Skepticism: The Missing Medieval Background* (Leiden: Brill, 2010), and Katherine Tachau, *Vision and Certitude in the Age of Ockham* (Leiden: Brill, 1988). See also Charles Bolyard, "Augustine, Epicurus, and External World Skepticism," *Journal of the History of Philosophy* 44:2 (2006): 157–68.

93. Augustine, *Against the Academicians and The Teacher,* tr. Peter King (Cambridge: L. Hackett, 1995), 160. This did not mean that people—mystics, devotional readers, and the like—might not come to wrong conclusions: if the intellect were not in the proper position to oversee them properly, they might err, as in the case of the mentally ill.

94. In addition to the Lollards in England, the Beguines and the followers of the *Devotio Moderna* in the Low Countries, Marguerite Porete, and those who belonged to the Brethren of the Free Spirit were all members of groups that sought to personalize religious experience. To counteract the potential heresy of vernacular mysticism, treatises on the discernment of spirits—texts that quite literally taught how to properly perceive sensibles— were written in an attempt to simultaneously interpret and entrain sense-perception among the laity. For instance, Jean Gerson, a contemporary of Walter Hilton, wrote a series of treatises on the subject—*De probatione spirituum, De distinctione verarum visionum a falsis,* and *De examinatione doctrinarum*—all of which consider the work of discerning the truth-value of sense-perception to be of the utmost importance for a critical evaluation of both revelatory experience and more mundane private reading practice. See Jean Gerson, *De probatione*

*spirituum, De distinctione verarum visionum a falsis,* and *De examinatione doctrinarum,* in *Opera Omnia,* ed. L. Ellis du Pin (The Hague, 1728), vol. 1; Gerson, "On Distinguishing True from False Revelations," in *Jean Gerson: Early Works,* tr. Brian Patrick McGuire (Mahwah, NJ: Paulist Press, 1998), 334–64; See also Caciola, *Discerning Spirits;* and Rosalynn Voaden, *God's Words, Women's Voices: The Discernment of Spirits in the Writing of Late-Medieval Women Visionaries* (York: York Medieval Press, 1999).

95. In the final chapter of this book, I will consider how Chaucer invokes the types of disabilities and impossibilities in order to imbue texts with a musical power. See Chapter 6.

CHAPTER 3

Note to epigraph: *Vel dicitur musica a "muso, sas", quod est "dubitare", vel "cum silentio murmurare", vel potius "cogitando alquid inquirere", quod magis ad musicam pertinet theoricam.* Jacobus Leodiensis, *Speculum musicae,* 19–20.

1. George Harne, "The Ends of Theory and Practice"; Noel Swerdlow, "*Musica dicitur a Moys, quod est aqua,*" *Journal of the American Musicological Society* 20:1 (1967): 3–9.

2. Quintilian, *Institutio Oratoria,* tr. Harold Edgeworth Butler (Cambridge, MA: Harvard University Press, 1996), I.vi.38, 128–29: *Quidam non dubitaverunt etymologiae subiicere omnem nominis causam: ut ex habitu, quemadmodum dixi . . . ex sono strepere, murmurare.* Some scholars do not hesitate to have recourse to etymology for the origin of every word, deriving . . . verbs such as '*strepere*' or '*murmurare*' from the sounds which they represent.

3. Jacques Attali, *Noise: The Political Economy of Music,* tr. Brian Massumi (Minneapolis: University of Minnesota Press, 2009), 19. Attali also claims that there was no "legislation for the suppression of noise and commotion" and that "the right to make noise was a natural right, an affirmation of each individual's autonomy." This is historically inaccurate.

4. Lisbeth Lipari, *Listening, Thinking, Being: Toward an Ethics of Attunement* (University Park: Pennsylvania State University Press, 2014), 50–51. See also Lipari, "Rhetoric's Other: Levinas, Listening, and the Ethical Response," *Philosophy and Rhetoric* 45 (2012): 227–45, 233. "Hearing denotes a capacity to discriminate characteristics of one's environment through aural sense perception, but listening is a relationally oriented phenomenon; it 'connects and bridges.'" In this sense, it is similar to Heidegger's differentiation of *horchen* (to hear) and *hören* (to listen, to understand) out of which conscience—and being—arise. Martin Heidegger, *Being and Time,* tr. Joan Stambaugh (New York: State University of New York Press, 1996), especially 250–76. For a cursory account of "hearing" versus "listening," see Michael Inwood, *A Heidegger Dictionary* (Oxford: Blackwell Press, 1999), s.v. "hearing," 86–87.

5. *Nisi enim ab homine memoria teneantur soni, pereunt, quia scribi non possunt.* Isidore of Seville, *Etymologies,* tr. Stephen A. Barney, W. J. Lewis, J. A. Beach, and Oliver Berghof (Cambridge: Cambridge University Press, 2006), III.xv, 95; Isidore of Seville, *Etymologiarum sive Originum Libri XX,* ed. W. M. Lindsay (Oxford: Clarendon Press, 1911), III.xv, n.p.

6. This phrase is Cheryl Glenn and Krista Ratcliffe's. See Glenn and Ratcliffe, eds., *Silence and Listening.* For Glenn and Ratcliffe, rhetoric has power because of silence, and listening is at the heart of all communicative acts.

7. *The Book of Margery Kempe: Annotated Edition,* ed. Barry Windeatt (Woodbridge: D. S. Brewer, 2006), Book I, P, 46.

8. For the bowdlerized and shortened version of Margery's text, see Henry Pepwell, *The Cell of Self-Knowledge,* ed. E. Gardner (London: Chatto and Windus, 1910). Early critics saw

Margery's desire to weep and wail as an indication of hysteria or postpartum depression, as a female voice that disrupted normal sociality, but this diagnosis has long been put to rest by contemporary scholarship, beginning with Karma Lochrie, *Margery Kempe and Translations of the Flesh* (Philadelphia: University of Pennsylvania Press, 1991) and Lynn Staley, *Margery Kempe's Dissenting Fictions* (State College: Pennsylvania State University Press, 1994), and continuing with recent studies, such as Rebecca Krug, *Margery Kempe and the Lonely Reader* (Ithaca, NY: Cornell University Press, 2017).

9. In addition to Karma Lochrie (1991) and Lynn Staley (1994), see David Lawton, "Voice, Authority, and Blasphemy in *The Book of Margery Kempe*," in *Margery Kempe: A Book of Essays*, ed. Sandra J. McEntire (New York: Garland, 1992), 93–115, who argues that Kempe's "unique voice as a woman" is preserved even if her speech is mediated; Diana R. Uhlman, "The Comfort of Voice, the Solace of Script: Orality and Literacy in *The Book of Margery Kempe*," *Studies in Philology* 91:1 (1994): 50–69, who argues that the *Boke* neutralizes the materiality of writing in a power-play between Margery's oral voice and the text's written one, allowing the "trewe sentence" of her words to be "trewly drawyn out" (55); as well as Karma Lochrie, "From Utterance to Text," in *The Book of Margery Kempe: A New Translation, Contexts, Criticism*, ed. Lynn Staley (New York: W.W. Norton, 2001), 243–56.

10. Liz Herbert McAvoy argues that Margery leverages the paradoxes of the "authority of the female voice" in the medieval period to attain rhetorical power; see Liz Herbert McAvoy, *Authority and the Female Body in the Writings of Julian of Norwich and Margery Kempe* (Cambridge: D. S. Brewer, 2004), 172; see also Felicity Riddy, "Text and Self in *The Book of Margery Kempe*," in *Voices in Dialogue: Reading Women in the Middle Ages*, ed. Linda Olson and Kathryn Kerby-Fulton (South Bend, IN: University of Notre Dame Press, 2005), 435–53; and Nicholas Watson, "The Making of the *Book of Margery Kempe*," in Olson and Kerby-Fulton, *Voices in Dialogue*, 395–434.

11. Orlemanski, "Margery's 'Noyse,'" 123–38.

12. P. R. Robins, "Discerning Voices in the Trial of Joan of Arc and *The Book of Margery Kempe*," in *Fifteenth-Century Studies* 38, ed. Barbara I. Gusick (Woodbridge: Boydell & Brewer, 2013), 175–234.

13. Julia Marie Smith, "*The Book of Margery Kempe* and the Rhetorical Chorus: An Alternative Method for Recovering Women's Contributions to the History of Rhetoric," *Advances in the History of Rhetoric* 17:2 (2014): 179–203.

14. Kathy Lavezzo, "Sobs and Sighs Between Women: The Homoerotics of Compassion in *The Book of Margery Kempe*," in *Premodern Sexualities*, ed. Louise O. Fradenburg and Carla Freccero (New York: Routledge, 1996), 175–98.

15. Corinne Saunders, "Voices and Visions: Mind, Body, and Affect in Medieval Writing," in *The Edinburgh Companion to the Critical Medical Humanities*, ed. Anne Whitehead, Angela Woods, Sarah Atkinson, Jane Macnaughton, and Jennifer Richards (Edinburgh: Edinburgh University Press, 2016), 411–27; Corinne Saunders and Charles Fernyhough, "Reading Margery Kempe's Inner Voices," *postmedieval* 8:2 (June 2017): 209–17.

16. See, for instance, *The Saintliness of Margery Kempe*, an adaptation of the *Boke*, that premiered off-Broadway on July 5, 2018, at The Duke on 42nd Street in New York City, and ran through August 26, 2018, to mixed reviews. See Michael Sommers, "The Saintliness of Margery Kempe: Holy Rolling amid Medieval Times," *New York Stage Review*, July 12, 2018, http://nystagereview.com/2018/07/12/the-saintliness-of-margery-kemp-holy-rolling-amid -medieval-times/. In September of that same year, Elizabeth Macdonald produced *Skirting Heresy* at Lynn Minster. See "Troubled Margery's Life Story Told in Play," *Lynn News*, June 30,

2018, https://www.lynnnews.co.uk/whats-on/troubled-margery-s-life-story-told-in-play
-9002993/. See also Heide Schreck, *Creature* (New York: Samuel French, 2011); and Dana
Bagshaw, *Cell Talk: A Duologue Between Julian of Norwich and Margery Kempe* (Santa Fe: Radius, 2002).

    17. *The Book of Margery Kempe*, I.13, 93.

    18. *The Book of Margery Kempe*, I.28, 164–65.

    19. *The Book of Margery Kempe*, I.35, 190.

    20. *The Book of Margery Kempe*, I.14, 100.

    21. *The Book of Margery Kempe*, I.14, 101.

    22. *The Book of Margery Kempe*, I.5, 73.

    23. *The Book of Margery Kempe*, I.6, 5.

    24. *The Book of Margery Kempe*, I.84, 366.

    25. *The Book of Margery Kempe*, I.3, 62.

    26. *The Book of Margery Kempe*, I.61, 289–90.

    27. *The Book of Margery Kempe*, I.58, 279.

    28. *The Book of Margery Kempe*, I.83, 360–61.

    29. *The Book of Margery Kempe*, I.27, 158.

    30. *The Book of Margery Kempe*, I.51, 246. For background on such letters and concerns
over vagrancy, see Susan S. Morrison, *Women Pilgrims in Late Medieval England: Private Piety as Public Performance* (New York: Routledge, 2000), especially "Legal Documentation
and Restriction: Disruption and Control," 43–82; Anne Middleton, "Acts of Vagrancy: The
C Version 'Autobiography' and the Statute of 1388," in *Written Work: Langland, Labour, and
Authorship*, ed. Steven Justice and Kathryn Kerby-Fulton (Philadelphia: University of Pennsylvania Press, 1997), 208–317.

    31. *The Book of Margery Kempe*, I.17, 115.

    32. *The Book of Margery Kempe*, I.59, 284.

    33. Spivak, *Can the Subaltern Speak?* 66–111.

    34. Katherine J. Lewis, "Model Girls? Virgin-Martyrs and the Training of Young Women
in Late Medieval England," in *Young Medieval Women*, ed. Katherine J. Lewis, Noël James
Menuge, and Kim M. Phillips (New York: St. Martin's Press, 1999), 25–46; Sheila Delaney,
*Impolitic Bodies: Poetry, Saints, and Society in Fifteenth-Century England. The Work of Osbern
Bokenham* (Oxford: Oxford University Press, 1998); Karen A. Winstead, *Virgin Martyrs: Leg-
ends of Sainthood in Late Medieval England* (Ithaca, NY: Cornell University Press, 1997);
Thomas J. Heffernan, *Sacred Biography: Saints and Their Biographers in the Middle Ages* (New
York: Oxford University Press, 1988). There is a huge bibliography on women, violence, and
speech in the medieval period. See, among others, Carissa Harris, *Obscene Pedagogies: Trans-
gressive Talk and Sexual Education in Late Medieval England* (Ithaca, NY: Cornell University
Press, 2018); Geri L. Smith, *The Medieval French Pastourelle Tradition: Poetic Motivations and
Generic Transformation* (Gainesville: University Press of Florida, 2009); Ruth Mazo Karras,
*Sexuality in Medieval Europe: Doing unto Others* (Abingdon: Routledge, 2005); Anna Kłosowska
and Anna Roberts, *Violence Against Women in Medieval Texts* (Gainesville: University Press of
Florida, 1998); Kathryn Gravdal, *Ravishing Maidens: Writing Rape in Medieval French Litera-
ture and Law* (Philadelphia: University of Pennsylvania Press, 1991).

    35. Emily Rebekah Huber and Elizabeth Robertson, eds., *The Katherine Group from
Oxford, Bodleian Library MS Bodley 34* (Kalamazoo: Medieval Institute Publications, 2016).

    36. John Capgrave, *The Life of Saint Katherine*, ed. Karen Winstead (Kalamazoo: Medi-
eval Institute Publications, 1999), II.197, IV.965.

37. Geoffrey Chaucer, "The Second Nun's Tale," in *The Riverside Chaucer*, VIII.473–83, 526–46.

38. Fred Moten, *The Undercommons: Fugitive Planning and Black Study* (New York: Minor Compositions, 2013).

39. Quintilian, *Institutio Oratoria*, XI.iii.121, 309. "In addition to these faults, there are those which spring not from nature, but from nervousness, such as struggling desperately with our lips when they refuse to open, making inarticulate sounds, as though something were sticking in our throat, when our memory fails us, or our thoughts will not come at our call; rubbing the end of our nose, walking up and down in the midst of an unfinished sentence, stopping suddenly and courting applause by silence, with many other tricks which it would take too long to detail, since everybody has his own particular faults." *Taciturnitas*, what one commentator defines as "a certain reserve or discretion in speech resulting from the love of silence," is central to Benedictine spirituality. See G. A. Simon, *Commentary for Benedictine Oblates on the Rule of St. Benedict* (Eugene: Wipf and Stock, 2009), 98.

40. In particular, Afro-pessimism, postcolonial studies, LGBTQ studies, and immigrants' rights movements—and this chapter is informed by the liberatory and emancipatory work that scholars like Fred Moten, Homi Bhabha, Dipesh Chakrabarty, Gayatri Spivak, and many others have done.

41. Sean L. Field, *The Beguine, the Angel, and the Inquisitor: The Trials of Marguerite Porete and Guiard of Cressonessart* (South Bend, IN: University of Notre Dame Press, 2012), 217.

42. Joan of Arc's trial may have been in Margery's mind as she passed through East Anglia, where the Norwich heresy trials of 1428–31 had been overseen by Bishop William Alnwick, an assessor at Joan's inquisition. Both Nancy Bradley Warren and Beverley Boyd have written about Margery, women's speech, and heresy in the context of Joan of Arc. See Nancy Bradley Warren, *Spiritual Economies: Female Monasticism in Later Medieval England* (Philadelphia: University of Pennsylvania Press, 2001), 163–82; Beverly Boyd, "Wyclif, Joan of Arc, and Margery Kempe," *Mystics Quarterly* 12:3 (1986): 112–18; as well as Henry Asgar Kelly, "The Right to Remain Silent: Before and After Joan of Arc," *Speculum* 68:4 (1993): 992–106.

43. *The Book of Margery Kempe*, I.54, 261.

44. *The Book of Margery Kempe*, I.54, 265.

45. *The Book of Margery Kempe*, I.54, 266.

46. *The Book of Margery Kempe*, I.55, 269.

47. A monograph devoted to the rest in medieval music has not been written. But the following studies provide invaluable information about the development of the notated rest (or *pausa*) in the thirteenth century, and on silence in the context of increasing metrical complexity of music in the late medieval period: Emma Hornby, "Preliminary Thoughts About Silence in Early Western Chant," in *Silence, Music, Silent Music*, ed. Nicky Losseff and Jenny Doctor (New York: Routledge, 2007), 141–54; Anna Maria Busse Berger, *Mensuration and Proportion Signs: Origins and Evolution* (Oxford: Oxford University Press, 1993); Willi Apel, *The Notation of Polyphonic Music, 900–1600* (Cambridge: The Medieval Academy of America, 1961).

48. "Rhetoric is the art of speaking well" (*Rhetorice ars est bene dicendi*). Quintilian, *Institutio Oratoria*, II.xiv.5 and II.xvii.37; Albertanus of Brescia, *Tractatus de arte loquendi et tacendi*, in Thor Sundby, *Della vita e delle opere di Brunetto Latini* (Florence: Successori Le Monnier, 1884), 475–509. Brunetto Latini adopted part of Albertanus's treatise in his *Livres dou Tresor*, which Geoffrey Chaucer in turn used in his *Tale of Melibee*. Brunetto Latini, *Li*

*livres dou tresor de Brunetto Latini*, ed. Francis J. Carmody (Berkeley: University of California Press, 1948). Geoffrey Chaucer, "The Tale of Melibee," in *The Riverside Chaucer*, VII.967–1887.

49. Albertanus, *Ars loquendi et tacendi*, 490: *Sit itaque verbum tuum efficax, non inane, rationabile, dulce, suave, molle et non durum, pulchrum et non turpe vel malum, et non obscurum, non ambiguum, non sophisticum, non injuriosum nec seditiosum, non irrisorium nec dolosum, non superbum nec otiosum.*

50. Albertanus, *Ars loquendi et tacendi*, 487: *Verbum dulce multiplicat amicos et mitigat inimicos.* See Ecclesiasticus 6:5.

51. Albertanus, *Ars loquendi et tacendi*, 487: *Tibiae et psalterium suavem faciunt melodiam, super utraque autem lingua suavis.* See Ecclesiasticus 40:21.

52. Nicolaus Dybinus, "*Declaractio oracionis de beata Dorothea* (ca. 1369)," in *Medieval Grammar and Rhetoric: Language Arts and Literary Theory AD 300–1475*, ed. Rita Copeland and Ineke Sluiter (Oxford: Oxford University Press, 2012), 821–32, 826–27.

53. Isidore of Seville, *Etymologiae*, II.vii: *Inchoandum est itaque taliter, ut benivolum, docilem, vel adtentum auditorem faciamus.*

54. For the *pausa* as a "refreshment," see Anonymous (thirteenth century), *De expositione musice*, in *Ein anonymer glossierter Mensuraltraktat 1279*, ed. Heinrich Sowa, Königsberger Studien zur Musikwissenschaft, vol. 9 (Kassel: Bärenreiter, 1930), 1–132, 107.

55. *Quemadmodum enim defatigatum auditorem sepius ioco quodam lenit orator et gratum reddit, sic auditorem cantus doctus cantor moras quasdam cantabilibus intermiscens vocibus avidum magis et intentum ad reliquas cantilene partes iniciendas facit. Moras has sive quietes a cantu pausas nominant.* Georgius Anselmus, *Georgii Anselmi Parmensis De musica: Dieta prima de celesti harmonia, dieta secunda de instrumentali harmonia, dieta tertia de cantabili harmonia*, ed. Giuseppe Massera, Historia Musicae Cultores Biblioteca, vol. 14 (Florence: Leo S. Olschki, 1961), 190, tr. Timothy J. McGee, *The Sound of Medieval Song: Ornamentation and Vocal Style According to the Treatises* (Oxford: Clarendon Press, 1998), 78. According to the fourteenth-century *Ceremonia Sublacenses*, these *morula* should be long enough for the singers to exhale and inhale again, long enough for the sound of the preceding line of chant to die away in the architectural space. Emma Hornby, "Preliminary Thoughts About Silence in Early Western Chant" in Losseff and Doctor, *Silence, Music, Silent Music*, 141–54, 142.

56. Quoted in Sarah Fuller, "'*Delectabatur in hoc auris*': Some Fourteenth-Century Perspectives on Aural Perception," *Musical Quarterly* 82:3 (1998): 466–81, 467.

57. Franchino Gaffurio, *Practica musice Franchini Gafori Laudensis* (Milan: Ioannes Petrus de Lomatio, 1496; reprint, New York: Broude Bros., 1979), II.6, ff. aavv. *Hanc [sc. pausam] musici et ad oportunam quietam atque refectionem vocis post laboriosam elationem: et ad cantus suauitatem instituerunt. Namque quemadmodum fastiditum auditorem saepius ioco quodam diuini verbi concionator oratorve lenit gratiorem et attentiorem reddens: sic cantilenarum auditores cantor moras quasdam vocibus intermiscens ad reliquas cantilenae partes praestat attentiores.* Tr. John Hawkins, *A General History of the Science and Practice of Music*, vol. 2 (London: T. Payne and Son, 1776), 318.

58. *The Book of Margery Kempe*, I.13, 96.

59. *The Book of Margery Kempe*, I.51, 242–43.

60. Jeffrey Jerome Cohen, "The Becoming-Liquid of Margery Kempe," in *Medieval Identity Machines* (Minneapolis: University of Minnesota Press, 2003), 154–87, 156.

61. Cohen, "The Becoming-Liquid," 157.

62. This is a privilege she invokes twice earlier, when the mayor of Leicester also asks her why she wears white clothes: "'Syr,' sche seyth, 'ye schal not wetyn of my mowth why I

go in white clothys; ye arn not worhty to wetyn it'" (*The Book of Margery Kempe*, I.48, p. 236); and when a woman from Lambeth accuses her of Lollardy, wishing that she would be burned at the stake: "this creatur stod stylle and answeryd not, and hir husbond suffred wyth gret peyn and wa ful sory to heryn hys wyfe so rebukyd" (*The Book of Margery Kempe*, I.16, p. 110).

63. *The Book of Margery Kempe*, I.P, 46; I.15, 105.

64. Lochrie, *Translations of the Flesh*, 100.

65. In *Translations of the Flesh*, Karma Lochrie points to this poignant moment of readerly engagement with the *Boke*. Lochrie, who is primarily interested in the relationship between Margery's English text and its Latin paratexts, argues that this is a reference to the Rollean phrase *clamor iste canor est*. By referring to the earlier male mystic, the marginal annotation imbues Margery's *Boke* and her tears with a Latinity that Margery and her *Boke* deliberately eschewed. "We might understand Rolle[, in referring to *canor*,] to mean something quite different from Kempe's boisterous cries," Lochrie argues, even though "the late medieval reader clearly did not." For her part, Lochrie ends her observation with an aporetic query, a question raised as a statement in order to refute its very terms. "This reading," she says, "raises the question of whether Kempe regards her own cries as the mystical *clamores* of which Rolle speaks." To Lochrie, Margery's crying is inimical to song; for her sixteenth-century reader and annotator, it was *canor*. The difference here does not stem from the sounds that Margery made, but instead from differences of attunement, and to the role of the listener in an intersubjective ethics that creates musical meaning. See Lochrie, *Translations of the Flesh*, 121. Here, Lochrie cites Hope Emily Allen's reading in *The Book of Margery Kempe: The Text from the Unique MS Owned by Colonel W. Butler-Bowdon*, ed. Sanford Brown Meech and Hope Emily Allen, EETS o.s. 212 (Oxford: Early English Text Society, 1961), 323. See British Library, Add. MS 61823, fol. 33v for the annotation. On the brown-ink annotator, see Joel Fredell, "Design and Authorship in the *Book of Margery Kempe*," *Journal of the Early Book Society* 12 (2009): 1–28. See also Adin Lears's discussion of the annotator in her *World of Echo: Noise and Knowing in Late-Medieval England* (Ithaca, NY: Cornell University Press, 2020).

66. See the entry for *clamour* in Lewis et al., *The Middle English Dictionary*.

67. Mark Ormrod, "Murmur, Clamour, and Noise," in *Medieval Petitions: Grace and Grievance*, ed. W. Mark Ormrod, Gwilym Dodd, and Anthony Musson (Woodbridge: Boydell and Brewer, 2006), 125–55; John M. Ganim, "Chaucer and the Noise of His People," *Exemplaria* 2 (1990): 71–88; Valerie J. Allen, "Broken Air," *Exemplaria* 16 (2004): 305–22; David Aers, "*Vox populi* and the Literature of 1381," in *The Cambridge History of Medieval English Literature*, ed. David Wallace (Cambridge: Cambridge University Press, 1999), 432–53.

68. Emily Steiner, "Commonalty and Literary Form in the 1370s and 1380s," *New Medieval Literatures* 6 (2003): 199–221, 200.

69. Carissa Harris discusses *clamour* briefly in "Rape and Justice in *The Wife of Bath's Tale*," in *The Open Access Companion to* The Canterbury Tales, ed. Candace Barrington, Brantley Bryant, Richard Godden, Daniel Kline, and Myra Seaman (2017), https://opencanterburytales .dsl.lsu.edu/wobt1/.

70. See Nadeem Badshah, "Guernsey Resident Halts Roadwork with Ancient Plea," *The Guardian*, August 14, 2018, https://www.theguardian.com/uk-news/2018/aug/14/guernsey -resident-halts-road-works-with-ancient-plea.

71. H. T. Riley, *Memorials of London and London Life in the XIIIth, XIVth, and XVth Centuries* (London: Longmans, Green, 1868), 86, 88.

72. Reginald R. Sharpe, ed., *Calendar of the Letter-Books of the City of London: Letter Book D [1309–14]* (London: John Edward Francis, 1902), 267.

73. *Quartas quatuor, videlicet ee ff gg aa, superacutas aut duplicatas primo ideo, quia magis pleniore voce cantantur quam acutae, secundo, quia super litteras acutas locuntur vel quia litterae in eis duplicantur. Ultimas quatuor excellentes primo ideo, quia earum voces tantum excedant humanas voces, ut iam non cantus per eas, sed magis clamor proferatur, secundo ideo, quia nullus cantus cuiuscumque toni de ratione ad eas ascendit.* Anonymous, *Tractatus de musica*, ed. Andres Briner, "Ein anonymer unvollständiger Musiktraktat des 15. Jahrhunderts in Philadelphia, USA," *Kirchenmusikalisches Jahrbuch* 50 (1966): 27–38, 29; tr. Andrew Hicks.

74. *The Book of Margery Kempe*, I.62, 297.

75. Richard Kostelanetz, ed., *John Cage, Writer: Previously Uncollected Pieces* (New York: Limelight Editions, 1993).

76. David Revill, *Roaring Silence: John Cage, a Life* (New York: Arcade Publishers, 1992), 166.

77. Kostelanetz, *John Cage, Writer.*

78. Jonathan D. Katz, "John Cage's Queer Silence; Or, How to Avoid Making Matters Worse," in *Writings Through John Cage's Music, Poetry, and Art*, ed. David W. Bernstein and Christopher Hatch (Chicago: University of Chicago Press, 2001), 41–60, 54.

79. *The Book of Margery Kempe*, I.28, 163–64.

CHAPTER 4

Note to epigraph: British Library, Additional MS 61823, fol. 33v.

1. Mount Grace Priory's ruins sit within what is now the North York Moors National Park, a 554-square-mile expanse of heather moorland, with a population of under 24,000 people as of the 2011 census.

2. Norton first entered the Coventry Charterhouse, but moved to Mount Grace soon thereafter, where he later became procurator, and then prior in 1509. Though it is not known exactly when Norton moved from the Coventry Charterhouse to Mount Grace, it is likely that this move occurred soon after his profession, and probably in 1483/4. The compiler of the Lincoln manuscript, a Carthusian monk named Robert Fletcher, notes that Norton was a monk in Mount Grace when he wrote the first two treatises in the Lincoln manuscript, the *Musica monachorum* and the *Thesaurus cordium vere amantium*; however, the dates for these texts, or the visions that might have precipitated them, are also unknown.

3. Brantley, *Reading in the Wilderness*, 197 and elsewhere. The bibliography on medieval monasticism is too large to include a complete one here. For purposes of orientation, see, for instance, Margot Fassler and Rebecca A. Baltzer, eds., *The Divine Office in the Latin Middle Ages: Methodology and Source Studies, Regional Developments, Hagiography* (Oxford: Oxford University Press, 2000); C. H. Lawrence, *Medieval Monasticism: Forms of Religious Life in Western Europe in the Middle Ages* (New York: Routledge, 1984).

4. William of Saint-Thierry, *The Golden Epistle of Abbot William of St. Thierry to the Carthusians of Mont Dieu* (London: Sheed and Ward, 1930), 14.

5. Ethel Margaret Thompson, *A History of the Somerset Carthusians* (London: John Hodges, 1895), 35–36.

6. For a study of earlier forms of monastic silence as both normative and aspirational, see Paul F. Gehl, "*Competens Silentium:* Varieties of Monastic Silence in the Medieval West," *Viator* 18 (1987): 125–60. Recent work on monastic sign language has opened new ways of thinking about the embodiment of language in nonsonic forms. See, for instance,

Scott G. Bruce, *Silence and Sign Language in Medieval Monasticism: The Cluniac Tradition c. 900–1200* (Cambridge: Cambridge University Press, 2007).

7. *Consuetudines Guigones*, 28.3–4: *Libros quippe tamquam semptiernum animarum nostrarum cibum cautissime custodiri et sudiosissime volumus fieri, ut quia ore non possumus, dei verbum manibus predicemus.* Quoted in Brantley, *Reading in the Wilderness*, 48.

8. Brantley, *Reading in the Wilderness*, 6.

9. Much work has been done on the refrain, particularly its influence on the "formal and widespread hybridity" of late medieval poetry and music. See Jennifer Saltzstein, *The Refrain and the Rise of the Vernacular in Medieval French Music and Poetry* (Cambridge: D. S. Brewer, 2013), 2. See also Ardis Butterfield, "The Refrain and the Transformation of Genre in the *Roman de Fauvel*," in *Fauvel Studies: Allegory, Chronicle, Music, and Image in Paris, Bibliothèque Nationale MS français 146*, ed. Margaret Bent and Andrew Wathey (Oxford: Clarendon Press, 1998), 105–59.

10. See Chapter 5.

11. For *amore langueo*, see Richard Rolle, "The Form of Living," in *Richard Rolle, Prose and Verse Edited from MS Longleat 29 and Related Manuscripts*, ed. S. J. Ogilvie-Thomson, EETS no. 293 (Oxford: Oxford University Press, 1988); see also Anonymous, "In a Valley of This Restless Mind," in *Moral Love Songs and Sonnets*, ed. Susanna Greer Fein (Kalamazoo: Medieval Institute Publications, 1998); and Felicity Riddy, "The Provenance of *Quia Amore Langueo*," *Review of English Studies* 18:72 (November 1967): 429–33. For *ego dormio*, see Richard Rolle, "*Ego Dormio*," in Ogilvie-Thomson, *Richard Rolle, Prose and Verse*.

12. Barbara Newman's edition and translation of Richard Methley's diaries is currently forthcoming, and will, hopefully, remedy the paucity of studies of his Latin treatises. See Barbara Newman, ed. and tr., *The Works of Richard Methley* (Collegeville, MN: Liturgical Press, 2021). In addition, see Laura Saetveit Miles, "Richard Methley and the Translation of Vernacular Religious Writing into Latin," in *After Arundel: Religious Writing in Fifteenth-Century England*, ed. Vincent Gillespie and Kantik Ghosh (Turnhout: Brepols, 2011), 449–67; Katherine Zieman, "Monasticism and the Public Contemplative in Late Medieval England: Richard Methley and His Spiritual Formation," *Journal of Medieval and Early Modern Studies* 42:3 (Fall 2012): 699–724. I am particularly indebted to Barbara Newman's translations in this chapter. For Methley's Latin, see James Hogg, "The *Scola Amoris Languidi* of Richard Methley of Mount Grace Charterhouse Transcribed from Cambridge, Trinity College MS O.2.56," in *Analecta Cartusiana* 55:2 (Salzburg: Institut für Anglistik und Amerikanistik, Universität Salzburg, 1981), 138–65; Hogg, "The *Dormitorium Dilecti Dilecti* of Richard Methley of Mount Grace Charterhouse Transcribed from Cambridge, Trinity College MS O.2.56," in *Analecta Cartusiana* 55:5 (Salzburg: Institut für Anglistik und Amerikanistik, Universität Salzburg, 1981), 79–103; and Hogg, "A Mystical Diary: The *Refectorium Salutis* of Richard Methley of Mount Grace Charterhouse," in *Analecta Cartusiana* 55:1 (Salzburg: Institut für Anglistik und Amerikanistik, Universität Salzburg, 1981), 208–38.

13. Zieman, "Monasticism and the Public Contemplative," 720.

14. See the Appendix.

15. Norton, *Thesaurus cordium vere amantium* (hereafter *TCVA*), fol. 43r: *Quia quociens cordialiter cantatur continue in cordibus caste amancium demones contristat, purgandos letificat et multos a penis liberat, angelis & sanctis in celis cum omnium beatorum spirituum agminibus magnum et mirabile gaudium prestat. . . . et sic facit eos celico sapore sonare suas peticiones, et dulciter diliciis diuinis ditari, et in deo durantur sine diminucione.* For translations of Norton, my deep gratitude to Elizabeth Lyon, whose expert translations from the Latin run throughout this chapter.

16. Norton, *TCVA*, fol. 44v: *Ideo dico o dulcis fili constanter age in custodia celle silentii et sensuum tuorum persolo amore meo mellifluo. Et cane me cordialiter in casto amore cum cantu ameno sine motu merorum in omnibus actibus tuis et anime et corporis et sine respectu alicuius creature cordialiter capto multifare meditando de mea passione.*

17. Methley, *Refectorium salutis*, fol. 51v: *Hodierna die id est crastino post festum sancti dionisii magni contemplatiui cito post horam octavam diei secundum quod anglicanus usus est horologium computare, incepi terciam horam diei dicere solus in choro clausis oculis corporalibus et apertis spiritualibus descenditque in me canor iubilens, et iubilus canorus amorosusque languor qui sanet omnia, nec discedunt a me adhuc cum scilicet presencia scribo, sed tripudeat sensibiliter et modo scribendo cor meum in pectore meo est enim eadem die tempus post decimam horam ante meridiem.*

18. *Dormitorium dilecti dilecti* (hereafter *DDD*), fol. 28r: *Est tamen uirtus que omnes excellit omnibus nimirum preponitur, quia sola perficit hominem fortassis dicit aliquis eam esse charitatem, Ego autem dico obedienciam ueram; que quidem communiter fit inter regulares singulariter, aut inter deum et eius anacoritam summum.*

19. For this chronology and an argument for Rolle's evolving style, see Watson, *Invention of Authority*.

20. *Scola amoris languidi* (hereafter *SAL*), fol. 7v: *Quomodo potest aliquis intelligere quomodo languor amoris est in dileccione nisi didicerit diligere?*

21. *SAL*, fols. 7v–8r: "Christ languishes because of delay, for he waits patiently to crown his lover in due time—the very best time, no doubt. How can anyone understand how love languishes in delay unless he has learned to love? There are many signs that reveal a person's great love for another. But undoubtedly someone who has experienced love's delay learns more in a moment than someone else learns from these signs in a lifetime. Yet what of that? Just because you are still ignorant, does that mean you cannot learn to love? Or because you have not yet experienced it, should you blush to learn? Experience is given by God, but the way to it is paved with ignorance. So learn from the signs how God languishes for love, waiting to crown his beloved with glory and honor in great and marvelous sweetness, and sometimes even with angelic song."

22. *SAL*, fols. 7v–8r: "How God languishes for love, waiting to crown his beloved with glory and honor in great and marvelous sweetness, and sometimes even with angelic song."

23. See Ian Cornelius, "The Rhetoric of Advancement: *Ars dictaminis, Cursus*, and Clerical Careerism in Late Medieval England," *New Medieval Literatures* 12 (January 2010): 289–330; Malcolm Richardson, "The *ars dictaminis*, the Formulary, and Medieval Epistolary Practice," in *Letter-Writing Manuals and Instruction from Antiquity to the Present: Historical and Bibliographic Studies*, ed. Carol Poster and Linda Mitchell (Columbia: University of South Carolina Press, 2007), 52–66.

24. *SAL*, fols. 21v–22r:

O Jesus, good ruler of morals
And savior of the ages,
*iubilus* of those who deserve you:
May the holy wound of your right hand
End the lament of our hearts
After the way of lovers.

Eternal, exalted King
And most delicious bread,

Food of those who enjoy you:
May the wound of your left hand
Bless us, lest the infernal Vulcan
Burn the hearts of believers.

Hail Jesus, hail Jesus,
Music to the ear, honey in the mouth,
Health of those who love you:
May the broad wound of your right foot
Purge our guilt away,
Salvation of the weak and sick.

Burn our loins, breath of holy fire,
Our helper and advocate,
Life of those who behold you:
May the open wound of your left foot
Expose the hidden wound of our hearts
In the way of confessors.

Hail Jesus, good Jesus,
In the union of love,
Holiness of those who live in you:
May the wound of your pierced heart
Heal the wounds of the desperate
And the hearts of those who sing.

25. On the Cult of the Holy Name, see Elizabeth Anne New, "The Cult of the Holy Name of Jesus in Late Medieval England, with Special Reference to the Fraternity in St Paul's Catheral, London c. 1450–1558" (Ph.D. diss., University of London, 1999); Denis Renevey, *The Moving of the Soul: Function of Metaphors of Love in the Writings of Richard Rolle and the Medieval Mystical Tradition* (Oxford: Oxford University Press, 1993); Richard W. Pfaff, *New Liturgical Feasts in Later Medieval England* (Oxford: Clarendon Press, 1970).

26. Norton, *TCVA*, fol. 54v: "To the roads leading the pilgrims, once they have been made perfect, to the gate of the beforementioned castle . . ."

27. Norton, *Musica monachorum*, fol. 16r: The love of God perfects the monks in "the glorious choruses of angels in the unity of true love and in the sight of the Supreme Author, in the purest and most chaste obedience of the glorious heavenly court."

28. Norton, *TCVA*, fol. 43r: "Because as often as there is continuous singing in the hearts of those loving chastely, it saddens demons, cheers those in purgatory and frees many from punishment, and furnishes a great and wonderful joy for the angels and saints in heaven, (along) with the multitude of all the blessed spirits. And it makes my mother, the sweetest Mary, with the whole court of heaven pray mellifluously through the spheres [of heaven] for my lovers, meditating in various ways in memory of my passion. And thus the singing makes them sound out their petitions with heavenly elegance, and sweetly to be enriched with divine delights, and they endure in God without diminishment."

29. For more on repetition and musicality, see "Sound-Objects" in Chapter 5.

30. *Vel quod iubilus inconditos sonos proferens nequaquam sensus per verba distinguat.* Jerome, "Psalm 88," in *Commentarioli in Psalmos*, ed. D. Germanus Morin (Oxford: J. Parker,

1895), 67–68; Augustine, "Psalm 100," in *Exposition on the Book of Psalms*, ed. and tr. Philip Schaff, Nicene and Post-Nicene Fathers, vol. 8 (Grand Rapids, MI: Christian Classics Ethereal Library, 2016), 965. Augustine speaks elsewhere about the *iubilus*. See his commentary on Psalm 32: *Iubilum sonus quidam est significans cor parturire quod dicere non potest. Et quem decet ista iubilatio, nisi ineffabilem Deum?* ("The *iubilus* is the sound signifying that the heart is giving birth to what it cannot say. And whom does jubilation befit but the ineffable God?") Augustine, *Expositions on the Book of Psalms*, ed. Philip Schaff, tr. A. Cleveland Coxe (Grand Rapids, MI: Eerdmans, 1956), 254.

31. *SAL*, fol. 7r-v: *Et sicut qui periculum metuunt ignis non clamant, "Ignis inuasit domum meam. Venite et adiuuante me," quia in angustia uel potius agonia positi uix possunt unum uerbum loqui sed clamant "ignis ignis ignis" uel si forcior est spiritus impetus clamant "a a a," in hoc uoce simul uolentes intelligi periculum suum. Sic ego secundum meum modulum. Nam in primis sepius commendaui spiritum meum deo dicens 'In manus tuas' aut uocaliter aut (quod magis puto) spiritualiter. Sed inualescente languore amoris, uix cogitare potui formans in spiritu hec uerba, "amor, amor, amor." Et tandem deficiens ab hac forma expsectaui quando totaliter spiritum exspirare possem "a, a, a" tantummodo aut consimili modo canens pocius quam clamans in spiritum pre gaudio.*

32. *Devota lamentatio* (hereafter *DL*), fol. 80v: *In quadam die in sanctissimo temporum quadragesima in spiritu raptus ad locum ualde delectabilem suauitate celica ditatum ineffabiliter . . .*

33. *DL*, fol. 84r: *O uirgo et mater et omnium domina potentissima sapientissima et benignissima. Audi. Audi. Audi. Audi. Audi. Audi. et exaudi me lamentabiliter et cordialiter clamantem ad te et educ me de corpore isto.*

34. *DL*, fol. 85r: *Igitur ut infans dico. A. A. A. accipe me mater mea misericordissima.*

35. *DL*, fol. 86r: *Scio namque quia pia es, et uere fateor quia pia es. A. A. A. O dulcissima domina, quid ultra fari ualeo?*

36. *DL*, fol. 87r: *"A. A. A. quid ultra dicere valeo?*

37. Bruce R. Smith, *The Acoustic World of Early Modern England: Attending to the O-Factor* (Chicago: University of Chicago Press, 1999), 8. Smith's poetic analysis of the phenomenology of sound brings body and text, listening, silence, and sound-production into productive tension. See also my later discussion of syllables and the sound-object ("Sound-Objects," Chapter 5).

38. Hollywood here is citing Bataille on religion in general, but Hollywood plays with this notion, and its relationship specifically to medieval women's mysticism, throughout her book. See Amy Hollywood, *Sensible Ecstasy: Mysticism, Sexual Difference, and the Demands of History* (Chicago: University of Chicago Press, 2002), 104.

39. Mikko Lagerspetz, "Music as Intersubjectivity—a Problematic for the Sociology of the Arts," *Musciology/Muzikologija* 1:20 (2016): 223–38.

40. The notion that manuscripts—and, in particular, the medieval tradition of commentary—might house something of a queer ethic or queer temporality has, of course, already been argued by other scholars. In a recent special issue of *postmedieval* devoted to queer philologies, Jonathan Hsy argues for the tradition of commentary and response as "queer" in the context of material textuality. See Jonathan Hsy, "Queer Environments: Reanimating 'Adam Scriveyn,'" *postmedieval* 9:3 (2018): 289–302. In that same issue, Lucy Allen Goss argues that textual collaboration among women in the medieval period is "something qualitatively and queerly different" from masculine paradigms of commentary, where *pagina* is female and the *pen* is male. See Lucy Allen-Goss, "Queerly Productive: Women and Collaboration in Cambridge, University Library, MS Ff.1.6," *postmedieval* 9:3 (2018): 334–48. See also Carolyn Dinshaw, *How Soon Is Now?* (Durham, NC: Duke University Press, 2012); Karma Loch-

rie, *Heterosyncracies: Female Sexuality When Normal Wasn't* (Minneapolis: University of Minnesota Press, 2005). Manuscripts are, like Eve Kosofsky Sedgwick's formulation of queer desire, spaces of "overlapping, contradictory, and conflictual definitional forces." See Eve Kosofsky Sedgwick, *Epistemology of the Closet* (Berkeley: University of California Press, 2008), 45.

41. For a critique of the exclusionary nature of normative binary friendships, see Jacques Derrida, *The Politics of Friendship*, tr. George Collins (London: Verso, 2005).

42. *SAL*, fol. 1r: *Omnium creaturarum summum studium est amare et amari*. There is a bookmark pasted to the manuscript at this line, suggesting that this sentence was held in some high esteem by at least one of its readers. Another reference to *amare et amari* appears on fol. 33v: *Et si generaliter hominem rectum, ergo naturaliter amabilem actiue scilicet ac passiue, id est habilem amare et amari*. ("If man in general is righteous, then he is by nature lovable, namely both actively and passively—that is, able to love and be loved.")

43. Aristotle, *The Art of Rhetoric*, tr. H. C. Lawson-Tancred (London: Penguin Books, 1991), VI.2.4, 1381a1–2, 150.

44. This mutual affection, Cicero goes on to claim, is most powerful in those who are alike: *Ut bonos boni diligant adsciscantque sibi quasi propinquitate coniunctos atque natura*. ("And therefore, the good love the good and attach them to themselves as though they were united by blood and nature.") See Marcus Tullius Cicero, *De amicitia*, tr. W. A. Falconer, Loeb Classical Library 154 (Cambridge, MA: Harvard University Press, 1923), I.14.

45. For more on the notion of friendships as binary pairs, see Ronald F. Hock, *Jesus, the Beloved Disciple, and Greco-Roman Friendship Conventions*, in *Christian Origins and Greco-Roman Culture: Social and Literary Contexts for the New Testament*, ed. Stanley E. Porter and Andrew Pitts (Leiden: Brill, 2013), 195–212, especially 199–206.

46. Lorraine Smith Pangle, *Aristotle and the Philosophy of Friendship*, ed. John von Heyking and Richard Avramenko (Cambridge: Cambridge University Press, 2003); Albrecht Classen and Marilyn Sandidge, eds., *Friendship in the Middle Ages and Early Modern Age: Explorations of a Fundamental Ethical Discourse* (Berlin: Walter de Gruyter, 2010). For a discussion of the *Nicomachean Ethics* in the medieval period, see Jon Miller, ed., *The Reception of Aristotle's Ethics* (Cambridge: Cambridge University Press, 2013), especially chapters 4–8.

47. Derrida, *The Politics of Friendship*, 28.

48. *Et quid erat quod me delectabat, nisi amare et amari*, Augustine. *Confessiones*, ed. James O'Donnell (Oxford: Oxford University Press, 1992), 2.2.2.

49. *Exhalabantur nebulae de limosa concupiscentia carnis et scatebra pubertatis, et obnubilabant atque obfuscabant cor meum, ut non discerneretur serenitas dilectionis a caligine libidinis*. Augustine, *Confessiones*, 2.2.2.

50. See, for instance, Martín Hugo Córdova Quero, "Friendship with Benefits: A Queer Reading of Aelred of Rievaulx and His Theology of Friendship," in *The Sexual Theologian: Essays on Sex, God, and Politics*, ed. Marcella Althaus-Reid and Lisa Isherwood (London: T&T Clark International, 2004), 26–46; Marilyn McCord Adams, "Trinitarian Friendship: Same-Gender Models of Godly Love in Richard of St. Victor and Aelred of Rievaulx," in *Theology and Sexuality: Classic and Contemporary Readings*, ed. Eugene F. Rogers (Oxford: Wiley, 2002), 322–40.

51. One of the chief sources for the monastic reticence toward particular friendship is Cassian, who in his sixteenth conference on *De amicitia* elides Christian friendship into a broader discussion of Christian charity. It is difficult not to do this, of course, for all Christians—unlike their pagan ancestors—have available to them a discourse of charitable, perfect love in the image of God that is easily abstractable from particular love of an individual. See Classen and Sandige, *Friendship in the Middle Ages*, 41. The problems associated

with friendship within the monastery were understood to be manifold: close personal bonds could cause favoritism, and in turn rancor, among a group of men who were supposed to be in harmony at all times. See Brian Patrick McGuire, "The Charm of Friendship in the Monastic Institution: A Meditation on Anselm and Bernard," In *Institution und Charisma*, ed. Franz Felten, Annette Kehnel, and Stefan Weinfurter (Vienna: Bohlau Verlag, 2009), 425–36.

52. *Nonne quaedam beatitudinis portio fuit, sic amare et sic amari; sic iuvare et sic iuvari; et sic ex fraternae caritatis dulcedine in illum sublimiorem locum dilectionis divinae splendorem altius euolare; et in scala caritatis nunc ad Christi ipsius amplexum conscendere, nunc ad amorem proximi ibi suaviter repausaturum descendere? In hac igitur amicitia nostra quam exempli gratia inservimus, si quid cernitis imitandum, ad vestrum id retorquete profectum.* See Aelred of Rievaulx, *Spiritual Friendship*, tr. Lawrence C. Braceland, S.J., ed. Marsha L. Dutton (Collegeville, MN: Liturgical Press, 2010), III.127, n.p.

53. Aelred, *Spiritual Friendship*, II.67.

54. Aelred, *Spiritual Friendship*, II.5.

55. *SAL*, fol. 8v: *Impossibile est enim languentem amore fratri inuidere.*

56. *SAL*, fol. 7v: *Vos igitur o amatores scitote, quod amore langueo et uere cupio dissolui et esse cum christo, ipsi gloria in secula. Ipse dedit michi donum humilitatis et fraterne charitatis et ideo amore langueo.*

57. *Musica monachorum* (hereafter *MM*), fols. 12v–16r.

58. *MM*, fol. 12r: *Caritas materia tocius saluacionis et omnium bonorum operum est. Sapiencia uero operatrix illius materie et instrumentum operandi et manifestandi opera eiusdem. Et graciosus amor ardescens est claritas coniunccio et perfectio uniuersorum predicte materie operum.*

59. The "operant wisdom" (*sapiencia . . . operatrix*) to which Norton refers here is Christ.

60. *MM*, fol. 5v: *Sine dubio si caste perseuerant ambo in celis gloriose coronabuntur et in benediccione mea sine fine gaudebunt cum angelis et sanctis celorum in secula sempeterna. Amen.*

61. *Refectorium salutis* (hereafter *RS*), fol. 62v: *Et post mense refeccionem in refectorio cum fratribus, ad litteram intellige, deveni in cellam et nouo adhuc modo uenit in me alia sensacio. Ita scilicet quod mente et corpore canerem in canore et iubilo cum gaudio valde magno quasi intrassem in paradisum domini. Sic inquam exultaui per graciam dilecti iesu christi.* ("After dining at table in the refectory with my brothers (in the literal sense), I came to my cell and another sensation came upon me, in yet another new way. I was enabled to sing in mind and body, in melody and jubilation with very great joy, as if I had entered into the Lord's paradise. In this way I exulted, I say, through the grace of Jesus Christ the Beloved.")

62. *RS*, fol. 52r: *Inde meum cor fere conscissum et conlateratum quia amore magno iam langueo dum hec vobis o dulcissimi fratres scribo.*

63. *RS*, fol. 67v: *Itaque senciens me sic in spiritu agentem nolui propter huiusmodi sensacionem uoluntarie leccionem et fratres dimittere, nisi forcius laboraret in me spiritus et fervor amoris et doloris.*

64. *DDD*, fol. 26r: *per gradus inquam O fratres mei in hoc dormitorium ascendendum est.*

65. *RS*, 70r-v: *Ecce fratres charissimi, scripsi vobis hoc refectorium salutis. Si necesse sit corrigite et deo gracias agite et orate pro me. Si scripseritis bene corrigite quod scripseritis alioquin rogo ne scribatis. Laus et honor deo.*

66. *RS*, fol. 67v: *Et subito motum est cor meum quasi gladio percussum.*

67. *RS*, fol. 67v: *Itaque senciens me sic in spiritu agentem nolui propter huiusmodi sensacionem voluntarie leccionem et fratres dimittere, nisi forcius laboraret in me spiritus et fervor amoris et doloris.*

68. For instance, see *MM*, fol. 3r: *Quadam die mihi sedenti more solito in cella mea* ("On a certain day, to me, sitting in my cell in the usual manner") versus fol. 8r: *Nota quod quodam tempore in oratorio stans . . .* ("Note that at a certain time, standing in the oratory . . .").

69. Glynn Coppack, "Make Straight in the Desert a Highway for Our God—Carthusians and Community in Late Medieval England," in *Monasteries and Society in the British Isles*, ed. Janet K. Burton and Karen Stöber, Studies in the History of Medieval Religion 35 (Woodbridge: Boydell, 2008), 168–79.

70. Zieman, "Monasticism and the Public Contemplative"; and Vincent Gillespie, "Monasticism," in *Cultural Reformations: Medieval and Renaissance in Literary History*, ed. Brian Cummings and James Simpson (Oxford: Oxford University Press, 2010), 480–501, 486.

71. The fullest biography of Melton can be found in Richard Rex, "Melton, William (d. 1528)," in *The Oxford Dictionary of National Biography* (Oxford: Oxford University Press, 2004). A theologian, Catholic priest, and authority on Euclid whose lectures at Cambridge were remarked upon by contemporaries, this reforming humanist had ties to John Fisher, John Constable, Ralph Collingwood, and John Colet; he became the chancellor of York in 1496, and at the time of his death owned over one hundred books, among them new favorites of the humanist movement, from Plato and Thomas More (*Utopia*) to Pico della Mirandola, Jacques Lefèvre d'Étaples, Erasmus, and John Fisher (contra Luther). That a humanist scholar had chosen to write an introduction to Norton's work indicates the degree of respect beyond the charterhouse that his visionary experiences garnered.

72. *MM*, fol. 2r-v: *Hec scripsi frater flecherus ut intelligas me libellum tuum perlegisse non prorsus indiligenter. sed cum grato fauore et fraterna caritate, quam nobis inuicem conseruet in eternum deus et dominus redemptor noster ihsus christus amen.*

73. *MM*, fol. 27r: *Sequitur libellus ab eodem et eodem tempore editus.* ("A treatise follows, by the same (person) and produced at the same time.")

74. *TCVA*, fol. 50r: *Ideo beatissimi uocantur qui in hoc opere usque ad mortem iugiter transalpinati fuerunt in amore casto, et in mortis sue tempore erunt puri contemplationi sine aliqua iniquitacione.*

75. *SAL*, fol. 13r-v: *O tediose frater mi, remedium queris contra temptaciones diaboli. Noli desperationem deici. Quia frater tuus sum quondam temptatus sicut tu, sed nunquam victus in hac parte si bene memini.*

76. *SAL*, fol. 21v: *Fratres mei orthodoxi et catholici, si necesse sit opus hoc corrigite; si vobis placuerit, scribite. Mecum precor deum in perpetuum laudate quia amore langueo et cetera.*

77. Mount Grace was one of the few monastic establishments founded, in 1389, between the Black Death and the Reformation. What is particularly interesting about this is the fact that the few others that were founded during this time also end up using Rolle extensively in their libraries and in their understanding of religious experience.

78. *RS*, fols. 55v–56r: *Cumque missam finissem, iterum atque iterum defeci totus languidus effectus, nam vita mea consistit in amore languore dulcore feruore, canore. Rarius tamen in sensibili feruore quia dilectus michi promisit quod frequencius in languore sicut et ille almus Ricardus dictus de hampol frequencius in calore de quo non legi quod tam frequens fuit in languore.*

79. For instance, Bonaventure used the word *communicatio* to signify the bond uniting two people through charity (*lex caritatis*) in contrast with the law of society (*lex socialis*). See John Dunn and Ian Harris, eds., *Aquinas*, Great Political Thinkers, vol. 4 (Cheltenham: Edward Elgar, 1997), 93. In this one phrase, Bonaventure connects obedience with love and, beyond this, with the language. Aelred of Rievaulx talks in some detail in Book II of the *De spirituali amicitia* about maintaining friendship at a distance, and many of the great "friend-

ships" of the medieval period can be discerned through the *ars dictaminis,* or the epistolary genre. See also Jens Rueffer, "Aelred of Rievaulx and the Institutional Limits of Monastic Friendship," in *Perspectives for an Architecture of Solitude: Essays on Cistercians, Art, and Architecture in Honour of Peter Fergusson,* ed. Terryl Kinder (Turnhout: Brepols, 2004), 55–62; Martin Camargo, *Ars dictaminis, ars dictandi* (Turnhout: Brepols, 1991); James Jerome Murphy, *Rhetoric in the Middle Ages: A History of Rhetorical Theory from Saint Augustine to the Renaissance* (Berkeley: University of California Press, 1974).

80. Alan Bray, *The Friend* (Chicago: University of Chicago Press, 2003), 4.

81. Margery Kempe, *The Book of Margery Kempe,* I.28, 163.

82. Margery Kempe, *The Book of Margery Kempe,* I.28, 164–65.

83. Katie Bugyis, "Handling the Book of Margery Kempe: The Corrective Touches of the Red Ink Annotator," in *New Directions in Medieval Manuscript Studies and Reading Practices,* ed. Kathryn Kerby-Fulton, John Thompson, and Sarah Baechle (Notre Dame, IN: University of Notre Dame Press, 2014), 138–58; Barry Windeatt, "1412–1534: Texts," in *The Cambridge Companion to Medieval English Mysticism* (Cambridge: Cambridge University Press, 2011), 195–225.

84. John S. Garrison, "On Friendship," *GLQ: A Journal of Lesbian and Gay Studies* 25:1 (January 2019): 79–83, 82.

85. This incompleteness and disjointed temporality are what José Esteban Muñoz recognizes as queer futurity, a utopian vision he outlines as a form of the coming community. José Esteban Muñoz, *Cruising Utopia: The Then and There of Queer Futurity* (New York: NYU Press, 2009), 11. This stands in sharp contrast to what Lee Edelman would call the heteronormative futurities of the present. See Lee Edelman, *No Future: Queer Theory and the Death Drive* (Durham, NC: Duke University Press, 2004).

CHAPTER 5

Note to epigraphs: François Rabelais, *Gargantua and Pantagruel,* tr. Burton Raffel (New York: W. W. Norton, 1990), IV.56, 496–97; Thomas Gascoigne, *Here after folowith the boke callyd the myrroure of Oure Lady very necessary for all relygyous persones* (1530), fol. 25r.

1. François Rabelais, *Gargantua and Pantagruel,* tr. Burton Raffel (New York: W. W. Norton, 1990), IV.55, 495.

2. For more on these sources and on the role of commonplace books in "freezing" useful phrases, see Eric MacPhail, "Words Frozen and Thawed," in his *Dancing Around the Well: The Circulation of Commonplaces in Renaissance Humanism* (Leiden: Brill, 2014), 44–74; Gina Bloom, "From Excitable Speech to Voice in Motion," in her *Voice in Motion: Staging Gender, Shaping Sound in Early Modern England* (Philadelphia: University of Pennsylvania Press, 2007), 1–20; Tonino Tornitore, "Interpretazioni novecentesche dell'episodio delle *Parolles Gelées,*" *Études Rabelaisiennes* 18 (1985): 179–204.

3. Dolar argues against the voice as necessary presence. See Dolar, *A Voice and Nothing More,* especially 36–52.

4. Chion, *Sound,* 30.

5. Geoffrey Chaucer, "The House of Fame," in *The Riverside Chaucer,* I.770.

6. For Chaucer, see "The House of Fame"; Arthur Brandeis, ed., *Jacob's Well: An English Treatise on the Cleansing of Man's Conscience,* Early English Text Society, o.s. 155 (London: Kegan Paul, Trench, Trübner, 1900), 115. For more on the Titivillus myth, see Marc Drogin,

"The Patron Demon of Calligraphy," in his *Medieval Calligraphy: Its History and Technique* (New York: Dover, 1980), 17–20.

7. Both Walter Ong and Don Ihde talk at length about the movement between aural/ oral cultures and literate/textual ones, which understand words as either events or objects, respectively. But I see no reason that these two systems might not coexist, in some matter, in all societies—are we all not always maneuvering between the world of sound and the world of inscription? Walter Ong, *Orality and Literacy* (New York: Routledge, 2002); Don Ihde, *Listening and the Voice: A Phenomenology of Sound* (Athens: Ohio University Press, 1976).

8. In descriptions of rhetorical allegory and rhetorical frameworks of allegorical analysis, such as Robert Hollander's notion of verbal figuralism, allegory is said to arise through the gradual accretion of meanings that attach to words, building itself out of the mutability of signifiers that accrete around puns, connotations, and larger semantic webs. See Robert Hollander, *Allegory in Dante's* Commedia (Princeton, NJ: Princeton University Press, 1969), as well as Jill Mann, "Langland and Allegory," in *The Cambridge Companion to* Piers Plowman, ed. Andrew Cole and Andrew Galloway (Cambridge: Cambridge University Press, 2014), 83–118. *Sonic allegory*, with its investment in the ways that *sound, voice,* and *music* arrive in the text in a state of already passing away, is ontologically prior to and serves as the ground of rhetorical analysis. It is in the mutability and always-becoming-absence of the text's sonic bodies that the mutability of the written word arises. Sonic allegory destabilizes the relationship between inanimate matter and animating form.

9. Jonathan Sterne, *The Audible Past: Cultural Origins of Sound Production* (Durham, NC: Duke University Press, 2003). This does not mean that earlier music writers did not note the objectival properties of sound. See not only the examples discussed in this chapter, but also the occult or mystical power that Marsilio Ficino ascribes to music in Book 3 of his *De triplici vita*. Marsilio Ficino, *De vita libri tres (Three Books on Life, 1489)*, tr. Carol V. Kaske and John R. Clarke (Tempe: The Renaissance Society of America, 2002), 3.21.

10. Tom Phillips and Armand D'Angour, *Music, Text, and Culture in Ancient Greece* (Oxford: Oxford University Press, 2018), especially Armand D'Angour, "The Musical Setting of Ancient Greek Texts" in that volume, 47–72.

11. For an account, Kane, *Sound Unseen*, as well as Schaeffer, *Treatise on Musical Objects*.

12. Schaeffer initially sorted these qualities, which he called the "morphology" of sounds, into seven categories. See Brian Kane, "Pierre Schaeffer, the Sound Object, and the Acousmatic Reduction," in his *Sound Unseen*, 15–44.

13. Kane, *Sound Unseen*, 8.

14. Kane, *Sound Unseen*, 149.

15. Schaeffer called the resulting musical compositions *musique concrete*, or concrete music.

16. As Suzanne Conklin Akbari notes, scholarship tends to understand allegory in two orthogonally invested ways: either as a visual form or as a rhetorical one. In the first case, allegory is understood to work through ekphrasis, eidetic memory, and the *imaginatio* as an image-based model of cognition; in the second, rhetorical type, wordplay, polysemy, and the particularities of language are foregrounded. Suzanne Conklin Akbari, *Seeing Through the Veil: Optical Theory and Medieval Allegory* (Toronto: University of Toronto Press, 2004), 7–8. In very broad terms, allegory of the early medieval period (roughly to the late thirteenth century) tends toward the eidetic or visual, whereas later medieval and early modern allegories, inspired by Aristotelian philosophy and nominalist theories of language and cognition, tend toward the rhetorical. For a collection of essays on the development of allegory, see Rita Copeland and Peter T. Struck, eds., *The Cambridge Companion to Allegory* (Cambridge: Cam-

bridge University Press, 2011); John Whitman, *Interpretation and Allegory, Antiquity to the Modern Period* (Leiden: Brill, 2000).

17. Isidore of Seville, *Etymologies*, I.xxxvii: *Ironia est sententia per pronuntiationem contrarium habens intellectum.*

18. Hugh of St. Victor, *Expositio super Prologum Ieronimi*, quoted in Hugh Feiss and Juliet Mousseau, eds., *A Companion to the Abbey of Saint Victor in Paris* (Leiden: Brill, 2018), 215: *Aliud dicitur et aliud significatur.*

19. *Hyponoia* (under-sense), *symoblon* (symbol), *figura* ("igure), *signum* (sign), *imago* (image), *eikon* (icon), and *aenigma* (enigma). This list is taken from Ann Raftery Meyer, *Medieval Allegory and the Building of the New Jerusalem* (Cambridge: D. S. Brewer, 2003), 2.

20. William Langland, *Piers Plowman*, ed. A. V. C. Schmidt (London: J.M. Dent, 1995). "Lo," B.18.328; "Harrow," B.20.88; "Help," B.20.88; "Alarme," B.20.92; "clergial speech," B.P.124; "jangle," B.P.130; Reson "rouning" in B.4.14; Anima in B.15.20, "loude and crie," B.18.262; there are snippets of song in B.P.225–30; Activa B.13.437–52; God's minstrels, B.13.436–46; Activa Vita, B.13. On *Piers Plowman* and performance, see Emily Steiner, *Reading* Piers Plowman (Cambridge: Cambridge University Press, 2013), 70–73; Ruth Nissé, "Reversing Discipline: *The Tretise of Miracles Pleyinge,* Lollard Exegesis, and the Failure of Representation," *Yearbook of Langland Studies* 11 (1997): 163–94; C. David Benson, *Public Piers Plowman: Modern Scholarship and Late Medieval English Culture* (Philadelphia: University of Pennsylvania, 2003), 113 ff.

21. Langland, *Piers Plowman*, B.P.1–4, 7–10.

22. Chion, *Sound,* 105.

23. Chion, *Sound,* 105.

24. Langland, *Piers Plowman*, B.P.217–18. William Langland, *Piers Plowman: The C-Text*, ed. Derek Pearsall (Exeter: University of Exeter Press, 1994), C.P.224: "Al Y say slepynge as ye shal here heraftur."

25. Langland, *Piers Plowman*, B.5.22–23.

26. Langland, *Piers Plowman*, B.12.66; John 3:11; B.13.64–67. See Nicolette Zeeman, Piers Plowman *and the Medieval Discourse of Desire* (Cambridge: Cambridge University Press, 2006), 19–20.

27. Reason governs the senses while recognizing that its operation depends on the presence of God, and Truth, as a higher power. See Michelle Karnes, "Will's Imagination in *Piers Plowman," Journal of English and Germanic Philology* 108:1 (2009): 27–58. She is referring to Augustine's *De libero arbitrium*, II.17 here. "In Aristotle's thought, truth resides within nature and is discovered through nature, not symbolically but actually. Nature accordingly becomes the object not just of the senses but also of the intellect" (Karnes, "Will's Imagination," 32).

28. Langland, *Piers Plowman*, B.1.12.

29. Langland, *Piers Plowman*, B.8.57–58.

30. Langland, *Piers Plowman*, B.11.9–10.

31. Ymaginatif's function as the "spokesman of Reason" has a long but vexed tradition in *Piers Plowman* scholarship. See Ernest N. Kaulbach, "The *Vis Imaginativa* and the Reasoning Power of Ymaginatif in the B-Text of *Piers Plowman," Journal of English and Germanic Philology* 84:1 (1985): 16–29.

32. Quintilian would say that the person who looked at images without paying attention to their attendant speech was a fool. Allegorical figures are *mutam effigiem,* or mute idols. See Quintilian, *Institutio Oratoria,* tr. H. E. Butler, Loeb Classical Library (Cambridge, MA: Harvard University Press, 1996), VI.I.32. In her work on medieval allegory, Maureen Quilligan

focuses on the punning nature of allegory to avert an ideational collapse: "In the Middle Ages, when allegorical texts were used for oral recitation, the puns which form the basis of the narrative could be sensed as true puns with meanings connected by auditory likeness, not merely strained spelling. This auditory effect does not detract from, but rather adds to the verbal emphasis of the narrative's action." Maureen Quilligan, *The Language of Allegory: Defining the Genre* (Ithaca, NY: Cornell University Press, 1992), 241.

33. Stephen Connor, *Dumbstruck: A Cultural History of Ventriloquism* (Oxford: Oxford University Press, 2000), 15.

34. See, in addition to the texts already cited, David Lawton, *Voice in Later Medieval Literature: Public Interiorities* (Oxford: Oxford University Press, 2017).

35. Mann, "Langland and Allegory," 65–82, 80; Alastair Minnis, *Translations of Authority in Medieval English Literature: Valuing the Vernacular* (Cambridge: Cambridge University Press, 2009), 38–67.

36. Lawton, *Voice*, 103.

37. Bodleian Library, MS Douce 104, fols. 8r, 15r, 38r.

38. Anima at B.15.13, Pacience at B.13.29, Piers at B.19.6, and Elde at B.11.27, and later, "the hoore" at B.20.95.

39. Kathryn Kerby-Fulton and Denise L. Despres, *Iconography and the Professional Reader: The Politics of Book Production in the Douce* Piers Plowman (Minneapolis: University of Minnesota Press, 1999), 119.

40. Reson and Wisdom are laconically described and speak, much as they do in *Piers Plowman*; there *is* speech in the poem. Reson speaks for eight lines (ll. 69–76), and, near the end of the unfinished poem, a group of citizens air their grievances about job and salary prospects (ll. 46–52). James M. Dean, ed., "Richard the Redeless," in *Richard the Redeless and Mum and the Sothsegger* (Kalamazoo: Medieval Institute Publications, 2000).

41. The King:

> Of a comliche kynge crowned with golde,
> Sett one a silken bynche, with septure in honde,
> One of the lovelyeste ledis, whoso loveth hym in hert,
> That ever segge under sonn sawe with his eghne.
> This kynge was comliche clade in kirtill and mantill -
> Bery-brown was his berde - brouderde with fewlys,
> Fawkons of fyne golde, flakerande with wynges,
> And ichone bare in ble blewe als me thoghte
> A grete gartare of ynde gerede full riche.
> Full gayly was that grete lorde girde in the myddis:
> A brighte belte of ble broudirde with fewles,
> With drakes and with dukkes - daderande tham semede
> For ferdnes of fawkons fete, lesse fawked thay were.

See Warren Ginsberg, ed., "Winnere and Wastoure," in *Winnere and Wastoure, and the Parlement of the Thre Ages* (Kalamazoo: Medieval Institute Publications, 1992), ll. 86–98. The Baron:

> He dothe hym doun one the bonke, and dwellys awhile
> Whils he busked and bown was one his beste wyse.

He laped his legges in yren to the lawe bones,
With pysayne and with pawnce polischede full clene,
With brases of broun stele brauden full thikke,
With plates buklede at the bakke the body to yeme,
With a jupown full juste joynede by the sydes,
A brod chechun at the bakke; the breste had another,
Thre wynges inwith wroghte in the kynde,
Umbygon with a gold wyre. When I that gome knewe,
What! he was yongeste of yeris and yapeste of witt
That any wy in this werlde wiste of his age.

See Ginsberg, "Winnere and Wastoure," ll. 109–20.

42. I am including here only figures that Will meets and speaks to on his journey. Some readers might argue that Piers Plowman is not a personification and that Haukyn is; we might also include Will himself in this list. At any rate, while the exact figures who should be included in this list are debatable, I count them at around thirty-six: Holi Church, Truth, Lady Mede, False, Conscience, Reason, the Seven Deadly Sins, Piers Plowman, Hunger, Thought, Kynde Wit, Dame Study, Clergy, Scripture, Fortune, Kynde, Imaginatif, Patience, Anima, Hope, the Four Daughters of God, Pride, Need, Old Age, Death, Pestilence, Grace.

43. See Stefan Gullatz, "Exquisite Ex-timacy: Jacques Lacan vis-à-vis Contemporary Horror," *Off/Screen* 5:2 (March 2001), https://offscreen.com/view/lacan.

44. Isidore of Seville, *Etymologies*, III.xvi.1: *Quarum sonus quia sensibilis res est praeterfluit in praeteritum tempus, imprimiturque memoriae, inde a poetis Jovis et Memoriae filias Musas esse confictum est. Nisi enim ab homine memoria teneantur soni, pereunt, quia scribi non possunt.*

45. In the B-text, these come at the beginning of Passus 5, 8, 13, 18, 19, 20, and at the end of Passus 20.

46. Langland, *Piers Plowman*, B.13.1–20. I'd like to stress that I am *not* primarily concerned with signification per se, but instead am concerned with the degree to which *things* or *concepts* might themselves be pictured as sonic rather than as eidetic. Boethius translates the "signifying concepts" of Aristotle into the phrase *passiones animae*—affections of the soul; Abelard calls them *significatio intellectuum* (signification of concepts). "Now spoken sounds are symbols of affections in the soul, and written marks symbols of spoken sounds. . . . What these are in the first place signs of—affections of the soul—are the same for all; and what these affections are likenesses of—actual things—are also the same." Aristotle, *De interpretatione*, tr. J. L. Ackrill, *Categories and De interpretatione* (Oxford: Clarendon Press, 1963), I.16.a3, 43.

47. Langland, *Piers Plowman*, B.13.19.

48. Echoic traces are precategorical, sensory memories of sound that allow it to be processed over time. The ability to process spoken language depends on the mind's ability to retain, analyze, and then make judgments about the relationship between a series of sounds over time without losing the memory of the initial sounds in the duration. See Ronald T. Kellogg, *Fundamentals of Cognitive Psychology* (Los Angeles: SAGE Publications, 2007), 98–99.

49. For a fuller discussion of music and paraphrase, see Elizabeth Hellmuth Margulis, *On Repeat: How Music Plays the Mind* (Oxford: Oxford University Press, 2014).

50. Scholarship on Langland's personifications, as is the case for so many other elements of the poem, has not reached a consensus; however, as with all medieval personifications, scholarship tends to divide into two roughly distinct groups. In the first group, personification

is a trope that binds the world of language to the material, sensorial world. In the second, personification is defined as verbal play; here, language creates, through formal means, graded levels of "substance-ness" in words without necessitating a connection to the body, sense-data, or the world of objects. For a longer discussion of this subject and for a more inclusive bibliography of Langlandian personification scholarship, see Tekla Bude, "Wet Shoes, Dirty Coats, and the Agency of Things: Thinking Personfication Through New Materialism," *Yearbook of Langland Studies* 33 (2019): 205–30.

51. Langland, *Piers Plowman*, B.12.293–95.

52. For a further discussion of apostraphe, see Barbara Johnson, "Apostraphe, Animation, and Abortion," *Diacritics* 16:1 (1986): 22–47.

53. Masha Raskolnikov, "Promising the Female, Delivering the Male: Transformations of Gender in *Piers Plowman*," *Yearbook of Langland Studies* 19 (2005): 81–105. See also Barbara Newman, *God and the Goddesses: Vision, Poetry, and Belief in the Middle Ages* (Philadelphia: University of Pennsylvania Press, 2003), 36, on the distinction between *Anima* and *Animus*.

54. Langland, *Piers Plowman*, B.5.78.

55. Langland, *Piers Plowman*, B.18.167, 171.

56. Judith Butler, "The Social Construction of Gender," in *Theorizing Gender* (Oxford: Blackwell, 2002), 64–93.

57. Lavinia Griffiths, *Personification in* Piers Plowman (Woodbridge: Boydell and Brewer, 1985), 5.

58. A caveat here: while *Piers Plowman* often includes rubrication, underlining, or other minimal forms of letter-decoration to indicate Latin phrases, *quod*s, and, in some cases, personifications, these names are generally not hyphenated.

59. "Dykeres and delveres[. . .] dryveth forth the longe day with *Dieu save Dame Emme*'"; cooks cry "hote pies, hote"; and taverners sing the praises of their potables (B.P.224–30). In her study of the landscapes of medieval sound, Emma Dillon engages in an in-depth analysis of the specific soundscapes that construct location and civic identity. She refers explicitly to Guillaume de Villeneuve's *Crieries de Paris* and street cries as one of these forms of civic aural phenomena that depict "urban glory in terms so superlative as to surpass language." Dillon, *The Sense of Sound*, 91.

60. Langland, *Piers Plowman*, B.9.102, B.5.507, B.13.225, B.14.27, B.3.311–12.

61. Priscian, *Institutiones grammaticae* 1.3, in *Medieval Grammar and Rhetoric*, ed. Rita Copeland and Ineke Sluiter (Oxford: Oxford University Press, 2009), 167–89, 173. *Litera est pars minima vocis compositae, [hoc est quae constat compositione literarum, minima autem, quantum ad totam comprehensionem voci literatae . .]. vel quod omnium est brevissimum eorum, quae dividi possunt, id quod dividi non potest.* Priscian, *Institutiones grammaticae*, ed. Heinrich Keil, (Leipzig: B.G. Teubner, 1855), 6.

62. Priscian, *Institutiones grammaticae*, 46, 47.

63. Aristotle, *De Anima* tr. R. D. Hicks (Cambridge: Cambridge University Press, 1907), 420.b.10, 87.

64. Isidore of Seville, *Etymologies*, III.xvi.1, 95: *Quarum sonus quia sensibilis res est praeterfluit in praeteritum tempus, imprimiturque memoriae.*

65. Isidore of Seville, *Etymologies*, III.xiv.1, III.xvi.1: *Nisi enim ab homine memoria teneantur soni, pereunt, quia scribi non possunt.* The mnemonic potential of sound has wide-ranging effects in medieval literature, not least in the context of Margery Kempe's *Boke*, as I discuss in Chapter 3, where Margery asks her readers to tune themselves to her text; her audiences'

memories of her roaring and anticipation of noise in silence not only make her outbursts musical, but give an intersubjective body to that music.

66. Reduced listening cannot be compelled; Schaeffer's project is always open to failure. Neither Schaeffer's *musique concrete* nor poetry is ever fully severed from intentional or discursive frameworks—there is no such thing as pure Schaefferian *entendre* or "purely musical" listening when it comes to poetry.

67. Martin J. Duffell, *A New History of English Metre* (London: Modern Humanities Research Association and Maney Publishing, 2008), 2.

68. One might also think here of Garrett Stewart's keen discussion of silent reading's always-conjuring of vocalized reading and how it is reliant on syllabization—the breakdown of words into constituent parts—which he calls "phonemic reading." See Garrett Stewart, *Reading Voices: Literature and the Phonotext* (Berkeley: University of California Press, 1990), 22, as well as his chapter, "The Ear Heretical," 100–143.

69. Langland, *Piers Plowman*, B.P.100–127.

70. Macklin Smith, "Langland's Alliterative Line(s)," *Yearbook of Langland Studies* 23 (2009): 163–216, 196.

71. This is a passage that is notably nonalliterative, so much so that it even presses the Middle English verse into Latin hexameters: "And thanne gan al the commune crye in vers of Latyn." For a thorough discussion of this passage, see Fiona Somerset, "'Al the comonys with o voys atonys': Multilingual Latin and Vernacular Voice in *Piers Plowman*," *Yearbook of Langland Studies* 19 (2005): 107–36.

72. George Kane, *Chaucer and Langland: Historical and Textual Approaches* (Berkeley: University of California Press, 1989), 85.

73. Macklin Smith, "Langland's Alliterative Line(s),"

74. Anonymous, *Iuxta artem conficiendi [compositiones]. Anonymi Tractatus de cantu figurativo et de contrapuncto (c. 1430–1520),* ed. Christian Meyer, Corpus scriptorum de musica, vol. 41, (N.p.: American Institute of Musicology; Hänssler-Verlag, 1997), 98–115, 98. *Componere sic diffinitur: est diversarum specierum sive concordantiarum iuxta perfectionem et imperfectionem, ascensuum et descensuum proportionata et debita positio, vel sic: compositio est armonia iuxta diversitatem plurimarum vocum perfectione et imperfectione regulata constructio.*

75. Margaret Bent, "What Is Isorhythm?," in *Quomodo Cantabimus Canticum? Studies in Honor of Edward H. Roesner,* Ed. David Butler Cannata, Gabriela Ilnitchi Currie, Rena Charnin Mueller, and John Louis Nádas, Publications of the American Institute of Musicology: Miscellanea, no. 7 (Middleton, WI: American Institute of Musicology, 2008), 121–43.

76. For a far more modern example, we might think of Adam Smith, who notes in his *Essay on the Imitative Arts*: "Poetry and Eloquence . . . produce their effect always by a connected variety and succession of different thoughts and ideas; but Music frequently produces its effects by a repetition of the same idea, and the same sense expressed in the same, or nearly the same, combination of sounds." Adam Smith, *Essays* (London: Murray & Son, 1869), 419. For more on the relation of repetition to musical meaning, see Margulis, *On Repeat*; David Huron, *Sweet Anticipation: Music and the Psychology of Expectation* (Cambridge, MA: MIT Press, 2006).

77. This phrase is taken from Anonymous II, *Tractatus de discantu (Treatise Concerning Discant)*, ed and tr. Albert Seay (Colorado Springs: : Colorado College Music Press, 1978), 32; for declamation in medieval music, see David Maw, "'Bona Cadentia Dictaminium': Reconstructing Word Setting in Machaut's Songs," *Music and Letters* 94:3 (August 2013): 383–432.

78. Elizabeth Eva Leach, "Music and Verbal Meaning: Machaut's Polytextual Songs," *Speculum* 85:3 (July 2010): 567–91, 573, 79.

79. *Cum enim eo, quod in nobis est iunctum convenienterque coaptatum, illud excpimus, quod in sonis apte convenientrque coniunctum est, eoque delectamur, nos quoque ipsos eadem similitudine compactos esse cognoscimus.* Boethius, *De institutione arithmetica libri duo, De institutione musica libri quinque,* ed. Godofredus Friedlein (Frankfurt: Minerva, 1966), 180. For Augustine: "When I remember the tears I shed at the psalmody of Thy church, when I first recovered my faith, and how even now I am moved not by the singing but by what is sung, when it is sung with a clear voice and apt melody, I then acknowledge the great usefulness of this custom. Thus I hesitate between dangerous pleasure and approved wholesomeness, though I am inclined to approve of the use of singing in the church (yet I would not pronounce an irrevocable opinion upon the subject), so that the weaker minds may be stimulated to devout thoughts by the delights of the ear. Yet when I happen to be moved more by the singing than by what is sung, I confess to have sinned grievously, and then I wish I had not heard the singing." Augustine, *Confessions,* tr. Edward Bouverie Pusey (Waiheke Island: The Floating Press, 1921), 299. *Verum tamen cum reminiscor lacrimas meas, quas fudi ad cantus ecclesiae in primordiis recuperatae fidei meae, et nunc ipsum quod moveor non cantu, sed rebus quae cantantur, cum liquida voce et convenientissima modulatione cantantur, magnam instituti huius utilitatem rursus agnosco. Ita fluctuo inter periculum voluptatis et experimentum salubritatis magisque, adducor; non quidem inretractabilem sententiam proferens, cantandi consuetudinem approbare in ecclesia, ut per oblectamenta aurium infirmior animus in affectum pietatis adsurgat. tamen cum mihi accidit, ut me amplius cantus quam res, quae canitur, moveat, poenaliter me peccare confiteor, et tunc mallem non audire cantantem. ecce ubi sum! flete mecum et pro me flete qui aliquid boni vobiscum intus agitis, unde facta procedunt. nam qui non agitis, non vos haec movent. tu autem, domine deus meus, exaudi et respice et vide et miserere et sana me, in cuius oculis mihi quaestio factus sum, et ipse est languor meus.* Augustine, *Confessions,* 1.10.50.

80. *Quamvis autem, in aliquibus consonantiis, delectetur sensus, et tristetur in aliis, omnium tamen cognitio placet intellectui.* Jacobus Leodiensis, *Speculum musicae,* 17.

81. Leach, "Music and Verbal Meaning," 586.

82. Smith, "Langland's Alliterative Line(s)," 211.

83. Alan T. Gaylord, "Some Prosodic Observations on the Peculiar Metric of *Pearl,*" in *Approaches to the Metres of Alliterative Verse,* ed. Judith Jefferson and Ad Putter, Leeds Texts and Monographs 17 (Leeds: Leeds Studies in English, 2009), 187–218.

84. Alan T. Gaylord, "Scanning the Prosodists: An Essay in Metacriticism," in *Essays on the Art of Chaucer's Verse,* ed. Alan T. Gaylord (New York: Routledge, 2001), 79–129, 79.

85. Adin Lears, "Noise, Soundplay, and Langland's Poetics of Lolling in the Time of Wycliff," *SAC* 38 (2016): 165–200, 194.

86. Smith, "Langland's Alliterative Line(s)," 190.

87. Although some scholars see in the performance of the liturgy a unifying practice, and one that interpellates medieval subjects before the law, Bruce Holsinger has argued for the fractious and antijuridical nature of the liturgy. See Bruce Holsinger, "Langland's Musical Reader: Liturgy, Law, and the Constraints of Performance," *Studies in the Age of Chaucer* 21:1 (1991): 99–141.

88. Langland, *Piers Plowman,* B.18.8–9.

89. "The symbolic experience of the unity of the senses enables a culture to entertain itself with the idea of the unity of meaning." Lawrence Sullivan, "Sound and Senses: Toward a Hermeneutics of Performance," *History of Religions* 26 (1986): 1–33, 8.

90. Salisbury, Chartres, and Rome were particularly ornate. See Clyde W. Brockett, "*Osanna!* New Light on the Palm Sunday Processional Antiphon Series," *Plainsong and Medieval Music* 9:2 (October 2000): 95–129, 99. Sources for Sarum practices can be found as far back as 1210, with the *De officiis ecclesiasticis tractatus* (a consuetudinary), but liturgical practices were established as early as Bishop Osmand (1079–99), which drew on continental practices while being respectful of insular traditions, and Anglo-Saxon practices can be traced back to Leofric's missal (1050–62) and the Rule of St. Dunstan (ca. 970). The first station was at the lay cemetery, where a subprocession was waiting; the second station went to the great west doors where the *Gloria, laus* was sung. W. H. Frere, *The Use of Sarum* (Cambridge: Cambridge University Press, 1898).

91. Similar processions around town occurred in Amiens, Bayeux, Laon, Metz, Paris, Reims, Rouen, Sens, and Soissons. Craig Wright, "The Palm Sunday Procession in Medieval Chartres," in *The Divine Office in the Latin Middle Ages: Methodology and Source Studies, Regional Developments, Hagiography,* ed. Rebecca A. Baltzer and Margot E. Fassler (Oxford: Oxford University Press, 2000), 343–64. For a full discussion of the use of music in mystery cycles and in late medieval theater, see Richard Rastall, *The Heaven Singing: Music in Early English Religious Drama* (Suffolk: Boydell and Brewer, 1996); as well as John Stevens, "Music in Mediaeval Drama," *Proceedings of the Royal Musica Association* 84 (1958): 81–95. Indeed, the Corpus Christi cycle, with its guild involvement and focus on spectacle, places the civic practice of religion in a spatiotemporal language that mimicked the daily processions of professed religious. See Margreta de Grazia, "World Pictures, Modern Periods, and the Early Stage," in *A New History of Early English Drama,* ed. John D. Cox and David Scott Kastan (New York: Columbia University Press, 1997), 7–24.

92. At York, this structure was temporary, and built out of wood; while at Wells and Salisbury, this *eminens locus* was permanent, built into the west facade of the church itself. Pamela Blum, "Liturgical Influences on the Design of the West Front at Wells and Salisbury," *Gesta* 25:1 (1986): 145–50.

93. "Every emission of the voice," Dolar says, "is by its very essence ventriloquism." Dolar, *A Voice and Nothing More,* 79.

94. The liturgical Latin of B.18 not only provides a useful historical locus for understanding Will's experience of acousmatic song, but might also help us consider the potential object-voicing of the other rubricated textual tags or Latin quotations in *Piers Plowman* manuscripts. But we might also argue that the Latin tags throughout the poem are themselves sound-objects. Because of their Latinity, they would have circulated with a different relationship to semiotics that aided in the type of *reduced listening* that privileges sonic units over the meaning of words—and that might circulate, separated from their original intended environment, nevertheless carrying the weight of their sonic import into new environments. In recalling, too, the rubrication of liturgical manuscripts and the coloration of music manuscripts, such as that of MS Egerton 3307—which contains, among other carols, the *Gloria, laus* in polyphony at folio 10v—where red ink is a semantic marker that must be *seen through* in order to arrive at the proper sonic performance of the text. *Piers Plowman*'s B.18 and the eschatological passus that follow it incorporate the reader through an act of reading that is, at the same time, listening and performance, recalling moments in other medieval material forms—such as liturgical books or music manuscripts—where the proper decoding of rubrication is key to understanding how the text is performed. *Piers Plowman*'s Latin quotations operate as a type of acousmatic veil out of which the sound-object emerges just as the songs of the children do during the singing of the *Gloria, laus* on Palm Sunday. See the Egerton

3307 MS on DIAMM at https://www.diamm.ac.uk/sources/207/#/images. These manuscripts of song in medieval England all involve red ink: the Ritson manuscript, British Library, Additional MS 5665 is a late fifteenth-century example containing thirty-six polyphonic *caroles* along with a series of Latin sequences, antiphons, hymns, motets, parts of the Mass, and some secular pieces. Cambridge, Trinity College MS O.3.58 also includes *caroles* on a roll from the fifteenth century. Arch. Selden B.26 includes coloration (probably 1425), and also includes twenty-five *caroles*; was probably copied at Worcester Abbey (this manuscript includes red coloration and also some words in red). The Old Hall manuscript (ca. 1415–21) is an earlier version of an English book of polyphony (one of the few in existence). The Egerton MS 3307, which contains not only twelve carols, but also liturgical music for Holy Week, is in choir-book and score layout, with a *Gloria, laus et honor* in polyphony at 10v. There is a beautiful example of red coloration at folio 17v (the *Sanctus*), and the *Agnus Dei* (folio 18v) does the introit in a really interesting way. Beginning on folio 53r with *Novus sol de virgine*, there are a series of motets/carols in English/Latin.

95. Langland, *Piers Plowman*, B.20.383.

96. Jean-Luc Nancy, *Listening*, tr. Charlotte Mandell (New York: Fordham University Press, 2007), 42.

CHAPTER 6

Note to epigraph: Geoffrey Chaucer, "The Book of the Duchess," in *The workes of Geffray Chaucer newlye printed, wyth dyuers workes whych were neuer in print beofre: As in the table more playnly doth appere* (London: Wyllyam Bonham, 1542), cclxix.

1. Alison Kafer, *Feminist, Queer, Crip* (Bloomington: Indiana University Press, 2013), 16.

2. Vicki Kirby, *Telling Flesh: The Substance of the Corporeal* (New York: Routledge, 1997), 63.

3. Kirby, *Telling Flesh*, 63.

4. For this, see Glennie's TED talk, "How to Truly Listen," from May 2017, https://www.youtube.com/watch?v=IU3V6zNER4g.

5. Kirby, *Telling Flesh*, 63.

6. "Interlude," *Oxford English Dictionary* (Oxford: Oxford University Press, 2019), and "interlude," in Lewis et al., *The Middle English Dictionary*.

7. Kafer, *Feminist, Queer, Crip*, quoted on 26, but this is the argument of the book as a whole.

8. Kafer, *Feminist, Queer, Crip*, 28.

9. See, for instance, Christopher Page's discussion of the distinction between *musicus* and *cantor*, noting that the *musicus* denoted, from the fifth century, a singer who knew the mathematical underpinnings of music; over time, the term *cantor* developed into a derogatory term for a singer who was ignorant of music theory. Christopher Page, "*Musicus* and *cantor*," in *Companion to Medieval and Renaissance Music*, ed. Tess Knighton and David Fallows (Berkeley: University of California Press, 1992), 74–78; see also Boethius, *De musica*, Patrologiae Cursus Completus, Series Latina (Paris: Garnier, 1844–1904), 63:1167–96, 1172.

10. Jan W. Herlinger, ed. and tr., *The* Lucidarium *of Marchetto of Padua: A Critical Edition, Translation, and Commentary* (Chicago: University of Chicago Press, 1985), 549, 551. *Musicus dicitur ille, testante Boetio, cui adest facultas secundum speculationem et rationem ipsius scientie musice de modis atqui rithimis deque generibus cantilenarum. . . . Musicus enim cognoscit virtutem*

*et rationem proportionum musicalium, et secundum hoc iudicat, et non solum per sonum. Cantor vero est sicut instrumentum quoddam ipsius musici; in quo instrumento operatur, artifex; sed musicus praticando ea que iam per rationem cognovit. Est itaque musicus ad cantorem sicut iudex ad preconem, nam iudex ordinat et per preconem preconizari mandat. Sic et musicus ad cantorem, nam musicus cognoscit, sentit, discernti, religit, ordinat et disponit omnio, quae ipsam tangunt scientiam: et per cantorem iubet tamquam per suum nuntium practicari."* Herlinger, 548, 550.

11. The distinction was so commonplace as to make an exhaustive list of music theorists who espoused it impossible, and it is included in the texts of Isidore of Seville to Guido d'Arezzo and many others. See Dolores Pesce, "Guido d'Arezzo, *Ut queant laxis*, and Musical Understanding," in *Musical Education in the Middle Ages and Renaissance*, ed. Russell E. Murray, Jr., Susan Forscher Weiss, and Cynthia J. Cyrus (Bloomington: Indiana University Press, 2010), 25–36, as well as Page, *"Musicus* and *cantor,"* 74–78 for a partial list.

12. See Lennard J. Davis, *Bending over Backwards: Disability, Dismodernism, and Other Difficult Positions* (New York: NYU Press, 2002).

13. *Aliquando, quod pudet dicere, in equinos hinnitus cogitur, aliquando virili vigore deposito in femineae vocis gracilitates acuitur. Speculum caritatis* II.23, quoted in Timothy J. McGee, *The Sound of Medieval Song: Ornamentation and Vocal Style According to the Treatises* (Oxford: Clarendon Press, 1998), 156.

14. This fundamentally ableist formulation excludes any number of performing bodies that a modern audience might recognize as musical, from what Joseph Straus terms the "supercrip" musical savant to the street musician with no formal musical training but years of performance experience. Joseph Straus, "Idiots Savants, Retarded Savants, Talented Aments, Mono-Savants, Autistic Savants, Just Plain Savants, People with Savant Syndrome, and Autistic People Who Are Good at Things: A View from Disability Studies," *Disability Studies Quarterly* 34:3 (2014): n.p.

15. Kafer, *Feminist, Queer, Crip*, 33.

16. *Horum aliqui nimis hoketant, nimis voces suas in consonantiis frangunt, scandunt et dividunt, et in locis inopportunis saltant, hurcant, iupant et, ad modum canis, hawant, latrant et, quasi amentes, incompositis et anfractis pascuntur vexationibus, harmonia utuntur a natura remota.* Jacobus Leodiensis, *Speculum musicae*, 23. Rob C. Wegman, *The Mirror of Music: Book the Seventh* (N.p.: Lamotte, 2017), 20.

17. See Bruce Holsinger's chapters devoted to Chaucer in *Music, Body, and Desire*, in particular 137–90, 259–92; as well as Carolyn Dinshaw, *Chaucer's Sexual Poetics* (Madison: University of Wisconsin Press, 1989), 157 ff.

18.   And Arcita anon his hand up haf,
      And moore encens into the fyr he caste,
      With othere rytes mo; and ate laste
      The statue of Mars bigan his hauberk rynge,
      And with that soun he herde a murmurynge.
      Full owe and dym, and seyde thus, "Victorie!"

Geoffrey Chaucer, "The Knight's Tale," in *The Riverside Chaucer*, I.2428–32. See also Alastair Minnis, *Chaucer and Pagan Antiquity* (Cambridge: Cambridge University Press, 1982) for the foundational study of Chaucer in a classical context.

19. Holsinger, *Music, Body, and Desire*, 290; Geoffrey Chaucer, "The Prioress' Tale," in *The Riverside Chaucer*, VII.541–73.

20. Geoffrey Chaucer, "The Second Nun's Tale," in *The Riverside Chaucer*, VIII.135.

21. Geoffrey Chaucer, "The Nun's Priest's Tale," in *The Riverside Chaucer*, VII.2821–3446. When, in the General Prologue, the Pardoner and Summoner appear, they are singing a duet—"Come hider, love, to me!" This song is, as Bruce Holsinger notes, an outbreak of homoeroticism, a queer threat to the newly formed social group on its pilgrimage. Geoffrey Chaucer, "The General Prologue," in in *The Riverside Chaucer*, I.672. See Bruce Holsinger, "Polyphones and Sodomites: Music and Sexual Dissidence from Leoninus to Chaucer's Pardoner," in *Music, Body, and Desire*, 137–90.

22. Jonathan Hsy, "Diverging Forms: Disability and the Monk's Tales," in *Chaucer and the Subversion of Form*, ed. Thomas Prendergast and Jessica Rosenfield (Cambridge: Cambridge University Press, 2018), 85–98, 86. For the origin of narrative prosthesis, see David T. Mitchell and Sharon L. Snyder, *Narrative Prosthesis: Disability and Dependencies of Discourse* (Ann Arbor: University of Michigan Press, 2001).

23. Hsy, "Diverging Forms," 96.

24. The original quotation from Julie Avril Minich, "Enabling Whom? Critical Disability Studies Now," *Lateral* 5:1 (2016): n.p.; Schalk uses Minich's formulation in her discussion of critical disability work not as a content area of expertise, but as a method, approach, or theoretical framework—not exclusively a study of disabled people—that takes intersectional account of difference, and how society encodes difference. See Sami Schalk, "Critical Disability Studies as Methodology," *Lateral* 6:1 (2017): n.p.

25. Hsy, "Diverging Forms," 86.

26. See D. H. Green, *The Beginnings of Medieval Romance: Fact and Fiction, 1150–1220* (Cambridge: Cambridge University Press, 2002), 10–12.

27. Jonathan Hsy, "Disability," in *The Cambridge Companion to the Body in Literature*, ed. David Hillmann and Ulrika Maude (Cambridge: Cambridge University Press, 2015), 24–40, 27; and Julie Orlemanski, "Literary Genre, Medieval Studies, and the Prosthesis of Disability," *Textual Practice* 30:7 (2016): 1253–72, 1264. Her argument hinges on the resistance of characters in *exempla* to narrative closure as a form of disability, but I interpret her trenchant critique as much more broadly applicable, as it forges a convincing link between the "physical forms" within texts to narratology more generally.

28. Juliana Chapman, "Melodye and Noyse: An Aesthetic of *Musica* in *The Knight's Tale* and *The Miller's Tale*," *Studies in Philology* 112:4 (Fall 2015): 633–55.

29. Geoffrey Chaucer, "The Retraction," in *The Riverside Chaucer*, X.1086. See Liza Strakhov's forthcoming *Continental England: Form, Translation, and Chaucer in the Hundred Year's War* (Columbus: Ohio State University Press) for potential counterexamples, such as the *Ch* ballades, which may have been written by Chaucer.

30. T. Atkinson Jenkins, "Deschamps' Ballade to Chaucer," *Modern Language Notes* 33:5 (May 1918): 268–78, 270.

31. Both "embodied asynchrony" and "temporally disjointed" are Kafer's terms, at *Feminist, Queer, Crip*, 48 and 49, respectively.

32. Geoffrey Chaucer, "The Franklin's Tale," in *The Riverside Chaucer*, V.868.

33. Shawn Normandin, *Chaucerian Ecopoetics: Deconstructing Anthropocentrism in the Canterbury Tales* (Cham: Palgrave Macmillan, 2018), 127–28.

34. Normandin, *Chaucerian Ecopoetics*, 132.

35. Geoffrey Chaucer, "The Franklin's Tale," V.944, 48–49.

36. Aristotle, *De anima*, 420.b.5, 87.

37. Ranulph Higden, *Polychronicon Ranulphi Higden Monachi Cestresnsis: English Translations of John Trevisa and of an Unknown Writer of the Fifteenth Century*, ed. Churchill Babington (London: Longman, Green, Longman, Roberts, and Green, 1865), 188–89.

38. *Quod si sono generato occurrat obstaculum, retunditur aer et quasi novus consimilis priori generatur sonus qui echo dicitur.* Jacobus Leodiensis, *Speculum musicae*, 81. Johannes Grocheio calls the *hoquetus* (the fashionable musical style of the thirteenth and fourteenth centuries in which one clipped voice would copy another) an echo. See Johannes de Grocheio, *De musica*, 41–67, 57.

39. "Echo," *The Middle English Dictionary*.

40. "Echo," *The Middle English Dictionary*.

41. Higden, *Polychronicon*, 188–89.

42. *Vox manet, ossa ferunt lapidis traxisse figuram / inde latet silvis nulloque in monte videtur,/ omnibus auditur: sonus est, qui vivit in illa.* Ovid. *Metamorphoses*, tr. Frank Justus Miller, Loeb Classical Library 42 (Cambridge, MA: Harvard University Press, 1916), III.398–401.

43. Elizabeth Dobbs, "Re-Sounding Echo," *Chaucer Review* 40:3 (2006): 289–310.

44. Pamela Gradon, ed., *Dan Michel's Ayenbite of inwyt; or, Remorse of conscience*, EETS no. 1, (London: Oxford University Press, 1866; reprint, 1965), 60.

45. In Western critical paradigms, Echo has been largely overlooked; Narcissus, not Echo, finds his way into Freudian and Lacanian critique and is central (as a negative presence) to the proper formation of the psychoanalytic subject. Narcissus, not Echo, captures our collective attention with tweets and with self-centered aggressive behavior; it is Narcissus, not Echo, for whom we now name a personality disorder. Tellingly, though, narcissism is figured by Freud and Lacan as a problem primarily of women, the socially repressed, and the colonial subject in the service of imperialism; Gayatri Spivak trenchantly critiques Freud and Lacan's misreading of the story of Narcissus through its inability to recognize Echo as central to psychoanalysis's failure as a critical methodology. For Spivak, taking account of Echo—the way Echo might or might not control her own voice—is central to taking account of the subject. Echo calls listeners to construct ethics, intent, and subjectivity *into* sound in spite of her fundamental *refusal* to host ethics, intent, or subjectivity in a body that, after all, is marked by its own absence. Echo's agency is disembodied, stolen from her, and assigned to those who speak to her in an extreme and violent reframing of the *cantor* to Marchettus's *musicus*. Echo's absent body is forced to give voice to sounds that are not her own. This body is made passive, disabled, by myth. See Gayatri Spivak, "Echo," *New Literary History* 24:1 (1993): 17–43, 23: "The account of Echo is a story of a punishment that is finally a dubious reward quite outside of the borders of the self."

46. Geoffrey Chaucer, "The Franklin's Tale," in *The Riverside Chaucer*, V.942–52.

47. In one particularly powerful retelling of the myth, Christine de Pisan, in the *Epistre Othea*, makes Echo into a desiring, plaintive subject, pleading to Narcissus for mercy, in an attempt to undermine the revisionist version of Guillaume de Lorris. See Marilynn Desmond and Pamela Sheingorn, *Myth, Montage, & Visuality in Late Medieval Manuscript Culture: Christine de Pizan's* Epistre Othea (Ann Arbor: University of Michigan Press, 2006), 70–77.

48. Ovid, *Metamorphoses*, X.252.

49. Hsy, "Diverging Forms," 96.

50. Geoffrey Chaucer, "Fortune," in *The Riverside Chaucer*, l. 8.

51. Geoffrey Chaucer, "Fortune," l. 70.

52. Cambridge, University Library MS Ii.3.2; Bodleian Library, MS Bodley 638; Bodleian Library, MS Fairfax 16.

53. Paul Zumthor, quoted in Thomas Stillinger, *The Song of Troilus: Lyric Authority in the Medieval Book* (Philadelphia: University of Pennsylvania Press, 1992), 11.

54. Geoffrey Chaucer, "Fortune," ll. 8, 16, 24.

55. Geoffrey Chaucer, "Fortune," ll. 6–7.

56. See also Philip Knox, "Hyt am y": Voicing Selves in the *Book of the Duchess*, the *Roman de la rose*, and the *Fonteinne Amoureuse*, in *Chaucer's 'Book of the Duchess': Contexts and Interpretations*, ed. Jamie Fumo, Chaucer Studies 45 (Cambridge: Boydell and Brewer, 2018), 135–56.

57. Geoffrey Chaucer, "Fortune," l. 74.

58. Anne Walters Robertson, *Guillaume de Machaut and Reims: Context and Meaning in His Musical Works* (Cambridge: Cambridge University Press, 2003), 299. The motet's theme is one of lost love, pitiful remembrance, and consequent yearning for death. Chaucer used it to structure his *Book* as well as to provide him with the *matière* of the text: Machaut's *dits*—particularly the *Fonteinne amoureuse*, the *Remede de Fortune*, the *Dit du vergier*, and the *Jugement dou roi de Behaingne*—as well as his third and eighth motets, from Froissart's *Paradys d'amours*, Machaut's first *Complainte*, the *Ovide moralise*, the *Roman de la Rose*, and Alain de Lisle's *De planctu naturae* along with the other, more complete borrowings from Machaut.

59. Geoffrey Chaucer, "The Book of the Duchess," in *The Riverside Chaucer*, ll. 470–71.

60. Geoffrey Chaucer, "The Book of the Duchess," ll. 481–86. The *aabaab* structure was troubling to early modern editors, as Thynne's edition of 1536 shows. His early printed text of *The Book of the Duchess* rearranges the lines and adds one at l. 479 (which most modern editions omit while numbering the lines as if it were included). This was ostensibly done to maintain the rhyming couplets of the rest of the poem, indicating that Chaucer's readership in the century after his death may not have had a taste for varying *formes* as employed in embedded lyric.

61. Chaucer's many complaints or embedded *lais* is specifically described as being spoken, rather than sung. See Thomas Campbell, "Machaut and Chaucer: *Ars Nova* and the Art of Narrative," *Chaucer Review* 24 (1990): 275–89, 276.

62. See Adin Lears, "Something from Nothing: Melancholy, Gossip, and Chaucer's Poetics of Idling in the *Book of the Duchess*," *Chaucer Review* 48:2 (2013): 205–21, for an overview of the scholarship on this point.

63. For a helpful overview of late medieval medicinal approaches to melancholy, see Timo Joutsivuo, "How to Get a Melancholy Marquess to Sleep? Melancholy in Scholastic Medicine," in *Mental (Dis)order in Late Medieval Europe*, ed. Sari Katajala-Peltomaa and Susanna Niiranen (Leiden: Brill, 2014) 21–46; in the introduction to this book, Sari Katajala-Peltomaa and Susanna Niiranen note that melancholia was recognized both as a humoral predisposition toward, and as an actual manifestation of, chronic, embodied, and psychological illness. Katajala-Peltomaa and Niiranen, *Mental (Dis)order in Late Medieval Europe*. The keynote study on *acedia* is still Siegfried Wenzel, *The Sin of Sloth: Acedia in Medieval Thought and Literature* (Durham, NC: Duke University Press, 1967), but see also Stanley W. Jackson, "*Acedia* the Sin and Its Relationship to Sorrow and *Melancholia* in Medieval Times," *Bulletin of the History of Medicine* 55 (1981): 172–85.

64. Melancholia as an artistic *habitus* of genius arises in the Renaissance, but for a medieval readership, such connections would not have been as readily available. See Jennifer Radden, ed., *The Nature of Melancholy from Aristotle to Kristeva* (Oxford: Oxford University Press, 2000), whose brief introductions to excerpted readings from the medieval period help to contextualize *acedia* and melancholy on the period's own, often complex and shifting, terms. For

Hoccleve, see Thomas Hoccleve, "My Compleinte," in *The Norton Anthology: English Literature, Volume A*, ed. James Simpson and Alfred David (New York: W. W. Norton, 2012). For Ofhuys's account, see Faith Wallis, tr., "Gaspar Ofhuy's Account of Hugo van der Goes's Mental Illness," in *Medieval Medicine, A Reader*, ed. Faith Wallis (Toronto: University of Toronto Press, 2010), 352–56.

65. The idea of singing "withoute noote" is not unique to the *Book of the Duchess*. It also appears in the Carthusian miscellany, British Library, Additional MS 37049, and, as Anna Zayaruznaya thoughtfully argues, in the *Roman de Fauvel*. She also argues for a relative "stillness" in the deeply plaintive *Dueil Angoisseus* by Binchois/Christine de Pizan. See Anna Zayaruznaya, "'*Sanz Note*' and '*Sanz Mesure*,'" 155–75.

66. Geoffrey Chaucer, "The Book of the Duchess," ll. 848–49, 927–31, 1182.

67. Geoffrey Chaucer, "The Book of the Duchess," ll. 743–44.

68. Geoffrey Chaucer, "The Book of the Duchess," ll. 50–51.

69. We might think here about the ways in which a poem, when recited, carefully treads the line between song and poetic recitation, as is evidenced even today in performances like, for instance, Patience Agbabi's "Slam Remix" of the Prologue to the *Canterbury Tales*, https://www.youtube.com/watch?v=-U-ozgjZfjQ.

70. Geoffrey Chaucer, "The Book of the Duchess," ll. 39–40.

71. Lears, "Something from Nothing," 221.

72. The poem has been called an "illogical solution of the philosophical problem[s]" outlined in the poem's narrative, where classical historiography, Boethian philosophy, and a Dantean cosmos are expected to exist side by side. See John W. Conlee, "Troilus' Ascension to the Eighth Sphere," *Chaucer Review* 7:1 (Summer 1972): 27–36, 28.

73. Kafer, *Feminist, Queer, Crip*.

74. Geoffrey Chaucer, "Troilus and Criseyde," in *The Riverside Chaucer*, I.396–99.

75. There are other songs, too: in Book II, Criseyde is made more open to the idea of love by Antigone's song, after which Criseyde is lulled asleep to the "loude song" of a nyghtyngale (II.920) and then dreams of having her heart viciously ripped out by an eagle, a dream that, once more, is *not* taken from the *Filostrato*. When Troilus and Criseyde enjoy their brief romance in Book III, Troilus sings a song taken from Boethius's *Consolation of Philosophy*. Geoffrey Chaucer, "Troilus and Criseyde," III.1742; Boethius, *The Consolation of Philosophy*, tr. Victor Watts (London: Penguin, 1999), 2.m.8, 45–46.

76. David Aers, "The Self Mourning: Reflections on *Pearl*," *Speculum* 68:1 (1993): 54–73.

77. Geoffrey Chaucer, "Troilus and Criseyde," V.1807–13, 1821–22.

78. Orlemanski, "The Prosthesis of Disability," 1253–72; Geoffrey Chaucer, "Troilus and Criseyde," I.8–11.

79. Chaucer and Deschamps were known to each other prior to 1391. It is well known that the two had an amicable sort of literary relationship, with Chaucer borrowing from Deschamps's *lais* and *Miroir de mariage* for a number of his texts; Eustache's "Ballade adressée a Geoffroy Chaucer, en lui envoyant ses ouvrages" is often cited as evidence of Chaucer's fame beyond England. Eustache Deschamps, *L'Art de Dictier*, ed. Deborah Sinnreich-Levi (East Lansing: Colleagues Press, 1994), 5–6. The *Miroir* was used in "The Merchant's Tale" as well as in "The Wife of Bath's Prologue," and the "Lai de franchise" served as a partial model for the prologue to *The Legend of Good Women*.

80. Deschamps, *L'Art de Dictier*, 63.

81. Deschamps, *L'Art de Dictier*, 103.

82. Deschamps, *L'Art de Dictier*, 65.

83. Deschamps, *L'Art de Dictier*, 65.

84. Giorgio Agamben, *The Time That Remains: A Commentary on the Letter to the Romans* (Stanford, CA: Stanford University Press, 2005), 62. Agamben, pace Derrida, argues for the importance of the "time that remains," that is, the "time that contracts itself and begins to end, . . . the time that remains between time and its end."

CODA

1. "From this it follows that, since there happen to be four mathematical disciplines, the other three share with music the task of searching for truth; but music is associated not only with speculation but with morality as well." Boethius, *Fundamentals of Music*, tr. Calvin M. Bower, ed. Claude V. Palisca (New Haven, CT: Yale University Press, 1989), I.1, 2. *Unde fit ut, cum sint quattuor matheseos disciplinae, ceterae quidem in investigatione veritatis laborent, musica vero non modo speculationi verum etiam moralitati coniuncta sit.* Boethius, *De institutione musica*, in *De institutione arithmetica libri duo, De institutione musica libra quinque*, ed. Godofredus Friedlein (Frankfurt: Minerva, 1966), I.i, 179.

2. Jan W. Herlinger, ed. and tr., *The Lucidarium of Marchetto of Padua: A Critical Edition, Translation, and Commentary* (Chicago: University of Chicago Press, 1985), 549. *Musicus enim cognoscit virtutem et rationem proportionum musicalium, et secundum hoc iudicat, et non solum per sonum. Cantor vero est sicut instrumentum quoddam ipsius musici.* Herlinger, 548.

3. Geraldine Heng, *The Invention of Race in the European Middle Ages* (Cambridge: Cambridge University Press, 2018), 90. See also Elizabeth Eva Leach, "Gendering the Semitone, Sexing the Leading Tone: Fourteenth-Century Music Theory and the Directed Progression," *Music Theory Spectrum* 28:1 (2006): 1–21, where she argues for both the gendering and the racing of particular intervals and harmonies.

4. Holsinger, *Music, Body, and Desire*, 137–87.

5. Sarah Roche-Mahdi, ed. and tr., *Silence: A Thirteenth-Century French Romance* (East Lansing: Colleagues Press, 1992).

6. David J. Eshelman, "'Great mowrning and mone': Spectatorship in the Towneley Scourging," *Baylor Journal of Theatre and Performance* 2 (2005): 23–34; Sarah Beckwith, *Signifying God: Social Relation and Symbolic Act in York's Play of Corpus Christi* (Chicago: University of Chicago Press, 2001).

7. Dante Alighieri, *De Vulgari Eloquentia: Dante's Book of Exile*, tr. Marianne Shapiro (Lincoln: University of Nebraska Press, 1990).

8. Leach, *Sung Birds*.

9. Thomas Hoccleve, *The Regiment of Princes*, ed. Charles R. Blyth (Kalamazoo: Medieval Institute Publications, 1999), ll. 995–98, 1013–19.

10. Hoccleve, *Regiment*, l. 1015.

11. Thomas Hoccleve, "My Compleinte," in *The Norton Anthology: English Literature, Volume A*, ed. James Simpson and Alfred David (New York: W. W. Norton, 2012), 360–69, l. 51.

12. For a recent example of work in this field, see Katharine Jager, ed., *Vernacular Aesthetics in the Later Middle Ages: Politics, Performativity, and Reception from Literature to Music* (Cham: Palgrave, 2019).

## APPENDIX

1. *SAL*, fol. 7r is a good example: *In festo sancti petri aduincula in monte gracie corporaliter fui in ecclesia.* ("On the feast of St. Peter in Chains, I was physically in the church at Mount Grace.")

2. There are a number of instances of marginal glossing. I give an example of one here: the *Scola* declares that the true lover of God can never become tired; and the marginal comment provides elaboration: *SAL*, fol. 5v, *Quia amore langueo, impossibile est ut fatigeris* ("It is impossible for you to grow weary if you deign to keep faith with your beloved"), with the comment, *Quia aut dulcedinem subministrat deus aut pacienciam*" ("Because God supplies either sweetness or patience"). Rita Copeland is the authority on the role of commentaries and glosses as a primary method of medieval *inventio*. See Rita Copeland, *Rhetoric, Hermeneutics, and Translation in the Middle Ages: Academic Traditions and Vernacular Texts* (Cambridge: Cambridge University Press, 1991).

3. *Canticum Canticorum* 5:2.

4. *DDD*, fol. 34v and elsewhere. Methley did not think he could speak about spiritual wakefulness as part of corporeal sleep until Christ assured him that he would speaking *through* him, using him as a prophetic mouthpiece. *DDD*, fol. 25v: *Ego dormio et cor meum vigilat cum in principio littera impossibilitatem habeat de necessitate ad spiritualem intellectum vertimus stilum. Et quia non discipulum sed magistrum decet docere. Peto et obsecro, ut doceas me et alios per me; scio et vere scio voluntatem tuam quia hic scribere me vis tecum nouo loquendi modo (quamquam verissime) tuum secundum aliquid non ut prius per inspiracionem tuum proposito nomine utriusque ut patet in libris multis quos scripsi per te.* ("'I sleep and my heart is awake.' At the very beginning, the literal sense proves to be impossible, so we must turn our pen to a spiritual understanding. Because it is the master who is supposed to teach, not the student, I beg you to teach me—and through me, teach others. Truly I know your will: in this book you want me to write with you in a new mode of speaking, a most truthful mode. Sometimes this will be through inspiration, though differently than before. At other times it will be in dialogue, as in the many books I have already written through you.")

5. *SAL*, fol. 28v: *Qui dormit corporaliter non cogitat naturaliter sicut uigilantes de amore mundi, et qui sic delectatur in amore dei ut obliuiscatur amorem mundi, uigilat in amore dei et dormit ab amore mundi.* ("He who sleeps in the body does not think naturally, like those waking from the love of the world; and he who thus delights in the love of God so that he forgets the love of the world, wakes in the love of God, and sleeps from the love of the world.")

6. *MM* includes an *ihc* in a heart (fol. 22v) and on a shield (fol. 40v), and has a shield with the five wounds of Christ (fol. 40v), a ladder with seven rungs (fol. 41r), a manicule (fol. 63v), and an *ihc* inscribed within a heart (fol. 66r).

7. *MM*, fol. 16r: *istorum omnium obedientiis ordinatus fuit a deo ille ordo purissimus carthusiensis quam ab angelis uocatus est excellentissimus.* ("This purest order, the Carthusian [order], which is called by the angels the most excellent, was appointed by God for [acts of] obedience of all these things.")

8. *DL*, fol. 64r: *et manifestabo tibi meipsum cum mira melodia cordis tui mirificati per nimio amore.* ("I will manifest myself to you with a wonderful/miraculous melody of your heart, made wonderful through love beyond measure.")

9. *DL*, fol. 79v: *in die ueneris ante festum penticostes anno tercio ingressionis mee ad hanc sanctam religionem. anno domino millesimo cccco lxxxvo immediate post missam sedenti in cella apparuit mihi in spiritu repente rapto glorissima domina angelorum maria mater ihesu ueri dei et*

*ueri hominis piisima induta habitum monialium nostri ordinis cum magna multitudine uirginum eodem habitu.* ("On the Friday before the feast of Pentecost, in the third year of my entrance into this religious life [= holy orders at Mount Grace], in the year of the Lord 1485, after Mass, sitting in my cell, there appeared to me in spirit, seized suddenly, the most glorious queen of the angels, Mary, mother of Jesus, true God and true man—[Mary], most loving, dressed in the habit of nuns of our order with a great multitude of virgins in the same habit.")

10. *DL,* fol. 80r.

11. *DL,* fol. 95r: *Et in custodiendo cellam et silencium et ceteras obseruancias sue religionis deuotissime secundum statum suum. Et ideo iam coronatus est inter summos choros angelorum. ubi nulla cogitatio anime sue bona et amorosa absque sempiterna remuneratione transit.* ("And by most devotedly keeping his cell and the silence, and the other observances of his religious (order) according to his station . . . on this account, now he has been crowned amongst the highest choirs of the angels, where no thought of his soul that is good and full of love passes away without eternal remuneration.")

12. *SAL,* fol. 7r-v; *DL,* fol. 84r.

13. *DDD,* 30r: *Anno eiusdem millesimo quadringentesimo octogesimo quinto, etatis mee ut arbitror tricesimo quarto, ingressionis in ordinem cartusiensem nono.* ("This year was 1485, and I judge my age at this time to be thirty-four, nine years after my entry into the Carthusian order.")

14. *RS,* 49v: *Hinc est quod hodierna die scilicet anno domini millesimo quadringentesimo octogesimo septimo in festo translacionis sancti hugonis lincolniensis cum ad primam dicendam in cella mea, in monte gracie surrexissem subito venit in me canor angelicus cum carmine sancto.* ("This is the day before, namely, in the year of the Lord 1487, on the feast of the translation of St. Hugh of Lincoln, while I was speaking Prime in my cell in Mount Grace, I had arisen, when, suddenly, an angelic song with a holy melody came upon me.") These include the feast of the translation of St. Hugh of Lincoln (fol. 49v), St. (Pope) Mark the Confessor (fol. 51r), St. Dennis (fol. 51v), St. Wilfrid (fol. 54r), St. Crispin (fol. 54v), the feast of Simon the Apostle (fol. 56v), the feast of all Saints (fol. 57v), all Souls (fol. 58v), the feast of Abbot Leonard, for whom he has special affection and after which he talks about his spiritual *canor* (fol. 59v), the feast of relics (fol. 60r), the feast of St. Theodore, Martyr (fol. 60r), St. Brice (fol. 59v), St. Edmund of Canterbury (fol. 60r), and then again St. Hugh of Lincoln (fol. 62r), St. Edmund, King of England (fol. 63v), the Vigil of St. Andrew (fol. 64v), St. Nicholas (fol. 66v), the Sunday after the feast of the Conception of the Virgin (fol. 67v), St. Eulalie (fol. 68r), St. Lucy (fol. 68v), the Third Sunday of Advent (fol. 69v).

15. In writing the *ODNB* entry for Richard Methley, Michael Sargent dates the composition of the *Scola,* using "internal references," to August 1481. I assume that the internal reference to which Sargent is referring occurs on fol. 11r: *Ego quondam fui tedio temptatus, sed si bene memini nunquam victus ex quo primum intravi hunc heremum annos septem complevi octavo currente, die ante sancti oswaldi regis festum in heremo montis gracie hec tibi scribens. Quia carthusiensis sum, te invito ad eundem propositum.* Indeed, August—August 5 in particular—seems to be the correct month for the penning of the manuscript, but I take issue with Sargent's calculation of the year. Methley says above that he has completed his seventh year at Mount Grace and has begun his eighth by the time he begins writing the *Scola.* If Methley entered Mount Grace before August 5 of 1476, this would make the completion of his seventh year in the monastery on or before St. Oswald's Day in 1483 and the correct year should be 1483; if he entered the monastery after August 5 of 1476, this would mean that he began writing in August of the following year, 1484. See Michael Sargent, "Richard Methley," in *The Oxford Dictionary of National Biography* (Oxford: Oxford University Press, 2004).

16. Francis Donald Logan, *Runaway Religious in Medieval England, c. 1240–1540* (Cambridge: Cambridge University Press, 1996), 49. One Thurstan Lofthous, identified as Thurstan Watson, is recorded as having left the Cistercians of Kirkstall and transferred to Mount Grace before 1489. A papal mandate exists from February 23, 1489, but he was allowed to remain a Carthusian. The only known manuscript of Methley's *Cloud* and *Mirror* is Cambridge, Pembroke College MS 221, in the hand of William Darker (d. 1512), a Carthusian of Sheen. See A. I. Doyle, "William Darker: The Work of an English Carthusian Scribe," in *Medieval Manuscripts, Their Makers, and Users* (Turnhout: Brepols, 2011).

17. *MM*, fols. 1r, 27r, 79v.

# Bibliography

MANUSCRIPTS

Baltimore, Walters MS W.102
Cambridge, Trinity College
  MS O.2.56
  MS O.3.58
Cambridge, University Library MS Ii.3.2
Lincoln, Cathedral Library MS 57
London, British Library
  Add. MS 5665
  Add. MS 37049
  Add. MS 47682
  Add. MS 57950
  Add. MS 61823
  Add. MS 88929
  Egerton MS 3307
  Egerton MS 5665
  Royal MS 2.B.xv
  Stowe MS 12
Oxford, Bodleian Library
  MS Arch. Selden B.26
  MS Bodley 638
  MS Douce 104
  MS Fairfax 16
Paris, Bibliothèque nationale de France, NAF 16251

BOOKS AND ARTICLES

Adams, Marilyn McCord, "Trinitarian Friendship: Same-Gender Models of Godly Love in Richard of St. Victor and Aelred of Rievaulx," in *Theology and Sexuality: Classic and Contemporary Readings*, ed. Eugene F. Rogers (Oxford: Wiley, 2002), 322–40.
Adorno, Theodor, "On Jazz," tr. Jamie Owen Daniel, *Discourse* 12:1 (1989–90): 45–69.
Aelred of Rievaulx, *Spiritual Friendship*, tr. Lawrence C. Braceland, S.J., ed. Marsha L. Dutton (Collegeville, MN: Liturgical Press, 2010).
Aers, David, "The Self Mourning: Reflections on *Pearl*," *Speculum* 68:1 (1993): 54–73.

Aers, David, "*Vox populi* and the Literature of 1381," in *The Cambridge History of Medieval English Literature*, ed. David Wallace (Cambridge: Cambridge University Press, 1999), 432–53.

Agamben, Giorgio, *The Time That Remains: A Commentary on the Letter to the Romans* (Stanford, CA: Stanford University Press, 2005).

Ahmed, Sara, and Jackie Stacey, eds., *Thinking Through Skin* (London: Routledge, 2001).

Ahuja, N. K., "It Feels Good to Be Measured: Clinical Role-Play, Walker Percy, and the Tingles," *Perspectives in Biology and Medicine* 56:3 (2013): 442–51.

Akbari, Suzanne Conklin, *Seeing Through the Veil: Optical Theory and Medieval Allegory* (Toronto: University of Toronto Press, 2004).

Alaimo, Stacey, and Susan Hekman, eds., *Material Feminisms* (Bloomington: Indiana University Press, 2008).

Albertanus of Brescia, *Tractatus de arte loquendi et tacendi*, in Thor Sundby, *Della vita e delle opere di Brunetto Latini* (Florence: Successori Le Monnier, 1884).

Albin, Andrew, "Auralities: Sound Cultures and the Experience of Hearing in Late Medieval England" (PhD diss., Brandeis University, 2010).

Albin, Andrew, "Canorous Soundstuff: Hearing the *Officium* of Richard Rolle of Hampole," *Speculum* 91:4 (2016): 1026–39.

Albin, Andrew, *Richard Rolle's Melody of Love: A Study and Translation with Manuscript and Musical Contexts* (Toronto: Pontifical Institute of Medieval Studies, 2018).

Alighieri, Dante, *De Vulgari Eloquentia: Dante's Book of Exile*, tr. Marianne Shapiro (Lincoln: University of Nebraska Press, 1990).

Alighieri, Dante, *The Divine Comedy* (Richmond: Alma Classics, 2012).

Allen, Judson Boyce, *The Ethical Poetic of the Later Middle Ages* (Toronto: University of Toronto Press, 1982).

Allen, Valerie, "Broken Air," *Exemplaria* 16 (2004): 305–22.

Allen-Goss, Lucy, "Queerly Productive: Women and Collaboration in Cambridge, University Library, MS Ff.1.6," *postmedieval* 9:3 (2018): 334–48.

Amerus, *Practica artis musice*, ed. Cesarino Ruini, Corpus scriptorum de musica, vol. 25 (N.p.: American Institute of Musicology, 1977), 19–112, www.chmtl.indiana.edu/tml.

Anderson, Joceline, "Now You've Got the Shivers: Affect, Intimacy, and the ASMR Whisper Community," *Television and New Media* 16 (2015): 683–700.

Anonymous, *The Cloud of Unknowing*, ed. Patrick J. Gallacher (Kalamazoo: Medieval Institute Publications, 1997).

Anonymous, *Commendacio artis musicae secundum quendam Gregorium*, in *Commentum Oxoniense in musicam Boethii: Eine Quelle zur Musiktheorie an der spätmittelalterlichen Universität*, ed. Matthias Hochadel, Bayerische Akademie der Wissenschaften, Veröffentlichungen der Musikhistorischen Kommission, vol. 16 (Munich: Bayerische Akademie der Wissenschaften, C. H. Beck, 2002), 414–32, www.chmtl.indiana.edu/tml.

Anonymous, *De expositione musice*, in *Ein anonymer glossierter Mensuraltraktat 1279*, ed. Heinrich Sowa, Königsberger Studien zur Musikwissenschaft, vol. 9 (Kassel: Bärenreiter, 1930), 1–132.

Anonymous, "In a Valley of This Restless Mind," in *Moral Love Songs and Sonnets*, ed. Susanna Greer Fein (Kalamazoo: Medieval Institute Publications, 1998).

Anonymous, *Iuxta artem conficiendi [compositiones]. Anonymi Tractatus de cantu figurativo et de contrapuncto (c. 1430–1520)*, ed. Christian Meyer, Corpus scriptorum de musica, vol. 41 (N.p.: American Institute of Musicology; Hänssler-Verlag, 1997), 98–115.

Anonymous, *Musica compendium*, transcribed by Oliver B. Ellsworth (*Thesaurus Musicarum Latinarum*, 2002), Salzburg, St. Peter's Abbey, a.VI.44, ff. 23r–41r, www.chmtl.indiana .edu/tml.

Anonymous, "Pearl," in *The Poems of the Pearl Manuscript: Pearl, Cleanness, Patience, Sir Gawain and the Green Knight*, ed. Malcolm Andrew and Ronald Waldron (Exeter: University of Exeter Press, 2002), ll. 58–59, 57.

Anonymous, *Speculum cantancium siue psallencium*, transcribed by Peter M. Lefferts (*Thesaurus Musicarum Latinarum*, 1996), www.chmtl.indiana.edu/tml.

Anonymous, *Tractatus de musica*, ed. Andres Briner, "Ein anonymer unvollständiger Musiktraktat des 15. Jahrhunderts in Philadelphia, USA," *Kirchenmusikalisches Jahrbuch* 50 (1966): 27–38.

Anonymous, "A Treatise on the Mensuration of Heights and Distances," in *Rara mathematica; or, a collection of treatises on the mathematics and subjects connected with them*, ed. James Orchard Halliwell-Phillipps (London: John William Parker, 1839), 56–71.

Anonymous, "Troubled Margery's Life Story Told in Play," *Lynn News*, June 30, 2018.

Anonymous II, *Tractatus de discantu (Treatise Concerning Discant)*, ed. and tr. Albert Seay (Colorado Springs: Colorado College Music Press, 1978).

Anzieu, Didier, *The Skin Ego*, tr. Chris Turner (New Haven, CT: Yale University Press, 1989).

Apel, Willi, *The Notation of Polyphonic Music, 900–1600* (Cambridge: The Medieval Academy of America, 1961).

Aquinas, Thomas, *Commentary on Aristotle's De anima*, ed. and tr. Kenelm Foster, Silvester Humphries, and Ralph McInerny (New Haven, CT: Yale University Press, 1994).

Aquinas, Thomas, *In Aristoteles Libros: De Sensu et Sensato, De Memoria et Reminiscentia, Commentarium*, ed. Angeli M. Pirotta (Turin: Libraria Marietta, 1820).

Aquinas, Thomas, "On Sense and What Is Sensed," in *Commentaries on Aristotle's "On Sense and What Is Sensed" and "On Memory and Recollection,"* tr. Edward M. Macierowski and Kevin White (Washington, DC: Catholic University of America Press, 2005).

Aquinas, Thomas, *The Power of God*, tr. Richard J. Regan (Oxford: Oxford University Press, 2012).

Aquinas, Thomas, *Quaestiones Disputatae de Potentia Dei* (Westminster: The Newman Press, 1952).

Aquinas, Thomas, *Summa Theologiae: Latin Text and English Translation, Introductions, Notes, Appendices, and Glossaries* (New York: McGraw-Hill, 1964).

Aquinas, Thomas, *Treatise on Separate Substances*, tr. Francis J. Lescoe (West Hartford: St. Joseph College, 1959).

Aristotle, *The Art of Rhetoric*, tr. H. C. Lawson-Tancred (London: Penguin Books, 1991).

Aristotle, *De Anima*, ed. and tr. Robert Drew Hicks (Cambridge: Cambridge University Press, 1907).

Aristotle, *De Interpretatione*, in *Categories and De Interpretatione*, tr. J. L. Ackrill (Oxford: Clarendon Press, 1963).

Aristotle, *Nichomachean Ethics*, ed. Julian Barnes (Princeton, NJ: Princeton University Press, 1984).

Arnovick, Leslie, *Written Reliquaries: The Resonance of Orality in Medieval English Texts* (Amsterdam: John Benjamins, 2006).

Ashley, Kathleen, "The French *Enseignemenz A Phelippe* and *Enseignement a Ysabel* of Saint Louis," in *Medieval Conduct Literature: An Anthology of Vernacular Guides to Behavior for*

*Youths, with English Translations*, ed. Mark David Johnston (Toronto: University of Toronto Press, 2009).

Attali, Jacques, *Noise: The Political Economy of Music*, tr. Brian Massumi (Minneapolis: University of Minnesota Press, 2009).

Atwood, Craig, "Little Side Holes," *Journal of Moravian History*, no. 6 (Spring 2009): 61–75.

Augustine, *Against the Academicians and The Teacher*, tr. Peter King (Cambridge: L. Hackett, 1995).

Augustine. *Confessiones*, ed. James O'Donnell (Oxford: Oxford University Press, 1992).

Augustine, *Confessions*, tr. Edward Bouverie Pusey (Waiheke Island: The Floating Press, 1921).

Augustine, *Expositions on the Book of Psalms*, ed. Philip Schaff, tr. A. Cleveland Coxe (Grand Rapids, MI: Eerdmans, 1956).

Augustine, "Psalm 100," in *Exposition on the Book of Psalms*, ed. and tr. Philip Schaff, Nicene and Post-Nicene Fathers, vol. 8 (Grand Rapids, MI: Christian Classics Ethereal Library, 2016).

Augustine, "Sermon 194.2," in *The Works of St. Augustine: Sermons* III/6, tr. Edmund Hill, ed. John E. Rotelle (New York: New City Press, 1993).

Avicenna, *Liber Canonis* (Basil: Johannes Heruagios, 1556).

Bacon, Roger, *Opus maius*, ed. John Henry Bridges (Oxford: Clarendon Press, 1897).

Bacon, Roger, *Opus maius*, tr. Robert Belle Burke (New York: Russell and Russell, 1962).

Badshah, Nadeem, "Guernsey Resident Halts Roadwork with Ancient Plea," *The Guardian*, August 14, 2018, https://www.theguardian.com/uk-news/2018/aug/14/guernsey-resident-halts-road-works-with-ancient-plea.

Bagshaw, Dana, *Cell Talk: A Duologue Between Julian of Norwich and Margery Kempe* (Santa Fe: Radius, 2002).

Barad, Karen, *Meeting the Universe Halfway: Quantum Physics and the Entanglement of Matter and Meaning* (Durham, NC: Duke University Press, 2017).

Barratt, Emma L., and Nick J. Davis, "Autonomous Sensory Meridian Response (ASMR): A Flow-Like Mental State," *PeerJ* 3:e851 (2015).

Beck, Julie, "How to Have a 'Brain Orgasm,'" *The Atlantic*, December 16, 2013, https://www.theatlantic.com/health/archive/2013/12/how-to-have-a-brain-orgasm/282356/.

Beckwith, Sarah, *Signifying God: Social Relation and Symbolic Act in York's Play of Corpus Christi* (Chicago: University of Chicago Press, 2001).

Bennett, Jane, *Vibrant Matter* (Durham, NC: Duke University Press, 2009).

Benson, C. David, *Public Piers Plowman: Modern Scholarship and Late Medieval English Culture* (Philadelphia: University of Pennsylvania Press, 2003).

Bent, Margaret, *Magister Jacobus de Ispania, Author of the* Speculum Musicae (New York: Routledge, 2016).

Bent, Margaret, "What Is Isorhythm?," in *Quomodo Cantabimus Canticum? Studies in Honor of Edward H. Roesner*, ed. David Butler Cannata, Gabriela Ilnitchi Currie, Rena Charnin Mueller, and John Louis Nádas, Publications of the American Institute of Musicology: Miscellanea, no. 7 (Middleton, WI: American Institute of Musicology, 2008), 121–43.

Benthien, Claudia, *Skin: On the Cultural Border Between Self and the World*, tr. Thomas Dunlap (New York: Columbia University Press, 2002).

Berger, Anna Maria Busse, *Mensuration and Proportion Signs: Origins and Evolution* (Oxford: Oxford University Press, 1993).

Berlant, Lauren, "Cruel Optimism," in *The Affect Theory Reader*, ed. Melissa Gregg and Gregory J. Seigworth (Durham, NC: Duke University Press, 2010), 93–117.

Bernard of Clairvaux, "Sermon 5: On the Four Kinds of Spirits," in *Commentary on the Song of Songs*, ed. and tr. Killian J. Walsh and Irene M. Edmonds (Spencer: Cistercian Publications, 1971).

Bernard of Clairvaux, *Sermones in Cantica canticorum* (Paris: Libraria Academica Wagneriana, 1888).

Bernard of Clairvaux, *Sermons on the Canticle of Canticles*, tr. a Priest of Mount Melleray (Dublin: Browne and Nolan, 1920).

Besseler, Heinrich, "Studien zur Musik des Mittelalters I," *Archiv für Musikwissenschaft* 7 (1925): 180–81.

Bhabha, Homi, *The Location of Culture* (New York: Routledge, 1994).

Bloom, Gina, *Voice in Motion: Staging Gender, Shaping Sound in Early Modern England* (Philadelphia: University of Pennsylvania Press, 2007).

Blum, Pamela, "Liturgical Influences on the Design of the West Front at Wells and Salisbury," *Gesta* 25:1 (1986): 145–50.

Boenig, Robert, "St Augustine's *Jubilus* and Richard Rolle's *Canor*," in *Vox Mystica: Essays in Honor of Valerie M. Lagorio*, ed. Anne Clark Bartlett (Cambridge: D. S. Brewer, 1995), 75–86.

Boethius, *The Consolation of Philosophy*, tr. Victor Watts (London: Penguin, 1999).

Boethius, *De institutione arithmetica libri duo, De institutione musica libra quinque*, ed. Godofredus Friedlein (Frankfurt: Minerva, 1966).

Boethius, *Fundamentals of Music*, tr. Calvin M. Bower, ed. Claude V. Palisca (New Haven, CT: Yale University Press, 1989).

Bolyard, Katherine, "Augustine, Epicurus, and External World Skepticism," *Journal of the History of Philosophy* 44:2 (2006): 157–68.

Borland, Jennifer, "Unruly Reading: The Consuming Role of Touch in the Experience of a Medieval Manuscript," in *Scraped, Stroked, and Bound: Materially Engaged Readings of Medieval Manuscripts*, ed. Jonathan Wilcox (Turnhout: Brepols, 2013), 97–114.

Boyd, Beverley, "Wyclif, Joan of Arc, and Margery Kempe," *Mystics Quarterly* 12:3 (1986): 112–18.

Brandeis, Arthur, ed., *Jacob's Well: An English Treatise on the Cleansing of Man's Conscience*, Early English Text Society, o.s. 155 (London: Kegan Paul, Trench, Trübner, 1900).

Brantley, Jessica, *Reading in the Wilderness: Private Devotion and Public Performance in Late Medieval England* (Chicago: University of Chicago Press, 2007).

Bray, Alan, *The Friend* (Chicago: University of Chicago Press, 2003).

Bridget of Sweden, *The Revelations of St Birgitta of Sweden*, vol. 4, *The Heavenly Emperor's Book to Kings, The Rule, and Minor Works*, ed. and tr. Bridget Morris (Oxford: Oxford University Press, 2015).

Brockett, Clyde W., "*Osanna!* New Light on the Palm Sunday Processional Antiphon Series," *Plainsong and Medieval Music* 9:2 (October 2000): 95–129.

Brower, Jeffrey, "Medieval Theories of Relations," in *The Stanford Encyclopedia of Philosophy*, ed. Edward N. Zalta (Winter 2018), https://plato.stanford.edu/archives/win2018/entries/relations-medieval.

Bruce, Scott G., *Silence and Sign Language in Medieval Monasticism: The Cluniac Tradition c. 900–1200* (Cambridge: Cambridge University Press, 2007).

Brunetto Latini, *Li livres dou tresor de Brunetto Latini*, ed. Francis J. Carmody (Berkeley: University of California Press, 1948).

Bude, Tekla, "Wet Shoes, Dirty Coats, and the Agency of Things: Thinking Personification Through New Materialism," *Yearbook of Langland Studies* 33 (2019): 205–30.

Bugyis, Katie, "Handling the Book of Margery Kempe: The Corrective Touches of the Red Ink Annotator," in *New Directions in Medieval Manuscript Studies and Reading Practices*, ed. Kathryn Kerby-Fulton, John Thompson, and Sarah Baechle (Notre Dame, IN: University of Notre Dame Press, 2014), 138–58.

Burgwinkle, Bill, "Medieval Somatics," in *The Cambridge Companion to the Body in Literature*, ed. David Hillmann and Ulrika Maude (Cambridge: Cambridge University Press, 2015), 10–23.

Butler, Judith, "The Social Construction of Gender," in *Theorizing Gender* (Oxford: Blackwell, 2002), 64–93.

Butler, Shane, and Alex C. Purves, "Introduction," in *Synaesthesia and the Ancient Senses*, ed. Shane Butler and Alex C. Purves (New York: Routledge, 2014).

Butterfield, Ardis, "The Refrain and the Transformation of Genre in the *Roman de Fauvel*," in *Fauvel Studies: Allegory, Chronicle, Music, and Image in Paris, Bibliothèque Nationale MS français 146*, ed. Margaret Bent and Andrew Wathey (Oxford: Clarendon Press, 1998), 105–59.

Bynum, Caroline Walker, *Christian Materiality: An Essay on Religion in Late Medieval Europe* (Brooklyn: Zone Books, 2015).

Bynum, Caroline Walker, *The Resurrection of the Body in Western Christianity, 200–1336* (New York: Columbia University Press, 1994).

Byrne, James Steven, "Angels and the Physics of Place in the Early Fourteenth Century," in *Conversations with Angels: Essays Towards a History of Spiritual Communication, 1100–1700*, ed. Joad Raymond (New York: Palgrave Macmillan, 2011).

Caciola, Nancy, *Discerning Spirits: Divine and Demonic Possession in the Middle Ages* (Ithaca, NY: Cornell University Press, 2003).

Camargo, Martin, *Ars dictaminis, ars dictandi* (Turnhout: Brepols, 1991).

Cambon, Glauco, "Synaesthesia in the *Divine Comedy*," in *Dante Studies, with the Annual Report of the Dante Society* 88 (1970): 1–16.

Campbell, Thomas, "Machaut and Chaucer: *Ars Nova* and the Art of Narrative," *Chaucer Review* 24 (1990): 275–89.

Capgrave, John, *The Life of Saint Katherine*, ed. Karen A. Winstead (Kalamazoo: Medieval Institute Publications, 1999).

Carruthers, Mary, *The Book of Memory: A Study of Memory in Medieval Culture* (Cambridge: Cambridge University Press, 2008).

Carter, Ronald, Malcolm MacRae, and John McRae, eds., *The Routledge History of Literature in English: Britain and Ireland* (New York: Routledge, 1997), 235–39.

Casas, Ghislain, "Language Without Voice: *Locutio angelica* as a Political Issue," in *Voice and Voicelessness in Medieval Europe*, ed. Irit Ruth Kleiman (New York: Palgrave Macmillan, 2015) 13–28.

Chaganti, Seeta, *Strange Footing: Poetic Form and Dance in the Late Middle Ages* (Chicago: University of Chicago Press, 2018).

Chapman, Juliana, "Melodye and Noyse: An Aesthetic of *Musica* in *The Knight's Tale* and *The Miller's Tale*," *Studies in Philology* 112:4 (Fall 2015): 633–55.

Chaucer, Geoffrey, *Collected Works*, in *The Riverside Chaucer*, ed. Larry D. Benson (New York: Houghton Mifflin, 1987).

Chen, Mel Y., *Animacies* (Durham, NC: Duke University Press, 2012).

Chillingsworth, William, *Religion of Protestants* (Printed by Leonard Lichfield, sold by John Clarke, 1638).

Chion, Michel, *Sound: An Acoulogical Treatise*, tr. James A. Steintrager (Durham, NC: Duke University Press, 2016).

Chow, Rey, "Listening after 'Acousmaticity': Notes on a Transdisciplinary Problematic," in *Sound Objects*, ed. James A. Steintrager and Rey Chow (Durham, NC: Duke University Press, 2019), 113–29.

Cicero, Marcus Tullius, *De amicitia*, tr. W. A. Falconer, Loeb Classical Library 154 (Cambridge, MA: Harvard University Press, 1923).

Ciconia, Johannes, *Nova musica, liber primus de consonantiis*, in Johannes Ciconia, *Nova musica and De proportionibus*, ed. and tr. Oliver B. Ellsworth, Greek and Latin Music Theory, vol. 9 (Lincoln: University of Nebraska Press, 1993), www.chmtl.indiana.edu/tml.

Classen, Albrecht, and Marilyn Sandige, eds., *Friendship in the Middle Ages and the Early Modern Age: Explorations of a Fundamental Ethical Discourse* (Berlin: Walter de Gruyter, 2010).

Cohen, Jeffrey Jerome, ed., *Animal, Vegetable, Mineral: Ethics and Objects* (Washington, DC: Oliphaunt Books, 2012).

Cohen, Jeffrey Jerome, "The Becoming-Liquid of Margery Kempe," in *Medieval Identity Machines* (Minneapolis: University of Minnesota Press, 2003), 154–87.

Coleman, Joyce, "Interactive Parchment: The Theory and Practice of Medieval English Aurality," in *The Yearbook of English Studies*, vol. 25, *Non-Standard Englishes and the New Media Special* (1995): 63–79.

Conlee, John W., "'Troilus' Ascension to the Eighth Sphere," *Chaucer Review* 7:1 (Summer 1972): 27–36.

Connor, Stephen, *Dumbstruck: A Cultural History of Ventriloquism* (Oxford: Oxford University Press, 2000).

Coolman, Boyd Taylor, *Knowing God by Experience: The Spiritual Senses in the Theology of William of Auxerre* (Washington, DC: Catholic University of America Press, 2004).

Copeland, Rita, *Rhetoric, Hermeneutics, and Translation in the Middle Ages: Academic Traditions and Vernacular Texts* (Cambridge: Cambridge University Press, 1991).

Copeland, Rita, and Peter T. Struck, eds., *The Cambridge Companion to Allegory* (Cambridge: Cambridge University Press, 2011).

Coppack, Glynn, "Make Straight in the Desert a Highway for Our God—Carthusians and Community in Late Medieval England," in *Monasteries and Society in the British Isles*, ed. Janet K. Burton and Karen Stöber, Studies in the History of Medieval Religion 35 (Woodbridge: Boydell, 2008), 168–79.

Cornelius, Ian, "The Rhetoric of Advancement: *Ars dictaminis, Cursus*, and Clerical Careerism in Late Medieval England," *New Medieval Literatures* 12 (January 2010): 289–330.

Cottington, David, *Cubism and Its Histories* (Manchester: Manchester University Press, 2004).

Craig, A. D., "How Do You Feel? Interoception: The Sense of the Physiological Condition of the Body," *Neuroscience* 3 (2002): 655–66.

Craig, A. D., "Interoception: The Sense of the Physiological Condition of the Body," *Current Opinion in Neurobiology* 13 (2003): 500–505.

Dailey, Patricia, *Promised Bodies: Time, Language, and Corporeality in Medieval Women's Mystical Texts* (New York: Columbia University Press, 2013).

Davidson, Clifford, ed., *The York Corpus Christi Plays* (Kalamazoo: Medieval Institute Publications, 2011).

Davis, Lennard J., *Bending over Backwards: Disability, Dismodernism, and Other Difficult Positions* (New York: NYU Press, 2002).

Dean, James M., ed., "Richard the Redeless," in *Richard the Redeless and Mum and the Sothsegger* (Kalamazoo: Medieval Institute Publications, 2000).

de Coussemaker, Edmond, ed., *Scriptorum de musica medii aevi nova series a Gerbertina altera,* 4 vols. (Paris: A. Durand, 1864–76).

DeFord, Ruth, *Tactus, Mensuration, and Rhythm in Renaissance Music* (Cambridge: Cambridge University Press, 2015).

de Grazia, Margreta, "World Pictures, Modern Periods, and the Early Stage," in *A New History of Early English Drama*, ed. John D. Cox and David Scott Kastan (New York: Columbia University Press, 1997), 7–24.

Delaney, Sheila, *Impolitic Bodies: Poetry, Saints, and Society in Fifteenth-Century England. The Work of Osbern Bokenham* (Oxford: Oxford University Press, 1998).

del Campo, Marissa A., and Thomas J. Kehle, "Autonomous Sensory Meridian Response (ASMR) and Frisson: Mindfully Induced Sensory Phenomena That Promote Happiness," *International Journal of School and Educational Psychology* 4 (2016): 99–105.

Deleuze, Gilles, and Félix Guattari, *A Thousand Plateaus,* tr. Brian Massumi (Minneapolis: University of Minnesota Press, 1987).

Derrida, Jacques, *The Politics of Friendship*, tr. George Collins (London: Verso, 2005).

Deschamps, Eustache, *L'Art de Dictier,* ed. Deborah Sinnreich-Levi (East Lansing: Colleagues Press, 1994).

Desmond, Karen, *Music and the Moderni, 1300–1500: The* Ars Nova *in Theory and Practice* (Cambridge: Cambridge University Press, 2018).

Desmond, Karen, "New Light on Jacobus, Author of *Speculum Musicae*," *Plainsong and Medieval Music* 9:1 (2000): 19–40.

Desmond, Marilynn, and Pamela Sheingorn, *Myth, Montage, & Visuality in Late Medieval Manuscript Culture: Christine de Pizan's* Epistre Othea (Ann Arbor: University of Michigan Press, 2006), 70–77.

Deutsch, Diana, "The Speech-to-Song Illusion: Crossing the Borderline Between Speech and Song," in *Musical Illusions and Phantom Words: How Music and Speech Unlock Mysteries of the Brain* (Oxford: Oxford University Press, 2019).

de Zamora, Juan Gil, *Ars musica*, ed. M. Gerbert, Scriptorium Ecclesiastici Musica, vol. 2 (St. Blaise: Typis San-Blasianus, 1784).

Dillon, Emma, "Representing Obscene Sound," in *Medieval Obscenities*, ed. Nicola McDonald (York: York University Press, 2006), 55–84.

Dillon, Emma, *The Sense of Sound: Musical Meaning in France, 1260–1330* (Oxford: Oxford University Press, 2012).

Dinshaw, Carolyn, *Chaucer's Sexual Poetics* (Madison: University of Wisconsin Press, 1989).

Dinshaw, Carolyn, *How Soon Is Now?* (Durham, NC: Duke University Press, 2012).

Dobbs, Elizabeth, "Re-Sounding Echo," *Chaucer Review* 40:3 (2006): 289–310.

Dolar, Mladen, *A Voice and Nothing More* (Cambridge, MA: MIT Press, 2006).

Doyle, A. I., "Carthusian Participation in the Movement of Works of Richard Rolle Between England and Other Parts of Europe in the 14th and 15th Centuries," *Kartausermystik und -mystiker*, Analecta Cartusiana 55 (Salzburg: Institut for Anglistik und Amerikanistik, University of Salzburg, 1981).

Doyle, A. I., "William Darker: The Work of an English Carthusian Scribe." *Medieval Manuscripts, Their Makers, and Users* (Turnhout: Brepols, 2011).

Doty, Brant Lee, "An Edition of British Museum MS Additional 37049: A Religious Miscellany" (PhD diss., Michigan State University, 1969).

Drogin, Marc, *Medieval Calligraphy: Its History and Technique* (New York: Dover, 1980).

Duffell, Martin J., *A New History of English Metre* (London: Modern Humanities Research Association and Maney Publishing, 2008).

Dunn, John, and Ian Harris, eds., *Aquinas*, Great Political Thinkers, vol. 4 (Cheltenham: Edward Elgar, 1997).

Dybinus, Nicolaus, "*Declaractio oracionis de beata Dorothea* (ca. 1369)," in *Medieval Grammar and Rhetoric: Language Arts and Literary Theory, AD 300–1475*, ed. Rita Copeland and Ineke Sluiter (Oxford: Oxford University Press, 2012), 821–32.

Dyer, Joseph, "Speculative *Musica* and the Medieval University of Paris," *Music & Letters* 90:2 (2009): 177–204.

Edelman, Lee, *No Future: Queer Theory and the Death Drive* (Durham, NC: Duke University Press, 2004).

Elders, Willem, *Symbolic Scores: Studies in the Music of the Renaissance* (Leiden: Brill, 1994).

Eliot, T. S., "Dry Salvages," in *Four Quartets* (New York: Harcourt, 1971).

Erasmus, Desiderius, *The Praise of Folly*, tr. Hoyt Hopewell Hudson (Princeton, NJ: Princeton University Press, 2015).

Eshelman, David J., "'Great mowrning and mone': Spectatorship in the Towneley Scourging," *Baylor Journal of Theatre and Performance* 2 (2005): 23–34.

Eyler, Josh, "Introduction," in *Disability in the Middle Ages: Reconsiderations and Reverberations* (New York: Routledge, 2010), 1–8.

Farb, Norman, Jennifer Daubenmier, et al., "Interoception, Contemplative Practice, and Health," *Frontiers in Psychology* 6 (2015): 1–26.

Fassler, Margot, and Rebecca A. Baltzer, eds., *The Divine Office in the Latin Middle Ages: Methodology and Source Studies, Regional Developments, Hagiography* (Oxford: Oxford University Press, 2000).

Feiss, Hugh, and Juliet Mousseau, eds., *A Companion to the Abbey of Saint Victor in Paris* (Leiden: Brill, 2018).

Ficino, Marsilio, *De vita libri tres (Three Books on Life, 1489)*, tr. Carol V. Kaske and John R. Clarke (Tempe: The Renaissance Society of America, 2002).

Field, Sean L., *The Beguine, the Angel, and the Inquisitor: The Trials of Marguerite Porete and Guiard of Cressonessart* (South Bend, IN: University of Notre Dame Press, 2012).

Freccero, Carla, *Queer/Early/Modern* (Durham, NC: Duke University Press, 2006).

Fredborg, Beverly, Jim Clark, and Stephen D. Smith, "An Examination of Personality Traits Associated with Autonomous Sensory Meridian Response (ASMR)," *Frontiers in Psychology* 8 (2017): 1–9.

Fredell, Joel, "Design and Authorship in the *Book of Margery Kempe*," *Journal of the Early Book Society* 12 (2009): 1–28.

Freeman, Elizabeth, "The Priory of Hampole and Its Literary Culture: English Religious Women and Books in the Age of Richard Rolle," *Parergon: Journal of the Australian and New Zealand Association for Medieval and Early Modern Studies* 29:1 (2012): 1–25.

Frere, W. H., *The Use of Sarum* (Cambridge: Cambridge University Press, 1898).

Fuller, Sarah, "'Delectabatur in hoc auris': Some Fourteenth-Century Perspectives on Aural Perception," *Musical Quarterly* 82:3 (1998): 466–81.

Gaffurio, Franchino, *Practica musice Franchini Gafori Laudensis* (Milan: Ioannes Petrus de Lomatio, 1496; reprint, New York: Broude Bros., 1979).

Ganim, John M., "Chaucer and the Noise of His People," *Exemplaria* 2 (1990): 71–88.

Garrison, John S., "On Friendship," *GLQ: A Journal of Lesbian and Gay Studies* 25:1 (January 2019): 79–83.

Gascoigne, Thomas, *Here after folowith the boke callyd the myrroure of Oure Lady very necessary for all relygyous persones* (1530).

Gavrilyuk, Paul, and Sarah Coakley, eds., *The Spiritual Senses: Perceiving God in Western Christianity* (Cambridge: Cambridge University Press, 2012).

Gaylord, Alan T., "Scanning the Prosodists: An Essay in Metacriticism," in *Essays on the Art of Chaucer's Verse*, ed. Alan T. Gaylord (New York: Routledge, 2001), 79–129.

Gaylord, Alan T., "Some Prosodic Observations on the Peculiar Metric of *Pearl*," in *Approaches to the Metres of Alliterative Verse*, ed. Judith Jefferson and Ad Putter, Leeds Texts and Monographs 17 (Leeds: Leeds Studies in English, 2009), 187–218.

Gehl, Paul F., "*Competens Silentium:* Varieties of Monastic Silence in the Medieval West," *Viator* 18 (1987): 125–60.

Georgius Anselmus, *Georgii Anselmi Parmensis De musica: Dieta prima de celesti harmonia, dieta secunda de instrumentali harmonia, dieta tertia de cantabili harmonia*, ed. Giuseppe Massera, Historia Musicae Cultores Biblioteca, vol. 14 (Florence: Leo S. Olschki, 1961).

Gerson, Jean, *De probatione spirituum, De distinctione verarum visionum a falsis*, and *De examinatione doctrinarum*, in *Opera Omnia*, ed. L. Ellis du Pin (The Hague, 1728).

Gerson, Jean, "On Distinguishing True from False Revelations," in *Jean Gerson: Early Works*, tr. Brian Patrick McGuire (Mahwah, NJ: Paulist Press, 1998), 334–64.

Giancarlo, Matthew, *Parliament and Literature in Late Medieval England* (Cambridge: Cambridge University Press, 2007).

Giger, Andreas, "Ludovicus Sanctus," in *Grove Music Online*, ed. Deane L. Root (Oxford: Oxford University Press, 2001).

Giles of Corbeil, *Carmina medica* (Leipzig: Leopold Voss, 1826).

Gill, Meredith J., *Angels and the Order of Heaven in Medieval and Renaissance Italy* (Cambridge: Cambridge University Press, 2014).

Gillespie, Vincent, "Monasticism," in *Cultural Reformations: Medieval and Renaissance in Literary History*, ed. Brian Cummings and James Simpson (Oxford: Oxford University Press, 2010), 480–501.

Gillette, Amy, "The Music of Angels in Byzantine and Post-Byzantine Art," *Peregrinations: Journal of Medieval Art and Architecture* 6:4 (2018): 26–78.

Ginsberg, Warren, ed., *Winnere and Wastoure, and the Parlement of the Thre Ages* (Kalamazoo: Medieval Institute Publications, 1992).

Glenn, Cheryl, and Krista Ratcliffe, eds., *Silence and Listening as Rhetorical Arts* (Carbondale and Edwardsville: Southern Illinois University Press, 2011).

Gower, John, *Cinkante Balades*, in *The French Balades*, ed. R. F. Yeager (Kalamazoo: Medieval Institute Publications, 2011).

Gradon, Pamela, ed., *Dan Michel's Ayenbite of inwyt; or, Remorse of conscience*, EETS no. 1, (London: Oxford University Press, 1866; reprint, 1965).

Grant, Roger, *Beating Time and Meausring Music in the Early Modern Era* (Oxford: Oxford University Press, 2014).

Gravdal, Katherine, *Ravishing Maidens: Writing Rape in Medieval French Literature and Law* (Philadelphia: University of Pennsylvania Press, 1991).

Green, D. H., *The Beginnings of Medieval Romance: Fact and Fiction, 1150–1220* (Cambridge: Cambridge University Press, 2002).

Green, Garth, "Nicholas of Cusa," in *The Spiritual Senses: Perceiving God in Western Christianity*, ed. Paul Gavrilyuk and Sarah Coakley (Cambridge: Cambridge University Press, 2012), 210–23.

Green, Richard Firth, *A Crisis of Truth: Literature and Law in Late Medieval England* (Philadelphia: University of Pennsylvania Press, 2002).

Greene, Richard Leighton, *The Early English Carols*, 2nd ed. (1935; Oxford: Clarendon Press, 1977).

Griffiths, Lavinia, *Personification in* Piers Plowman (Woodbridge: Boydell and Brewer, 1985).

Gruner, Oskar Cameron, tr., *A Treatise on the Canon of Medicine of Avicenna* (New York: AMS Press, 1930).

Gullatz, Stefan, "Exquisite Ex-timacy: Jacques Lacan vis-à-vis Contemporary Horror," *Off/Screen* 5:2 (March 2001), https://offscreen.com/view/lacan.

Gustafson, Kevin, "Richard Rolle's English Psalter and the Making of a Lollard Text," *Viator: Medieval and Renaissance Studies* 33 (2002): 294–309.

Hamburger, Jeffrey, *Nuns as Artists: The Visual Culture of a Medieval Convent* (Berkeley: University of California Press, 1997).

Hammerstein, Reinhold, *Die Musik der Engel: Untersuchungen zur Musikanschauung des Mittelalters* (Bern: Francke, 1962).

Hanna, Ralph, "The Transmission of Richard Rolle's Latin Works," *Library: The Transactions of the Bibliographical Society* 14:3 (2013): 313–33.

Harman, Graham, *Guerrilla Metaphysics: Phenomenology and the Carpentry of Things* (Chicago: Open Court, 2005).

Harne, George, "The Ends of Theory and Practice in the *Speculum Musicae*," *Musica Disciplina* 55 (2010): 5–31.

Harne, George, "Unstable Embodiments of Musical Theory and Practice in the *Speculum musicae*," *Plainsong and Medieval Music* 21:2 (2012): 113–36.

Harris, Carissa, *Obscene Pedagogies: Transgressive Talk and Sexual Education in Late Medieval England* (Ithaca, NY: Cornell University Press, 2018).

Harris, Carissa, "Rape and Justice in *The Wife of Bath's Tale*," in *The Open Access Companion to* The Canterbury Tales, ed. Candace Barrington, Brantley Bryant, Richard Godden, Daniel Kline, and Myra Seaman (2017), https://opencanterburytales.dsl.lsu.edu/wobt1/.

Hatter, Jane, "*Col tempo*: Musical Time, Aging, and Sexuality in 16th-Century Venetian Paintings," *Early Music* 39:1 (2011): 3–14.

Hawkins, John, tr., *A General History of the Science and Practice of Music*, vol. 2 (London: T. Payne and Son, 1776).

Heffernan, Thomas J., *Sacred Biography: Saints and Their Biographers in the Middle Ages* (New York: Oxford University Press, 1988).

Heidegger, Martin, *Being and Time*, tr. Joan Stambaugh (New York: State University of New York Press, 1996).

Helene, Henricus, *Summula*, transcribed by Peter M. Lefferts (*Thesaurus Musicarum Latinarum*, 2008), www.chmtl.indiana.edu/tml.

Heng, Geraldine, *The Invention of Race in the European Middle Ages* (Cambridge: Cambridge University Press, 2018).

Herlinger, Jan W., ed. and tr., *The Lucidarium of Marchetto of Padua: A Critical Edition, Translation, and Commentary* (Chicago: University of Chicago Press, 1985).

Hesse, Dag Nikolaus, "The Soul's Faculties," in *The Cambridge History of Medieval Philosophy*, ed. Robert Pasnau (Cambridge: Cambridge University Press, 2014), 305–19.

Hicks, Andrew, *Composing the World: Harmony in the Medieval Platonic Cosmos* (Oxford: Oxford University Press, 2017).

Higden, Ranulph, *Polychronicon Ranulphi Higden Monachi Cestresnsis: English Translations of John Trevisa and of an Unknown Writer of the Fifteenth Century*, ed. Churchill Babington (London: Longman, Green, Longman, Roberts, and Green, 1865).

Hildegard von Bingen, *Symphonia Armonie Celestium Revelationum*, ed. and tr. Barbara Newman (Ithaca, NY: Cornell University Press, 1988).

Hilles, Carroll, "The Sacred Image and the Healing Touch: The Veronica in Julian of Norwich's *Revelation of Divine Love*," *Journal of Medieval and Early Modern Studies* 28:3 (1998): 553–80.

Hilton, Walter, "De imagine peccati," in *Walter Hilton's Latin Writings*, vol. 1, ed. John P. H. Clark and Cheryl Taylor (Salzburg: Institut für Anglistik und Amerikanistik, 1987).

Hilton, Walter, *Of Angels' Song*, in *English Mystics of the Middle Ages*, ed. Barry Windeatt (Cambridge: Cambridge University Press, 1994), 131–36.

Hilton, Walter, *The Scale of Perfection*, tr. John P. H. Clark and Rosemary Dorward (New York: Paulist Press, 1991).

Hoccleve, Thomas, "My Compleinte," in *The Norton Anthology: English Literature, Volume A*, ed. James Simpson and Alfred David (New York: W. W. Norton, 2012).

Hoccleve, Thomas, *The Regiment of Princes*, ed. Charles R. Blyth (Kalamazoo: Medieval Institute Publications, 1999).

Hock, Ronald F., "Jesus, the Beloved Disciple, and Greco-Roman Friendship Conventions," in *Christian Origins and Greco-Roman Culture: Social and Literary Contexts for the New Testament*, ed. Stanley E. Porter and Andrew Pitts (Leiden: Brill, 2013), 195–212.

Hogg, James, ed., "The *Dormitorium Dilecti Dilecti* of Richard Methley of Mount Grace Charterhouse Transcribed from Cambridge, Trinity College MS O.2.56," in *Analecta Cartusiana* 55:5 (Salzburg: Institut für Anglistik und Amerikanistik, Universität Salzburg, 1981), 79–103.

Hogg, James, ed., "A Mystical Diary: The *Refectorium Salutis* of Richard Methley of Mount Grace Charterhouse," in *Analecta Cartusiana* 55:1 (Salzburg: Institut für Anglistik und Amerikanistik, Universität Salzburg, 1981), 208–38.

Hogg, James, ed., "The *Scola Amoris Languidi* of Richard Methley of Mount Grace Charterhouse Transcribed from Cambridge, Trinity College MS O.2.56," in *Analecta Cartusiana* 55:2 (Salzburg: Institut für Anglistik und Amerikanistik, Universität Salzburg, 1981), 138–65.

Holden, Stephen, "How Sound Feels to a Musician Who Lost Her Hearing," *New York Times*, September 7, 2005, https://www.nytimes.com/2005/09/07/movies/how-sound-feels-to -musician-who-lost-her-hearing.html.

Hollander, Robert, *Allegory in Dante's Commedia* (Princeton, NJ: Princeton University Press, 1969).

Hollywood, Amy, *Sensible Ecstasy: Mysticism, Sexual Difference, and the Demands of History* (Chicago: University of Chicago Press, 2002).

Holsinger, Bruce, "Langland's Musical Reader: Liturgy, Law, and the Constraints of Performance," *Studies in the Age of Chaucer* 21:1 (1991): 99–141.

Holsinger, Bruce, *Music, Body, and Desire in Medieval Culture: Hildegard of Bingen to Chaucer* (Stanford, CA: Stanford University Press, 2001).

Hornby, Emma, "Preliminary Thoughts About Silence in Early Western Chant," in *Silence, Music, Silent Music*, ed. Nicky Losseff and Jenny Doctor (New York: Routledge, 2007), 141–54.

Horstmann, Carl, *Yorkshire Writers: Richard Rolle of Hampole and His Followers* (Cambridge: Brewer, 1999).

Hsy, Jonathan, "Close Listening: Talking Books, Blind Readers, and Medieval Worldbuilding," *postmedieval: A Journal of Medieval Cultural Studies* 7:2 (Summer 2016): 181–92.

Hsy, Jonathan, "Disability," in *The Cambridge Companion to the Body in Literature*, ed. David Hillmann and Ulrika Maude (Cambridge: Cambridge University Press, 2015), 24–40.

Hsy, Jonathan, "Diverging Forms: Disability and the Monk's Tales," in *Chaucer and the Subversion of Form*, ed. Thomas Prendergast and Jessica Rosenfield (Cambridge: Cambridge University Press, 2018), 85–98.

Hsy, Jonathan, "Queer Environments: Reanimating 'Adam Scriveyn,'" *postmedieval* 9:3 (2018): 289–302.

Huber, Emily Rebekah, and Elizabeth Robertson, eds., *The Katherine Group from Oxford, Bodleian Library MS Bodley 34* (Kalamazoo: Medieval Institute Publications, 2016).

Huron, David, *Sweet Anticipation: Music and the Psychology of Expectation* (Cambridge, MA: MIT Press, 2006).

Ihde, Don, *Listening and the Voice: A Phenomenology of Sound* (Athens: Ohio University Press, 1976).

Inwood, Michael, *A Heidegger Dictionary* (Oxford: Blackwell Press, 1999).

Iribarren, Isabel, and Martin Lenz, eds., *Angels in Medieval Philosophical Inquiry: Their Function and Significance* (New York: Routledge, 2016).

Isidore of Seville, *Etymologiarium sive Originum Libri XX*, ed. W. M. Lindsay (Oxford: Clarendon Press, 1911).

Isidore of Seville, *Etymologies*, tr. Stephen A. Barney, W. J. Lewis, J. A. Beach, and Oliver Berghof (Cambridge: Cambridge University Press, 2006).

Jackson, Stanley W., "*Acedia* the Sin and Its Relationship to Sorrow and *Melancholia* in Medieval Times," *Bulletin of the History of Medicine* 55 (1981): 172–85.

Jacobus Leodiensis, *Speculum musicae, Liber primus: Jacobi Leodiensis Speculum musicae*, ed. Roger Bragard, Corpus scriptorum de musica, vol. 3/7 (Rome: American Institute of Musicology, 1973), 3–142.

Jager, Katharine, ed., *Vernacular Aesthetics in the Later Middle Ages: Politics, Performativity, and Reception from Literature to Music* (Cham: Palgrave, 2019).

Jenkins, T. Atkinson, "Deschamps' Ballade to Chaucer," *Modern Language Notes* 33:5 (May 1918): 268–78.

Jerome, "Psalm 88," in *Commentarioli in Psalmos*, ed. D. Germanus Morin (Oxford: J. Parker, 1895).

Jerome of Moravia, *Tractatus de musica*, ed. S. M. Cserba, Freiburger Studien zur Musikwissenschaft, vol. 2 (Regensburg: Pustet, 1935), 3–179, www.chmtl.indiana.edu/tml.

Johannes de Grocheio, *Die Quellenhandschriften zum Musiktraktat des Johannes de Grocheio: Im Faks. hrsg. nebst Übertr. d. Textes u. Übers. ins Dt., dazu Bericht, Literaturschau, Tab. u. Indices*, ed. Ernst Rohloff (Leipzig: Deutscher Verl. f. Musik, 1972).

Johannes de Muris, *Speculum musicae, Liber primus*, in *Die einleitenden Kapitel des Speculum Musicae von Johannes de Muris: Ein Beitrag zur Musikanschauung des Mittelalters*, ed. Walter Grossmann (Leipzig: Breitkopf und Härtel, 1924; reprint, Nendeln/Liechtenstein: Kraus, 1976), 53–93, www.chmtl.indiana.edu/tml.

Johannes Velendrinum, *Opusculum de musica*, in *Opusculum de musica ex traditione Iohannis Hollandrini. A Commentary, Critical Edition and Translation*, ed. Alexander Rausch,

Musical Theorists in Translation, vol. 15 (Ottawa: Institute of Mediaeval Music, 1997), 26–80, www.chmtl.indiana.edu/tml.

John Damascene, *De Fide Orthodoxa,* ed. Eligius M. Buytaert (St. Bonaventure, NY: The Franciscan Institute, 1955).

Johnson, Barbara, "Apostrophe, Animation, and Abortion," *Diacritics* 16:1 (1986): 22–47.

Johnson, Eleanor, *Practicing Literary Theory in the Middle Ages: Ethics and the Mixed Form in Chaucer, Gower, Lydgate, and Hoccleve* (Chicago: University of Chicago Press, 2013).

John Trevisa, *On the Properties of Things, John Trevisa's Translation of Bartholomaeus Anglicus De Proprietatibus Rerum, a Critical Text,* ed. M. C. Seymour et al. (Oxford: Clarendon Press, 1975).

Joutsivuo, Timo, "How to Get a Melancholy Marquess to Sleep? Melancholy in Scholastic Medicine," in *Mental (Dis)order in Late Medieval Europe,* ed. Sari Katajala-Peltomaa and Susanna Niiranen (Leiden: Brill, 2014), 21–46.

Julian of Norwich, "A Revelation of Love," in *The Writings of Julian of Norwich: A Vision Showed to a Devout Woman and a Revelation of Love,* ed. Nicholas Watson and Jacqueline Jenkins (State College: Pennsylvania State University Press, 2006).

Justice, Steven, "Did the Middle Ages Believe in Their Miracles?," *Representations* 103:1 (2008): 1–29.

Kafer, Alison, *Feminist, Queer, Crip* (Bloomington: Indiana University Press, 2013).

Kane, Brian, *Sound Unseen: Acousmatic Sound in Theory and Practice* (Oxford: Oxford University Press, 2014).

Kane, George, *Chaucer and Langland: Historical and Textual Approaches* (Berkeley: University of California Press, 1989).

Kantorowicz, Ernst, *The King's Two Bodies: A Study in Medieval Political Theology* (Princeton, NJ: Princeton University Press, 2016).

Karáth, Tamas, *Richard Rolle: The Fifteenth-Century Translations* (Leiden: Brepols, 2018).

Karnes, Michelle, "Will's Imagination in *Piers Plowman,*" *Journal of English and Germanic Philology* 108:1 (2009): 27–58.

Karras, Ruth Mazzo, *Sexuality in Medieval Europe: Doing unto Others* (Abingdon: Routledge, 2005).

Katz, Jonathan D., "John Cage's Queer Silence; Or, How to Avoid Making Matters Worse," in *Writings Through John Cage's Music, Poetry, and Art,* ed. David W. Bernstein and Christopher Hatch (Chicago: University of Chicago Press, 2001), 41–60.

Kaulbach, Ernest N., "The *Vis Imaginativa* and the Reasoning Power of Ymaginatif in the B-Text of *Piers Plowman,*" *Journal of English and Germanic Philology* 84:1 (1985): 16–29.

Kay, Sarah, and Miri Rubin, *Framing Medieval Bodies* (Manchester: Manchester University Press, 1994).

Keats, John, *Ode on a Grecian Urn,* in *The Broadview Anthology of British Literature: Concise Edition,* vol. B, ed. Joseph Black et al. (Buffalo: Broadview Press, 2013), 453–54.

Keck, David, *Angels and Angelology in the Middle Ages* (Oxford: Oxford University Press, 1998).

Kellogg, Ronald T., *Fundamentals of Cognitive Psychology* (Los Angeles: SAGE Publications, 2007).

Kelly, Henry Asgar, "The Right to Remain Silent: Before and After Joan of Arc," *Speculum* 68:4 (Oct, 1993): 992–106.

Kempe, Margery, *The Book of Margery Kempe: Annotated Edition,* ed. Barry Windeatt (Woodbridge: D. S. Brewer, 2006).

Kerby-Fulton, Kathryn, and Denise L. Despres, *Iconography and the Professional Reader: The Politics of Book Production in the Douce* Piers Plowman (Minneapolis: University of Minnesota Press, 1999).

Kessler, Herbert L., *Spiritual Seeing: Picturing God's Invisibility in Medieval Art* (Philadelphia: University of Pennsylvania Press, 2000).

Kirby, Vicki, *Telling Flesh: The Substance of the Corporeal* (London: Routledge, 2014).

Kłosowska, Anna, and Anna Roberts, *Violence Against Women in Medieval Texts* (Gainesville: University Press of Florida, 1998).

Kluchko, Marina, and Elvira Brattico, "Interoception in the Sensory Sensitivities: Evidence from the Auditory Domain," *Cognitive Neuroscience* 10:3 (2019): 166–68.

Knox, Philip, "Hyt am y": Voicing Selves in the *Book of the Duchess*, the *Roman de la rose*, and the *Fonteinne Amoureuse*," in *Chaucer's 'Book of the Duchess': Contexts and Interpretations*, ed. Jamie Fumo, Chaucer Studies 45 (Cambridge: Boydell and Brewer, 2018), 135–56.

Knuutila, Simo, "Medieval Conceptions of Emotions from Abelard to Aquinas," in *Emotions in Ancient and Medieval Philosophy* (Oxford: Oxford University Press, 2004), 177–254.

Koelsch, Stefan, Peter Vuust, and Karl Friston, "Predictive Processes and the Peculiar Case of Music," *Trends in Cognitive Sciences* 23:1 (2019): 63–77.

Kostelanetz, Richard, ed. *John Cage, Writer: Previously Uncollected Pieces* (New York: Limelight Editions, 1993).

Krug, Rebecca, *Margery Kempe and the Lonely Reader* (Ithaca, NY: Cornell University Press, 2017).

Lagerlund, Henrik, ed., *Rethinking the History of Skepticism: The Missing Medieval Background* (Leiden: Brill, 2010).

Lagerspetz, Mikko, "Music as Intersubjectivity—a Problematic for the Sociology of the Arts," *Musciology/Muzikologija* 1:20 (2016): 223–38.

Lane, Eleanor, et al., *The Ritson Manuscript: Liturgical Compositions, Votive Antiphons, Te Deum* (Newton Abbot: Antico Edition, 2001).

Langland, William, *Piers Plowman*, ed. A. V. C. Schmidt (London: J.M. Dent, 1995).

Langland, William, *Piers Plowman: The C-Text*, ed. Derek Pearsall (Exeter: University of Exeter Press, 1994).

Lavezzo, Kathy, "Sobs and Sighs Between Women: The Homoerotics of Compassion in *The Book of Margery Kempe*," in *Premodern Sexualities*, ed. Louise O. Fradenburg and Carla Freccero (New York: Routledge, 1996), 175–98.

Lawrence, C. H., *Medieval Monasticism: Forms of Religious Life in Western Europe in the Middle Ages* (New York: Routledge, 1984).

Lawton, David, "Voice, Authority, and Blasphemy in *The Book of Margery Kempe*," in *Margery Kempe: A Book of Essays*, ed. Sandra J. McEntire (New York: Garland, 1992), 93–115.

Lawton, David, *Voice in Later Medieval Literature: Public Interiorities* (Oxford: Oxford University Press, 2017).

Leach, Elizabeth Eva, "Gendering the Semitone, Sexing the Leading Tone: Fourteenth-Century Music Theory and the Directed Progression," *Music Theory Spectrum* 28:1 (2006): 1–21.

Leach, Elizabeth Eva, "Music and Verbal Meaning: Machaut's Polytextual Songs," *Speculum* 85:3 (July 2010): 567–91.

Leach, Elizabeth Eva, *Sung Birds: Music, Nature, and Poetry in the Later Middle Ages* (Ithaca, NY: Cornell University Press, 2007).

Lears, Adin, "Noise, Soundplay, and Langland's Poetics of Lolling in the Time of Wycliff," *SAC* 38 (2016): 165–200.

Lears, Adin, "Something from Nothing: Melancholy, Gossip, and Chaucer's Poetics of Idling in the *Book of the Duchess*," *Chaucer Review* 48:2 (2013): 205–21.

Lears, Adin, *World of Echo: Noise and Knowing in Late-Medieval England* (Ithaca, NY: Cornell University Press, 2020).

Leech-Wilkinson, Daniel, *The Modern Invention of Medieval Music: Scholarship, Ideology, Performance* (Cambridge: Cambridge University Press, 2002).

Lenz, Martin, "Why Can't Angels Think Properly? Ockham Against Chatton and Aquinas," in *Angels in Medieval Philosophical Inquiry: Their Function and Significance*, ed. Isabel Iribarren and Martin Lenz (New York: Routledge, 2016), 155–70.

Lerer, Seth, "'Representyd Now in Yower Syght,' the Culture of Spectatorship in Late Fifteenth-Century England," in *Bodies and Disciplines*, ed. Barbara Hanawalt and David Wallace (Minneapolis: University of Minnesota Press, 1996), 29–62.

Levinas, Emmanuel, *Otherwise Than Being, or, Beyond Essence*, tr. Alphonso Lingis (Pittsburgh: Duquesne University Press, 1998).

Lewis, Katherine J., "Model Girls? Virgin-Martyrs and the Training of Young Women in Late Medieval England," in *Young Medieval Women*, ed. Katherine J. Lewis, Noël James Menuge, and Kim M. Phillips (New York: St. Martin's Press, 1999), 25–46.

Lewis, Robert E., et al., eds., *The Middle English Dictionary* (Ann Arbor: University of Michigan Press, 1952–2001).

Lipari, Lisbeth, *Listening, Thinking, Being: Toward an Ethics of Attunement* (University Park: Pennsylvania State University Press, 2014).

Lipari, Lisbeth, "Rhetoric's Other: Levinas, Listening, and the Ethical Response," *Philosophy and Rhetoric* 45 (2012): 227–45.

Lochrie, Karma, "From Utterance to Text," in *The Book of Margery Kempe: A New Translation, Contexts, Criticism*, ed. Lynn Staley (New York: W.W. Norton, 2001), 243–56.

Lochrie, Karma, *Heterosyncracies: Female Sexuality When Normal Wasn't* (Minneapolis: University of Minnesota Press, 2005).

Lochrie, Karma, *Margery Kempe and Translations of the Flesh* (Philadelphia: University of Pennsylvania Press, 1991).

Logan, Francis Donald, *Runaway Religious in Medieval England, c. 1240–1540* (Cambridge: Cambridge University Press, 1996).

Luria, Alexander, *The Mind of a Mnemonist: A Little Book About a Vast Memory*, tr. Lynn Solotaroff (Cambridge, MA: Harvard University Press, 1968).

Machon, Josephine, "Defining (Syn)aesthetics," in *(Syn)aesthetics: Redefining Visceral Performance*, ed. Josephine Machon (London: Palgrave Macmillan UK, 2009).

MacPhail, Eric, *Dancing Around the Well: The Circulation of Commonplaces in Renaissance Humanism* (Leiden: Brill, 2014).

Malo, Robyn, *Relics and Writing in Late Medieval England* (Toronto: University of Toronto Press, 2013).

Mann, Jill, "Langland and Allegory," in *The Cambridge Companion to* Piers Plowman, ed. Andrew Cole and Andrew Galloway (Cambridge: Cambridge University Press, 2014), 65–82.

Margulis, Elizabeth Hellmuth, *On Repeat: How Music Plays the Mind* (Oxford: Oxford University Press, 2014).

Maw, David, "'*Bona Cadentia Dictaminium*': Reconstructing Word Setting in Machaut's Songs," *Music and Letters* 94:3 (August 2013): 383–432.

McAvoy, Liz Herbert, *Authority and the Female Body in the Writings of Julian of Norwich and Margery Kempe* (Cambridge: D. S. Brewer, 2004).

McGee, Timothy J., *The Sound of Medieval Song: Ornamentation and Vocal Style According to the Treatises* (Oxford: Clarendon Press, 1998).

McGinn, Bernard, "The Language of Inner Experience in Christian Mysticism," *Spiritus: A Journal of Christian Spirituality* 1:2 (2001): 156–71.

McGinn, Bernard, *Presence of God: A History of Western Christian Mysticism*, 6 vols. (New York: Crossroad, 1991–2016).

McGuire, Brian Patrick, "The Charm of Friendship in the Monastic Institution: A Meditation on Anselm and Bernard." In *Institution und Charisma*, ed. Franz Felten, Annette Kehnel, and Stefan Weinfurter (Vienna: Bohlau Verlag, 2009), 425–36.

McIlroy, Claire Elizabeth, *English Prose Treatises of Richard Rolle* (Cambridge: D. S. Brewer, 2004).

McInroy, Mark, *Balthasar on the Interior Senses: Perceiving Splendor* (Oxford: Oxford University Press, 2014).

Meech, Sanford Brown, and Hope Emily Allen, eds., *The Book of Margery Kempe: the Text from the Unique MS Owned by Colonel W. Butler-Bowdon*, EETS o.s. 212 (Oxford: Early English Text Society, 1961).

Mengozzi, Stefano, *The Renaissance Reform of Medieval Music Theory: Guido of Arezzo Between Myth and History* (Cambridge: Cambridge University Press, 2010).

Merleau-Ponty, Maurice, *The Visible and the Invisible: followed by working notes*, ed. Claude Lefort, tr. Alphonso Lingis (Evanston, IL: Northwestern University Press, 1968).

Metzler, Irina, *Disability in Medieval Europe: Thinking about Physical Impairment During the High Middle Ages, c. 1100–1400* (London: Routledge, 2006).

Meyer, Ann Raftery, *Medieval Allegory and the Building of the New Jerusalem* (Cambridge: D. S. Brewer, 2003).

Middleton, Anne, "Acts of Vagrancy: The C Version 'Autobiography' and the Statute of 1388," in *Written Work: Langland, Labour, and Authorship*, ed. Steven Justice and Kathryn Kerby-Futlon (Philadelphia: University of Pennsylvania Press, 1997), 208–317.

Miles, Laura Saetveit, "Richard Methley and the Translation of Vernacular Religious Writing into Latin," in *After Arundel: Religious Writing in Fifteenth-Century England*, ed. Vincent Gillespie and Kantik Ghosh (Turnhout: Brepols, 2011), 449–67.

Miller, Jon, ed., *The Reception of Aristotle's Ethics* (Cambridge: Cambridge University Press, 2013).

Milton, John, *Paradise Lost*, ed. Barbara K. Lewalski (Oxford: Blackwell, 2007).

Minich, Julie Avril, "Enabling Whom? Critical Disability Studies Now," *Lateral* 5:1 (2016): n.p.

Minnis, Alastair, *Chaucer and Pagan Antiquity* (Cambridge: Cambridge University Press, 1982).

Minnis, Alastair, *Medieval Theory of Authorship: Scholastic Literary Attitudes in the Later Middle Ages* (Philadelphia: University of Pennsylvania Press, 1988).

Minnis, Alastair, *Translations of Authority in Medieval English Literature: Valuing the Vernacular* (Cambridge: Cambridge University Press, 2009).

Mitchell, David T., and Sharon L. Snyder, *Narrative Prosthesis: Disability and Dependencies of Discourse* (Ann Arbor: University of Michigan Press, 2001).

Morrison, Susan S., *Women Pilgrims in Late Medieval England: Private Piety as Public Performance* (New York: Routledge, 2000).

Morton, Timothy, *Hyperobjects: Philosophy and Ecology After the End of the World* (Minneapolis: University of Minnesota Press, 2013).

Moten, Fred, *The Undercommons: Fugitive Planning and Black Study* (New York: Minor Compositions, 2013).

Muñoz, Jose Esteban, *Cruising Utopia: The Then and There of Queer Futurity* (New York: NYU Press, 2009).

Murphy, James Jerome, *Rhetoric in the Middle Ages: A History of Rhetorical Theory from Saint Augustine to the Renaissance* (Berkeley: University of California Press, 1974).

Myers, Nancy, "Purposeful Silence and Perceptive Listening: Rhetorical Agency for Women in Christine de Pizan's *The Treasure of the City of Ladies*," in *Silence and Listening as Rhetorical Arts*, ed. Cheryl Glenn and Krista Ratcliffe (Carbondale and Edwardsville: Southern Illinois University Press, 2011), 56–74.

Nancy, Jean- Luc, *Listening*, tr. Charlotte Mandell (New York: Fordham University Press, 2007).

New, Elizabeth Anne, "The Cult of the Holy Name of Jesus in Late Medieval England, with Special Reference to the Fraternity in St Paul's Cathedral, London c. 1450–1558" (PhD diss., University of London, 1999).

Newman, Barbara, *God and the Goddesses: Vision, Poetry, and Belief in the Middle Ages* (Philadelphia: University of Pennsylvania Press, 2003).

Newman, Barbara, ed. and tr., *The Works of Richard Methley* (Collegeville, MN: Liturgical Press, 2021).

Nissé, Ruth, "Reversing Discipline: *The Tretise of Miracles Pleyinge*, Lollard Exegesis, and the Failure of Representation," *Yearbook of Langland Studies* 11 (1997): 163–94.

Normandin, Shawn, *Chaucerian Ecopoetics: Deconstructing Anthropocentrism in the* Canterbury Tales (Cham: Palgrave Macmillan, 2018).

Nusbaum, Emily C., Paul J. Silvia, et al., "Listening Between the Notes: Aesthetic Chills in Everyday Music Listening," *Psychology of Aesthetics, Creativity, and the Arts* 8:1 (2014): 104–9.

Oldfather, Elizabeth, "'Ode to a Nightingale': Poetry and the Particularity of Sense," *European Romantic Review* 30 (2019): 557–72.

Ong, Walter, *Orality and Literacy* (New York: Routledge, 2002).

Origen, *Contra Celsum*. tr. Henry Chadwick (Cambridge: Cambridge University Press, 1953).

Orlemanski, Julie, "Literary Genre, Medieval Studies, and the Prosthesis of Disability," *Textual Practice* 30:7 (2016): 1253–72.

Orlemanski, Julie, "Margery's 'Noyse' and Distributed Expressivity," in *Voice and Voicelessness in Medieval Europe*, ed. Irit Ruth Kleiman (New York: Palgrave Macmillan, 2015), 123–38.

Orlemanski, Julie, *Symptomatic Subjects: Bodies, Medicine, and Causation in the Literature of Late Medieval England* (Philadelphia: University of Pennsylvania Press, 2019).

Orlemanski, Julie, "Who Has Fiction? Modernity, Fictionality, and the Middle Ages," *New Literary History* 50:2 (Spring 2019): 145–70.

Ormrod, Mark, "Murmur, Clamour, and Noise," in *Medieval Petitions: Grace and Grievance*, ed. W. Mark Ormrod, Gwilym Dodd, and Anthony Musson (Woodbridge: Boydell and Brewer, 2006), 125–55.

Ovid, *Metamorphoses*, tr. Frank Justus Miller, Loeb Classical Library 42 (Cambridge, MA: Harvard University Press, 1916).

Page, Christopher, "*Musicus* and *cantor*," in *Companion to Medieval and Renaissance Music*, ed. Tess Knighton and David Fallows (Berkeley: University of California Press, 1992), 74–78.

Pangle, Lorraine Smith, *Aristotle and the Philosophy of Friendship*, ed. John von Heyking and Richard Avramenko (Cambridge: Cambridge University Press, 2003).

Parkin, Gabrielle, "Read with Your Hands and Not with Your Eyes: Touching Books of Hours," in *Later Middle English Literature, Materiality, and Culture: Essays in Honor of James M. Dean*, ed. Brian Gastle and Erick Kelemen (Newark: University of Delaware Press, 2018), 147–66.

Pepwell, Henry, *The Cell of Self-Knowledge*, ed. E. Gardner (London: Chatto and Windus, 1910).

Pesce, Dolores, "Guido d'Arezzo, *Ut queant laxis*, and Musical Understanding," in *Musical Education in the Middle Ages and Renaissance*, ed. Russell E. Murray, Jr., Susan Forscher Weiss, and Cynthia J. Cyrus (Bloomington: Indiana University Press, 2010), 25–36.

Peter Lombard, *The Sentences, Book 2: On Creation*, tr. Giulio Silano (Toronto: Pontifical Institute of Medieval Studies, 2008).

Pfaff, Richard W., *New Liturgical Feasts in Later Medieval England* (Oxford: Clarendon Press, 1970).

Phillips, Tom, and Armand D'Angour, *Music, Text, and Culture in Ancient Greece* (Oxford: Oxford University Press, 2018).

Poulain, Augustin, *Des grâces d'oraison: Traité de théologie mystique* (Paris: G. Beauchesne, 1922).

Poulain, Augustin, *The Graces of Interior Prayer*, tr. L. L. Yorke Smith (London: Kegan Paul, Trench, Trübner, 1950).

Priscian, *Institutiones grammaticae*, ed. Heinrich Keil (Leipzig: B.G. Teubner, 1855).

Priscian, *Institutiones grammaticae* 1.3, in *Medieval Grammar and Rhetoric*, ed. Rita Copeland and Ineke Sluiter (Oxford: Oxford University Press, 2009), 167–89.

Pseudo-Dionysius, *The Complete Works*, tr. Colm Luibhéid (New York: Paulist Press, 1987).

Quero, Martín Hugo Córdova, "Friendship with Benefits: A Queer Reading of Aelred of Rievaulx and His Theology of Friendship," in *The Sexual Theologian: Essays on Sex, God, and Politics*, ed. Marcella Althaus-Reid and Lisa Isherwood (London: T&T Clark International, 2004), 26–46.

Quilligan, Maureen, *The Language of Allegory: Defining the Genre* (Ithaca, NY: Cornell University Press, 1992).

Quintilian, *Institutio Oratoria*, ed. G. P. Goold (Cambridge, MA: Harvard University Press, 1996).

Quintilian, *Institutio Oratoria*, tr. Harold Edgeworth Butler, Loeb Classical Library (Cambridge, MA: Harvard University Press, 1996).

Rabelais, François, *Gargantua and Pantagruel*, tr. Burton Raffel (New York: W. W. Norton, 1990).

Radden, Jennifer, ed., *The Nature of Melancholy from Aristotle to Kristeva* (Oxford: Oxford University Press, 2000).

Rahner, Karl, "Le debut d'une doctrine des cinq sens spirituels chez Origène," *RAM* 13 (1932): 113–45.

Raskolnikov, Masha, "Promising the Female, Delivering the Male: Transformations of Gender in *Piers Plowman*," *Yearbook of Langland Studies* 19 (2005): 81–105.

Rastall, Richard, *The Heaven Singing: Music in Early English Religious Drama* (Suffolk: Boydell and Brewer, 1996).

Raymond, Joad, *Conversations with Angels: Essays Towards a History of Spiritual Communication, 1100–1700* (New York: Palgrave MacMillan, 2011).

Renevey, Denis, *The Moving of the Soul: Function of Metaphors of Love in the Writings of Rich-ard Rolle and the Medieval Mystical Tradition* (Oxford: Oxford University Press, 1993).

Revill, David, *Roaring Silence: John Cage, a Life* (New York: Arcade Publishers, 1992).

Rex, Richard, "Melton, William (d. 1528)," *The Oxford Dictionary of National Biography* (Oxford: Oxford University Press, 2004).

Richardson, Malcolm, "The *ars dictaminis*, the Formulary, and Medieval Epistolary Practice," in *Letter-Writing Manuals and Instruction from Antiquity to the Present: Historical and Bibliographic Studies*, ed. Carol Poster and Linda Mitchell (Columbia: University of South Carolina Press, 2007), 52–66.

Rico, Gilles, "'*Auctoritas Cereum habet Nasum*': Boethius, Aristotle, and the Music of the Spheres," in *Citation and Authority in Medieval and Renaissance Musical Culture: Learning from the Learned. Essays in Honour of Margaret Bent*, ed. Suzannah Clark and Elizabeth Eva Leach (Woodbridge: Boydell and Brewer, 2005), 20–28.

Rico, Gilles, "Music in the Arts Faculty of Paris in Thirteenth and Early Fourteenth Centuries" (PhD diss., Oxford University, 2005).

Riddy, Felicity, "The Provenance of *Quia Amore Langueo*," *Review of English Studies* 18:72 (November 1967): 429–33.

Riddy, Felicity, "Text and Self in *The Book of Margery Kempe*," in *Voices in Dialogue: Reading Women in the Middle Ages*, ed. Linda Olson and Kathryn Kerby-Fulton (South Bend, IN: University of Notre Dame Press, 2005), 435–53.

Riley, H. T., *Memorials of London and London Life in the XIIIth, XIVth, and XVth Centuries* (London: Longmans, Green, 1868).

Ritchie, J. Brendan, and Peter Carruthers, "The Bodily Senses," in *The Oxford Handbook of Philosophy of Perception*, ed. Mohan Matthen (Oxford: Oxford University Press, 2015), 353–70.

Robbins, Rossell Hope, "Middle English Carols as Processional Hymns," *Studies in Philology* 56:4 (October 1959): 559–82.

Robertson, Anne Walters, *Guillaume de Machaut and Reims: Context and Meaning in His Musical Works* (Cambridge: Cambridge University Press, 2003).

Robertson, Elizabeth, "*Noli Me Tangere:* The Enigma of Touch in Middle English Religious Literature and Art for and about Women," in *Reading Skin in Medieval Literature and Culture*, ed. Katie Walter (New York: Palgrave Macmillan, 2013), 29–55.

Robertson, Kellie, "Medieval Materialism: A Manifesto," *Exemplaria* 22:2 (2010): 99–118.

Robins, P. R., "Discerning Voices in the Trial of Joan of Arc and *The Book of Margery Kempe*," in *Fifteenth-Century Studies* 38, ed. Barbara I. Gusick (Woodbridge: Boydell & Brewer, 2013), 175–234.

Roche-Mahdi, Sarah, ed. and trans., *Silence: A Thirteenth-Century French Romance* (East Lansing: Colleagues Press, 1992).

Rolle, Richard, *The* Contra amatores mundi *of Richard Rolle of Hampole*, ed. Paul F. Theiner (Los Angeles: University of California Press, 1968).

Rolle, Richard, *Ego Dormio*, in *Richard Rolle, Prose and Verse Edited from MS Longleat 29 and Related Manuscripts*, ed. S. J. Ogilvie-Thomson, EETS no. 293 (Oxford: Oxford University Press, 1988).

Rolle, Richard, *Emendatio Vitae; Orationes ad Honorem Nominis Ihesu, Edited from Cambridge University Library MSS Dd.v.64 and Kk.vi.20*, ed. Nicholas Watson (Toronto: Centre for Medieval Studies, 1995).

Rolle, Richard, "The Form of Living," in *Richard Rolle, Prose and Verse Edited from MS Long-leat 29 and Related Manuscripts*, ed. S. J. Ogilvie-Thomson, EETS no. 293 (Oxford: Oxford University Press, 1988).

Rolle, Richard, *The Incendium Amoris of Richard Rolle of Hampole*, ed. Margaret Deanesly (Manchester: Manchester University Press, 1915).

Rolle, Richard, *The Melos Amoris of Richard Rolle of Hampole*, ed. E. J. F. Arnould (Oxford: Blackwell, 1957).

Rolling, Bern, "Angelic Language and Communication," in *A Companion to Angels in Medi-eval Philosophy*, ed. Tobias Hoffmann (Leiden: Brill, 2011), 223–60.

Roman, Christopher Michael, *Queering Richard Rolle: Mystical Theology and the Hermit in Fourteenth-Century England* (New York: Palgrave Macmillan, 2017).

Rozenski, Steven, Jr., "Authority and Exemplarity in Henry Suso and Richard Rolle," in *The Medieval Mystical Tradition in England, Exeter Symposium VIII*, ed. E. A. Jones (Cambridge, D. S. Brewer, 2013), 93–108.

Rudy, Gordon, *The Mystical Language of Sensation in the Later Middle Ages* (New York: Routledge, 2002).

Rueffer, Jens, "Aelred of Rievaulx and the Institutional Limits of Monastic Friendship," in *Perspectives for an Architecture of Solitude: Essays on Cistercians, Art, and Architecture in Honour of Peter Fergusson*, ed. Terryl Kinder (Turnhout: Brepols, 2004), 55–62.

Saltzstein, Jennifer, *The Refrain and the Rise of the Vernacular in Medieval French Music and Poetry* (Cambridge: D. S. Brewer, 2013).

Sargent, Michael, "Richard Methley," in *The Oxford Dictionary of National Biography* (Oxford: Oxford University Press, 2004).

Sauer, Michelle M., "Audiotactility and the Medieval Soundscape of Parchment," *Sounding Out!* (October 2016), https://soundstudiesblog.com/author/ndanchoress/.

Sauer, Michelle M., "Touching Jesus: Christ's Side Wound and Medieval Manuscript Tradition," *Women's Literary Culture and the Medieval Canon: An International Network Funded by the Leverhulme Trust* (January 2016), http://blogs.surrey.ac.uk/medievalwomen/2016/01/05/touching-jesus-christs-side-wound-medieval-manuscript-tradition/.

Saunders, Corinne, "Voices and Visions: Mind, Body, and Affect in Medieval Writing," in *The Edinburgh Companion to the Critical Medical Humanities*, ed. Anne Whitehead, Angela Woods, Sarah Atkinson, Jane Macnaughton, and Jennifer Richards (Edinburgh: Edinburgh University Press, 2016), 411–27.

Saunders, Corinne, and Charles Fernyhough, "Reading Margery Kempe's Inner Voices," *post-medieval* 8:2 (June 2017): 209–17.

Sayers, Edna Edith, "Experience, Authority, and the Mediation of Deafness: Chaucer's Wife of Bath," in *Disability in the Middle Ages: Reconsiderations and Reverberations*, ed. Joshua Eyler (New York: Routledge, 2010), 81–107.

Scarry, Elaine, *The Body in Pain: The Making and Unmaking of the World* (Oxford: Oxford University Press, 1987).

Schaeffer, Pierre, *Treatise on Musical Objects: An Essay Across Disciplines*, tr. Christine North and John Dack (Oakland: University of California Press, 2017).

Schalk, Sami, "Critical Disability Studies as Methodology," *Lateral* 6:1 (2017): n.p.

Schreck, Heide, *Creature* (New York: Samuel French, 2011).

Sclater, William, *An exposition with notes vpon the first Epistle to the Thessalonians* (Printed by William Sclater for John Parker, 1619).

Sears, Elizabeth, "The Iconography of Auditory Perception in the Early Middle Ages: On Psalm Illustration and Psalm Exegesis," in *The Second Sense: Studies in Hearing and Musical Judgment from Antiquity to the Seventeenth Century*, ed. Charles Burnett, Michael Fend, and Penelope Gouk (London: The Warburg Institute, 1991), 19–38.

Sedgwick, Eve Kosofsky, *Epistemology of the Closet* (Berkeley: University of California Press, 2008).

Segerman, Ephraim, "Tempo and Tactus After 1500," in *Companion to Medieval and Renaissance Music*, ed. Tess Knighton and David Fallows (Berkeley: University of California Press, 1992), 337–44.

Serres, Michel, *The Five Senses: A Philosophy of Mingled Bodies*, tr. Margaret Sankey and Peter Cowley (London: Bloomsbury Academic, 2016).

Sharpe, Reginald R., ed., *Calendar of the Letter-Books of the City of London: Letter Book D [1309–14]* (London: John Edward Francis, 1902).

Shen, Yeshayahu, and Ravid Aisenman, "'Heard melodies are sweet, but those unheard are sweeter': Synaesthetic Metaphors and Cognition," *Language and Literature* 17:2 (2008): 107–21.

Shuffelton, George, *Codex Ashmole 61: A Compilation of Popular Middle English Verse* (Kalamazoo: Medieval Institute Publications, 2008).

Simon, G. A., *Commentary for Benedictine Oblates on the Rule of St. Benedict* (Eugene: Wipf and Stock, 2009).

Singer, Julie, "Playing by Ear: Compensation, Reclamation, and Prosthesis in Fourteenth-Century Song," in *Disability in the Middle Ages: Reconsiderations and Reverberations*, ed. Joshua Eyler (New York: Routledge, 2010), 39–52.

Siraisi, Nancy, "The Music of Pulse in the Writings of Italian Academic Physicians (Fourteenth and Fifteenth Centuries)," *Speculum* 1 (1975): 689–710.

Smith, Adam, *Essays* (London: Murray & Son, 1869).

Smith, Bruce R., *The Acoustic World of Early Modern England: Attending to the O-Factor* (Chicago: University of Chicago Press, 1999).

Smith, Geri L., *The Medieval French Pastourelle Tradition: Poetic Motivations and Generic Transformation* (Gainesville: University Press of Florida, 2009).

Smith, Julia Marie, "*The Book of Margery Kempe* and the Rhetorical Chorus: An Alternative Method for Recovering Women's Contributions to the History of Rhetoric," *Advances in the History of Rhetoric* 17:2 (2014): 179–203.

Smith, Macklin, "Langland's Alliterative Line(s)," *Yearbook of Langland Studies* 23 (2009): 163–216.

Somerset, Fiona, "'Al the comonys with o voys atonys': Multilingual Latin and Vernacular Voice in *Piers Plowman*," *Yearbook of Langland Studies* 19 (2005): 107–36.

Sommers, Michael, "The Saintliness of Margery Kempe: Holy Rolling amid Medieval Times," *New York Stage Review*, July 12, 2018, http://nystagereview.com/2018/07/12/the-saintliness-of-margery-kemp-holy-rolling-amid-medieval-times/.

Spivak, Gayatri, *Can the Subaltern Speak?*, in *Colonial Discourse and Post-Colonial Theory: A Reader*, ed. Patrick Williams and Laura Chrisman (New York: Columbia University Press, 1993), 66–111.

Spivak, Gayatri, "Echo," in *New Literary History* 24:1 (1993): 17–43.

Staley, Lynn, *Margery Kempe's Dissenting Fictions* (State College: Pennsylvania State University Press, 1994).

Steiner, Emily, "Commonalty and Literary Form in the 1370s and 1380s," *New Medieval Literatures* 6 (2003): 199–221.

Steiner, Emily, *Reading Piers Plowman* (Cambridge: Cambridge University Press, 2013).

Sterne, Jonathan, *The Audible Past: Cultural Origins of Sound Production* (Durham, NC: Duke University Press, 2003).

Stevens, John, "Music in Mediaeval Drama," *Proceedings of the Royal Musica Association* 84 (1958): 81–95.

Stewart, Garrett, *Reading Voices: Literature and the Phonotext* (Berkeley: University of California Press, 1990).

Stillinger, Thomas, *The Song of Troilus: Lyric Authority in the Medieval Book* (Philadelphia: University of Pennsylvania Press, 1992).

Straus, Joseph, "Idiots Savants, Retarded Savants, Talented Aments, Mono-Savants, Autistic Savants, Just Plain Savants, People with Savant Syndrome, and Autistic People Who Are Good at Things: A View from Disability Studies," *Disability Studies Quarterly* 34:3 (2014): n.p.

Sullivan, Lawrence, "Sound and Senses: Toward a Hermeneutics of Performance," *History of Religions* 26 (1986): 1–33.

Sutton, Anne, and Livia Visser-Fuchs, "The Cult of Angels in Late Fifteenth-Century England: An Hours of the Guardian Angel Presented to Queen Elizabeth Woodville," in *Women and the Book: Assessing the Visual Evidence*, ed. Lesley Smith and Jane H. M. Taylor (London: The British Library; Toronto: University of Toronto Press, 1996), 230–65.

Swerdlow, Noel, "*Musica dicitur a Moys, quod est aqua*," *Journal of the American Musicological Society* 20:1 (1967): 3–9.

Tachau, Katherine, *Vision and Certitude in the Age of Ockham* (Leiden: Brill, 1988).

Tanay, Dorit, *Noting Music, Marking Culture: The Intellectual Context of Rhythmic Notation, 1240–1400* (Holzgerlingen: Hänssler, 1999).

Thompson, Anne B., ed., "Homily 14, Septuagesima Sunday," in *The Northern Homily Cycle* (Kalamazoo: Medieval Institute Publications, 2008).

Thompson, Ethel Margaret, *A History of the Somerset Carthusians* (London: John Hodges, 1895).

Tornitore, Tonino, "Interpretazioni novecentesche dell'episodio delle *Parolles Gelées*," *Études Rabelaisiennes* 18 (1985): 179–204.

Trachsler, Richard, "Orality, Literacy, and Performativity of Arthurian Texts," in *Handbook of Arthurian Romance: King Arthur's Court in Medieval European Literature*, ed. L. Tether and J. McFadyen (Berlin: De Gruyter, 2017), 273–91.

Tremain, Shelley, "On the Government of Disability," *Social Theory and Practice* 27:4 (2001): 617–36.

Tsur, Reuven, *Playing by Ear and the Tip of the Tongue: Precategorical Information in Poetry* (Amsterdam: John Benjamins, 2012).

Uhlman, Diana R., "The Comfort of Voice, the Solace of Script: Orality and Literacy in *The Book of Margery Kempe*," *Studies in Philology* 91:1 (1994): 50–69.

Verdicchio, Massimo, *The Poetics of Dante's Paradiso* (Toronto: University of Toronto Press, 2010).

Voaden, Rosalynn, *God's Words, Women's Voices: The Discernment of Spirits in the Writing of Late-Medieval Women Visionaries* (York: York Medieval Press, 1999).

von Henneberg, Josephine, "Saint Francesca Romana and Guardian Angels in Baroque Art," *Religion and the Arts* 2 (1998): 467–87.

Wallis, Faith, tr., "Gaspar Ofhuy's Account of Hugo van der Goes's Mental Illness," in *Medieval Medicine, A Reader*, ed. Faith Wallis (Toronto: University of Toronto Press, 2010), 352–56.

Walter, Katie L., "Fragments for a Medieval Theory of Prosthesis," in *Prosthesis in Medieval and Early Modern Culture*, ed. Chloe Porter, Katie Walter, and Margaret Healey (London: Routledge, 2018), 5–23.

Walter, Katie L., *Middle English Mouths: Late Medieval Medical, Religious, and Literary Traditions* (Cambridge: Cambridge University Press, 2018).

Walter, Katie L., ed., *Reading Skin in Medieval Literature and Culture* (New York: Palgrave Macmillan, 2013).

Warren, Nancy Bradley, *Spiritual Economies: Female Monasticism in Later Medieval England* (Philadelphia: University of Pennsylvania Press, 2001).

Watson, Nicholas, "The Making of the *Book of Margery Kempe*," in *Voices in Dialogue: Reading Women in the Middle Ages*, ed. Linda Olson and Kathryn Kerby-Fulton (South Bend, IN: University of Notre Dame Press, 2005), 395–434.

Watson, Nicholas, "The Middle English Mystics," in *The Cambridge History of Medieval English Literature*, ed. David Wallace (Cambridge: Cambridge University Press, 1999), 539–65.

Watson, Nicholas, *Richard Rolle and the Invention of Authority* (Cambridge: Cambridge University Press, 1991).

Wegman, Rob C., "Jacobus de Ispania and Liège," *Journal of the Alamire Foundation* 8:2 (2016): 254–76.

Wegman, Rob C., *The Mirror of Music: Book the Seventh* (N.p.: Lamotte, 2017).

Wenzel, Siegfried, *The Sin of Sloth: Acedia in Medieval Thought and Literature* (Durham, NC: Duke University Press, 1967).

Whitman, John, *Interpretation and Allegory, Antiquity to the Modern Period* (Leiden: Brill, 2000).

Wiens, Stefan, "Interoception in Emotional Experience," *Current Opinion in Neurology* 18:4 (2005): 442–47.

William of Saint-Thierry, *The Golden Epistle of Abbot William of St. Thierry to the Carthusians of Mont Dieu* (London: Sheed and Ward, 1930).

Williamson, Beth, "Sensory Experience in Medieval Devotion: Invisibility and Silence," *Speculum* 88:1 (2013): 1–43.

Windeatt, Barry, "1412–1534: Texts," in *The Cambridge Companion to Medieval English Mysticism* (Cambridge: Cambridge University Press, 2011), 195–225.

Winstead, Karen A., *Virgin Martyrs: Legends of Sainthood in Late Medieval England* (Ithaca, NY: Cornell University Press, 1997).

Wippel, John F., "Metaphysical Composition of Angels in Bonaventure, Aquinas, and Godfrey of Fontaines," in *A Companion to Angels in Medieval Philosophy*, ed. Tobias Hoffman (Leiden: Brill, 2012), 45–78.

Wiskus, Jessica, *The Rhythm of Thought: Art, Literature, and Music After Merleau-Ponty* (Chicago: University of Chicago Press, 2013).

Witkin, Robert W., "Why Did Adorno 'Hate' Jazz?," *Sociological Theory* 18:1 (2000): 145–70.

Woolley, Reginald Maxwell, ed., *The Officium et Miracula of Richard Rolle of Hampole* (New York: Macmillan, 1919).

Wright, Craig, "The Palm Sunday Procession in Medieval Chartres," in *The Divine Office in the Latin Middle Ages: Methodology and Source Studies, Regional Developments, Hagiography*, ed. Rebecca A. Baltzer and Margot E. Fassler (Oxford: Oxford University Press, 2000), 343–64.

Yudkin, Jeremy, "The Influence of Aristotle on French University Music Texts," in *Music Theory and Its Sources: Antiquity and the Middle Ages*, ed. André Barbera (South Bend, IN: Notre Dame University Press, 1990), 173–89.

Zayaruznaya, Anna, *The Monstrous New Art* (Cambridge: Cambridge University Press, 2015).

Zayaruznaya, Anna, "'*Sanz Note*' and '*Sanz Mesure*': Toward a Premodern Aesthetics of the Dirige," in *Voice and Voicelessness in Medieval Europe*, ed. Irit Ruth Kleiman (New York: Palgrave MacMillan, 2015), 155–75.

Zeeman, Nicolette, Piers Plowman *and the Medieval Discourse of Desire* (Cambridge: Cambridge University Press, 2006).

Zieman, Katherine, "Monasticism and the Public Contemplative in Late Medieval England: Richard Methley and His Spiritual Formation," *Journal of Medieval and Early Modern Studies* 42:3 (Fall 2012): 699–724.

Zieman, Katherine, "The Perils of *Canor*: Mystical Authority, Alliteration, and Extragrammatical Meaning in Rolle, the *Cloud*-Author, and Hilton," *Yearbook of Langland Studies* 22 (2008): 133–66.

Zieman, Katherine, *Singing the New Song: Literacy and Liturgy in Late Medieval England* (Philadelphia: University of Pennsylvania Press, 2008).

Žižek, Slavoj, *The Parallax View* (Cambridge, MA: MIT Press, 2006).

# Index

Page numbers in italics indicate illustrations. Titles of works will be found under the author's name; anonymous works are listed by title.